Social Organization of the Western Pueblos

MAP OF THE PUEBLO REGION

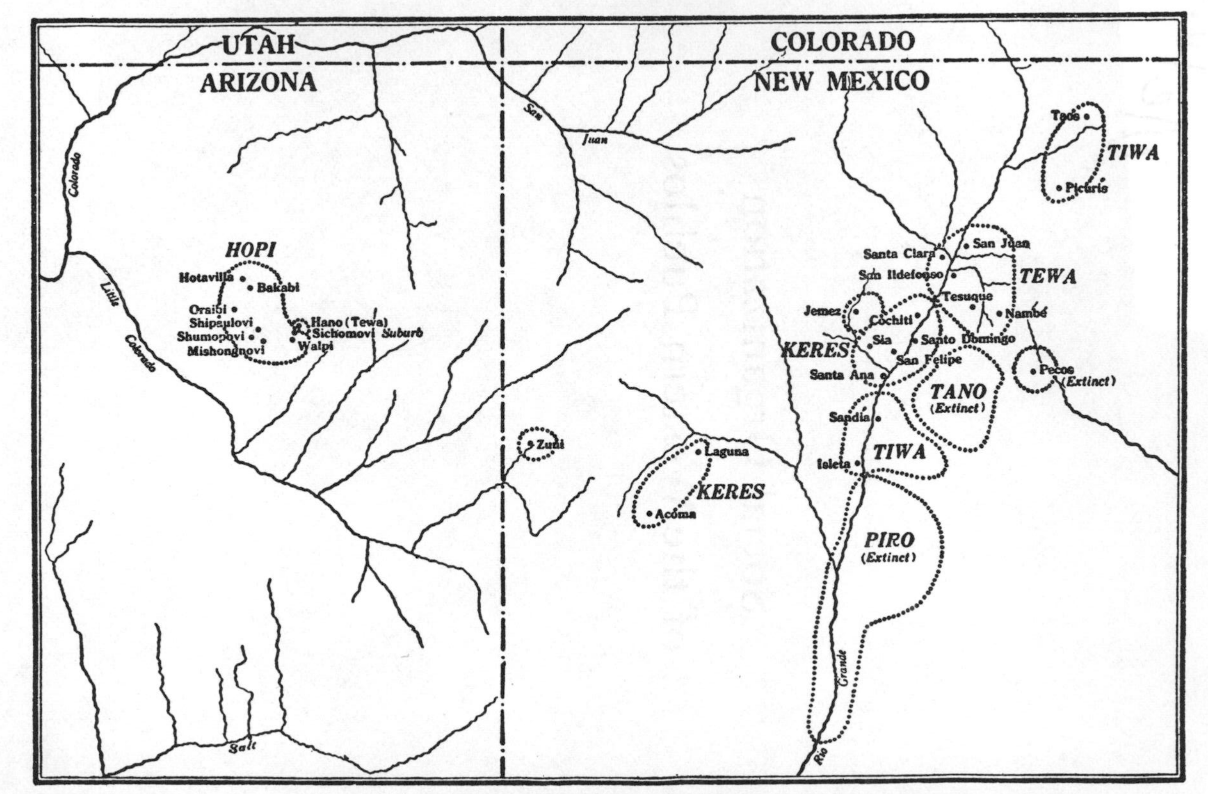

(After Parsons, *Pueblo Indian Religion*)

Social Organization

of the

Western Pueblos

By

FRED EGGAN

THE UNIVERSITY OF CHICAGO PRESS

CHICAGO AND LONDON

THE UNIVERSITY OF CHICAGO PRESS, CHICAGO 60637
The University of Chicago Press, Ltd., London

 Published 1950. *Sixth Impression* 1973
Printed in the United States of America

International Standard Book Number: 0-226-19075-7 (Clothbound)
Library of Congress Catalog Card Number: 50-9388

To R.-B.

Preface

THIS study was originally presented as a doctoral thesis in the Department of Anthropology of the University of Chicago in 1933. Field work was carried out among the Hopi of Third Mesa under the auspices of a field-training fellowship from the Laboratory of Anthropology at Santa Fe, New Mexico, during the summer of 1932. A research assistantship provided by the Social Science Research Committee of the University under the direction of Professor A. R. Radcliffe-Brown made it possible, among other things, to become acquainted with comparable data for other Pueblo groups during the following year.

In the period since 1933 I have had an opportunity to widen my knowledge and deepen my perspective through both teaching and further field research. The winter season of 1933–34 was spent among the Hopi, partly with Mischa Titiev on Third Mesa and partly on Second Mesa. The following year and a half I was in the Philippines, but the summer of 1937 was spent with the Peabody Museum Expedition to Awatovi, with briefer visits in the following years. In 1940 my wife and I began a study of social and cultural change at New Oraibi—a study to which we have only recently returned. The process of rewriting the thesis has been interrupted by the war and its aftermath, but its completion has been greatly aided by the facilities generously offered by the Laboratory of Anthropology.

I would like to express my appreciation to the above-mentioned institutions for underwriting the field and library research on which this monograph is based. To Professor Leslie A. White, leader of the Laboratory of Anthropology field-training party, I am greatly indebted for my first introduction to field work. To the members of the field party, Edward A. Kennard, Jess Spirer, Mischa Titiev, and George Devereaux, I am indebted for much information as well as for many stimulating discussions. The original field materials on which my thesis was based were gathered in collaboration with Dr. Titiev, who returned the following year for a longer stay. His recent monograph on *Old Oraibi* is the first adequate detailed study of the social and ceremonial organization of Third Mesa; from the manuscript which he generously allowed me to read and from numerous discussions I have had with him I have gained a great deal.

The debt I owe to my former teachers and colleagues in the Department of Anthropology of the University of Chicago is not one that can be dismissed in a sentence. Professors Fay-Cooper Cole, A. R. Radcliffe-Brown, Robert Redfield, Harry Hoijer, Leslie Spier, Edward Sapir, and Manuel J. Andrade all had a hand in my anthropological education, and these and others have provided intellectual stimulation ever since. To Professor Radcliffe-Brown I owe a special debt with reference to the problems and concepts utilized in the present study and for the legacy of a project in North American social organization which he had initiated and in which he was particularly interested. A. L. Kroeber, R. H. Lowie, E. C. Parsons, and M. E. Opler, among others, have been kind enough to read this manuscript in its original form and offer criticisms and suggestions. To Dorothy Eggan, my wife, I owe a great deal in the way of insight into Hopi life and culture. She has given me new perspective on many aspects of Hopi behavior, as well as contributing independently to the field of Hopi personality and culture. I have had many stimulating conversations with H. P. Mera, Erik Reed, and Stanley Stubbs as to the development of culture in the Rio Grande region. To Mr. and Mrs. John Connelly I am indebted for much information on Hopi problems. Finally, I would like to express my appreciation of the many students of Pueblo culture who have contributed so much in the way of information and interpretation and to the various Hopi friends and informants who have made field work not "work" but an experience to be long remembered.

In my absence from the country, Mr. Charles Leslie assisted in preparing the manuscript for publication and is responsible for the Index.

The present study differs in several important ways from the original one. The detailed presentation of social and ceremonial life in Titiev's monograph partially releases me from the obligation to present my data in standard form and makes it possible to provide a more theoretically oriented analysis and comparison. In addition, various problems have been considered beyond those dealt with originally. This monograph is part of a projected series of papers which will attempt to cover systematically the social organization of the North American Indian and to consider various historical and scientific problems which arise in connection with it. As such, there are many loose ends which I hope some day to be able to tie down.

FRED EGGAN

CHICAGO, ILLINOIS

Table of Contents

List of Illustrations

List of Tables

Chapter I

INTRODUCTION

The Pueblos

THE Pueblo Indians of New Mexico and Arizona, having managed to preserve a good deal of their complex and colorful culture, have been the object of intensive and varied ethnological investigation over several decades. This investigation will undoubtedly continue for a long time to come, but it is worth while from time to time to make preliminary assemblies and analyses of the data with a view to noting gaps and formulating problems and hypotheses. Anthropological vistas widen to the extent that we see new problems and gather materials which bear upon them. Parsons has recently assembled and analyzed the ritual and ceremonial life of the Pueblos in her monumental study of *Pueblo Indian Religion*, emphasizing the problems of variability and the theme of cultural change.[1] This present study attempts an assembly and comparison of the data on social organization for the western Pueblos, with a greater emphasis on the underlying uniformities of social structure and the factors responsible for them.

Despite the voluminous literature available, the social organization of the Pueblos, except in broad outline, is but imperfectly understood. For many groups we have no detailed information at all; for others the accounts are conflicting or confused. The current classifications of Pueblo social organization reflect this situation and are therefore neither comprehensive nor accurate, with the result that historical inferences are frequently misleading and that wider generalizations rest on a faulty base. There are various reasons for this situation—the complexity of Pueblo social structures, the difficulties in the way of ethnographical investigations, particularly in the eastern Pueblos, and the interest of many investigators in other problems and aspects of Pueblo life. The following study is an attempt to remedy this situation, so far as the data allow, for one group of villages—the western Pueblos.

The Pueblos form a cultural unit for comparison with other groups, but closer examination makes it possible to establish various divisions based upon differences in location, language, or institutions. The basic cultural division which is recognized is that between the eastern Pueblos of the Upper Rio Grande drainage and the western Pueblos of the mesa and canyon country to the west. From the standpoint of social organization the situation is more complex. It is not possible at present to deal adequately with the eastern Pueblos—a preliminary survey suggests two or possibly three types of social structure for this group. The far western Pueblos, on the other hand, appear to conform to a single basic type of social structure. To this type the more western Keresan-speaking villages of Acoma and Laguna also belong, so that, for our purposes, the western Pueblos consist of the Hopi villages, Hano, Zuni, Acoma, and Laguna.[2] The line of cleavage is not a sharp one; rather there is a gradual shift in most social institutions as one travels from west to east.[3] Jemez, which is intermediate in certain respects, I have arbitrarily classed with the eastern groups. The significance of this shift is one of the problems with which we will be concerned.

These western Pueblos, with the exception of Hano and Laguna, were found by Coronado and his followers in essentially the same locations which they occupy today. Hano was settled by Tewa-speaking peoples who migrated from the Rio Grande region around 1700; Laguna was founded at about the same time by Keresan-speaking migrants from the same region. In historic times these villages have been more isolated from Spanish and American contacts than their eastern neighbors, a factor which needs to be considered in evaluating differences in social organization as well as in religion.

Four linguistic stocks are represented in the Pueblos. In the east are villages speaking various dialects of Tanoan—Tiwa, Tewa, and Towa, the Tewa-speaking Hano being settled among the Hopi. The bulk of the Keresan-speaking villages are likewise in the Rio Grande region, though we have classed Acoma and

Laguna with the west. Zuni has its own language, while the Hopi belong with the extensive Uto-Aztekan stock. These linguistic differences suggest different historical origins for certain of the Pueblo peoples and furnish a control for comparisons within the group.[4]

The geographical environment is remarkably uniform throughout the Pueblo area, particularly in the western portions. Here is a high plateau with a distinctive topography—mesas, canyons, and dry washes. The climate is solar and semiarid, with daily and seasonal extremes of temperature and a scanty precipitation distributed primarily in the form of local thundershowers during the summer months. In the east the higher altitude provides a somewhat greater rainfall and cooler temperature; more important, the Rio Grande and its tributaries furnish a relatively constant water supply in contrast to the greater dependence upon rainfall and seepage in the western villages. The vegetation is characteristic of semiarid regions; the fauna is less specialized than the flora and not very numerous. In the recent past antelopes, deer, mountain sheep, mountain lions, wolves, coyotes, wildcats, bears, badgers, rabbits, and numerous smaller mammals and birds were to be found in the region. Despite their present primary dependence on agriculture, the Pueblo peoples formerly made considerable use of the available flora and fauna, and, as symbols, they pervade the social and ceremonial life.

The external adjustment of the Pueblos to this environment, with minor differences, follows one pattern. The people live in compact communities with stone or adobe houses grouped around plazas, often rising in terraced tiers. These dwellings not only affect the outward appearance of the villages but often reflect their internal organization as well. Each pueblo depends primarily on agriculture for subsistence, corn, beans, and squash being the primary crops, supplemented by plants and animals introduced by the Spaniards. Material culture, including the arts of weaving, pottery, and basketry, is everywhere unmistakably Pueblo. Internal organization, on the other hand, follows several patterns, as we have noted above.

Within the geographical and ecological area which houses the

Pueblos are other peoples who are sharply separated in many respects, despite the opportunities for contact and the similarities in environment. For the Pueblo area, itself, it may be said that in material culture, on the one hand, and in the ideas, beliefs, and sentiments, on the other, there is a remarkable unity. Each village has achieved a social integration which has been strong enough to keep the society from disintegration, if not from change. That these results have been reached through varying types of social organization is important for theoretical purposes. Before considering these groups and problems in detail, we might present some observations as to our own point of view.[5]

The Study of Social Organization

The student of social organization has made some progress in developing concepts, formulating problems, and establishing procedures for gathering and analyzing relevant data. His primary data are individuals behaving in social situations; his most general concepts are society and culture. These three—the individual, society, and culture—are all interrelated in one ongoing process, and to get from one to the other requires analysis and abstraction. A society is a group of individuals who have adjusted their interests sufficiently to co-operate in satisfying their various needs. Culture is the set of conventional attitudes and behavior patterns by which the mutual adaptation and co-operation is carried out. On the human level a society cannot exist without culture, nor a culture without the individuals of a social group.[6]

The units of social behavior in any society are the social usages—behavior patterns expectable between different individuals or groups under given conditions. A Hopi father's mother presents her son's child to the rising sun on the twentieth day of its life and gives it a name from her clan; a father's sister provides piki and other food on occasions when her brother's son dances; etc. These social usages are organized into patterns which mold the behavior of individuals and groups over longer periods of time; these in turn make up the "social" culture of the group. This social culture is of course only a portion of the total cultural behavior, which is, itself, an abstraction from the sum total of all kinds of behavior in the social group.

The units of social structure in any society are the social relations which develop through the recurring expression in behavior of social usages. Conventional behavior between individuals or groups establishes social relations which may be abstracted from the behavior in which they are imbedded and, for certain purposes, treated separately. Such relationships may be characterized both in terms of the individuals or groups represented and by the type of relation involved. These social relations are frequently recognized by the social group and, as such, become part of the social structure in the form of status positions. Such relations as those of parent and child, buyer and seller, and ruler and governed are examples of this process; other relations may remain unformulated but nevertheless important. These social relations between individuals and groups form a network which we can call the social structure, the organizational or configurational aspect of society.[7] Institutions partake of both aspects: they are composed of individuals organized in a social structure, with a set of attitudes and behavior patterns through which the structure is exemplified and the institutional ends are achieved.

While social relations are related to social usages, they differ from them in important respects. In the first place, similar social relations, whether of superordination, subordination, co-operation, etc., may be derived from objectively and historically different cultural behavior. The parent-child relationship, for example, has a similar form in a great number of societies where the social usages are objectively different, and the "caste" relations in our South are maintained by social customs historically different from those in India. Conversely, it is possible for similar social usages in different societies to support different types of social relations. A rule against eating together might maintain a superordinate-subordinate relationship in one society and express a social difference without subordination in another. More important, for our purposes, is the probability that there are a limited number of possible social relations and that these can combine to form a social structure in a limited number of ways. To have social relations, there must be *mutual* adaptations of behavior. It is difficult to co-operate if one party avoids the other; respect relationships cannot be maintained in the face of jesting and familiarity. Similar limitations apply in the field of culture but on a much less extensive scale, since there is less social necessity for precise definition and agreement on beliefs and practices within the minds of individuals.

The above analysis suggests that social structures have a limited number of forms which may operate with different sets of social usages. If this be so, we can begin to see why similar social structures recur in widely separated areas along with objectively different cultural elements and patterns. On the other hand, we also find examples of old structural forms persisting despite the partial replacement of social usages with new patterns. It seems probable that borrowing and invention play somewhat different roles with regard to social structures. Social relations are more subtle, more abstract, and more difficult to grasp than are social usages; social structures as such are no more subject to ready borrowing than are linguistic structures, whereas social usages, like linguistic vocabulary, may be more easily taken over.

The concept of integration likewise has a somewhat different meaning with reference to social structure and to culture. If the social structure is a network of relations binding the individuals of a social group together for certain purposes, then social structures may differ in the number of individuals bound together and in the character and complexity of the ties uniting them with one another. Cultural integration, on the other hand, refers to the degree to which beliefs, attitudes, and behavior patterns are mutually adjusted and form a single system without contradictions or loose ends. Here the process of rationalization plays an important role. Not only are social integration and cultural integration measured by different criteria but they can vary independently of one another.[8]

Different social structures allow variant adjustments of conflicting interests; hence some structures will be more efficient for certain purposes and less so for others. Thus small bilateral family structures have a difficult problem in providing social continuity and in the transmission of property and position, whereas unilateral extended family structures provide efficient mechanisms for both but find difficulty in reacting to changed conditions. Here, as in the biological world, specialization in structure brings about efficiency in adjusting to certain conditions but a relative inability to meet changes.

The role of the individual in relation to a society and its culture is an ambiguous one. Individuals are of course necessary to the maintenance and perpetuation of both society and culture, but these may continue long beyond the lifetime of any particular individual or generation.[9] Society, through the psychological processes by which the social heritage is transmitted by the individuals of one generation to those of the next, tends toward stability; major changes come about only at crises, occasions when there are conflicts which the society cannot resolve with its own resources. At such times individual personalities loom larger and may bring about far-reaching changes in both social structure and cultural behavior, though under normal conditions they might find difficulties in introducing innovations. And, at all times, as Linton points out, although the structures of societies "bear little relation to the special qualities of individuals, they bear a very close relation to the general qualities of our species."[10]

One of the important problems facing the student is to be able to "explain" the social organization of a given tribe in one way or another. One form of explanation is historical and attempts to work out the sequences of events which lead to certain end results. Such studies are exceedingly valuable, both as ends in themselves and as means to the control of comparative studies designed for other ends; they give us bases from which to operate and a type of insight or understanding of social phenomena not achieved by any other approach. An alternate method of achieving insight into the nature of social organization is by means of the comparative study of correlated phenomena in a series of tribes. Studies in correlation and covariation of social phenomena may lead to hypotheses which when adequately tested and verified may be considered generalizations or even "laws."

Much has been written, pro and con, about generalizations and "laws" for society, but they at least seem worth looking for. Morris Cohen has laid down some of the minimum requirements as follows:

> As a condition of useful generalization, I should emphasize first the identifiability of the repeatable elements. Unless elements can be repeated there is no science. What is ultimately unique or unrepeatable is not the object of a generalization. But the repeatable escapes us if it is not identified. When social scientists, therefore, wish to formulate laws or generalizations, they must make sure that the terms which enter into these laws can be either directly perceived or else identified as the results of logical construction on the basis of definitions and postulates, so that the question of their applicability is a determinate one.[11]

He goes on to point out that the value of any generalization depends on our ability to verify it, a procedure which is not too easy in the social field. Further, since social science materials are ultimately dependent on physical, biological, and, above all, historical factors, the formulas for social relations are inherently more complicated. "Whether we can find laws or not in the latter field depends upon whether we can isolate simple enough relations to which some arrangement of the actual phenomena can significantly correspond or approximate."[12]

Generalizations do not have to be universal in order to be useful. If we can formulate the conditions under which social phenomena correlate or covary, such information will be found to be extremely valuable not only as a lead to further research but in giving an understanding of social phenomena which is different from that attained by historical inquiries. The partial testing of such generalizations is made possible by the diversity of types of societies in the world, a social laboratory which has only begun to be utilized in terms of its potentialities.

The relation between historical inquiries and studies directed toward the establishment of generalizations needs some discussion. Both make use of the same raw materials—the ethnographic data—but each orders this material in different ways and analyzes it for different ends. Logically each procedure may be carried out separately, but in practice the two are often carried out together; indeed, many students have so fused them that they consider them a single process. More desirable is the recognition of them as different procedures giving different results, but aiding and abetting each other when properly utilized.[13] Historical studies not only furnish valuable controls for comparative studies but also supply historical sequences for possible generalization. In turn comparative investigations may increase the adequacy of historical interpretations by suggesting additional factors and by setting limits to historical processes under certain conditions. In achieving new knowledge the two methods are complementary rather than antagonistic.[14]

In order for the comparative study of correlated social phenomena in a series of tribes to be valid, it is necessary to make the first comparisons between phenomena which belong to the same class or type or, alternately, between phenomena derived from the same historical source. Only by exercising such controls can we be sure that the phenomena compared are comparable for scientific purposes. Hence one of the first important problems is an adequate classification of social organizations. Ideally such a classification should be based on similarities and differences in the total social structure. Social structures differ in range and complexity, and ultimately it should be possible to arrange them on a continuum of relative complexity. For preliminary purposes, since the social structure is known in detail for very few tribes, it is necessary to utilize various criteria as indexes of social structure. Some of these are limiting factors: the size of the social group, the density of its population, and the territorial arrangement. More important as indexes are various subdivisions of the social structure, the sex and age divisions, the kinship system, and the various formal and informal organizations which the group may take.

The relative importance of these for purposes of classification remains to be assessed. Linton has recently called attention to the neglect of the influence of age and sex differences upon social structure and believes that "age and sex categories are probably more important for the understanding of the operation of most societies than are family systems."[15] While this remains to be determined by empirical study, the kinship system has proved, in many cases, to be the most useful index of social structure. In many societies the kinship system represents practically the entire social structure, and, even when there are elaborate developments of segmentary and associational structures, these are frequently closely associated with the kinship system. In some types of social structure (our own, for example) kinship plays a much less important role.

The kinship system consists of socially recognized relations between individuals who are genealogically and affinally connected, plus the set of social usages which normally prevails among them. These relations originate in the domestic family but are largely socially determined. Between each pair of relatives there are rights and duties which define their relation; these relations are usually organized in such a way that they are consistent with one another and result in a minimum of conflict under ordinary circumstances. In many societies these relationships, and the corresponding behavior patterns, are widely extended, making the kinship system coterminous in effect with the tribe. Kinship terms are part of the social usages but also symbolize the character of the relationships between relatives. Kinship terminology represents one means of organizing relations between kindred and for extending these for social purposes. From this standpoint the emphasis on terms of relationship as strictly linguistic phenomena is not warranted. Since, however, there is usually a fairly close correlation between the terminology and the social behavior of relatives, in the absence of information concerning social usages, some insight into the kinship system may be obtained by a study of the way in which relatives are classified terminologically.

By the analysis and comparison of various kinship systems a limited number of structural principles have been worked out which derive from the relations existing in the elementary family.[16] Such principles as the "equivalence of siblings," the "differentiation of sex," the "relationship of generations," the "unity of the lineage group," and others have been defined. These principles, representing descriptive summaries of social relations and social behavior, are found in varying proportions and arrangements in different kinship systems, and in other aspects of the social structure as well, and thus offer a basis for preliminary comparison and classification. Since such principles often lie behind diverse institutions, they may suggest explanations of particular correlated features.

The present study is primarily concerned with two related problems: (1) the nature and functions of the social organization in each of the western Pueblos and (2) the possibility of classifying these as varieties of a single specialized type of social structure and of explaining the variations in terms of sociological and historical factors. The first part of this study should furnish increased insight into the kinship system, as well as the relations between kinship and other aspects of social structure, in the western Pueblos. The second portion may give us some understanding of the factors responsible for variations in social institutions. The study as a whole should increase our knowledge of the integrative and disintegrative factors in Pueblo social life and serve as a basis for further interpretations of the complex social, economic, and ritual aspects of Pueblo culture and as the context for studies of individual behavior and personality. The present problems may likewise be seen as part of a wider problem: to define the types of social structure which are present in the Pueblos as a whole and to compare the nature of the social integration achieved by each. These types may then be compared with those for other areas. In this process various historical and conceptual problems arise, and it will be useful to indicate the significance of the Pueblo data for such theories and hypotheses as have been advanced in connection with these problems.

Previous Studies of Pueblo Social Organization

The great mass of literature available for the western Pueblos deals in the main with other aspects of life; only a handful out of the hundreds of published papers are concerned with kinship and social organization. While the information in these papers will be summarized in later sections, it is desirable to consider briefly the point of view of the writers concerned, since that viewpoint has profoundly influenced the type of data gathered.

The pioneer studies of social organization in the western Pueblos were those of Cushing for Zuni.[17] While his "mytho-sociological" system is presented in brief outline only, it is evident that Cushing has considerable insight into Zuni social structure, and it is therefore unfortunate for ethnology that he published so few details. No ethnologist has since had the same opportunities. The early studies of the Hopi by Fewkes[18] and by Mindeleff[19] contain valuable information, part of it collected by Stephen, whose *Journal* has recently been made available by Parsons,[20] but their uncritical attempts to utilize the mythology for historical reconstructions of Hopi society have been rightly criticized by Kroeber[21] and others.

The first writer to present a study of the kinship system of a western Pueblo was Barbara Freire-Marreco. Her study of "Tewa Kinship Terms from the Pueblo of Hano, Arizona," published in 1914, outlined the essentials of Hano kinship and made some acute observations on the nature of Hano social structure. Unfortunately, her more detailed papers have never appeared, a particularly serious loss, since she had a profound knowledge of eastern Tewa culture as well.

Kroeber's *Zuni Kin and Clan* appeared three years later; this has been perhaps the most influential paper written on kinship and social organization in the Southwest. Kroeber in earlier papers had rejected sociological interpretations almost completely:

> The causes which determine the formation, choice and similarities of terms of relationship are primarily linguistic. Whenever it is desired to regard terms of relationship as due to sociological causes and as indicative of social conditions, the burden of proof must be entirely with the propounder of such views.[22]

In addition to this emphasis upon the terms as such, and their linguistic causality, Kroeber believed that the ethnologist should consider the principles or categories of relationship which underlie the terms used. These categories of generation, descent, sex, relation by blood or marriage, etc., were for Kroeber "psychological" principles which served as end points in analysis and which had no necessary sociological correlates.

The application of this point of view to Zuni kinship terminology and clan organization, brilliant though it was, missed certain essential and important features of Zuni social organization. It is not merely desirable to know that the Zuni disregard the principle of "generation"; it is also important to understand the nature of this disregard and what social functions it may perform. The analysis of Pueblo clans on the principle of "polarity" is subject to the same criticism. If these "psychological" principles have sociological correlates, as has been suggested for other areas,[23] then more insight into Pueblo social structure will be gained by utilizing them.

Parsons' study of Laguna[24] made the following year was modeled on Kroeber's Zuni paper, with, however, more basic data in the form of genealogies and behavior of kindred. She gives considerable comparative material for other Keresan-speaking villages, but her comparisons are limited to the kinship terms rather than to the systems as such. She also questions Kroeber's analysis of Pueblo clans.

At the same time that Kroeber was studying Zuni, Lowie made a study of kinship and clan organization among the Hopi of First and Second mesas[25] which led him to quite different conclusions. By comparing the Hopi system with other Shoshonean systems, he came to the conclusion that "linguistic conservatism has been of slight importance in the history of the present Hopi nomenclature and that the clan concept has exerted a deep influence upon it."[26] These studies, however, were not published until 1929.

While Kroeber has since receded from his extreme position, he has left a significant mark upon later studies in the Pueblos. Monographs are published with a partial list of kinship terms and a genealogy or two, lists of terms are analyzed in the interests of the "standing controversy" between linguistic and sociological factors in kinship nomenclature,[27] and linguistic factors are still called upon to explain odd features of terminology.[28]

More valuable for studies of Pueblo social life, in our opinion, is the point of view expressed by Lowie:

> Relationship terms are studied by the Anthropologists not merely as so many words inviting philological analysis and comparison, but as correlates of social custom. Broadly speaking, the use of a specific kinship designation, e.g., for the maternal as distinguished from the paternal uncle, indicates that the former receives differential treatment at the hands of his nieces and nephews. Further, if a term of this sort embraces a number of individuals, the probability is that the speaker is linked to all of them by the same set of mutual duties and claims, though their intensity may vary with the closeness of the relationship. Sometimes the very essence of social fabric may be demonstrably connected with the mode of classifying kin. Thus kinship nomenclature becomes one of the most important topics of social organization.[29]

This point of view has several noteworthy advantages. It results in the collection of more adequate data on kinship, it considers the possibility that kinship is systematic, and it leads to the attempt to establish correlations between kinship terminology and social behavior. The attempt to correlate various aspects of social organization with kinship terminology in America has been primarily the work of Lowie, though Sapir, Gifford, Lesser, and others have made notable contributions. These writers have attempted to explain various types of kinship terminology as due to the influence of some particular institution, or combination of institutions, such as the clan, the levirate and sororate, and various forms of preferential marriage. Close comparative analysis is necessary to determine whether these causal arrangements of correlated data are adequate; it may be possible and profitable to abstract more general factors which are basic to a whole series of particular institutions.

This point of view also lends itself to the elucidation of the concepts of social integration and social function about which there has been so much confusion. According to Radcliffe-Brown,

> one of the fundamental problems of a science of culture or of human society is . . . the problem of social integration. This problem can only be approached by the study of a number of different cultures from this specific point of view by an intensive investigation of each culture

as an adaptive mechanism and a comparison one with another of as many variant types as possible.[30]

While such studies are not directly historical, they are in no sense "antihistorical." It would seem that both historical reconstructions and studies of recent social and cultural change would have greater validity when based on a fuller knowledge and understanding of social organization. With reference to kinship Lowie long ago remarked that

we are sadly in need of the intensive investigations of particular systems, giving all the connotations of every term, and indicating by comparison with closely related systems how and why kinship nomenclature changes. A comparative study of all the Siouan, or all the Athabaskan, or all the Southwestern systems would be of the greatest value in this respect.[31]

The present work makes a beginning in this direction for the Pueblo portion of the Southwest. Studies of recent and contemporary social and cultural change offer especial advantages in the Pueblo area, both because of the possibility of utilizing historical documents for purposes of control and because of the opportunities for observing the actual processes of change. Further, hypotheses as to change may be formulated with the real possibility of testing them, since Pueblo cultures will undoubtedly continue in existence for a long time to come.

Our procedure will consist of presenting the data on western Pueblo social organization in a common framework so that the similarities and differences will be more readily apparent. In addition, each Pueblo is considered in terms of its particular contribution to an understanding of the major problems of Pueblo organization. Hopi social organization is given in considerable detail, since the data are better controlled and since the Hopi present us with what appears to be the basic form of the Crow kinship system. For the first time there is sufficient material available from different villages so that an over-all Hopi pattern can be presented, and archeological and historical data allow for a preliminary interpretation of the development of Hopi social structure from Basin patterns. Hano social organization is analyzed in terms of a shift from eastern Tewa patterns toward Hopi patterns, and some reconstruction of the processes involved is attempted. Zuni, with perhaps the deepest roots of any of the western Pueblos, has experienced consolidation of all of its villages in historic times. The influence of these events on Zuni social structure and the resulting differences in comparison with Hopi present a hypothesis for further investigation. Acoma and Laguna are of crucial importance in understanding the relations between the eastern and western Pueblos, since the "Keresan bridge" spans the two regions. The fuller data on Laguna make it possible to reconstruct Acoma social organization with some confidence; the historical position of Laguna gives us a further key by which to understand the changes which have taken place among the Keresan villages.

In the final section the common elements of western Pueblo social organization are defined and the nature of the variations which occur are appraised. Some hypotheses as to the nature of social and cultural change are presented and various theoretical problems are considered, of which the relations between eastern and western Pueblos are of primary importance. As in all such studies, new problems are raised and certain limitations in our knowledge become apparent. But with this basis it should be possible to consider more profitably the relations of the Pueblo groups to the Southern Athabaskans and other groups in the Southwest and to groups elsewhere who have social systems with similar organizations.

Chapter II

THE SOCIAL ORGANIZATION OF THE HOPI INDIANS

Introduction

THE Hopi villages, most western and isolated of the Pueblo groups, are located on a series of finger-like projections from Black Mesa in northeastern Arizona. This region is part of the arid and dissected Colorado Plateau which here averages some 6,000 feet in height; drainage is southwestward into the Little Colorado. Rainfall is scarce and variable, averaging only some ten inches per year and falling largely during the summer months. Hack has discussed in detail the geological and geographical factors involved in the Hopi water supply;[1] these have enabled a small population to reside in this area since the later Basketmaker period, dating back to approximately the sixth century A.D.[2]

At the time of Coronado there were some seven Hopi villages on four mesas, but after the Pueblo Rebellion of 1680 important changes took place in the region. Awatovi was abandoned or destroyed around 1700, and other villages located on lower spurs moved to the mesa tops. At this time also a group of Tewa-speaking peoples from the Rio Grande settled Hano, and other refugees from the same region took up temporary abode. Population growth and internal dissension led to further village-building, with the result that today there are some eleven villages, distributed as follows: On First Mesa are Walpi, and its "suburb" Sichomovi,[3] and the Tewa-speaking Hano; on Second Mesa are Mishongnovi, Shongopavi, and the latter's semicolony, Shipaulovi; and on Third Mesa, down to 1906, was Oraibi. Oraibi had occupied the same location long before the arrival of the Spaniards and was by far the largest village; in 1906 internal dissension led to the founding of Hotevilla and Bakavi, and further defections to New Oraibi at the foot of the mesa and to the former summer colony at Moencopi left Oraibi a mere shell of its former self.[4]

The present population of the Hopi villages is around thirty-five hundred, an average of about three hundred to a village. The seventeenth- and eighteenth-century estimates were much larger and probably somewhat exaggerated, but famines and disease have operated to reduce the number severely on occasions. For a long time the population remained more or less stationary at a little over two thousand; in the last decade there has been a gradual increase, brought about by a number of factors. This increase threatens to intensify the situation with reference to their neighbors, the Navaho.

From both a cultural and a geographical standpoint the Hopi represent the westernmost outpost of Pueblo life. Their nearest Pueblo neighbors, the Zuni, are some two hundred miles to the southeast, while the Navaho, recent comers to the Hopi region, now completely surround them. Despite their geographical position, their culture is in no sense marginal but is thoroughly Pueblo. To the west there is a sharp cultural break, though the neighboring Navaho have borrowed much and have given much in return. Because the Spaniards did not return in any force after the Pueblo Rebellion, the Hopi lack certain political and religious institutions imposed on other Pueblos, though they have shared in the material benefits which the Spanish brought.

Each major village is politically independent; the Hopi have acted together only on occasions when their welfare has been seriously threatened or when forced by government pressure.[5] What tribal unity there is lies in their common language and culture. With the exception of Hano, there are only slight dialectic differences from mesa to mesa, and the social and cultural patterns encompass the entire tribe.

A preliminary examination reveals that each village is divided into a series of matrilineal, totemically named clans which are linked or grouped in nameless but exogamous phratries. Each clan is composed of one or more matrilineal lineages, which, though nameless, are of great importance. The basic local organization is the extended family based on matrilocal residence and occupying a household of one or more rooms in common. In addition, there are various associations, both societies and kiva groups, which are involved in the performance of the calendric ceremonies. The structure, social functions, and interrelations of these groups can be best seen in the light of an analysis of the kinship system.

The Kinship System[6]

For the Hopi the kinship system is the most important element in their social structure. If kinship is considered as based on genealogical relations which are socially recognized and which determine social relations of all kinds between persons so related, the Hopi have emphasized the *social recognition* at the expense of the *genealogical relations* and have used kinship relations and behavior in ceremonial as well as daily life.

TERMINOLOGY

Figures 1–2 illustrate the kinship system by means of the conventional genealogical diagrams. The Hopi terminological system is of the "classificatory" type, with the father being classed with the father's brother, and the mother with the mother's sister.[7] But within each generation there is a wide variety of relatives to be found. There are separate terms for grandfather and grandmother, but their siblings are classed in a variety of ways, some with the grandparents and others with the father, brother, or mother's brother. In the parental generation there are separate terms for the father's sister and the mother's brother, but the former's husband is considered a "grandfather" while the latter's wife is a "female relative-in-law." In ego's generation siblings are distinguished according to sex and age, except that a woman uses the same term for her younger siblings. Parallel cousins are treated as siblings, whereas cross-cousins are differentiated, the children of the father's sister being called "father" and "father's sister," while the children of the mother's brother are "children" (male speaking) or "grandchildren" (female speaking). In the children's and grandchildren's genera-

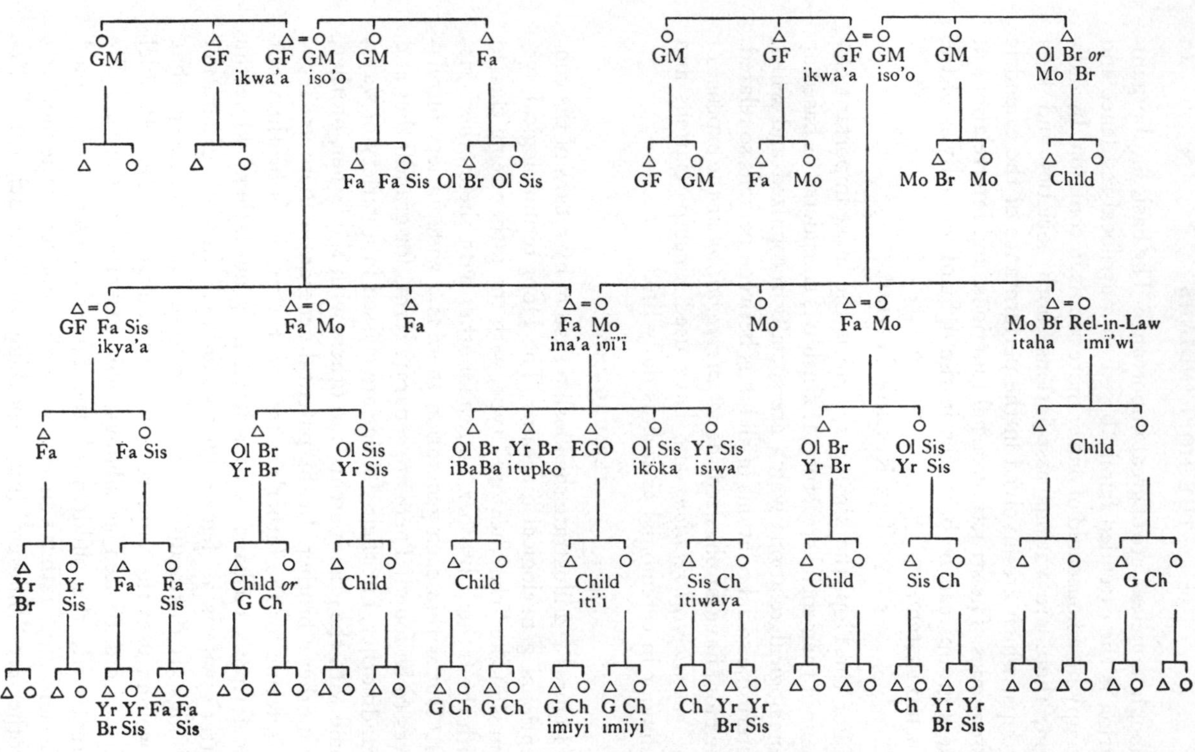

FIG. 1.—The Hopi kinship system. Ego = male. The Hopi terms are given in the first person possessive and in simplified phonetics. Fa = father; Mo = mother; GF = grandfather; etc.

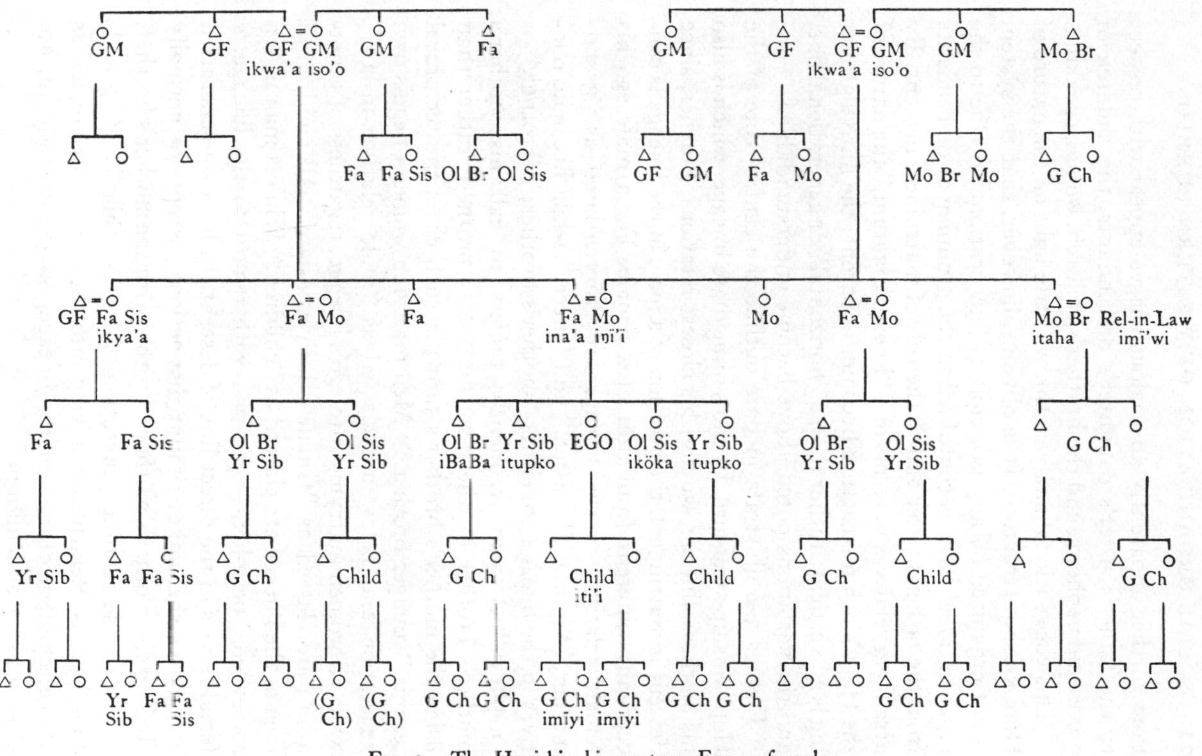

FIG. 2.—The Hopi kinship system. Ego = female

tions further apparently anomalous usages appear with respect to the father's sister's daughter's descendants, the children of nieces and nephews, and the brother's children, woman speaking.

This conventional analysis throws little light on the nature of Hopi kinship structure. It is obvious, however, that the system is not organized on any principle of "generation." A clue to the organizational basis is contained in the grouping of descendants from the father's sister and in the rule of matrilineal descent. By arranging relatives in terms of a "lineage diagram," the nature of the Hopi kinship structure becomes apparent: the native grouping is a "vertical" rather than a "horizontal" or generational one, and the variations noted above become understandable.[8]

Figures 3–6 illustrate in bare outline the central core of the Hopi kinship structure. In ego's immediate lineage, which is also his mother's lineage, we find his closest relations. Further, since descent is matrilineal, the position of a male in the lineage is conceptually different from that of a female. For a male ego his female relatives in the lineage are differentiated as "grandmother," "mother," "sister," and "niece," while his male relatives in the lineage are either "mother's brother," "brother," or "nephew." A man frequently prefers to call his mother's mother's brother by the term for "older brother" rather than using the mother's brother's term; in such cases the reciprocal term is "younger brother."[9] Men marrying women of ego's own generation and below are classed as "male relatives-in-law," while all women marrying into ego's lineage, regardless of generation, are classed as "female relatives-in-law." All children of men of the lineage are classed as "children." While a man is in a somewhat "peripheral" position with regard to the lineage, a female ego is in the direct line of descent. In her own generation and above she makes similar distinctions, except for normally classing the mother's mother's brother with the mother's brother, but in the descending generations she uses "child" and "grandchild" terms. Relatives marrying into the lineage are treated as above; children of men of the lineage, on the other hand, are classed as "grandchildren."

In ego's own lineage we find a considerable differentiation of

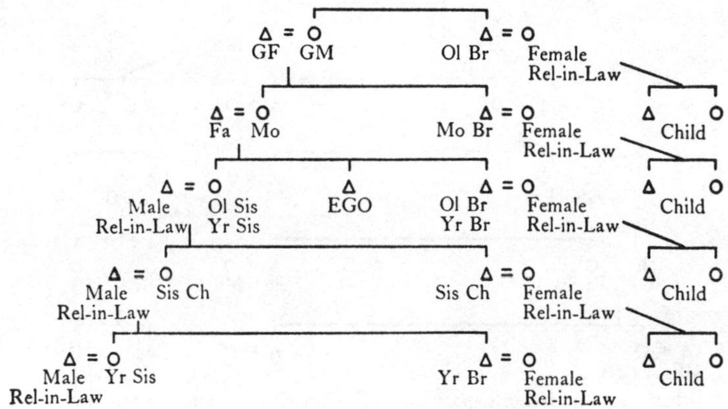

Fig. 3.—The mother's matrilineal lineage. Ego = male

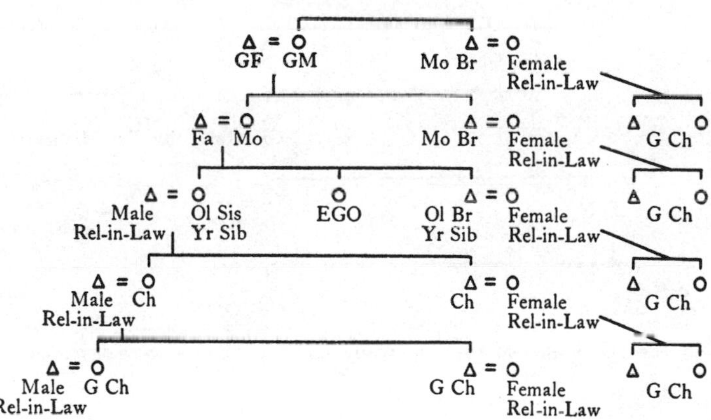

Fig. 4.—The mother's matrilineal lineage. Ego = female

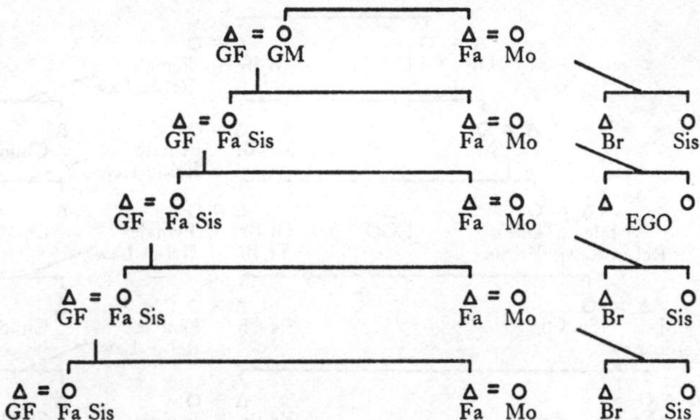

FIG. 5.—The father's matrilineal lineage. Ego = male or female

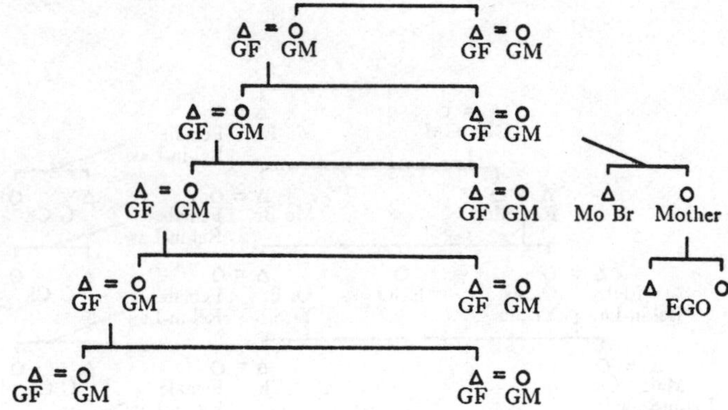

FIG. 6.—The mother's father's matrilineal lineage. Ego = male or female

relatives, but with reference to individuals marrying into the lineage we note that they are classed together in terminological usage. Generational distinctions are important only within the lineage; with reference to outsiders attached by marriage the lineage is conceived of as a unit. For a male ego, but not for a female, there is some tendency to reduce the number of male lineage relationships by classing alternate generations as "brothers," but this tendency is not thoroughly rooted in social usage at present.

With reference to the father's lineage, which becomes related through the marriage of ego's parents, the treatment of the lineage as a unit becomes clearer. In ego's father's lineage all the women are "grandmothers" or "father's sisters," and all the men of the lineage are "fathers," regardless of age or generation. Any man marrying a woman of the father's lineage is a "grandfather"; all wives of "fathers" are "mothers." Any child belonging to a man of the father's lineage is a "brother" or "sister." These terms are used by both male and female egos, except for the differences in sibling terminology noted above. In the mother's father's lineage, which is similarly related through the marriage of the mother's parents, the treatment of the lineage as a unity is carried still further. All the women of this lineage are "grandmothers" and all the men are "grandfathers"; their spouses are likewise "grandfathers" and "grandmothers."

We are now in a position better to understand certain of the "apparent anomalies" noted in the discussion of the conventional kinship charts. The father's mother's brother is classed as a "father" because he is a member of the father's matrilineal lineage; his children are "brothers" and "sisters" because any child of any man of the father's lineage is a "sibling." Similarly the children of the mother's brother and the mother's mother's brother are "children" (male speaking) or "grandchildren" (female speaking) because they are offspring of men of ego's own lineage. The differences in conceptual position of the father's sister's husband and the mother's brother's wife, of paternal and maternal cross-cousins, and of nephews and nieces and their respective children all become intelligible in terms of their different relationships to ego's lineage. Further, some at least of the differences in terminological usage between males and females are explicable in terms of their different conceptual positions in the matrilineal lineage structure; when we get away from ego's own lineage, these distinctions tend to disappear.

The lineage diagrams suggest that the father's matrilineal lineage and the mother's father's lineage are related to ego's lineage in conceptually similar ways. Each is attached to ego's lineage by a marriage of a man to a woman of the lineage, the difference in generation being relatively unimportant. With regard to the father's father's lineage, however, there is considerable difference; the father's father's lineage is a whole lineage removed from ego's lineage and is not socially recognized by the Hopi, though kinship terms are usually extended by courtesy to the father's father's siblings. Hence there are no terms for the father's father's sister's descendants, although these are just as close, from a strict genealogical standpoint, as the mother's mother's brother's children. This social rule also explains the variation in usage for the children of the father's brother's son, the relative unimportance of such relatives as the mother's brother's son's children, etc.

EXTENSIONS

These lineages—ego's own, his father's, and his mother's father's—form the central core or nucleus of the kinship structure and give the basic differentiation of relatives. They are not limited to the five generations portrayed; in Hopi theory they are timeless, stretching backward to the Emergence and continuing into the future. They also serve as units for the extension of the kinship structure which makes a Hopi related, in one way or another, to almost everybody in his village, to many people in other villages, and even to individuals of other tribes. The primary extension of kinship is to the clan; a person is considered to be related to everybody in his own clan, regardless of whether the clan consists of one lineage or several, and to the members of his father's and mother's father's clans. While a Hopi distinguishes between "own relatives" and "clan relatives," similar terms are extended to the latter, though on a somewhat simplified basis. Thus *all* women of the father's clan are "father's sisters," and any man marrying a clanswoman is a "male relative-in-law." In Hopi theory a clan is composed of individuals genealogically related through females, even though connections between component lineages cannot be traced at present.

Kinship is further extended to all the members of the associated or linked clans which make up the Hopi phratry, so that a person is related to his own, his father's, and his mother's father's phratry groups. The phratry groupings, in Hopi theory, consist of clans which met or shared in some experience during the period of wanderings which preceded the final settlement in the Hopi country; as such, they are "partners" rather than genealogically related clans, and the extension of kinship is on a more strictly social basis.

Since the same or similar clans and clan groupings exist in other Hopi villages, a Hopi at birth already has a large number of relatives to whom he can trace no direct genealogical connection, but which are socially recognized. Those of his own clan and phratry are most important and also those of his father's clan. The extensions of kinship to the mother's father's clan and phratry are less important and often ignored.

This, however, is only the beginning of the social extension of kinship. A "ceremonial father" is selected by the parents for a boy, and a "ceremonial mother" for a girl, to sponsor them in various organizations. The "ceremonial father" is chosen from outside the circle of clan relatives, in order, according to one informant, "to give the boy another group of relatives." He is chosen to be a "second father" to the boy, and the latter is adopted into the "ceremonial father's" clan and becomes related to the whole phratry group. For a girl the brother of the "ceremonial mother" acts when a male sponsor is needed, and she is similarly adopted. If a person is very ill, he may be "given" in adoption to the doctor who "brings him back to life." This adoption establishes a kinship relation with the "doctor father's" clan and phratry. It is further possible to have more than one "ceremonial father" or "doctor father."

Marriage results in the acquisition of an additional set of relatives, since, in theory at least, a man should marry outside his own, his father's, and his mother's father's clan. For his affinal relatives a man uses the same kinship terms which his wife employs for the members of her household and lineage, unless he happens to be otherwise related to them, and the wife similarly uses her husband's terms for his relatives. These relationships are felt as extending to the spouse's clan in certain circumstances, but such extensions are normally not important. This terminological usage is nonreciprocal, since the spouses are called "male relative-in-law" and "female relative-in-law" in return, a usage which is explicable in terms of the marriage situation and the obligations involved.

Ordinary adoption of a child may take place when parents die or separate, but generally in such cases the mother's sister or other close relatives care for the child, and there are no new relationships established. Where such is not the case, the adopted child is treated as a member of the household and uses corresponding kinship terms.

Within the village there are certain extensions of kinship of a symbolic sort. The village chief is considered as a "father" and may be so addressed on ritual occasions, and corresponding terms are employed for members of his immediate family such as his sisters and his wife. Likewise important medicine men or priests may be referred to as "fathers." Voth considered that special kinship relations were used between members of a fraternity during ritual smoking and thought that these corresponded to the rankings of their respective clans; but Titiev has demonstrated that the ordinary kinship and ceremonial relationships outlined above account for all such terms used in the ceremonies.[10] Between the members of the kiva groups there are no special kinship ties.

There is a further extension of kinship to the world of nature, certain of the phenomena of nature, particularly those which serve as clan names, being referred to as kindred by the Hopi. The sun is called "father," the earth and corn are called "mother," and the spider "grandmother" by all the Hopi, while the more important plant and animal species which serve as clan names are called "father," "mother," or "mother's brother" by the clanspeople. While this ritual extension of kinship is important in other directions, it also is one basis for the extension of kin relations outside the village and even the tribe. When similarly named clans exist among other Pueblo groups, or among the Navaho, they are considered as relatives, for certain purposes at least.

These extensions of kinship, largely on the basis of the clan as a unit, result in the individual having a very considerable number of relatives. In certain cases also the individuals concerned may stand in more than one relationship, in which case the choice is controlled by a variety of circumstances.[11] The Hopi have no definite rules, but Titiev has worked out the approximate order of closeness on the basis of indirect evidence as follows: (1) immediate family, (2) mother's sisters and children, (3) others of household, (4) own clan, (5) father's household, (6) own phratry, (7) father's clan and phratry, (8) "ceremonial father's" clan and phratry, and (9) "doctor father's" clan and phratry.[12] He points out that this order is confirmed by the incest regulations, marriage being forbidden with the first six groups, theoretically forbidden but tolerated with the seventh, and allowed with the last two.

THE HOUSEHOLD

We have now outlined the formal kinship structure as it is reflected in terminological usage and have indicated the main mechanisms of extension by which the structure becomes tribalwide. In this analysis the basic unit is the lineage, which as we shall see is of great importance in Hopi life. Of equal though different importance is the domestic or household group into which a Hopi is born and in which he receives his primary orientation. The basic family unit is an extended family based on matrilineal descent and matrilocal residence and thus may consist of a woman and her husband, married daughters and their husbands, unmarried sons, and children of the daughters. This group normally occupies a set of adjoining rooms which it uses in common and may thus be designated, for convenience, a "household." Though various factors may lead to further division, such as increased numbers, conflicts between sisters, and modern conditions, the *conceptual* unity of the household group still remains.[13]

The central core or axis of the household is composed of a line of women, a segment of a lineage. All the members of this segment, male or female, are born in the household and consider it their home, but only the women normally reside there after marriage. The men of the lineage leave at marriage to reside in the household of their wives, returning to their natal home on various ritual and ceremonial occasions or in case of separation or divorce. Into the household, in turn, come other men through marriage, who take over the economic support of the household, but not its ritual support. If they remain, they gradually achieve a more important role as they become fathers and grandfathers.

Thus the household groups, which from one point of view are merely a series of elementary families held together in the female line, achieve a more significant structure. We may view them as lines of women looking alternately to their brothers and to their husbands. On ritual occasions, when men return to their natal household, the household group becomes a lineage or a lineage segment; on ordinary occasions the household group is composed of these same women with their husbands and children. The household revolves about a central and continuing core of women; the men are peripheral, with divided residences and loyalties. They grow up in one household but live most of their adult lives in their wives' households.

There is no native term for the household, nor is it considered an independent unit by the Hopi.[14] But, despite being an ethnological abstraction, the household group is important in many contexts. Its correlation with the lineage has been noted; in terms of the lineage diagrams above we can see it overlapping the lineage groupings, uniting blood and affinal kin in a domestic group. A Hopi born into such a household finds there representatives of practically all his kin, and here he receives his basic orientation with regard to kinship which serves as a pattern for later extension and elaboration. If his mother's sisters should live in separate households, their homes are equally his, as to a lesser extent are those of other women belonging to his clan and phratry. Of importance also is the father's natal household, the women of which play a special role in ego's life, as well as the households of other father's sisters, whether clan or ceremonial. Here are additional relatives who complete the kinship outline, except for the experience of marriage. A Hopi is thus linked to a set of households which parallel the lineages and clans to which he is related, but which provide a somewhat different and more concrete orientation. The interrelations between these two organizations provide one key to Hopi social structure and social function.

KINSHIP BEHAVIOR

Having outlined the basic classification of relatives and the structural forms involved, we might now examine in more detail the social relations which make up the structure and the social usages in which they are embodied and maintained. The basic relationships are those between the members of the elementary family, but, because of conditions of descent and residence, certain other relationships of a more distant order come to have great importance among the Hopi. The general relationship and pattern of behavior prevailing between each pair or set of relatives will be outlined; this will be followed by a summary of the duties and obligations of relatives in connection with the life-cycle.[15] Such an account should illuminate the native values ascribed to the terminology, as well as the relation of the individual to the household and clan, and the nature of the correlation between kinship terminology and behavior.

The relation of a father to his child is of a different order from the relation of a woman to her children. A child belongs to the mother's lineage and clan but is a "child" of the father's clan; although both are recognized as kin, the two parental groups are rather sharply differentiated in attitudes, behavior, and residence. The father's obligations to his sons are primarily economic. While he helps select a "ceremonial father" and makes bows and arrows for his sons at Katcina ceremonies, he is mainly responsible for preparing them to make a living. He teaches them to farm and herd sheep, often going into partnership with them in herding activities. When a son marries, his father may give advice and aid in the preparations; frequently he will present him with a portion of the flock and a piece of spare land as well.

The position of a father in relationship to his son is something like that of an older comrade and teacher. There is affection but little in the way of punishment, and, while a boy respects his father, he does not ordinarily fear him. In certain respects the relationship is also conceived of as a reciprocal one. A father teaches his son how to make a living and furnishes him with sheep and other property; in return a father will be supported in his old age by his sons. A father likewise buries his sons, and he in turn is buried by one of them, the latter receiving a larger share of the father's personal property for this service.

The Hopi normally make little distinction between the father and the father's brothers,[16] although behavior toward more distant "fathers" may be much attenuated. Close ties are frequently found between a father's brother and his brother's son; other "fathers" may have close relations as the result of special circumstances. The "ceremonial father" has the special duty of seeing his "son" through the various initiations, while the doctor who brings a child back to life from a severe illness is also considered as a "father." A Hopi's primary obligation is to those "fathers" who have taken an interest in him and aided him on various occasions. Since all men of the father's clan and phratry are "fathers," it is possible to have "fathers" much younger than their "sons"; in such cases the Hopi preserve the same pattern of behavior but reverse the relationship, the "son" helping the "father" while the latter is growing up and the "son" being aided in turn when he is old.

The relations of a father to his daughter are more limited in scope. He contributes to his daughter's upbringing but has few specific duties, beyond making Katcina dolls and aiding in the activities surrounding her marriage. The relation of a daughter to her father is affected by his behavior toward her mother and the rest of the household. It is generally affectionate but not very close; when crises arise, the father is usually blamed and often treated as an outsider. Since divorce is common, a girl may have one or more stepfathers whose behavior may be variable.

The mother-daughter relationship, in contrast, is an exceedingly close one, based on clan ties, common activities, and lifelong residence together. Sex solidarity is strong among the Hopi, exemplified in the kinship groupings, division of labor, and attitudes toward children. A woman with a female child considers her life complete or at least well under way.

The mother is responsible for both the economic and the ritual training of her daughters. She teaches them to grind corn, to cook, to take care of babies, to plaster and repair houses, and to make baskets, plaques, and pottery. She chooses a "ceremonial mother" to look after their initiations into the Katcina cult and the woman's societies, and she may transmit ritual knowledge pertaining to the clan to one or more of them. At puberty, marriage, and the birth of her daughter's children, the mother has important duties.

A daughter's behavior in most cases is reciprocally one of respect and obedience as well as affection. A good daughter aspires to follow her mother's example and rarely acts in opposition to her wishes, even after she is married and has children. Normally she continued to reside with her mother after marriage, though modern conditions are making it easier to set up a separate household.

The position of the mother's sister is practically identical with that of the mother. She normally lives in the same household and aids in the training of her sister's daughter for adult life. Other clan "mothers" may help on occasion, but usually they are primarily concerned with their own children. The "ceremonial mother" has an important role on ritual occasions and often on others as well.

The relation of a mother to her son is almost as close as that with her daughter, particularly in early life. Even after he leaves home at marriage a son frequently returns for aid and advice. A mother encourages her son not to be lazy and to help his father. She has the primary decision as to his "ceremonial father" and repays the latter with food and gifts. While she does not control the marriage arrangements, she plays an important role in the wedding activities. Her home always remains his "real home"; here he keeps much of his personal and ritual property, here he brings guests, and here he returns in case of separation and divorce. A man shows great respect for his mother as head of the household, consulting her on all important questions. Rarely do mother and son fail to get along, though there may be occasional conflicts with more distant "mothers."

The bond between husband and wife varies with time and circumstances but is seldom very close. Their primary loyalties are to their own lineages and clans, and the ties holding them together are tenuous and easily broken to begin with. The marked sexual dichotomy gives them somewhat different spheres of interest and activity, and their relationship is one of co-operation rather than companionship. In Hopi theory the best farm lands are owned by clans and divided among the households; the women own the houses and the crops. A husband has the economic obligation of helping to support not only his wife but the whole household, and, as such, his efforts are often criticized, with resultant separations.

A wife has certain obligations to her husband. She must wash and care for her husband's hair, particularly for ceremonies, and she must prepare food and extend hospitality to his guests on feast days or other occasions. At such times there may be restrictions on sexual relations if the husband is a participant; there are similar restrictions for forty days after the birth of a first child. There is a good deal of individual freedom in the marriage relation. The main tie seems to be their children, and teknonymous usage is frequent. There is also a religious sanction for marriage—the marriage ceremony is essential in order to prepare a woman for entrance to the land of the dead.

Separation is easy, and there is a fairly high rate of divorce in all the villages—a rate which Titiev has computed at around 34 per cent for Old Oraibi.[17] When serious conflicts arise between spouses, the husband is usually treated as an outsider by the household of the wife and may be made unwelcome, or he may become aggrieved at her conduct. In either case he usually returns to his own household until reconciliation or remarriage. The serious social consequences of separation are cushioned by the extended family structure of the household, which makes such a rate of separation possible without disrupting the whole society. The wife and small children can fall back on the larger family for economic support until remarriage, older children being allowed to go with whichever parent they prefer. Modern conditions are rapidly modifying this situation, with serious social consequences, but the older attitudes often persist. One well-educated modern Hopi girl summed up the relationship as follows: "I don't need my husband any more now that I have my baby girl. My family has some extra land, and my brothers will plant it for me." Even children are not a strong enough tie in the face of lineage loyalties.

The sibling bond, in contrast, is a very strong one and one of the most fundamental in Hopi society, being based on common blood and residence and on mutual aid. The strongest and most permanent tie is that between two sisters; next is the relationship between brothers. Brothers frequently co-operate in economic and ritual activities throughout life, despite living in different households after marriage. An older brother should teach and look after a younger brother, although it is knowledge and not age that is important. They may tease each other, but it should not be carried too far; quarrels are thought to blow over quickly, and a brother's behavior is defended to outsiders. Brothers frequently combine their efforts in caring for a herd of sheep, often in collaboration with their father and their brothers-in-law.

Two brothers occasionally marry two sisters or marry into the same clan, although this is not a definite rule. Such marriages may increase the solidarity of the household group and are supposed to eliminate quarreling between the sisters-in-law. Brothers share equally in the personal property of their deceased father, except that the one carrying out the burial duties usually receives an additional amount. Next to the actual brothers, the mother's sister's sons are the closest, often living in the same household. The father's brother's sons, on the other hand, are "brothers" merely because their fathers are in the same clan.

For more distant "brothers" the feeling of relationship and obligation is usually much weaker, unless exceptional circumstances are involved.

The relation of sisters to one another—and to their mother—is the foundation of the Hopi household group. This relationship, based on the closest ties of blood, residence, and common occupation, lasts from birth to death and influences their lives each day. Their children are reared together and cared for as their own; if one sister dies, the other looks after her children and brings them up. When there is an age difference, an older sister may act as a "mother" to her younger sister, but ordinarily there is little difference in their behavior. They co-operate in all the tasks of the household, grinding corn together, plastering the house, cooking, and the like. An older sister helps with the preparations for marriage and initiations into the Katcina cult and the women's societies. Despite this close bond, sororal polygyny is not practiced, nor is there any tendency toward the sororate or levirate. A mother sometimes turns over the house to a favorite daughter, but usually the eldest sister inherits the control of the household. While quarrels occur, sisters generally manage to get along together. Any quarrels are usually settled by their brothers or their mother's brothers; if that is not possible, one may move out, but she usually continues to use the household equipment. The extensions of the sister relationship are similar to those for brothers.

The brother-sister bond, while close, is modified by the prevailing division of labor and the rules of residence after marriage. There are no restrictions or avoidances in their behavior, but their contacts are fewer in later life. Before marriage a brother works to support his sister and the other members of the household, and even after marriage he considers his sister's household as his own and is free to come and go as he pleases. The sister, in turn, looks to her brother for aid in various crises and often co-operates with him in ceremonial enterprises belonging to the lineage or clan or in the duties attendant upon "ceremonial parenthood."

An older brother has much in common with a younger brother but less with a younger sister. An older sister, on the other hand, engages equally in the task of taking care of her younger brothers and sisters as part of her training for parenthood.[18] When a brother participates in ceremonies and dances and when he marries, a sister aids in the preparation of food and in other ways. Each has a pride in the other's activities. The strong bond between them is the basis for their relationships to each other's children as well. Brothers and sisters share their patrimony, but sisters usually are given fewer of the sheep from their father's flock. With regard to marriage there is no tendency to brother-sister exchange between households.[19]

The relation of a mother's brother to his sister's children is likewise one of the most important in the Hopi kinship structure. As head of his sister's lineage and household, his position is one of authority and control; he is the chief disciplinarian and is both respected and obeyed. "Our old uncles told us" is sufficient explanation and sanction for custom. The mother's brother has the primary responsibility for transmitting the ritual heritage. He usually selects the most capable nephew as his successor and trains him in the duties of whatever ceremonial position he may control. To make him a good Hopi, he may get his nephew up early to run around the mesa and bathe in cold water; if he is lazy, he will pour water on him. In return a nephew is frequently afraid of his uncle, particularly where punishment is administered, but an uncle usually has his nephew's interests at heart.

A mother's brother has no special duties at birth or initiation but plays an important role at the time of his nephews' and nieces' weddings, especially the nieces'. He often is consulted on the choice of a spouse; he takes charge of the weaving of the wedding garments for his nephew's wife and instructs him in his new duties and the proper behavior toward his new relatives. At his niece's marriage he formally welcomes her husband to the household and looks after her interests in any disputes.[20] Normally a niece has less contact with her mother's brother, since she is more directly under her mother's supervision. She may "joke" or tease her mother's brother concerning his "father's sisters" (her mother's father's sisters). "They don't like you," she will tell him, intimating that she is stronger in affection.[21]

The mother's mother's brother is likewise an important relative. While alive he is the ritual head of the household and is considered to know more than the mother's brother. He may act as a teacher, particularly in regard to clan legends and stories, but he seldom punishes his sister's daughter's children, leaving such tasks to his sister's sons. The relations between the brother, mother's brother, and mother's mother's brother are important ones for Hopi ritual life. They belong to the same lineage and household and have the primary responsibility for the proper transmission of clan and ritual knowledge, including ceremonial offices and duties. Within this group the mother's brother has the primary obligation and disciplinary position; the mother's mother's brother has largely finished his tasks. The Hopi have partly taken him out of the mother's brother's classification and classed him as an "older brother," a comrade and helper rather than an authoritarian instructor and disciplinarian. He might have been considered a "grandfather" but that would not fit into the lineage structuring of the kinship system.[22] Parallel to this is the tendency to class the mother's mother's mother as an "older sister," though such cases are, naturally, quite rare.

The grandparent-grandchild relation is more varied, but in general it is one of great affection and attachment. By reason of residence a mother's father is usually closer to his grandson, often sleeping with him, instructing him in Hopi stories and legends, teaching him songs, and giving him gifts. There is some training in agricultural and herding activities but little in the way of punishment or authority involved. The father's father is in a similar relationship, though, being in a different household, he normally has fewer opportunities. He will take his grandson hunting and to his fields, instructing him in Hopi lore. This latter grandfather, along with the father's sister's husband, enters into a joking relationship with the grandson. The father's father may pour water on his grandson if he sleeps late or may roll him in the snow. When the grandson is older, he attempts to "get even" with his grandfather by doing the same thing. While the father's sister's husband enters into such joking and teasing, the special relations between a man and his father's sisters bring about an additional type of joking, outlined below. The mother's father, perhaps because of his position as husband of the head of the household, does not enter into such teasing to any great extent. The relations of grandfather to granddaughters are less extensive and less marked by teasing or joking but involve the same affection and interest.[23]

Grandmothers likewise treat their grandchildren with kindness and affection, teaching them Hopi ways and helping them out of difficulties. If the mother is too hard on her children, the grandmother will interfere on their behalf. The mother's mother occupies a dominant position in the household and as such must be respected, even by the granddaughters. On occasions of ceremony and marriage she aids in the preparation of food and presents. The father's mother is closer to her grandchildren and shows them more affection. As a woman of the father's household and clan she shares, with the father's sisters, an important joking relationship with the grandson, particularly at the time of marriage. Teasing relationships with the granddaughter seem more developed on First Mesa than on Second or Third. The mother's mother and the father's mother divide the duties attendant upon the introduction of a new grandchild into the world.

The grandparent-grandchild relation is widely extended and includes relatives in several conceptual categories. The grandparent term may be used for any very old person—these should be listened to, "since they know the important things." The father's parents occupy a similar position in a different household from that of the mother's parents; in terms of the differential relations of these households to ego we might expect a difference in terminology, but the Hopi have apparently ignored these differences and classed them together, while behaving somewhat differently toward them. The special position of the father's sister's husband will be further discussed below.

The relation between the father's sister and her brother's child is a very important one in Hopi life. With the father's mother, the father's sisters are involved in all the crises and ceremonial occasions in the life of their brother's child, from birth to death. At birth, puberty, marriage, initiations, ceremonial participation, and preparation for burial the father's sisters play an important role.[24] These relations are closer and more concerned with the brother's son than with his daughter. Not only is her home a second home to ego, but the relationship has a sexual tinge, with many references to sexual play between them, which may be symbolical or refer to actual relations.[25]

This relationship serves to illuminate the role of the father's sisters at marriage and the joking relationship with the father's sister's husband. At the time of the boy's marriage, besides aiding in the preparations, the father's sisters find fault with the bride, comparing her unfavorably to themselves. Sometimes all the women of the father's household and clan descend with mock ferocity on the boy's household, bedaubing the mother and her sisters with mud and disrupting the household, at the same time engaging in spirited repartee. Any damage done is later more than repaid, and, while the show is very realistic, "they don't mean it—it's a means of showing that they care more for the boy than the others." Similar expressions of their regard may continue, even after the groom has gone to live at the bride's household.[26]

This expression of jealousy and regard takes a reciprocal form in the joking and teasing between ego, his father's sisters, and their husbands. The latter, as a "grandfather," may have rolled his grandson in the snow and otherwise teased him as a child,[27] for which direct retaliations are in order. The boy may also tease his father's sister about her husband, telling her that her husband is lazy and "no good" and that he will look after her. The father's sister, in turn, may tell her husband that he is free to leave her at any time, since her "grandchild" will take care of her—"you can go home and I'll take my *imïyi* for my husband." A man is expected to stand up for all his "father's sisters" at all times.

The father's sister, while carrying out similar duties toward her brother's daughters, does not have the same close and intimate relationship with them. There are fewer ritual occasions, and there is no teasing or joking involved. Girls aid and co-operate with their father's sisters in plastering houses, in carrying water, and in doing other household tasks. Boys hunt rabbits for their "aunts" and in former times went on expeditions to furnish them with salt.

While a man has many "father's sisters," the closest ones are the actual sisters of his father, who usually reside in his natal household. The father's sister's daughters, when unmarried, are not teased; they choose favorite mother's brother's sons as partners in "Butterfly" and other social dances. A girl who receives aid from her unmarried "father's sisters" at the time of her marriage will reciprocate when the latter marry. More distant "father's sisters," whether clan, phratry, or ceremonial, are regarded with affection and joked with whenever occasions arise. The position of the father's sister in the father's lineage and in behavior is essentially that of a "grandmother," and occasionally she is called that.[28] She calls her brother's children "grandchild," and her husband in turn is called "grandfather." She might be considered as a "little grandmother"; the special terminology serves to segregate the women of the father's clan and phratry from the primary grandparents who have a direct genealogical relationship.

The relations with relatives by marriage, other than the father's sister's husband, take a somewhat different and nonreciprocal form. A man marrying into a household begins to share in the task of supporting the household by cultivating its land, hunting game, and gathering wood. To begin with, he is considered as a "male relative-in-law" and is judged by the household on the basis of his performance. If he gets along well in co-operative activities, there is a tendency for the wife's brothers to call him "brother" rather than "male relative-in-law," and, as he has children, he becomes a "father" to the generation below. At first, also, his connection with the household and lineage is solely through his wife, and he uses for them the same terms that his wife does, extending these to the clan. Two men married to sisters in the same household call each other "partners"; they have similar tasks in relation to the household.

The relations with female relatives-in-law are somewhat different, though equally nonreciprocal. Any woman marrying a man of the lineage (and clan) is considered as a "female relative-in-law" and must be called by the term *imï'wi* from the beginning of the marriage ceremony; in return she uses the terms her husband uses for his clanspeople. The "female relatives-in-law" do not form a localized group but are regarded with affection, except by the father's sisters of their husbands. They have important duties at marriage; whenever a woman of their husbands' clan is being married, they are expected to come and aid in the preparations which are necessary.[29]

The primary obligations of relatives-in-law are to the household and lineage with which they are immediately tied, but these obligations are further extended to the clan and phratry group. The obligations of the household and lineage, in return, amount to relatively little, nor is there any extension to the relatives of these in-laws of the relationships outlined above. These relationships become somewhat more "reciprocal," however, if we look at them from the standpoint of the two households (and lineages) united by a marriage. The husband's household loses an economic worker but gains a "female relative-in-law"; correlatively, the wife's household gains an economic support and furnishes a worker for marriage and other occasions. On a village-wide basis households lose brothers and gain "male relatives-in-law."

STRUCTURAL RELATIONSHIPS

The preceding account of the basic relationships and patterns of behavior between reciprocal pairs of relatives makes it possible to characterize further the kinship structure of the Hopi. That structure is remarkably uniform from mesa to mesa, more so perhaps than any other aspect of the socioceremonial system. Part of that uniformity is doubtless due to intermarriage between different villages, but the long period of relative isolation has also made it possible for the kinship structure to develop a high degree of consistency in the interrelations of its parts and a considerable efficiency in carrying out the social functions assigned to it.

If we now look at the structural pattern, we may further note the importance of the lineage and household groupings. The primary superordinate relationships, involving authority and control, are not organized on the basis of the elementary family or the parental generation but are confined to ego's own lineage and concentrated largely in the mother's generation. The line of women maintains authority over activities connected with the running of the household, but the primary authority and punishing power is concentrated in the hands of the mother's brother. The father and his sisters, on the other hand, are in a quite different relation despite their being in the same generation and genealogically as close. Correlated with these superordinate relationships is the primary responsibility for transmitting the ritual and social heritage of the lineage and clan, the heritage of highest value in the eyes of the Hopi. These relationships are extended to the clan and phratry, though the associated behavior patterns are largely potential rather than actualized.[30]

Within the same lineage and generation are found the basic co-operative relationships—those characteristic between siblings. In Hopi theory one should always be able to depend on one's brothers and sisters for aid and assistance. The relationship between two sisters is perhaps the most fundamental, being the closest and most permanent in Hopi thinking. Brothers maintain a close co-operation also in both economic and ritual matters, despite the responsibilities of marriage. A brother and a sister, on the other hand, have somewhat different but complementary duties relating to the household and lineage. Age differences between siblings, while partly recognized terminologically, are of no great importance socially; knowledge is considered of greater value than an age differential, generally speaking. The alternate classing of a mother's mother's brother as an "older brother" further illustrates the unimportance of actual age.

The sibling relationship is perhaps the most widely extended of any Hopi kinship relation. The position of the mother's sister as a second "mother," often indistinguishable from the biological mother in Hopi thought, is a reflection of the relationship between two sisters. The classing of the mother's mother's mother and the mother's mother's brother as "siblings" has been mentioned; this may furnish a mechanism for further integration, vertically, within the lineage. More significant is the extension of the sibling relationship to all the members of one's clan and phratry who are of roughly the same age or generation and also to the children of all men of the father's clan and phratry, including the clans and phratries of the ceremonial and doctor fathers, regardless of age. In addition, those brothers-in-law who co-operate well with their wife's brothers may be called "brothers" instead of "male relatives-in-law." These extensions, brought about by separate mechanisms, make available a vast number of potential sibling relationships and provide a lateral integration between a great number of separate lineages and clans.

The relations of a man to his father's lineage and household are of a somewhat different order. Here are more affectionate relations, involving economic and ceremonial obligations which must be reciprocated but which do not involve superordination or direct co-operation. The father's sister–brother's son relation is the most elaborated, involving affection and esteem tinged with sexual behavior, along with ceremonial obligations which are repaid by salt-gathering trips and hunting activities. The father's relation to his children is likewise one of affection; in addition, there are economic obligations which are part of his obligations to the household of his wife. These relations are extended to all the men and women of the father's clan and phratry and later to the ceremonial and doctor fathers' clans and phratries.

The grandparent-grandchild relation is likewise largely one of affection and comradeship without any particular obligations or exercise of authority, with the exception of the mother's mother, who is in the same lineage as her daughter's child. This relationship is rather widely extended, and the use of grandparental terms for any very old man or woman suggests that the Hopi look upon this relation as a rather generalized one.

The relations between spouses are nonreciprocal, tenuous, and brittle, in contrast to the enduring relations between relatives by blood. Between husband and wife there is little of love as we know it; on the other hand, sexual interest and economic advantage are both involved. Men marrying into a lineage and household offer it economic support and protection in exchange for sexual privileges and children; this relationship gradually becomes more co-operative as the husband acquires a greater stake in his wife's household. The wife, in turn, has certain obligations to her husband's lineage or clan, particularly at the time any of his clanswomen are married. Many affinal relatives, we might note, are classed with consanguineal relatives, in both terminology and behavior.

This brief analysis of the structural relationships in Hopi kinship illustrates the importance of the lineage in organizing and integrating the basic relationships within the group. Within the lineage associated with one's own household are the primary superordinate and co-operative relationships which are basic to the transmission of the social heritage and the operations of daily life; related to these are the affinal relationships which help maintain the household and lineage. The other related households and lineages share in a relation characterized by affection and interest, and involving many obligations which are later repaid, but with little or no superordination or direct co-operation.

Within the overlapping structures of the household and lineage the primary bonds and loyalties, in Hopi thinking, should lie with the lineage relatives; affinals are not tolerated if they interfere too much with the integrity of the lineage. This is particularly true in the case of women, who make up the core of both the lineage and the household.[31] Men, on the other hand, play a role in two households (or even more if they marry more than once), and their interests are normally much wider, going beyond these localized groups to the clan and associational structures in which they play an important and significant role, in contrast to their position in the household.

LIFE-CYCLE

Before considering the formal and associational structures in which men play a more important role, we might first examine the life-cycle in order to note the sequence of introduction of the individual to various institutions and activities in Hopi culture as well as to the occasions when, and the situations in which, the above relationships and behavior patterns are expressed. No attempt will be made to present a complete ethnographic account of the life-cycle, for which the reader is referred to the existing literature.[32]

Before the birth of a child there are behavioral restrictions on both the father and the mother, the disobeying of which may affect the prospective child in varying ways. At the time of delivery the women of the household care for the mother; in theory she should give birth to her child alone, but often she is aided by her mother or even her husband. A medicine man may be summoned in case of difficulty or to see that the position of the child in the womb is satisfactory. After the birth process is completed, the mother's mother takes charge of the infant and the afterbirth, cutting the umbilical cord on an arrow shaft (if a boy) or on a stirring stick (if a girl) and disposing of the placenta and blood at the edge of the village.

The father's mother (or one of his sisters) is then called in to take charge of the mother and newborn infant. She excludes the sun with a blanket, a practice at every transition rite, and proceeds to look after the infant, washing it in warm water and rubbing it with ashes and then placing it in a cradle made by the father. One or more corn-ear "mothers" are placed with the child, and lines of corn meal—or ashes—are made on each wall, forming a ritual house: "Now I have made a house for you. Now then must you stay there. That you may (survive) until twenty days we shall be waiting for you" (Oraibi). The father's mother then looks after the needs of the mother, preparing juniper tea and keeping her warm.

The mother and child must be kept indoors for twenty days away from the sun, and the mother must abstain from meat and salt during this period and from any contact with men. The father normally retires to the kiva for a somewhat longer period. During this period the father's mother, assisted by the father's sisters, takes complete charge of the mother and child. Early on the morning of the twentieth day they wash the child's head, and each, in turn, gives it a name referring to their clan. The father's mother then presents the infant to the rising sun and prays for its welfare and long life, mentioning all the names it has received. The mother does the same, and they return to enjoy a feast prepared by the mother's mother and the female relatives of the household, after which the villagers are usually invited as well. When the father's mother and the father's sisters go home, each is given a plaque filled with blue corn meal.[33]

Names given refer to the clan or phratry eponyms of the father's group, generally having a direct or symbolic reference to the father's clan. Of the various names given, one is selected by the parents for use as a childhood name and remains in use until the adult name is acquired from the "ceremonial father's" clanswomen during the Tribal Initiation. Names are seldom duplicated in a given village, but popular names are used over and over again in connection with later generations.

Hopi beliefs concerning birth and children are obscure and difficult to unravel. While conception is known to result from sexual intercourse, there is some evidence of other beliefs. On Third Mesa a female deity named Talatumsi is said to control births and send children.[34] She keeps all babies, in the form of little images, in her womb and sends these into the women of the village. Barren women may make offerings or rub their body with her image "to put a baby inside them"; continued barrenness means that the images fail to enter their body because they have a "bad heart." Of significance in this connection is the relation between Katcina dolls and children, mentioned for Second and First mesas.[35] Children are thought of generally as coming from the underworld, from whence the Hopi ancestors emerged long ago and to which they return at death. Talatumsi seems essentially an intermediary between the ancestors in the underworld and the Hopi. In this connection it is interesting that children who die in infancy, or before being initiated into the Katcina cult, are buried in different locations, and the spirits of the infants return to the mother's house, where they linger under the roof and are reborn in the mother's next child of opposite sex or, failing that, in the next child born into the household. Such beliefs are not incompatible. It is possible that the Hopi, aware of the general role of the father in reproduction, consider this of secondary or incidental importance.

All children are desired and taken care of, even illegitimate ones; but women frequently state a preference for female children, while their husbands often prefer sons. Twins, the result of two images being sent into the mother, are usually not desired because of the attendant difficulties at birth and later. On Third Mesa twins are believed to be related to antelopes and are considered to have various powers, particularly when small. The firstborn is considered the "older brother" and is named as usual, but the second is "adopted" and named by an unrelated clan, though the mother continues to care for them. The relations of twins are immortalized in the Little Twin War Gods and their exploits.

The act of birth introduces the child into the mother's household and clan, but a whole series of transition rituals intervenes between birth and full adult status in Hopi society. Birth itself is a transition for both mother and child, and each is segregated until the change in status and social personality is complete, the mother for the reason that she is considered to be both dangerous to the male community and in potential danger through loss of blood, and the child in order to protect it from the dangers attendant upon its new environment and life.[36] During the twenty-day seclusion from the sun "father" and the community, the child's nutritional needs are met by the real mother and, symbolically, by the corn "mother" (since corn gives life to the Hopi). Female representatives of the father's clan look after both mother and infant and on the twentieth day adopt it as a "child" of their clan by washing its head and giving it a name, and then they present both mother and child to the sun, who is "father" to all the Hopi. The whole procedure is likewise a symbolic re-enactment of portions of the Emergence Myth.

The training of the Hopi child takes place primarily within the household group and has, as we have seen, two main aspects: one connected with making a living and the other with ritual activities. The social division of labor allots different but complementary spheres of activity and interest in each of these. In the old days, at least, training for subsistence came primarily from the "fathers," aided by the "grandfathers," and ritual training came largely from the "mother's brothers" in the case of a boy. For a girl both economic and ritual training comes primarily from her "mothers" and mother's mother, with some aid from the "mother's brothers." The interests of a girl were concentrated on the affairs of the household and close relatives; those of a boy were diffused over a wider and more varied set of institutions.

The changing social status of a Hopi is marked by a series of initiation rituals which are held in connection with the ceremonial cycle, plus such social transitions as marriage, parenthood, and death. The "ceremonial parents" are the key to the complex of ceremonial associations to which a Hopi belongs, since they sponsor the latter in all the societies and groups to which they belong. The first major step is the introduction into the Katcina cult, which takes place for both boys and girls at around the ages of eight to ten. Children are taught that the Katcinas are gods who visit the village bringing the good things of Hopi life. Now they are to learn more about the Katcina, particularly that they are not gods but men impersonating gods.

The initiation takes place during the Powamu ceremony in February, and, while the ceremonial procedure varies somewhat from village to village,[37] the novices are ritually prepared by fasting and prayer offerings and then whipped with yucca switches by two Katcinas while their "ceremonial parents" stand by and support them. Their heads are then washed by their "ceremonial aunts," and they are given a Katcina name, which is used ceremonially. After morning offerings to the sun and continued fasting from salt and meat, the child observes the Powamu Katcinas dancing unmasked in the kivas. The novices are now in a position to act as Katcinas, though normally they should wait a year or so before actually participating, at which time there is said to be a second whipping. Following the ceremony the boy hunts rabbits to repay his "ceremonial aunts" for their help.

The Katcina initiations mark the introduction of the child to status in the tribe as a whole. He is here introduced to the ancestors, or "Cloud People," who return in the form of Katcinas, and the whipping impresses upon him the importance of the secrets he has learned and the necessity of keeping them from the younger children. The change in ritual status is marked by a new name and the privilege of returning to the underworld at death and is accompanied by the acquisition of a whole new set of relatives, the clan and phratry of the "ceremonial father," who will play an important role in the child's expanding life. From this joint beginning, however, the pathways of a boy and girl diverge.

Before the *kelehoya* ("little chicken hawk") can become a full-fledged adult by undergoing the Tribal Initiation, he is usually inducted into the various societies to which his "ceremonial father" belongs and to others which he may wish to join. Thus if his "ceremonial father" belongs to Blue Flute or Snake, or any of the half-dozen or more societies of the Hopi, a boy would normally join these, in each society receiving a name to be used in the ceremony. There are no puberty rituals for a boy, but a hunting initiation has been reported for Second Mesa.[38] Marriage can occur before the Tribal Initiation, but usually it comes later.

Changes in the status of girls were formerly marked by variations in headdress. On Second Mesa, and also on First, girls around ten years of age had their hair arranged in small whorls by their father's sister after grinding corn for one day. Later, around puberty or after, girls would grind corn for four days in their father's sister's house, with the sun excluded and the food taboos observed. At the end of four days the "aunts" washed the girl's hair and gave her a new name. On First Mesa this ritual began on the evening of the day of first menstruation, and the girl was assisted by other girls who had gone through the same procedure. On Second Mesa once a year, at the Summer Solstice ceremony, all girls who have arrived at puberty during the preceding year go to their father's sister's house to grind corn. On Third Mesa the ceremony is not thought to be connected with puberty and was organized somewhat differently, but with similar restrictions.[39] On all mesas, however, the rituals culminated with the arrangement of the hair in "butterfly whorls" and a feast for the villagers. In the old days these whorls were worn until marriage, and on Third Mesa, at least, this ritual was a necessary preliminary to marriage. The greater emphasis on puberty as one goes toward First Mesa is probably the result of greater Navaho influence, particularly intermarriage. Girls likewise join one or more of the three women's societies, under the sponsorship of their "ceremonial mother," but these play a minor role in the ceremonial cycle.

Throughout the period covered by these initiations and rituals the "ceremonial father" and his sisters look after their "child," pulling him through the various dangerous periods and in general acting as second "fathers" and "mothers." In return a boy helps his "ceremonial father" in his fields, while a girl helps her "ceremonial mother" grind corn. The parents of the child also return large quantities of corn meal and other food in payment for these services. These relations reach their climax in the Tribal Initiations, which were formerly held for young men in each major village every four years or so.

The Tribal Initiation is the most jealously guarded of all Hopi ceremonies and has never been observed in full at any village.[40] In each major village four important men's societies, Kwan, Ahl, Tao, and Wuwutcim, co-operate in periodic initiations of the young men of their own and colony villages in connection with their annual ceremonies in November. Each man normally joins the group to which his "ceremonial father" belongs and participates in that group's rituals; in addition, there is a joint initiation on the fourth night.

The novices are required to remain in the kivas under severe restrictions of behavior for four days, except for various supervised activities. They are *kelehoya*, "little chicken hawks," waiting for their quills to harden so they may leave the kiva nest. They are also being "reborn" under the care of their "ceremonial fathers," and many of the ritual activities are symbolic of the original Emergence of the Hopi from their underworld home. On the fourth night the spirits of the dead return to the barred and guarded village and "participate" in the rituals. In this atmosphere the climax of the initiation occurs. It is probable that the Kwan chief, in the role of the God of Death, "ritually kills" the neophytes, who are then brought back to life as "men" with the aid of their "ceremonial fathers." They are also introduced to the deceased members of the societies and prepared to take their special places in the afterworld which are assigned each society.

The following morning the "ceremonial fathers" take their "sons" to their natal households, where their sisters wash their heads and give each a new name from their clan, which is henceforth used as the adult name. The "ceremonial father" has woven a special *kele* shirt for his "son" and usually makes a dancing costume as well. For the succeeding four days of the initiation, the young men take part in the various public performances of their societies. After the ceremony the young man hunts rabbits for his ceremonial "father's sisters," and his parents and sisters prepare great quantities of corn meal to repay the ceremonial relatives for their aid.

The above initiation is a prerequisite to participation in the Soyal ceremony, the most important ceremony in the Hopi calendar. This ceremony, which follows the Wuwutcim group, involves the co-operation of all the men and households of the village and is designed to regulate and control Hopi life. Cooperating in this ceremony are the men's societies which participate in the Tribal Initiation, the main rituals being conducted in the chief kiva by the Soyal chief, who is usually also the village chief. Again members participating for the first time have their heads washed and are given Soyal names to be used in connection with the ceremony.

With the completion of the following cycle of Tribal Initiations the "boy" has completely become a "man," from a ritual standpoint at least, and assumes the full privileges and responsibilities of that status. An uninitiated individual is still ritually a "boy" regardless of marriage or children. The "ceremonial father's" task is now complete, but the kinship relations and obligations remain as permanent bonds.

In the old days it was possible to enhance one's status by taking a scalp and becoming a "warrior." The procedure in such cases paralleled that for other initiations, but the specific practices varied rather widely. The ceremonies in the Warrior Society on First Mesa after scalp-taking lasted twenty-five days and emphasized bravery and war magic; on Second Mesa the procedure parallels that for birth, the scalp-takers and scalps being kept in the kiva for twenty days under the care of the father's sisters, while on Third Mesa an *avowed* scalp-taker enters the kiva and sits with feet drawn up for four days with rituals to protect him from his "son" being carried out by the leaders of the War society.[41]

Membership in a kiva follows primarily from initiation into one of the men's societies involved in the Tribal Initiation. A boy normally frequents the kiva of his "ceremonial father" after the Katcina initiation and begins to take part in kiva group activities such as racing and dancing, as well as using it as a men's clubhouse. Kiva membership is somewhat amorphous, however, and a man may frequent any kiva of his choice, except that he must return to the kiva in which he was initiated for Wuwutcim, Soyal, and Powamu.

The series of initiations serves to introduce a boy—and to a lesser extent, a girl—to the ritual activities connected with Hopi life. Each initiation likewise brings the boy into relation with a new group of men, with whom he will be associated for ceremonial and social purposes for the rest of his life. The importance of ritual activities in Hopi society is brought out by the close relationship between status and participation in ritual activities. The bonds which bind these groups together are only partly kinship bonds, there is in addition the common interest in activities which furthers the welfare of the whole society.

Marriage is an important occasion among the Hopi, involving practically every relative in one way or another, but the activities are primarily social and economic rather than ritual in character.[42] Marriage is essential to the Hopi in order to facilitate the journey to the afterworld, and every Hopi should therefore go through the marriage ceremony and acquire the necessary objects—a wedding robe for the woman and a wedding plaque for the man—which will insure a safe journey. In addition, the reciprocal exchanges and activities of the relatives of the bride and groom establish bonds between the households and clans involved.

Courtship is almost completely in the hands of the individuals concerned. The primary restrictions are based on kinship: one should not marry in one's own clan or phratry, or in one's father's clan or phratry, though violations of the latter rule are more frequent. There is a further restriction in that a man once married should not court an unmarried girl, nor an unmarried man a widow, violation of which is punished in afterlife by the deceased spouse and in this life by the failure to secure the wedding garments essential for the afterlife.[43] Between the rather high standards of conduct expressed by the old people and the actual situation in regard to courtship in the present and recent past there is a wide discrepancy. At present there is great freedom in regard to premarital experiences, and the birth of children before marriage is common. In the old days there were formal occasions for courtship such as "picnics," certain ceremonies, and grinding parties, and at these the girls took the initiative in courtship. While there was also considerable freedom, the marriage ceremonies were held more promptly and usually took place before the child was born.[44]

After the couple are known to be going together, their respective relatives may try to dissuade them if they disapprove of the partner,[45] but such dissuasion should be exercised early if it is to be effective. When the girl wishes to marry, she prepares a great deal of corn meal, with the aid of various female relatives who will be helped in turn, and then goes to the boy's house where she remains for three days, secluded from the sun. During this period she grinds corn for her prospective mother-in-law and is called "female relative-in-law" by her husband's kin. Also during this period the boy's father's sisters "attack" the household, heaping insults on the bride and battling the boy's mother and clanswomen for allowing him to marry her, a procedure designed to show their affection and interest in their "grandson."

Early on the fourth morning the mothers of the couple prepare yucca suds, and the maternal female relatives, assisted by the father's sisters, bathe the couple and ritually mingle their hair so that they will cling together. After the joint hair-washing the bride is presented to the rising sun and then returns to bake piki for the wedding feast served by her clanswomen in the boy's mother's household. The girl's hair is now dressed by her mother in the married women's braids. She remains in her mother-in-law's household until the wedding garments are completed.

The preparation of the wedding outfit of belt, robes, and moccasins is in the hands of the groom's male relatives on both sides, led by his father and mother's brother. They prepare the yarn and weave the garments in the kiva, aided by any friends and relatives who wish to help. The bride's kinswomen bring corn and other food to the boy's household and there prepare feasts for the weavers, assisted by the "female relatives-in-law." These latter receive the surplus food and return trays of piki the next day. The boy's father usually provides the meat food in the form of a sheep or goat.

When the outfit is completed, the boy's uncle talks to his nephew's wife somewhat as follows: "Everything is well completed—we have given you clothing—now you may go to your own home. Be thankful for these things. When you go home, try not to forget us. When you stay here, we feel connected, you seem like a real daughter, and we love you. Come over any time you want to, so we may be happy together; don't leave us all alone. When you get home, your people will be glad. We are thankful for the food you have made for us; we were made healthy. The food you made we put into our bodies; it gave us strength to work for you."

The next morning the boy's mother washes the bride's hair, and she is then dressed in her new costume and escorted to her own home, where she is awaited by her mother and father's sisters. There is an exchange of food between the respective households. The boy is now ready to go to his wife's household, but, before he goes, his mother's brother reminds him of his obligations:

> You are no longer a boy; you must be diligent and watchful. You are going to a new house where you will have to look out for your wife's people and see that they have enough food. Be active and work

hard in the fields; if you do not, there will be complaints against you. We don't want people to say bad things about you. If you don't take my advice, I will be hard on you. Be thoughtful, faithful, and brave. Everything the woman wants to eat you will bring to your mother-in-law. Take care of your wife's people as you take care of your own people. Take your wife's father's place and work on his farm more than on your own. Make them happy so that they have no needs.[46]

The boy then goes to his wife's house to take up residence there. He must gather a load of wood for his wife's mother, which she receives with thanks; he is then a member of the household though still maintaining close contacts with his natal household. His father usually gives him a portion of his sheep, which they may continue to care for together.

The girl must pay for her bridal outfit by returning several plaques piled with corn meal. She goes in procession with her mother and mother's brothers, and the father's sister who cared for her as a child, and presents the plaques full of meal to her husband's mother, who receives them with thanks. At the time of the Niman ceremony the new bride takes corn meal to her mother-in-law and grinds corn for her all day. In the late afternoon she is dressed and taken by the mother-in-law to the plaza, where she stands with other new brides to watch the last dance. This is the last time the wedding clothes are worn until she is buried.

Marriage among the Hopi is strictly monogamous, in that only one marriage is permitted at a time, though frequent separation and remarriage is common. Divorce is at the desire of either party, and for a wide variety of reasons. Titiev estimates a divorce rate of between 30 and 40 per cent for Old Oraibi,[47] and data from other villages suggest a similar situation. This extreme "brittleness" of marriage seems an old pattern, although its tempo has probably increased in recent times. Since a wife may fall back temporarily on her household for support, the only deterrents to divorce are their objection to losing a helper and the fear of gossip. The husband may likewise return to his natal household until remarriage. For a second marriage there is no ceremony beyond the wife washing her husband's head.

Neither the sororate nor the levirate is recognized as an institution, nor do they occur with any frequency in the genealogies. Two brothers may sometimes marry into the same clan or even household, but this is perhaps due to greater opportunities for getting acquainted. Sister exchange between households is a chance affair, since there is no arrangement of marriages.

The enforcement of the rule against marriage within the clan and phratry is exceedingly strict in both theory and practice, although there are no direct sanctions applied. Marriage within the father's clan and phratry is likewise wrong in theory, but there are a number of instances of such marriages in all the villages.[48] Also marriage is not allowed within the range of close relatives such as father's brother's daughters, though more distant relatives whose fathers are in the same clan, or "ceremonial relatives," may marry. The mother's father's clan and phratry are exogamous in theory but not in practice.

Sickness is caused in a variety of ways—by quarreling and having bad thoughts, by trespass and sacrilege, and by witchcraft. The Hopi believe many of their fellow-villagers to be witches who prolong their own lives at the expense of others, particularly their own relatives.[49] Each society also has a particular disease which contact with it, or the society's paraphernalia, causes, and which the priests of the society can cure. For bad thoughts and quarrels, confession to the doctor or the mother's brother is necessary to avoid serious consequences.

Death may be from any of these causes, or from old age, the Hopi conception being that old people "become like a child" and finally "go to sleep," awakening in the underworld. Death is highly unwelcome, and the Hopi as individuals are extremely afraid of the dead; but the ritual of burial and mourning is simple. Only the women of the household lament; there is no formal wailing or ceremonial gathering. The body is prepared and buried immediately, if possible. A man should be wrapped in buckskin, a woman in her wedding robe. The father's sister on First and Second mesas washes the deceased's head for the last time, and prayer feathers are placed on the body and a "cloud mask" of raw cotton on the face. On First Mesa, at least, she also gives the deceased a new name. A father or son, or some close relative, normally does the actual burying, assisted by any men who will help. The grave is prepared at the burial grounds at the foot of the mesa, and the flexed body is interred with food and water along with a vertical stick to allow exit from the grave and symbolizing the Emergence.

On their return the men and women of the household purify themselves ritually and "propitiate the spirit of the dead so that it will forget the living and not worry them."[50] The next morning, meal and prayer sticks are placed on the grave, and the man placing them prays for rain and requests the spirit not to return to the village, closing the trail with charcoal lines. On his return the members of the household wash their hair and smoke themselves in piñon gum smoke. They should then try to forget the deceased and continue with life as usual.

The spirits of the dead are believed to remain in the grave for three days and then to rise on the fourth morning and follow the path to the land of the dead. The general home of the dead is believed to be in the Grand Canyon, the wedding garments allowing them to float down gently, where they join their dead relatives in the life of the afterworld. The dead are identified with the "Cloud People" and with the Katcinas[51] and are believed to bring rain and the good things of life to the living, as well as returning periodically for the Wuwutcim ceremonies.

The property of the deceased passes by inheritance to his or her relatives. The house and furnishings and the clan lands assigned to a household are corporate properties held in trust by the lineage, but personal property may be disposed of as desired. A woman generally leaves her personal belongings to her daughters and may select one of them to take her place as head of the household if there are no sisters living. A man leaves ritual properties to his brothers or nephews, but at present his personal property and sheep are usually divided among the children, the sons often taking the major share. The son who buries his father generally takes the deceased's turquoise-and-shell necklace.

The above survey of the life-cycle has indicated some of the transitions in status which occur in Hopi culture and the differences in the statuses achieved by males and females. Social status is associated primarily with initiation and marriage, unmarried individuals being called *tíyo* ("boy") and *mána* ("girl"), whereas initiated men are classed as *táka* ("man") and married women as *wúhti* ("woman") (cf. Table 1). There are also special

TABLE 1

HOPI STATUS TERMS

Condition	Male	Female
Cradle	*táka hoya*, "little man"	*mána hoya*, "little girl"
Out of cradle	*tíyo hoya*, "little boy"	*mána hoya*, "little girl"
Boyhood or girlhood	*tíyo*, "boy"	*mána*, "girl"
After initiation	*táka*, "man"	....
After marriage	....	*wúhti*, "woman"

terms for the divorced and widowed. More important is the series of ritual statuses through which an individual passes. They are social in that they involve membership in and relations with new groups, but they also involve relations with the gods and the ancestors and prepare the individual for a position in the afterworld. Here there are sharper differences between the sexes. While women enter the Katcina cult, they do not take an active part; they are excluded altogether from the Tribal Initiation. Men, on the other hand, may participate in a wide variety of ritual statuses which lead not only to activities in this world but also to specialized activities in the afterworld. These statuses will be more sharply defined later, but, in general, they are dependent on initiation rather than on marriage.

The changes in status are marked by transition rites. In practically all of them there is the seclusion of the novice, the period of training or waiting with its restrictions, and the reappearance of the initiate in his new "personality," with a new position and a new name. In most of these transitions, also, the novice is thought of as undergoing a "rebirth" under the guidance of the "ceremonial father," with important duties performed by the "father's sisters" and these services repaid by the novice's own maternal relatives. Even death is such a transition. At death a person does not die but merely changes residence, returning to the underworld from whence he came. Here his head is washed again, and from here he continues to aid his relatives and the Hopi generally.

Throughout the life-cycle, too, we see the continuing importance of the mother's and father's lineages and households, with the addition of the "ceremonial father's" lineage. On all important ritual occasions the father's sisters, whether own or ceremonial, play an important role in relation to ego and his lineage, and their efforts are repaid by the latter. The exchanges consequent upon initiations of various kinds furnish a goodly portion of the economic exchange of goods in Hopi society, and from each lineage and household there is a constant inflow and outgo of food, clothing, and other wealth.

SUMMARY

The kinship system may now be seen in larger perspective. The kinship system classifies relatives into groups, on the one hand, and regulates their social behavior, on the other. Toward each class of kindred there is a definite relationship, expressed in terms of duties, obligations, and privileges, which serves to order social life with a minimum of conflict. Within each class of relatives there are degrees of "closeness," and normally the intensity of the relationship varies accordingly.

The closest and most important set of relatives make up the lineage group, and within this group occur both the most varied obligations and ties and the greatest differentiations in terminology. The relation to the father's lineage and household is likewise important but socially simpler; the terminology, too, is much simpler. This relation also serves as a pattern for the various ceremonial relationships which are possible in Hopi society. The relation with the mother's father's lineage is still simpler in both behavior and terminology. The further extensions of kinship relations on the basis of marriage follow the pattern of one's own lineage and household.

While the elementary bilateral family can be isolated, the matrilineal lineage serves to organize these family relatives in a definite way, linking them together into a structure and giving them a continuity they lack by themselves. Such families stretch back into the past and prospectively forward into the future. The kinship system similarly is organized on a "vertical" plan, and even the "life-structure" of the individual reaches back into the past and prospectively forward into the afterworld.

The basic reciprocity in Hopi kinship terminology is reflected in the reciprocal or complementary behavior patterns between most pairs of relatives. When the relations are "nonreciprocal" in character, the terminology is likewise nonreciprocal. Only in the case of such genealogically distant relatives as "grandparents" have the Hopi classed groups of relatives with somewhat different positions under one set of terms.

In regard to the kinship system it may be said that there is a rather precise correlation between the present kinship terminology and the present social behavior of relatives. There is little reason to interpret the kinship system in terms of previous conditions, nor is it necessary or desirable to restrict the analysis to linguistic and psychological factors. We will see, however, that earlier conditions have left their mark.

The Clan System

We are now in a better position to investigate the Hopi clan and phratry structure and its relations to the kinship system, on the one hand, and the ceremonial organization, on the other. Hopi social organization has been approached largely from the standpoint of the clan and phratry, so that there is a considerable literature available, covering a span of almost sixty years.[52] The older writers were content to take Hopi statements about the historical movements and relationships of clans at their face value and, largely on the basis of First Mesa data, constructed "histories" of the Hopi villages based upon purported migrations and mythical events. The important kernel of truth in these accounts was lost in the attempts to reconcile contradictory data. A comparative analysis of the data for all the main villages makes it possible to determine the main patterns of clan organization and to see the mechanisms of conservation and change.

The clan is the outstanding feature of social life, in Hopi eyes. It is, as we have pointed out, a group of people united through the female line, with a name and definite functions. Each clan is composed of one or more matrilineal lineages which are not formally distinguished by the Hopi, who consider them all descended from a common ancestor. The clans, which are "totemically" named after some object or aspect of nature, are first of all kinship units. The members of the same clan are considered to be genealogically related, and kinship terms and behavior patterns, based on the relations existing within the lineage, are extended to them. The clans are also land-owning groups, each clan normally having certain lands reserved for the use of its members, lands traditionally given in exchange for services rendered to the village. The clan is likewise the basic ritual unit in that the control of ceremonies and ritual paraphernalia is in the keeping of certain clans. Each clan in the village has a main "clanhouse" which is regarded as the main home of the clan in that village. Here the head woman of the clan normally resides and the ritual objects pertaining to the clan are kept.

Each clan is also part of a larger grouping of "linked" or associated clans which may be called a "phratry." The phratry has no separate name, but it is nevertheless an important institution in Hopi life. The constituent clans are normally not considered to be descendants from a common ancestor but to have become "partners" as the result of common experiences during the mythical wanderings following the Emergence. Kinship is extended to all the clans comprising the phratry—it is thus the largest unit in kinship extension. The phratry is also the largest exogamic unit, marriage being forbidden with all clans in the phratry group. The phratry, on the other hand, has no economic functions and does not act as a ritual unit, nor does it have any political duties. It does serve to tie clan units together into larger structures and furnishes a mechanism for dealing with clan extinction, since "partner" clans normally take over the ceremonial obligations. There also develop rivalries between clans within the phratry which may cause serious trouble and even disorganization.

A similar phratry organization is found in all the major Hopi villages, and the Hopi themselves ignore the variations from village to village which actually exist in favor of a common plan. These variations are nevertheless important, since they show us something of the character of the changes taking place. The features common to all the villages also serve as a basis both for historical studies and for comparative studies. Many conclusions arrived at on the basis of First Mesa data are invalid for the Hopi as a whole, because these villages are in certain respects atypical.

One difficulty which has bothered every investigator of the Hopi phratry system is the large number of clan names which individuals will give for each phratry group. Sixty to one hundred or more names may be furnished by informants living in villages in which only a handful of clans actually exist. Some of these are actually existing clans, some of them belong to clans recently or long extinct, and some belong to "clans" which probably never existed. The genealogical approach is thus essential to a preliminary investigation of the clan-phratry problem, but, as Titiev points out, it is not in itself sufficient to solve the problems presented.[53]

The multiplicity of clan names and the changing patterns from village to village have confused the clan-phratry situation among the Hopi to such an extent that Parsons, for example, feels that "between clan naming and clan organization there is no consistent, uniform system whatsoever."[54] In every village, however, there is a conceptual grouping of clan names into phratries which is remarkably consistent, regardless of the actual clans now present. This conceptual grouping has two main aspects: it represents, on the one hand, a grouping of the population into segmental units and, on the other, a grouping of objects or aspects of nature which have some reference to Hopi life. Only from this dual standpoint do the clan-phratry groupings make complete sense.

PHRATRY GROUPINGS

The following summary of the clan-phratry situation in the major villages is presented as a basis for further discussion and analysis. It does not pretend to be exhaustive, but most of the relevant literature has been examined. There are many contradictions and variations in the accounts of different investigators for the same village—indeed, this was the experience of the Laboratory Field Party in 1932, when it devoted a good portion of its efforts to untangling the clan-lineage-phratry situation for one village. Table 2 is designed to summarize briefly the discussion.[55]

In all the major villages except Walpi the Bear clan is pre-eminent, furnishing the village chief and controlling the Soyal ceremony. In the myths, the Bear clan arrived first at the village site, and the chief allowed other clans to enter and gave them land in exchange for various services. Associated with the Bear clan in Hopi thinking are such clans as Carrying Strap, Spider, Bluebird, and possibly others. At Walpi in the 1880's the Bear clan was apparently long extinct, the last survivor who called himself "Bear" belonging to the linked Spider clan, which in itself was rapidly approaching extinction.[56] With the extinction of the Bear clan, the related Spider clan probably took over its main functions as well as its more important name, but with its own approaching extinction there were no further phratry representatives, and other clans in other phratries, notably the Horn and Snake clans, took over the position formerly occupied by the Bear clan.[57] The origin myths were modified to fit the new situation, and the shift in authority is dramatized and rationalized in the Blue Flute ceremony.

The Second Mesa villages have a somewhat different pattern of existing clans within the "Bear phratry." In all of them the Bear clan is flourishing and pre-eminent, but the Spider clan is not represented in any of them.[58] The Carrying Strap and Bluebird clans have representatives in Shongopavi and Mishongnovi, with similar legends, and possibly the Bear clan at Shipaulovi was originally Carrying Strap, in part at least. In Mishongnovi,

TABLE 2*

The Hopi Clan System

Phratry and Clan	First Mesa	Second Mesa		Third Mesa
	Walpi	Mishongnovi	Shongopavi	Oraibi
I. (Bear)				
Bear	†	×	×	×
Spider	×	...	†	×
Carrying Strap	...	×	×	...
Bluebird	...	×	×	...
II. (Katcina)				
Parrot	†	×	†	×
Katcina	×	×	×	×
Crow	†	†	†	†
(Rabbit-Tobacco)	...	...	...	×
III. (Snake)				
Snake	×	†?	†?	×
Lizard	×	×	†	×
Sand	†	†	†?	×
Cactus	†	...	...	...
Dove	†	...	...	...
IV. (Sun)				
Sun	×	†	×	×
Sun's Forehead	...	...	×	...
Eagle	†	×	†	×
Gray Hawk	...	×	†?	†
Owl	†	...	...	...
V. (Reed)				
Reed	×	...	[×]	×
Greasewood	†?	...	...	×
Bow	...	...	...	×
VI. (Kokop)				
Masau'u	†	†	...	×
Kokop	†	×	...	×
Coyote	×	†	...	×
Water Coyote	...	...	...	×
Millet (Lehu)	(×; see XI)	...	...	×
Cedar (Kwan)	...	...	...	×
VII. (Badger)				
Badger	×	×	...	×
Gray Badger	...	...	...	×
Navaho Badger	...	...	...	×
Butterfly	×	×	...	×
Moth	...	...	...	†
VIII. (Rabbit)				
Rabbit	×	†	†	(×; see II)
Tobacco	†	†	...	†

* Based primarily on Stephen, Fewkes, Parsons, Lowie, Forde, Titiev, and the writer's field notes. × = present or recently present; daggers (†) = recently extinct; square brackets ([ ]) = recent migrants via marriage; interrogation marks (?) = conflicting evidence for former presence.

TABLE 2—*Continued*

Phratry and Clan	First Mesa	Second Mesa		Third Mesa
	Walpi	Mishongnovi	Shongopavi	Oraibi
IX. (Patki)				
Patki	×	×	×	×
Pikyas	...	×	×	×
Corn	×	...	...	...
Cloud	†?	...	...	...
Fog	...	...	[×]	...
Snow	...	...	×	...
Sivapi	†	...	...	×
X. (Squash)				
Squash	†	×	...	×
Chicken Hawk (kele)	...	...	...	×
Crane	...	†?	...	×
Tubish	†	...	...	...
XI. (Horn-Flute)				
Horn	×	...	...	...
Deer	×	...	...	...
Millet	×	...	...	(×; see VI)
Mountain Sheep	†	...	...	...
Red Ant	†	...	...	...
XII. (Mustard)				
Mustard	×	...	...	...
Chakwaina	†	...	...	...
Roadrunner	†?	...	...	(†? in V)

Forde reported these three clans—Bear, Strap, and Bluebird—as a single clan recently formed by merging, but Bear and Bluebird, at least, maintain separate identities.[59]

On Third Mesa, on the other hand, only Bear and Spider are actually represented. At Oraibi a long-standing quarrel between the leaders of these two clans over ceremonial privileges, adoption of white ways, and land led in 1906 to a splitting of the village into two almost equal halves and the secession of the Spider clan and its faction to the new village of Hotevilla. Here the relations between the "partner" clans have shifted radically, and the mythology has been partly modified to fit the changed situation and "explain" the events which took place. The approaching extinction of the Bear clan at Old Oraibi will bring about further complications.[60]

The Parrot-Katcina-Crow phratry is represented in the early surveys of First Mesa by a Katcina or Crow lineage and is listed by Lowie as Katcina, though, since no names are recorded in the census list for this clan, it was perhaps extinct by 1915.[61] Parsons lists Katcina-Parrot as one clan with two names. The Hano Cottonwood clan is also considered as belonging to this phratry on First Mesa.

At Mishongnovi both the Parrot and the Katcina clans are represented, but the Katcina clan is practically extinct at present. Lowie reported only five Katcina people left in 1916; the Ravens (or Crow) are said to have formerly lived at Mishongnovi, the Katcina taking their land when they died out. Forde in 1929 found them regarded as a single clan recently merged, though their lands were still distinguished. Five years later Beaglehole reported that "the Parrot and Katsina clans are definitely dying out; there is no longer a woman in the Katsina clan and only two old women without daughters in the Parrot clan."[62] The Katcina clan is listed in all the reports available for Shongopavi.[63] The Parrots ("who arrived perched on the head of the Bears") are considered extinct; the Ravens are also listed as extinct, but the probability of their having existed as a group at Shongopavi is enhanced by the legend that many years ago they furnished the town chiefs, the chieftaincy passing to the Bear clan. Parsons listed Katcina-Parrot as a separate clan in 1920, but Forde later reports it as grouped with Corn-Water-Snow as a linked exogamous unit.

Both Parrot and Katcina families are represented in the surveys of Oraibi clans, with the further probability that a Crow clan existed in recent times, finally merging with Parrot. This grouping is an important one at Oraibi, and the Rabbit-Tobacco phratry has become attached to it, forming one enlarged phratry grouping. This combination is fairly old and may be in part the result of the reduction of the Tobacco clan and the lack of ceremonial standing of the Rabbits. These two subgroups are clearly distinguishable—they are separate but yet are "partners" and have a mythological sanction for their union.

The Snake-Lizard-Sand phratry is seen in most expanded

perspective from First Mesa. Here the Snake phratry is treated separately and considered to include, in addition to all kinds of snakes, the Mountain Lion, Mourning Dove, and various varieties of Cactus. The early surveys list five Snake families and one Cactus family in Walpi, but probably there were no real Snake people left, since the ceremonies belonging to this group were in the hands of the Dove and Cactus clans. With the decline of the Snake clans in numbers there was a merging with the Lizard-Sand phratry. The Lizard-Sand group was represented by one Lizard family in Stephen's 1883 survey of Walpi and by three lineages in Fewkes's 1900 survey. The traditional "history" of these clans is much confused, a reflection, I believe, of recent shifts in their ceremonial and social relations. The Lizard clan is reported by Lowie to have joined the Snake clan for ceremonial purposes; they do not intermarry, and the oldest Snake woman is said to belong really to the Lizard clan. Parsons lists Snake-Lizard-Cactus as one clan with several names in 1920, while in 1929 Forde reports Snake-Sand-Lizard as alternate names for a single clan, with their lands only partially distinguished. Incidentally, he lists clan land for the Snake and Sand clans but not for the Lizard, Dove, and others.

With the approaching extinction of the Bear clan and phratry, the Snake clan took over the village chieftainship for a while; but, before they could consolidate their position, they themselves became extinct or lost out to other clans. The ceremonially less important Lizard clan took over the name and the task of continuing the Snake group; whether Snake-Lizard-Sand is an old grouping on First Mesa is not clear from the accounts available for that village.

At Mishongnovi, Stephen's early survey reports only one Sand family of this phratry as being present. Lowie reports Lizard present with two lineages, Snake as never existing here, and Sand extinct but once present. Forde lists lands for all three clans but indicates that they have merged into one group under the name of Lizard, while Beaglehole's informant called this group "Snake." No people are reported for any of the clans of this phratry at either Shongopavi or its colony, Shipaulovi, though Forde lists Lizard as one of three clans merged with Bear at Shongopavi and hence presumably existing in the not too distant past. Since this is the only clan listed without traditional clan lands, however, the evidence is not too convincing.

On Third Mesa all three clans of this phratry are represented, though in Stephen's time the Snake clan was reduced to one family. Stephen also lists nine families for the Burrowing Owl clan in this phratry, in all probability a confusion of *koko* ("burrowing owl") with *kokop*, a clan in another phratry. In recent times the Snake clan has become almost extinct on Third Mesa, the Lizard clan taking over certain of its functions and, to some extent, the name.

The Sun-Eagle phratry group has a somewhat variable composition in the Hopi villages. In Walpi the Eagle, various Hawks, the Owl, Sun, Stars, Reed, Greasewood, and Turkey are all listed as clan names of the Eagle-Sun-Reed phratry, with the Eagle, Sun, Reed, and Owl clans being represented by families in Stephen's early survey. In 1915–16 Lowie reports no Sun clan people as living, though a Pumpkin clan woman had moved into the Sun clanhouse and "become" a Sun clanswoman. The Eagle clan also became extinct in 1914 with the death of the last survivor, and the sole survivor of the Greasewood clan had been reared by her stepmother and was considered as belonging to her clan. Only the Reed clan was well represented in 1916. By 1920 they were considered one clan with several names; by 1929 Forde lists them under Sun clan, with four lands belonging to Sun and three to Reed.

On Second Mesa the phratry picture for this group is confused. At Mishongnovi the Sun clan is represented by a single family in Stephen's survey, is not mentioned by Lowie, and is listed as a clan name in the Bear phratry, if I read Forde's table right. Stephen also lists two "Chicken Hawk" (better "Gray Hawk") families, eight Eagle families, and no Wild Turkey families; in Lowie's time the "Gray Hawk" clan is flourishing, the Eagle clan is reduced to three survivors, and the Wild Turkey is no longer remembered. By 1929 all three clans were considered merged in the "Chicken Hawk" ("Gray Hawk") group, though the Eagle lands were still distinguished; in 1934 the name "Eagle" was given for this group to Mrs. Beaglehole. Shongopavi and Shipaulovi share the Sun and Sun's Forehead clans, though the former is predominant in Shongopavi, and the latter makes up the bulk of the population in Shipaulovi. In Shongopavi the Eagle clan is mentioned as one of the clans merged with the Bear phratry and credited with one clan land; the Hawk clan is reported as extinct; the Sun and Sun's Forehead are merged into a single exogamous unit, though separate lands are listed for each.[64]

At Oraibi, Stephen lists Sun, Eagle, and Gray Hawk families. The one Gray Hawk family may have come from Second Mesa, but a clanhouse is recognized for it on Third Mesa, though it has not survived as a separate clan down to the present. Sun and Eagle lineages are still present, but no Turkey people are remembered.

The Reed-Greasewood-Bow phratry, which on First Mesa is merged inextricably with the Sun-Eagle-Hawk group, is on Third Mesa a separate phratry. Stephen's early survey listed some twenty-four Reed families and four Bow families but no Greasewood members; the investigations of White and Titiev, however, indicate that all these clans are, and were, represented on Third Mesa. The Bow clan on First Mesa is listed by Stephen as one of the clan names in the Kokop group. The Reed phratry is not represented in any of the Second Mesa villages, except for the anomalous situation reported recently for Shipaulovi by Mrs. Beaglehole where a woman of the Sun's Forehead clan quarreled with her clanmates and started calling herself "Reed," a shift which is intelligible only in terms of the First Mesa groupings. The Bow clan at Oraibi is felt to be somewhat "distant" from the other clans in the phratry because of the behavior of recent clan heads toward the village chief.

The Kokop[65]-Coyote-Masau'u phratry on First Mesa includes, as names, various kinds of foxes, as well as Piñon, Juniper, and Bow. Stephen's survey shows only Coyote people, though the lineage is variously called Cedarwood (Masau'u) or Cedarwood-Eototo, the latter deity being considered similar to Masau'u on

First Mesa. Lowie lists the Charcoal-Coyote clan, as "one clan with two names"; Parsons lists Coyote-Cedarwood-Fire-Masöwö as one clan with several names; while Forde groups these clans as merged under "Coyote," with three lands. While the Kokops figure in the traditional history, they have apparently been long extinct, along with the Masau'u clan, if it ever actually existed on First Mesa. An Eototo clan is also reported, but this is probably the reflection of the impersonation of Eototo by the Cedarwood-Coyote clan chief in certain ceremonies.

At Mishongnovi, Stephen reported three Firewood families and one Coyote family but no Masau'u clanspeople. In 1916 Lowie notes that the one surviving Coyote clansman joined the Kokop, along with a large family of Oraibi Coyotes. Forde, on the other hand, reports that, while "Fire" is the more usual name now (1929), most of the clanspeople are descended from Coyotes. In 1934 this group was called "Coyote," according to Mrs. Beaglehole. No members of this group are mentioned for Shongopavi or Shipaulovi.

On Third Mesa this phratry group has a more complete representation. Stephen recorded seventeen Coyote families and one Mescal Cake ("Kwan"), but later research has broken this grouping up into Masau'u, Real Coyote, Water Coyote, Kokop, Millet, and Kwan-Cedar-Hovakop, each group with separate lineages and clanhouses. One woman in a Coyote lineage insisted that she was Yellow Fox as a result of quarrels with her clansmates.

The Badger-Butterfly phratry is represented on all the mesas. On First Mesa the phratry theoretically includes Badger, all kinds of butterflies and moths, Porcupine, Turkey Buzzard, and Medicine. The early surveys report both Badger and Butterfly lineages here, but by 1915 the Badger survivors are said to have joined the Butterfly clan, using the latter name. Parsons reports Butterfly-Badger-Porcupine as one clan in 1920, but nine years later Forde found them being called "Badger," with no reference to merging or even to Butterfly lands.

On Second Mesa at Mishongnovi, we find eight Badger families in Stephen's survey but no Butterfly or Porcupine peoples.

Here, too, are grouped Tobacco and Rabbit, but without any representatives listed. Lowie has a dual division in this phratry in 1916—Badger with Tobacco and Rabbit and Butterfly with Porcupine—the two linked as an exogamous unit. Forde in 1929 listed the whole group under "Badger," with, however, the Butterfly lands separately recognized. In 1934 Mrs. Beaglehole listed six Badger and thirty-eight Butterfly clanspeople resident in Mishongnovi. None of these clans is listed for either Shongopavi or Shipaulovi, though one Butterfly woman has moved to the latter village from Mishongnovi recently, according to Mrs. Beaglehole.

Stephen's survey of Third Mesa clans noted thirteen Badger families and one Moth family, the latter equatable with "Butterfly." The Badger clan at present is divisible into Real Badger, Gray Badger, and Navaho Badger. The division between Real Badger and Gray Badger may be an old one, as both have clan-houses in Oraibi, but the Navaho Badger is a recent group which started with the adoption of an orphan Navaho girl by a Badger woman, the descendants of the girl being distinguished as Navaho Badgers. No Porcupine families are listed or remembered, though Porcupine is recognized as belonging to this lineage.

The Rabbit-Tobacco phratry has been mentioned above in connection with other phratry groups. On First Mesa it traditionally included the following clans: Tobacco, Jack Rabbit, Cottontail Rabbit, and Pipe. The early surveys show Tobacco and Cottontail Rabbit lineages at Walpi and Sichomovi, but by 1915 the former clan was reduced to a single male survivor who joined the Rabbit clan. In 1920 Parsons lists Rabbit-Tobacco as one clan, and by 1929 "Tobacco" was used as frequently as "Rabbit" and was considered the more proper name.

At Second Mesa we have noted that Rabbit and Tobacco are extinct but are linked with the Badger clan at Mishongnovi. In Shongopavi there are likewise no Rabbit or Tobacco people at present, but Rabbit is said to have merged with the Bear clan, and one Rabbit clan land is remembered.[66]

On Third Mesa, Stephen lists a dozen Rabbit families but no

Tobacco families. The latter is considered to be an extinct group merged with the Cottontail Rabbit clan. The Rabbit-Tobacco group here is attached to the Parrot-Katcina phratry to form an enlarged group, though the two subdivisions are distinguishable from one another.

The Patki-Pikyas-Corn-Cloud-Snow phratry group is well represented on all the mesas. This group is indefinitely expandable, as far as clan names are concerned, everything connected with rain or water or corn, as well as useful plants such as *sivapi* (rabbit brush), being considered to belong to this phratry. On First Mesa the early surveys indicate Patki ("Water House?"), Corn, Cloud, Snow, and Sivapi families, though there was a tendency to refer to them all as "Patki." Lowie lists "Cloud (Patki)-Corn" as one clan with two names,[67] and Parsons indicates only one clan for the entire group. Forde groups them under "Water" clan as plural names or merged clans.

At Mishongnovi, Stephen's survey lists five Pikyas ("Young Corn-Ear" or "Sprouting Corn"), four Patki, and no Sivapi families. Lowie groups Water Cloud (Patki) and Sivapi under Sprouting Corn, with the note that there is no remembrance of Sivapi. Forde lists two separate clan groups—Sprouting Corn, with Corn subsidiary, and Water, including Cloud, Snow, Frog, etc., each group with a set of lands. In 1934 Mrs. Beaglehole lists simply "Corn" and "Water." Presumably these are linked in a larger exogamous grouping, since they do not intermarry according to marriage data presented. This phratry is well represented at Shongopavi, where Corn, Water, and Snow clans are listed in Stephen's survey. Parsons recorded a Snow–Patki–Young Corn-Ear grouping in 1920; Forde's data (1929) indicate that Corn, Water, and Snow clans have separate lands but are linked—with Katcina into a larger exogamous unit or phratry.[68] A Water (Cloud) family is also listed in the early reports on Shipaulovi; this group was extinct in 1916 but remembered by Lowie's informants.

Stephen's survey for Third Mesa indicated some nine families classed as Corn or Pikyas clan but was uncertain as to possible Patki families. Titiev's more recent investigations indicate that there were both Pikyas and Patki peoples at Oraibi, and even a few Sivapi, with clanhouses for all three. The latter are now extinct, but the former two are quite separate, perhaps even more so than formerly, since they have engaged in several quarrels.

The Kele-Squash-Crane phratry group has long been extinct on First Mesa. No families are listed, even in the early surveys, but the Squash clan is remembered as having owned the Wuwutcim and Marau ceremonies. One of the clans of this group, the Tubish or "Sorrow-making" clan, is also said to have owned the Drab Flute ceremony. Lowie lists a Squash (Pumpkin) clan without any phratral associates, while Ford lists the Squash clan as extinct but with its clan land still remembered.

At Mishongnovi, Stephen lists three Squash families, with some question as to Kele families. The Cranes are extinct but reported by Lowie to have been once numerous according to tradition. The Kele (here translated as "pigeon hawks" but, better, "chicken hawk") are not known to have lived in Mishongnovi, but there was one lineage of Squash in 1916. Forde lists only the Squash clan, which Mrs. Beaglehole's informant refers to as "Pumpkin." No members of this phratry are known for Shongopavi,[69] but Forde lists one Squash family which was said to have come recently from Shongopavi to Shipaulovi. Mrs. Beaglehole also notes a Pumpkin clanswoman who moved from Mishongnovi to Shipaulovi; this may be the family to which Forde's informants were referring.

On Third Mesa, Stephen found one family each for Kele, Squash, and Crane but none for Duck, which is associated with this group at Oraibi. Titiev has confirmed the presence of all three clans in the period before 1906, though at present they seem to have largely merged into one lineage. Here also, as on First Mesa, this phratry group controls the Wuwutcim ceremony.

There are, in addition, two phratry groups which are represented on First Mesa only. The most important of these is the Horn-Flute phratry, including such clan names as Horn, Antelope, Mountain Sheep, Deer, Millet, Red Ant, Black Ant, Flute, etc. The early accounts differ somewhat. Stephen's genealogies in his *Hopi Journal* list Horn, Deer, Millet, and Mountain Sheep lineages, but his survey for Mindeleff indicates five Horn families, two Flute families, and seven Red Ant families in Walpi. Fewkes later lists two Horn lineages and six Flute lineages, though this is, in part, a condensation of Stephen's lineages. With the extinction of the Bear clan, this phratry ultimately acquired the village chieftaincy which became lodged in the Millet lineage. Since this lineage also controlled the Blue Flute ceremony, the chieftainship became associated with control of this ceremony, and the term "Flute" was applied to the clan and associated clans. This shift is recorded symbolically in the mythology and dramatized in the Flute ritual where the chief is received by the representatives of the Bear and Snake clans and invited to enter and take over the leadership of the village.

In 1915 Lowie reports Horn-Flute as one clan and notes that Snake, Horn, and Flute are said to have come from different places, but at the same time, so that they join together for ceremonies. As a result the Flutes are supposed to call the Snake clanspeople by kinship terms because of their early ceremonial relations, some informants even feeling they should not intermarry. Parsons lists Millet-Horn as one clan with two names, while Forde lists Deer as the main clan, with Horn, Flute, and Ant as subsidiary names or merged clans.

These names do not occur in Second and Third Mesa phratry groups for the most part, though Millet is listed as one of the Kokop-Coyote-Masau'u clans at Oraibi. When pressed, informants will say that they were formerly present but have died out, though this is unlikely in view of the distributions of the other phratries.

The last phratry to be considered is the Mustard phratry, in which is found such clan names as Chakwaina, Roadrunner, Magpie, Oak, and Throwing Stick. Both Mustard and Chakwaina clans seem to be present, though there is some doubt about the latter, which refers to the custody of the Chakwaina Katcina. The Mustard people live partly in Sichomovi and are thought to be latecomers, possibly from the Rio Grande region or from Zuni. Lowie reported this group as the Grass clan in 1915 with one lineage; Parsons reported the whole group as one clan or maternal family; while Forde found six separate lineages classed as Mustard, with Chakwaina, Acorn, and Rabbit Stick as subsidiary names. These names are likewise absent from the phratry groupings of Second and Third mesas, though the Roadrunner is listed as one of the Reed-Greasewood-Bow clan names at Oraibi.

If we now look beneath the variations resulting from the play of historical factors, we can discern a basic clan-phratry pattern for the Hopi, the definition of which is essential to the recognition and explanation of the variations themselves. This pattern is only partially represented in any one village but is more completely realized when all the major villages are considered. Out of the hundreds of clan names, some fifty clans are actually represented, or can be inferred to have existed recently, in the various Hopi villages. These clans, listed in Table 2 above, are grouped into some twelve phratries, two of which are restricted to First Mesa villages. Some of these phratry groups have recombined into larger groupings in certain villages, but, even so, they often retain a degree of separateness; others are completely absent from certain villages, suggesting either that they were never there or that they have died out. This clan-phratry pattern has had a long period to develop; in view of the relatively rapid changes noted in the last fifty years, it is very remarkable that there is any pattern left to define.

One answer lies in the analysis of the relations between lineage, clan, and phratry. Parsons notes that Stephen was confused in regard to clan classification "largely because he failed to grasp completely the importance of the maternal family, the group of blood kin, in the construction of the clan; because he did not analyze fully the relations, ceremonial and otherwise within the clan, or between the clans; and because the terminology he favored, phratry and gens, was misleading."[70] Her solution of the terminological difficulty is to substitute "clan" for phratry and "maternal family" for clan [gens], a solution which involves her in a greater confusion than Stephen's.

The structural composition of the Hopi clan is important from a number of standpoints. Parsons has advanced the theory that each named clan represents a matrilineal lineage of real blood kindred, and Lowie is inclined to agree with her, though he prefers to retain the term "clan" in his descriptive account. She is apparently basing her argument on the fact that the Hopi do not distinguish separate lineages within the clan terminologically (though they distinguish them in other ways) and on the hypothesis that Hopi clans have developed from lineages originally. My own feeling is that three terms are needed for an adequate analysis. Genealogical investigations by Fewkes, Lowie, Forde, White, and Titiev[71] leave no doubt that, of the totemically named clans represented in the various villages, at least half have more than one lineage, and the number of separate lineages may range as high as six. White's field party found thirty-nine lineages for twenty-one clans, and Lowie's data for Second Mesa are similar, only seven clans out of fifteen coinciding with single lineages.[72] It may be granted that there are a variety of mechanisms by which separate lineages arise, but unless it is assumed that Hopi clans originated recently, or did not begin to suffer change until a few years ago, this argument has little point. What is important is that where there are separate lineages within a named clan they are discriminated in regard to ownership and control of land, ceremonies, and ceremonial position, though they may be considered to be related ultimately by genealogical descent.

In some cases individual clans may have two or more names owing to merging of survivors of dying clans, the taking-over of ceremonial duties of extinct clans, or conceptual identifications based on Hopi logic. This situation is particularly true at First Mesa, where a relatively small population supports an extensive clan structure, but was less true of Old Oraibi, where the population was larger. This has led Parsons to state that "there are no facts to warrant anything but classification by clan" and to consider that there are no real phratries. Her basis seems to be exogamy: "Pity the anthropologist! His only safe criterion is exogamy. Let him count groups or lineages which do not intermarry as belonging to the same clan and let it go at that!"[73]

But this ignores the larger groupings which our comparative

survey indicates actually exist, and which are made up of separate clans or clan groups. This larger group is nameless, and the clans forming it are not considered to be genealogically connected but to be related because of common experiences in early times. Kinship relations are extended on the basis of "partnership" rather than on the basis of common descent, and exogamy is extended to this larger group; but to call it a "clan" is to ignore its structure and functions. On First Mesa the Bear phratry may be so reduced that it represents a single merged clan group, but that is not true on Second Mesa or on Third; in fact, the Bear and Spider clans on Third Mesa are so sharply separated that there is no possible confusion of the two at present, and the same thing is true of the Bear and Bluebird groups on Second Mesa. Similarly, while Tobacco-Rabbit have merged into a single clan on First Mesa but retain their "phratry identity," on Second Mesa they have been pretty completely incorporated as "names" with Badger-Butterfly, while on Third Mesa they have merged into one clan group but have affiliated with Parrot-Katcina as a definitely recognizable subdivision of this larger exogamous phratry group. To call these larger groups "clans" ignores the comparative facts and hamstrings historical as well as structural and functional analyses.

The basic phratry pattern is more clearly delimited for the Hopi than are the constituent clan patterns. Titiev, for example, has found that it is possible to reproduce Stephen's clan and phratry census of 1883 with a considerable degree of accuracy. It is evident that the phratry grouping has exerted an enormous stabilizing influence in Hopi society. Individual clans are subject to extinction from failure of the line or lines of women. This can happen rather rapidly, as the data for the last three generations indicate, particularly where the average population per clan group is small. The Hopi villages have been in existence since before 1540, and Oraibi at least probably before 1200. With our present knowledge of the mechanisms for clan change, the basic pattern presented can only be due to the importance and conservatism of the phratry pattern, unless we are willing to assume that the clan-phratry pattern is recent among the Hopi. This is denied by the central importance of the clan and the uniqueness of the phratry pattern for the Hopi—and Parsons assumes that the Hopi developed clanship and spread it to the other Pueblos.[74]

The history of clan-phratry groupings among the Hopi is tied up with an interpretation of the origin legends, the findings of archeology, and a comparative study of other Shoshonean-speaking communities. The origin legends of the Hopi follow a characteristic pattern. After the emergence of the various clans from the underworld they set out in various directions, ultimately arriving at one or another of the Hopi villages. During their migrations they met other clans with whom they became associated and lived at various of the ruins which dot the Southwest. The early ethnologists, particularly Fewkes,[75] accepted these legends at their face value and attempted to reconstruct Hopi history in accordance with them. But it soon became apparent that the origin legends of the same clan from different villages showed major contradictions and that even within the same village the stories of associated clans did not always correspond. And later research has suggested that the *order* of arrival of clans at various villages parallels their present ceremonial precedence.

It seems clear that the Hopi have accounted for their present social structure by projecting it back into the mythological past. It is not possible for clans to exist as independent units, the "unit-clan" houses of the archeologists notwithstanding, since a clan is made up of real (or assumed) blood relatives who are normally not allowed to intermarry. To the extent that local groups were clan (or lineage) organized, therefore, they would have to have at least two clan groups. Mindeleff, in attempting to account for the enormous number of small ruins scattered over the country, studied the development of farming villages in the historic period and concluded that they played an important role in earlier times. He assumed a long period of migration by small bands, as well as occasional aggregations into larger units for protection.[76]

The ancestors of the present inhabitants of the villages reached Tusayan in little bands at various times and from different directions. Their migrations occupied very many years, although there were a few movements in which the people came all together from some distant point. Related clans commonly built together, the newcomers seeking and usually obtaining permission to build with their kindred; thus clusters of rooms were formed, each inhabited by a clan or phratry.[77]

It is Mindeleff's reconstruction, rather than Fewkes's, which modern archeological and ethnological studies support. These latter will be summarized in a later section; here it may be suggested that the groups moving into the Hopi country may well have been organized around matrilocal households and matrilineal lineages as a base and that the more elaborated clan and phratry organization was developed to integrate the larger populations.[78]

CLASSIFICATION OF NATURE

Turning now to the classification of nature represented in the Hopi clan-phratry system, we can get some additional insight into the bases for phratral groupings. The application of the term "totemism" to Hopi clans has been resisted by most investigators. Thus Lowie states: "The relationship of a clan to the eponymous animal was so irregular as hardly to merit the term 'totemic.' Thus while the Butterfly people refrain from killing butterflies, the Rabbit people always kill rabbits and the Bear clan kill bears."[79]

But this is an exceedingly narrow and one-sided view of totemism; more useful in my opinion is Radcliffe-Brown's suggestion that "the problem of totemism is part of the wider problem of the relation of man to nature in ritual and myth, and must always be studied in reference to the larger problem."[80] Regardless of what term is used for the Hopi system, one of the important bases for clan-phratry unity lies in the relations of this social classification to the classification of natural phenomena.

Each Hopi clan is named after some object, personage, or aspect of nature. Titiev has summarized the situation as follows:

> The great majority of names on any clan list are those of plants, animals, or supernatural personages. These eponyms the Hopi call *wuya* or *n'atöla*, terms which seem to refer to ancestors or ancients. Some of them are represented by masks, figurines, or fetishes of various sorts, others have no tangible representation; but in either case there is a strong feeling of empathy and kinship between each group and its *wuya*.[81]

Between the clan group and the *wuya* a definite relationship exists—the *wuya* is personified in part and kinship terms extended to it. The *wuya* protects a Hopi; he will pray to it for strength and good crops. Some informants evince a belief in descent of the clan from its *wuya*, but the mythological explanations generally refer to the securing of *wuya* and clan names as a result of events occurring after the emergence of the clans from the underworld. Where the *wuya* are represented by masks, they are stored in the clanhouse and are regarded as the heart of the clan.[82]

There are no taboos on the utilization of *wuya* for necessary purposes, although they must always be treated with respect and with a certain amount of ritual.[83] During the Soyal ceremony each clan makes prayer sticks for its own, and associated, *wuya* and *natoila;* this is one of the major ritual duties of a clan head. When an animal or bird is killed for food or feathers by any Hopi, it is ritually treated so that the spirit will return again—eagles have a special ritual in which they are treated as if they were persons.

Titiev has discussed the dynamics of clan segmentation and union among the Hopi as a basis for phratral groupings.[84] He assumes that phratries arise chiefly from the splitting of lineages or clans which acquire a separate status but continue their interest in one another. Such a hypothesis accounts for the multiple clan *wuya* (it is probable that "each clan has one primary and several secondary *wuya*"), the common stock of names, and the exercise of phratral exogamy. But it does not explain the variations in phratry groupings from mesa to mesa; nor is it clear why the clan legends do not refer to common origins except in terms of common experiences.

The clan legends are of two general types: (1) after emergence a clan has a series of adventures which account for the several objects with which it is associated[85] or (2) a series of clans have somewhat different adventures with the same object which accounts for the clan groups in a particular phratry and for the relations between particular *wuya*.[86] There are no cases of legendary origins of phratry groupings in the underworld or by splitting of clan groups. Hence it may be useful to examine the nature of the groupings of natural objects or aspects of nature in terms of their position in Hopi thinking and culture.

The basis for the classification of *wuya* into groups seems to be related to the position and significance of the various species and objects in Hopi culture. The *wuya* and the people of the clan group are considered as if they were in a "partnership"; in fact, the *wuya* are often spoken of as "partners." Within the various groupings, the classification is expandable, so that there is a definite (or potential) place for everything that is important to the Hopi. Each clan group is closely associated with all the *wuya* of the phratry group, as well as with its own.

The nature of the relationships involved in the classification are not completely clear. The Hopi have a definite feeling that the sets of "clan names" in the various phratry groups go together in a logical manner, and they agree pretty well on the groupings, but the "reasons" they give for the groupings are in most cases merely the mythological sanctions. If the phratry groupings outlined above are carefully examined, certain inferences as to the bases of association can be made; others will require more adequate historical and ceremonial information.[87]

The Bear–Spider–Bluebird–Bear's Rope phratry grouping has a mythological sanction in the adventures of various clans with a dead bear;[88] in other accounts the Bear clan was aided by Spider Woman in the emergence from the underworld.[89] The bear is considered a strong animal with powerful "medicine"; in aboriginal times he was the only animal that the Hopi could not handle. Since he hibernates in winter, he is associated with seasonal changes. The "bear's rope" refers to the carrying strap or tumpline, formerly used for carrying loads. Spider Woman taught the Hopi how to spin and weave, as well as guiding them on various journeys. The trap-door spider, which lives in a "kiva," is specifically referred to in many of the myths. The bluebird is associated with summer and perhaps with wisdom.

The ceremonial relationships provide additional tieups in the Second and Third Mesa villages. The Bear clan controls the Winter Solstice chieftainship, while the "Summer Solstice" Flute and Antelope ceremonies are largely in the hands of other clans of this phratry. The bluebird is important in Blue Flute ritual, and the locust,[90] in both adult and immature forms, is represented in the Blue and Gray Flute ceremonies. The Spider "grandmother" is an important mythological figure—so important that she gave a strong sanction to the Spider clan in connection with the "split" at Oraibi and the founding of Hotevilla.[91] The primacy of the Bear clan in all the villages may be the result of colonization from one main village; the Oraibi traditions of separation from Shongopovi and the recent efforts of Walpi and Old Oraibi to re-establish the Bear clan by importing a Shongopovi Bear clan girl are indications in this direction.

The basis for the associations in the Katcina-Parrot-Crow phratry seems primarily ceremonial: in connection with the Katcina cult. The Katcina clan is generally in charge of the Katcinas; parrot feathers "belong" to the Katcinas and are an integral part of their costume. Spruce is also associated with this group for a similar reason; and cottonwood because it is associated with water and is used for making Katcina dolls. The crows or ravens were formerly associated with war[92]—and also with storm clouds, since they come in flocks an hour or two before a storm.[93] The Crow-Wing Katcina acts as "mother" of the Katcinas during the Katcina initiation. It is probable that the "extinction" of the Crow clan everywhere is in part a function of loss of war prestige and the deprecatory attitudes of whites; such clans have shifted to Katcina or Parrot in certain cases.[94]

The association of Rabbit and Tobacco with this group is found only at Oraibi and is probably the result of the extinction of the Tobacco clan and the lack of ceremonial importance of the Rabbit clan, particularly with the decline of hunting. Despite the relative separation of these two subgroups, they have developed a mythological sanction for their "partnership."

The Snake-Lizard-Sand phratry association is based on a "logical" relationship: the sand or earth is a "mother" who feeds the Hopi by producing crops; the snakes are "messengers" for rain as well as guardians of the springs; lizards likewise bring rain, as well as being associated with love-making. The burrowing owl and snake are thought to inhabit prairie-dog holes in common. On First Mesa, Snake, Cactus, and Dove form one subgroup, and Lizard, Horned Toad, and Sand another. In general, this phratry group is associated with the Snake ceremony, and there is a tendency to maintain this name in recent times because of the prestige of the latter.

The Sun-Eagle-Hawk phratry grouping has a general association with the "above" direction. The sun is one of the important Hopi deities, and offerings are frequently made to the "sun father"; the moon and stars are associated with the sun, and the "sun's forehead" symbolizes the importance of dawn. Eagles and hawks are powerful hunters; they are captured and kept for their feathers, which are used in prayer-stick-making. Turkeys, which were formerly domesticated, were also kept for their feathers, which are particularly used in making the "sun shield." The association of the Reed and Greasewood clans with this group on First Mesa seems a recent phenomenon, owing in part to partial extinction of both groups.

The Reed-Greasewood-Bow-Arrow-Roadrunner phratry grouping is intelligible in terms of the "bow-and-arrow complex." Reeds were used for arrows (as well as in weaving); greasewood may have been used for bows and is used for making arrows in connection with certain ceremonies. The roadrunner runs fast "like an arrow," and its track cannot be followed. The Bow clan is one of the few groups named after a cultural object or artifact; the arrow is logically associated but is not actually represented anywhere. At Oraibi Roadrunner and Greasewood are closely associated (perhaps an ecological association); and Reed and Bow form a subunit. The "social distance" of the Bow clan has been recently influenced by the behavior of its leaders.[95] On First Mesa we have noted the affiliation of Reed and Greasewood with the Sun-Eagle phratry group; the Roadrunner or Chaparral Cock, on the other hand, is here associated with the Mustard phratry, and the Bow with the Kokop grouping.

The Badger-Butterfly-Porcupine phratry grouping is at first sight a strange combination. The badger is the medicine animal par excellence and through his digging ability controls all roots; through the latter control he is also responsible for the early growth of wild plants. After the plants grow and flower, the butterflies appear and visit each flower, after which there are seeds or fruits. The Badger clan's control of Powamu, in which the plant growth for the coming year is ritually encouraged, is thus intelligible; on Third Mesa this serves in part to link the Badger and Katcina clans in the control of the Katcina cult.[96]

The Masau'u-Kokop-Coyote phratry group seems to be organized around war and death. Masau'u, one of the important Hopi deities, is in charge of the afterworld and is the "owner" of fire and the crops. Juniper and piñon ("cedar") are the major woods used for fire. The *kokop* is a small unidentified bird which belongs to Masau'u[97] and brings black clouds and rain. Kwan (agave) and yucca are used for food and for soap, respectively; their sharp-pointed leaves are symbols of protection. The Coyote clans are traditionally "fighters" on Third Mesa; associated with them are the various foxes and the wolf. There seem to be two subgroupings here, one associated with Masau'u and his activities, and the other with the coyote-fox species whose craft and skill are well known. On Third Mesa the two subgroups came from different directions; their association in one phratry is very probably in terms of protection and war.

The Rabbit-Tobacco phratry grouping has been mentioned above. The jackrabbit and the cottontail are differentiated, and the latter is more important, both in terms of food and ritually. The association of tobacco and pipe is clear, but the basis for the association of tobacco and rabbit is obscure. There may be some relation of rabbits and wild tobacco or some as yet unknown ceremonial association. We have noted the affiliation of this group with the Katcina-Parrot phratry on Third Mesa; at Mishongnovi they were linked with the Badger group.

The Patki-Pikyas-Corn-Cloud-Rain phratry is concerned primarily with the growth cycle of corn. As one informant said: "The clouds come, the rain falls, the corn grows and forms ears which feed the Hopi." The *patki* seems to refer to the rock cisterns of the Hopi and to the clouds, both of which are "water houses." *Pikyas* refers to the "milk" stage in the ripening of corn. Along with rain, clouds, thunder, lightning, rainbow, snow, hail, and other related phenomena, there are also listed frogs, tadpoles, and other water animals. *Sivapi*, a plant used in basketry and for many other purposes, is also included in this group. Stephen suggests that it refers to the Lakon society, whose chieftaincy is in the Patki group, but this would not explain the parallel inclusion on Third Mesa.

The Kele-Squash-Crane phratry group is traditionally associated with the Wuwutcim ceremony. The *kele* or chicken hawk is a symbol of bravery, since it attacks birds larger than itself; novices in the Wuwutcim initiation are *kelehoya*, "little chicken hawks," getting ready to leave their nest. The crane and duck, water birds, "belong" to the Wuwutcim ceremony; the nature of the affiliation of squash with *kele* is not clear.

The Horn-Deer-Flute phratry grouping includes various horned animals, deer, mountain sheep, and antelope, and *lehü*, a wild millet which probably served as food for these animals as well as for the Hopi. Millet is associated with the Masau'u group on Third Mesa, but otherwise the group is restricted to First Mesa. Various kinds of ants are associated with this phratry grouping, and early surveys show Ant clan families, but they are now extinct or have shifted to more "important" names.[98]

The Mustard-Chakwaina-Roadrunner phratry grouping is likewise restricted to First Mesa, and includes the throwing stick, oak, and magpie. The Chakwaina Katcina, in the custody of this group, has given its name to one of the clans. The mountain oak was used for the manufacture of curved throwing sticks. But this group seems a miscellaneous assortment of clans, in part probably recently introduced from elsewhere, which have been brought together under the phratry pattern.

The above survey suggests that the classification of nature for social purposes is rather complex. While there is some tendency among the Hopi to assign animals and objects to various directions for ceremonial purposes, there is no directional phratry grouping such as Cushing noted for Zuni.[99] Rather, the classification seems based on the significant activities of Hopi life as related to the external environment. The growth of crops, rain, war, hunting, and the control of ceremonies—these are the foci for the larger symbolic groupings. Each of these groupings has a rationale of its own, in Hopi eyes at least, but there is no apparent master-plan by which they are all tied together.

Laura Thompson, in a recent interpretation of Hopi culture, has proposed such a master-plan:

> An analysis of the phratry groupings in relation to the Hopi traditional symbol system as revealed in ceremony and myth, shows that they tend to follow an ideal pattern in which each unit, composed of a group of related clans, may also include as non-human partners one or more related species of animals and of plants, one or more orders of physical objects, one or more natural elements and one or more deities or parts of anthropomorphic deities. Moreover, ideally each unit appears also to be associated with certain character traits of their non-human partners; with one of the six world directions and its color (each direction has a color as well as other symbolic associations); with a season of the year; with an important activity (economic or ceremonial); with one or both sexes; and with some aspect of the reproduction and growth cycle.[100]

That all these are important the above survey indicates (Thompson's interpretations were in part based upon these data), but in my opinion her "ideal pattern" is at best incipient, and there is little evidence for the *systematic* associations which she assumes. The Hopi have never developed a central hierarchy of priests to organize and systematize the somewhat differing conceptions of the world which each clan or ceremonial group holds, and the variations from village to village add further complications.

By viewing the clan names in relationship to Hopi life, it is possible to see them as symbolizing certain social values. Various aspects of nature are personalized, and their characteristics are made use of in myth and ritual. By the use of masks or other means the *wuya* of the clan may be impersonated or represented and their influence enlisted for the aid of the group. The rich field of Hopi symbolism needs to be studied in terms of Hopi "logic," a procedure which requires a much greater knowledge of Hopi ceremonies than we yet possess. The key to certain of these ceremonies has been provided by Titiev in his analysis of the scheme of Hopi ceremonialism,[101] but we lack a detailed interpretative statement for any of the Hopi rituals.

The conception of the classification of nature embodied in the phratry groupings as concerned with significant aspects of Hopi life will ultimately allow us to see how they conceive of these activities and how they are related in Hopi thinking. From this knowledge we will be in a position to define the phratral classification more adequately. This conception of the classification of nature also has important implications for historical and theoretical problems. We have noted that the groupings are only partially dependent upon the actual clan groups existing at any one time. Hence Lowie's statement that "it is essential to distinguish actual clans, present or known to have become extinct within the memory of men still living, and mere clan *names* associated together by native theorizers,"[102] is only partially valid. They should be distinguished, but each is important.

Kroeber long ago pointed out that it is not necessary to assume that the names in a Hopi phratry correspond to actual existing, or formerly existing, bodies of people, nor is it necessary to assume that the mythology is history or that the phratry groupings represent pristine Hopi social organization. In his pioneer comparative study of the Pueblo clan system he came to the conclusion that "in essentials a single system of clan organization pervades all of the pueblos."[103] By using the key provided by Fewkes's compilation of Hopi clans[104] and using only clans listed by some authority as actually occurring, he found it possible to organize Pueblo clans in some dozen groups. The basis of the system, he believed, was a grouping of clans in pairs from which he assumed a principle of duality or polarity. Thus in his table of Pueblo clans he groups the Hopi clans into eleven paired sets, but he achieves his grouping by a judicious subordination and by putting together such clans as Bear and Badger. The fuller data for the Hopi found in Forde's review[105] of First and Second Mesa clans and Titiev's data[106] for Third Mesa (summarized above) throw considerable doubt on this grouping of clans by pairs. Kroeber's principle of duality or polarity is not, in my opinion, adequate to explain the Hopi data; its possible significance for other pueblos will be considered below.

The Hopi clan system, then, becomes more intelligible if it is considered (1) from the standpoint of a segmentary grouping of the population for certain purposes and (2) as a grouping of aspects of nature which have significance and value for Hopi life. We have noted the important unilineal groupings of lineage, clan, and phratry, the functions they perform, and the relations between them. In general, they confirm Forde's recent generalization that, where major unilineal groups occur, "it is found not only that there often is segmentation at a series of levels, but that with respect to the transmission of rights and duties, the more specific the claim or obligation, the narrower the segment involved."[107] The relations between these segments and the important aspects of nature is not completely understood but is mediated through kinship and "partnership" rather than descent. The dynamics of this interrelated system is affected by changes in population, changes in culture, changes in the prestige gradient, and other historical factors, some of which we have noted above.

The relations of the Hopi clan system to the ceremonial and political organization will be discussed below; the similarities with the systems of other Pueblos will be considered in the concluding chapter.

Ceremonial Organization

The ceremonial organization of the Hopi is highly complex and includes the Katcina cult, the men's societies concerned with Tribal Initiation, the Winter Solstice ceremony, and the various societies concerned with rain, war, clowning, and curing. The ritual activities are organized in terms of a ceremonial calendar, and each major ceremony is associated with a clan, a society, and a kiva. The First Mesa ceremonies have been described by Stephen, Fewkes, and Parsons, among others, and Voth has given meticulous descriptions of several Third Mesa rituals, plus a very few Second Mesa ceremonies. One of the important tasks still to be accomplished is the recording of the Second Mesa ceremonial cycles, but enough is known to make a preliminary analysis useful.

The interpretation of Hopi ceremonies has been inadequate except for Titiev's recent monograph, *Old Oraibi*. Since this volume is readily available, I have condensed my original discussion of the ceremonial system to emphasize the organizational aspects of the ceremonies, and the interrelations of clan, society, and kiva groupings in terms of the ceremony, not only at Oraibi but on all the Hopi mesas, so far as information is available.[108]

In Hopi theory each ceremony is owned or controlled by a single clan, though on Second Mesa there are important tendencies toward the sharing of ceremonial control by two or more clans. The ceremony was usually "given" to a clan before the emergence from the underworld by one or another of the deities, but some ceremonies, notably the Snake and Flute rituals, were received at a later time in connection with the adventures of certain cult heroes. The controlling clan takes charge of the ritual apparatus, which is normally kept in the clanhouse, and furnishes the chief priest. While control of the ceremony is phrased in terms of the clan, its actual transmission is normally within the important lineage occupying the clanhouse. The chief priest selects a sister's son—or other lineage relative—and trains him as his successor; selected women of the lineage are likewise intrusted with the special knowledge pertaining to the ceremony as well as the care of the paraphernalia. If the lineage should die out, another lineage of the same clan (or a clansman from another village) may take over the responsibility. In theory a ceremony should die out when a clan becomes extinct, but in the case of important ceremonies, at least, associated clans of the same phratry may take over the duties or, in their absence, a "child" of the clan. In extreme instances a ceremony may be offered to any individual who will take over the responsibilities and privileges of leadership.[109] In the case of the founding of a new village, the whole ceremonial cycle may be recreated, and responsibility for particular ceremonies assigned to new clans where necessary.[110] For certain ceremonies, at least, there is evidence that subordinate ceremonial positions are likewise associated with particular lineages and clans.[111]

Each ceremony is performed by a society or fraternity whose

membership cuts right across the clan-phratry system. Since the "ceremonial father" is selected from an unrelated clan and since he initiates his "ceremonial son" into all the societies to which he belongs, the initiation procedure automatically brings about such a distribution of membership. In the case of certain of the societies there is some tendency to consider the clanspeople of the controlling clan as potential members. Curing and trespass are alternative paths to membership, and any adult may request a member to initiate him if he so desires. Care is taken by the controlling clans to see that potential successors to leadership in the ceremonies are properly sponsored and initiated.

The Katcina cult is the only tribal-wide organization among the Hopi, both boys and girls being initiated, as we have noted, but the ritual and dancing activities are largely carried out by the men. The Katcinas are associated with the cult of the dead and are thought of as generalized ancestors who return with clouds and rain to help the community. They normally come in groups to dance in the plaza, being impersonated by the men; the more important Katcinas (the Chief Katcinas) are thought of as clan ancestors and are impersonated by clansmen in connection with the important ceremonies.[112] The large number of Katcinas representing animal and bird species, nowadays seldom impersonated, suggest a much closer relationship with the world of nature in the recent past.

The Katcina cult on all mesas is associated with the Powamu society and with the Katcina-Parrot phratry group. The Oraibi organization appears to be the most complex. Here the Powamu society is controlled by the Badger clan, whose members have a preferred right to membership and act as "fathers" of the Katcinas during their appearances in the village. The Katcina chief should be a member of the Katcina clan and is in charge of the Katcina initiation during the Powamu ceremony in February and of the Niman ceremony in July. The Badger clan and Powamu chief are in charge of the first half of the Katcina season, then control shifts to the Katcina clan and chief, though the two chiefs co-operate throughout. In the other major villages the Katcina (or Parrot) clan controls both Powamu and the

Katcina cult, and the Powamu chief acts also as Katcina chief. It is not clear whether there are separate initiations, as at Oraibi, but it is highly probable.

The simpler pattern found in the majority of villages may well be the basic form, with the Oraibi situation representing a specialized development in which the Badger clan has taken over a portion of the extensive responsibilities for the Katcina cult.[113] But, on the other hand, it is not usual for a single society to perform two ceremonies such as Powamu and Niman in a six-month period. It is possible that the elaboration of the Katcina cult which has occurred among the Hopi was in the process of being "rationalized" at Oraibi through a further division of labor. Why the Badger clan secured control of Powamu, if our conclusion is correct, is not too clear.[114] Badger is associated with medicines (via roots), and the "medicine chiefs" in the Niman ceremonies at Walpi and Mishongnovi are Badger clansmen. Also the privilege of whipping the children at initiation belongs to the Badger and Rabbit clans on First Mesa, according to Lowie.[115] With the elaboration of the Katcina cult there may well have been greater prestige involved in the Katcina cult than in Powamu. There may also be involved some secondary modification of clan names in the direction of the term "Katcina." The situation at Shongopovi exhibits some interesting features with regard to these problems. Here the Katcina clan is at present reduced to one old man who is in process of transferring the Katcina chieftaincy to a Parrot clansman who is married in from Mishongnovi. Leadership of the Powamu society seems to have been taken over temporarily by the village chief (Bear clan) and may later pass to another clan.

The kiva affiliations of the Powamu society vary from village to village. At Oraibi they met in Hotcitcivi,[116] "owned" by the Badger clan; at Shongopovi in the Parrot (chief) kiva, "owned" by Bear and Katcina clans; at Mishongnovi in the Kwan kiva; and at Walpi in the chief kiva, controlled by the Patki and Katcina clans. The responsibility for the Niman Dance, as well as for other Katcina activities during the winter season, rotates annually among the various kivas in each village in a fixed order.

The Tribal Initiation ceremony is performed periodically by four men's societies: Wuwutcim, Tao, Ahl, and Kwan, into one of which every young man is normally initiated. Each society has its separate ceremony, performed annually in November, but all co-operate in the initiation rituals held now at irregular intervals. Titiev has summarized the procedures for Third Mesa so far as they are known and has provided us with a preliminary interpretation of their significance.[117]

The role of these four societies in Hopi life has changed considerably in the last century. An early statement by Stephen[118] considers these groups as the concentric walls of a house: the Kwan, "the destroyers of the enemy," are the outer wall; the Ahl, or Horns, the heralds who bring information as to the enemy, are the second wall; the Wuwutcim, ancients and councilors, are the third wall; and the Tao, or Singers, are the fourth wall. To these four groups are added the Snake society, as the fifth wall, and the Warriors as the sixth, or inner wall.

The Hopi theory of defensive warfare placed primary reliance upon the help of various deities, and in time of war the Kwan and Ahl groups were relied upon to weaken the enemy. The Kwan are named after the agave or century plant, the central stalk of which is protected by bayonet-like leaves, and are associated with the god of death; the Ahl represent the horned animals, particularly the mountain sheep, which are noted for their sharpness of vision and hearing. These two societies, who once co-operated in protecting the village against external enemies, now play an important role in Tribal Initiation and in the ceremonial system.

The Wuwutcim and Tao societies are, in general, fertility societies, in contrast to the warlike character of the Kwan and Ahl groups. The Wuwutcim, whose name is usually applied to the November ceremonies, are especially associated with grass, as well as with fertility in general; the Tao are responsible for the songs during initiation and are said to be named after the mockingbird who taught the Hopi at the time of Emergence. These two societies co-operate in many activities during Tribal Initiation. The initiation rituals dramatize the emergence of the

Hopi from the underworld and prepare the novices for their position in the underworld after death.

The relative position of these societies varies considerably from village to village. At Oraibi the Wuwutcim division was by far the largest, and the Wuwutcim chief, of the Kele or Chicken Hawk clan, was in general charge of the Tribal Initiation; on First Mesa, the societies are roughly equal in size and the Tao chief, of the Tobacco clan, was in general charge; at Shongopovi the Ahl chief, in recent years a Fog clansman, has been in general charge, though the Wuwutcim group is the largest; and at Mishongnovi it is probable that the Tao chief is general manager. At Oraibi, and probably at all villages, the Kwan society must have at least one candidate before the full ceremony can be performed, since this group has the most important ceremonial role in initiation.

The Wuwutcim society is controlled by the Kele or Chicken Hawk clan at Oraibi, by the Corn clan (assisted by Bluebird, Snow, and Sun) at Shongopovi,[119] by the Coyote and Squash clans at Mishongnovi, and by the Squash clan formerly at Walpi, though, when this clan became extinct, a Mustard clansman, who was "child" of the Squash, assumed responsibility. Since Kele and Squash are in the same phratry group, it is probable that the Wuwutcim society has been associated with this group, and more specifically with Squash, for some time. The Shongopovi situation is aberrant in that rotation of chieftainship is apparently practiced; however, Forde lists a society field for this village under the term *kelvasa*.[120]

The Tao society is controlled by the Parrot clans at Oraibi and Mishongnovi and by the related Katcina clan at Shongopovi, though the principle of rotation has recently been applied to this society as well. At Walpi, however, the society is controlled by the Tobacco clan, whose chief claims that it was introduced by his ancestors from Awatovi.[121] While there is a Katcina-Parrot clan at Walpi, it was reduced in numbers and had its hands full, ceremonially speaking, with the Powamu ceremony and the Katcina cult. It is possible, therefore, that it may have given up the Tao ceremony, despite the legendary claims of the Tobacco clan chief.

The Ahl society has varied associations: the Bow clan at Oraibi; the Bear and, more recently, the Fog clan,[122] at Shongopovi; the Patki clan at Mishongnovi; and the Bear clan at Walpi, though in Stephen's time a Reed clansman, "child" of Bear, was acting as regent. The association with Bear on First Mesa seems old, since the Ahl society is the only one of the four societies to have a tiponi at Walpi, though the latter may belong primarily to the Bear clan chief.

The Kwan society is the most divergent and least known of Hopi societies. At Oraibi it was controlled by a clan of the Masau'u-Kwan group, at Shongopovi by the Katcina clan (though Sun and Snow have recently taken over responsibility), at Mishongnovi by the Lizard clan, and at Walpi by the Patki clan. The "logical" association is with the Masau'u-Kwan clan group, in view of the Kwan society's relation to the dead and to Masau'u, but the clans of this group at Mishongnovi and Walpi have other ceremonial associations.

Each of these four societies is associated with a kiva which is popularly known by the name of the society, though there are more formal names given by the clan or clans which "own" or look after them. At Oraibi the Tao, Ahl, and Kwan ceremonies were held in kivas owned by the controlling clans or by others in the same phratry group. The Wuwutcim society, on the other hand, required some five kivas, though the main rites were held in Hawiovi, owned by the Bow and Sand clans, the overflow being accommodated in the Blue Flute (Spider clan), Hano (Squash clan), and Snake (Snake clan) kivas. At Shongopovi the five kivas are all primarily associated with the Tribal Initiation societies: Tao in the Parrot (chief) kiva, controlled by the Katcina and Bear clans; Ahl in the Horn kiva, owned by the Fog-Water clans; Kwan in the Snow Mountain kiva, controlled by the Sun and Snow clans; and Wuwutcim in the Bluebird kiva, owned by the Corn and Bluebird clans. A second kiva, Snow kiva, was built by the Sun and Snow clans to take care of the Wuwutcim overflow. Mishongnovi likewise has five kivas, of which four, at least, are associated with these societies: Honani (Badger) kiva with Wuwutcim, Parrot kiva with Tao, Kochovi with Kwan, and Horn kiva with Ahl. Whether Chavwuna (chief) kiva is used during Tribal Initiation is not clear but is probable. At Walpi the chief kiva (owned by Patki and Katcina clans) houses the Tao society, Wikwalobi (Mustard clan) the Wuwutcim, Ahl kiva (Horn clan) the Ahl society, and Chivato or Goat kiva (Reed clan) the Kwan group. In addition, there are two kivas in Sichomovi, one an offshoot of Wikwalobi, which are owned by the Mustard and Corn clans, respectively.[123]

The kivas, and their relations to clan, society, and ceremony, have never been clearly defined for the Hopi, and there is much confusion in the literature on the subject. These underground rectangular chambers symbolize the underworld from whence the Hopi emerged, and the major ceremonies are carried out therein. Kivas are built or repaired to meet ceremonial needs, so that a member of a clan controlling a particular ceremony frequently takes the initiative in construction and the obligation of maintenance. He will be assisted by his clanspeople, and in some cases by the members of another clan, and the responsibilities will be inherited in normal Hopi fashion.

But while the kiva is thought of as "belonging" to a particular clan or clans, membership is not by clan, contrary to Parsons' implications: "Hopi kivas are associated primarily with clanship, only secondarily are they devoted to ceremonial usage, to ceremonies and kachina dances." She goes on further to note: "To be sure this secondary function has obscured the primary to such an extent that the use of kivas is perplexing."[124] In historical perspective Parsons may be correct, since the Hopi traditions associate ceremonies with particular clans, and both the ceremonies and the kivas are thought of as contributions by the clan for the village as a whole. But kiva *membership* is not primarily by clan—while men may join other ceremonies and participate in other kivas which are more congenial or more convenient, their basic affiliation is with the kiva into which they are initiated during the Tribal Initiation. As Voth remarks for Oraibi: "At present the men who occupy that kiva (Hawiobi) belong to many different clans, as is the case with every Hopi kiva, although the clan that built it is usually considered to be the owner of it."[125] That the normal membership is that of the

Wuwutcim societies is clearly indicated in Titiev's statement that a boy usually "associates himself with the kiva to which his ceremonial Katcina father belongs, but in later life he transfers his allegiance to that kiva which houses his particular branch of the Tribal Initiation rites."[126] And, in discussing the succession to the Walpi village chieftainship, Stephen notes that "Kopeli is opposed to any of the Goat kiva men, i.e., Agaves being Town chief."[127]

The survey of the kiva affiliations of the Tribal Initiation societies further suggests a basic relationship, since in the smaller villages all the kivas are directly associated with the four societies. Only at Oraibi were there many additional kivas associated with other ceremonies. In addition to housing the Wuwutcim ceremonies, various kivas were also used for other ceremonies at all villages, a factor responsible for some of the confusion.

Initiation into one of the four divisions of the Tribal Initiation ceremony is a prerequisite for participation in the Soyal, the great Winter Solstice ceremony. This ceremony is the keystone of the Hopi ceremonial system and includes every household in its activities and benefits. At Oraibi the Soyal ceremony is owned by the Bear clan and closely associated with the village chief who normally acts as chief priest, assisted by the chiefs of several important clans. The esoteric rituals were performed in chief kiva in the presence of the Wuwutcim members initiated in that kiva, so that the Soyal officers were all members of this group. But the other kiva groups likewise participated in prayer-stick-making, dancing, and various ritual activities, and they all co-operated in the special rituals which accompany Tribal Initiation years.[128] At Shongopovi there is apparently a similar relation between the Soyal ceremony and the Bear clan, though Parsons reported the Soyal as in charge of Katcina-Parrot people in 1920,[129] and the main rites are held in chief kiva. At Mishongnovi, on the other hand, the Lizard clan is reported to be in charge of Soyal, a reflection perhaps of the difficulties which that village has experienced in finding a village chief.

On First Mesa a somewhat different situation is found. The extinction of the Walpi Bear clan led to a considerable rearrangement of ceremonial control, with the Patki clan apparently taking over the Soyal ceremony, while the village chieftaincy came ultimately to rest in the Millet clan.[130] As a result, the Soyal performance at Walpi differs in important ways from that at Oraibi.[131] The Soyal chiefs are drawn from the Patki clan and rank well down in the village hierarchy, but the main rituals are held in chief kiva, and the major village chiefs are involved in part of the ceremony. The Soyal chiefs may include members of all four Tribal Initiation societies. As in the other villages, all kivas participate; Parsons states that every man goes into the kiva his clan is associated with to make prayer feathers,[132] but the societies participate as units in the ritual of initiation years and represent the kiva groups, according to Stephen's account.

The various societies associated with rain, war, curing, and clowning have a more restricted membership and a lesser role in the ceremonial cycle. The initiation procedures, altars, and ritual performances follow a common pattern, and some of the ceremonies dramatize the myth as to how the particular clan came to the village and offered its ceremony in exchange for land and a position in the village. But the relationships of clan and society vary considerably from mesa to mesa.

The two Flute societies, which perform a joint ceremony on alternate years, are classed as solstitial and solar ceremonies by Titiev,[133] but their avowed purpose is to produce rain for the maturing crops. The Blue Flute ceremony was controlled by the Spider clan at Oraibi and was held in Sakwalenvi (then chief) kiva; the Gray Flute ceremony was owned by the Patki clan and was held in Hawiovi kiva. At Shongopovi the Blue Flute ceremony is reported to be assigned to the Patki clan, and the Gray Flute is owned by the Bear clan; at Mishongnovi the Blue Flute is controlled by the Parrot clan and the Gray Flute by the Squash clan—in both these villages the rituals are held in the clanhouse of the controlling clan. On First Mesa the Millet clan controlled the Blue Flute ceremony, and, when the village chieftaincy came into the hands of this clan, the Blue Flute ceremony became associated with the village chieftaincy and came to involve a dramatization of the transfer of control from the

Bear clan to the Millet clan.[134] The Gray Flute ceremony is extinct but was formerly in the hands of the Squash clan. The Blue Flute ceremony is held in the Millet clanhouse, despite its association with the Town chieftainship.

The Snake and Antelope societies likewise perform a joint ceremony, alternating with the Flute ceremonies in the major villages, and the two sets have many parallels in their origin myths and in their rituals. At Oraibi the Snake and Antelope ceremonies were controlled by the Snake and Spider clans, respectively, and they used the Snake (owned by Snake clan) and Nasavi (owned by Bow clan) kivas for their rites. The Shongopovi association is Sun (or Sun's Forehead) clan with Snake and Carrying Strap with the Antelope ceremony,[135] and they use Nuvaovi (Snow) and Tao (chief) kivas, respectively. At Mishongnovi the Lizard clan controls the Snake ceremony and the Bear clan the Antelope ceremony; they use the Honani and Ahl kivas, respectively. The Walpi situation is better known and, in this case, simpler. Both Snake and Antelope ceremonies are controlled by clans of the Snake phratry—Cactus and Dove, respectively—the Snake clan itself having become extinct, and the rituals were held in Wikwalovi and Tao (chief) kivas. Parsons and others believe that the greater elaboration of the Snake ceremony on First Mesa and the possession of a tiponi by the Snake society chief at Walpi indicate a possible spread from First Mesa.[136]

The variety of Flute society clan affiliations among the Hopi is in contrast to the relative uniformity of the Snake-Antelope associations. There is no discernible pattern of clan control of the Flute ceremonies, and yet they are important enough in Hopi thinking to be associated with the village chieftaincy at Walpi, and it was the Blue Flute chief who led the opposition in Old Oraibi which resulted in the founding of Hotevilla and Bakavi. The Snake ceremony, on the other hand, has close conceptual and actual relations with the Snake and related clans, while the Antelope ceremony is in the hands of one of the clans of the Bear group, except at Walpi, where the latter is extinct.[137]

The greater ritual importance of the Flute societies and their more variable clan affiliations suggest that they may be older than the Snake-Antelope societies with their greater emphasis on war. Certainly the two groups have much in common, and there has been a good deal of borrowing in one direction or the other. There is also a greater tendency for clanspeople of the controlling clan to join these societies; Lowie reports that *all* the controlling clanspeople belong to the two Flute societies at Mishongnovi, as well as members from other clans,[138] and there is some evidence that Snake clansmen are expected to join the Snake society if membership is low. The use of clanhouses rather than kivas for the Flute ceremonies is puzzling; at Oraibi, where kivas were used, a special kiva was employed for the Blue Flute society, which had some forty-six members around 1900. The use of kivas for the Snake ceremony was probably necessary in view of the keeping and handling of snakes. The alternation of these two sets of ceremonies suggests further that they are conceptually similar and play a comparable role in the ceremonial calendar.

The women's societies are patterned after those of the men (though each has some participants of the opposite sex) and have similar functions. The Marau society is the most important; it is symbolically associated with the Wuwutcim society and has both fertility and curing functions. The other two women's societies, Oaqöl and Lakon, are similar in organization. There is great variation in the controlling clans from village to village, with no perceivable over-all pattern. The chief priestess is usually assisted by her brother (or husband) in the conduct of the rituals, and women might join one or more of the groups as desired, men joining temporarily as a result of being cured.

The Warrior society was formerly of great importance, but with the cessation of warfare around 1860 the organization gradually became extinct. At Oraibi, according to Titiev,[139] there were two organizations: (1) the ordinary Warrior society or Momtcit, which was divided into two groups, the regular Momtcit and the Stick-swallowers society; and (2) the *real* Warriors, who had avowedly to slay and scalp an enemy. The Spider and Kokop clans were in charge of the Momtcit and

Stick-swallowers rituals and paraphernalia, and the ceremonies were held in Wiklavi kiva. Whether the *real* Warriors had a separate organization is not clear; they were initiated in Hawiovi (Wuwutcim) kiva under the direction of the same two clans.

At Shongopovi the war group and the Snake society are reported as identical by Parsons,[140] and the Snake society chief is also the War Chief. She lists the War Chief as Reed clan, but he probably belongs to the associated Sun (or Sun's Forehead) clan, since Forde reports no Reed clan lands for Shongopovi. At First Mesa there is evidence of a parallel organization to that of Oraibi, called the "Kaletakwimkya," in charge of the Reed clan. This ceremony is performed following the Soyal and includes performances of the Stick-swallowers and a War Dance.[141]

The major Hopi societies all have curing functions (in connection with the disorders that they have the power to bring about), but these are subordinate to their rain-bringing and community welfare activities. Formerly there were also some curing societies among the Hopi; the Yaya, or Fire Doctor's society, and the Poboctu, or Eye-seekers society, existed on both First and Third mesas, and probably on Second Mesa also. The Yaya was controlled by the Greasewood clan at Oraibi, the Katcina clan (?) at Mishongnovi, and the Badger clan at Walpi, while the Poboctu survivors at Oraibi and Walpi were Kokop and Lizard clansmen, respectively. The Poboctu were said to be especially concerned with counteracting the activities of *powaka*, or witches, who were thought to be organized into a society of the typical Hopi pattern. In some accounts the witch society is "international" in scope, including Navahos, whites, and other Indians. The Yaya cured burns due to fire and indulged in fire magic.

The nature of the Clown organizations in the Hopi villages is not clear. Parsons notes that the Wuwutcim and Singers societies are ex officio members of the Chüka, or "Squatting" society, on First Mesa and that the Singers chief acted as their chief, but they are listed by Stephen as formerly a society in charge of the Katcina-Parrot clan.[142] On Third Mesa they have been associated with the Eagle clan. The Paiyatamu appear to be a

Keresan organization introduced, in all probability, by the Tewa on First Mesa. At Hano they are owned by the Cottonwood (Katcina) clan and act as "fathers" of the Katcina. Titiev[143] lists a Paiyatamu Clown society at Oraibi owned by the Eagle clan which formerly met in Hano kiva. The Tatcukti, or *koyemci*, are borrowed from Zuni, and the Piptü are temporary self-appointed grotesques who appeared with other clowns on various occasions.

In addition to the organized societies which performed regular rituals, there were other temporary groups whose activities were of a semiritual nature. Communal rabbit hunts were held, permission being secured from the Rabbit clan chief who controlled the animals; and work parties were organized to clean out springs and to plant and harvest for village officials. Formerly ritual expeditions to gather salt were made to the Grand Canyon or to Zuni Salt Lake.

Within the major ceremonies certain clans claimed prescriptive rights to particular ritual operations. Thus a Tobacco clansman should prepare the pipe for smoking, a Badger clansman should make medicine and sprinkle participants, the Patki clan should fetch water from the springs, a Sand clansman should bring sand for the altar, etc.

This brief survey is summarized in Table 3, which lists Hopi ceremonies; but it is impossible to indicate all the changes which have taken place or to reconcile the conflicting data in many instances. What is evident from the discussion above is a common pattern of societies and ceremonies at each major village. The association of particular ceremonies with particular clans is much less evident, though in certain instances there is a discernible pattern. The ceremonial calendar is likewise almost identical for the major villages despite minor variations in the Katcina cycle and other rituals from mesa to mesa.[144]

The processes by which this common pattern of societies and ceremonies became established can only be inferred, but an analysis of the modern situation gives us an indication of how the common patterns may be transferred at the same time that new associations of ceremonies with clans are established. Titiev

TABLE 3*

MAJOR HOPI CEREMONIES AND THEIR SOCIETY, CLAN, AND KIVA AFFILIATIONS

Ceremony and Society	Oraibi		Shongopovi		Mishongnovi		Walpi	
	Controlling Clan	Home Kiva	Controlling Clan	Home Kiva	Controlling Clan	Home Kiva	Controlling Clan	Home Kiva
Tribal Initiation:								
Wuwutcim	†Kele	Hawiovi	Corn and Bluebird	Bluebird	Coyote and Squash	Honani	[Squash] Mustard	Wikwalovi
Tao	Parrot	Tao	Bear and Katcina	Parrot	†Parrot	Parrot	†Tobacco	Chief
Ahl	Bow	Nasavi	†Fog and Patki	Ahl	Patki	Ahl	Bear and Reed	Ahl
Kwan	Masau'u	Kwan	Katcina Sun and Snow	Snow Mountain	Lizard	Kochovi	Patki	Chivato
Soyal	Bear	Sakwalenvi	Bear	Parrot	Bear? Lizard	Ahl	Patki	Chief
Powamu:								
Powamu	Badger	Hotcitcivi	Katcina and Bear	Parrot	Katcina	Kochovi	Katcina-Parrot	Chief
Katcina	Katcina	Hawiovi	Katcina	Parrot	Katcina	Kochovi	Katcina-Parrot	Chief
Niman	Katcina	Rotates	Katcina	Rotates	Katcina	Rotates	Katcina-Parrot	Rotates
Blue Flute	Spider	Sakwalenvi	Patki	Clanhouse	Parrot	Clanhouse	Millet	Clanhouse
Gray Flute	Patki	Hawiovi	Bear	Clanhouse	Squash	Clanhouse	[Squash]	....
Snake	Snake	Snake	Sun and Sun's Forehead	Nuvaovi	Lizard	Honani	Snake-Cactus	Wikwalovi
Antelope	Spider	Nasavi	Carrying Strap	Parrot	Bear	Ahl	Snake-Dove	Chief
Marau	Lizard	Marau	Bluebird	Parrot	Parrot	Honani	[Squash] Snake	Ahl
Oaqöl	Sand	Hawiovi	Bear	Parrot	Badger	Honani	Reed-Eagle	Young Corn Mound
Lakon	Parrot	Hawiovi	Snow	Parrot	Lizard	Kochovi	Patki	Chivato

* See text for variations. Oraibi is given as before 1900; others are brought up to more recent dates. Daggers (†) = group of chief in general charge; brackets ([ ]) = extinct clans.

has analyzed the sociological factors involved in the disintegration of Old Oraibi and has suggested that similar factors were operative in prehistoric periods.[145] In Oraibi tradition, Oraibi was settled by migrants from Shongopovi as a result of a quarrel between Matcito, the legendary founder, and his brother, the Shongopovi Bear chief. In general, the socioceremonial pattern, so far as we know it, seems closer between Oraibi and Shongopovi than between any other villages, though the controlling clans are identical in only one instance and of the same phratry in only three. The establishment of Hotevilla as an independent offshoot from Oraibi in 1906 gives a particularly instructive instance, since the objective was to establish a ceremonial cycle modeled as closely as circumstances would permit on that of Old Oraibi. Titiev has shown that almost the whole ceremonial cycle was re-established in properly named kivas and that every effort was made "to select chiefs from the traditional proprietary clans."[146] Even so, an analysis of the results shows only a bare majority of clan-ceremonial associations similar to those of Oraibi.

Given the tendency to rationalize the mythology to account for the present situation,[147] it is clear why it is impossible to take the clan legends at their face value. Only in the case of the Bear clan, and perhaps the Katcina and Snake clans, as well, is there any uniformity of socioceremonial associations from village to village, and these are not present in every instance. Even the "colony" villages such as Shipaulovi show few parallels with their parental villages despite their ceremonial dependence.

The central position of the ceremony in the interrelations of clan, society, and kiva groupings among the Hopi is evident from the above analysis. Each ceremony is performed by a society whose membership cuts across the clan-phratry system, and the ceremony contributes to the total welfare of the community. Each ceremony is owned by a particular clan (or clans), which furnishes the officers and ritual equipment and provides for its continuance and transmission. Each ceremony is normally performed in a kiva, though certain ceremonies are given in the clan households of the controlling clan. The clan, through its control of the ceremony, society, and, in some instances, the kiva, holds these groupings together in a particular configuration at any one village. The major kiva groupings are those of the Tribal Initiation societies which function in the Soyal ceremony and in the Katcina cycle; these groups periodically vacate the kivas to allow other societies to perform their rituals. Only at Oraibi were additional kivas developed to take care of ceremonies other than those connected with Tribal Initiation and the village chieftainship; several of these were constructed in connection with the ceremonial rivalry preceding the "split." While clan, kiva, and society frequently have the same name, they must be clearly distinguished in terms of both membership and activities if the operation of Hopi society is to be understood.

An interesting development, largely confined to the Second Mesa villages of Shongopovi and Mishongnovi, is the practice of rotation of ceremonial office. Parsons, in her visit to Shongopovi in 1920, noted the custom of rotation in office for several societies, including most of the Tribal Initiation groups—a custom with which her First Mesa interpreter was quite unfamiliar.[148] Lowie mentions a similar rotation for Mishongnovi in connection with village chieftainship, "representatives of the Bear, Cloud, and Parrot clans taking turns for about four years each."[149] The custom of "resting" from ceremonial duties is found elsewhere, particularly at Oraibi in connection with the village chief, but the rotation of ceremonial offices, the association of two clans with each of the Tribal Initiation ceremonies, and the multiple clan ownership of kivas has been carried farthest at Shongopovi. In part, this situation may have been brought about by the reduction in the number of clans and the consequent increase in ceremonial obligations. Thus, Parsons noted that "there are but three members of the *Kachina*-Parrot clan and their ceremonial obligations are heavy. A way out was found. The office of Singers chief is made to rotate between the three men, each holding it for four years."[150] But recent evidence indicates that this pattern has been more widely extended in recent decades, with important results in flexibility, integration, and reduced friction.

At the other extreme are the situations in such modern villages as New Oraibi, where the ceremonial system has been largely given up, under governmental and missionary influence. Along with the loss of the ceremonies has also gone much of the feeling for clanship and the obligations of extended kinship, as well as the society and kiva associations, and there has been a general disintegration of community life.

Political Organization

Hopi political organization[151] is difficult to characterize, because authority is phrased in ritual rather than in secular terms and is not concentrated in any single position. There is no central authority for the Hopi as a whole, nor is there any secular government annually elected such as the Spaniards instituted elsewhere among the Pueblos. Within each major village there is a hereditary group of priests or chiefs, but the order of this "hierarchy" varies from village to village, and they have a minimum of secular authority.

In most of the Hopi villages the village chieftainship is associated with the Bear clan, and the chiefs are installed by the Kwan society, the members of which cannot themselves become village chief. At Oraibi there is a further association of the village chieftainship with the Soyal ceremony, and the officers of the Soyal constitute the top religious hierarchy, a step perhaps in the direction of a central religious ruling group. At Shongopovi the village chief is likewise of the Bear clan and associated with Soyal, but the Tribal Initiation chiefs and the Katcina chief are his major advisers; the rotation of the village chieftaincy at Mishongnovi complicates the pattern, though there is a definite feeling that the Bear clan is the proper source for the village chiefs.[152] For Walpi we have noted the shift of the village chieftaincy from the Bear clan to the Millet clan and the subsequent association with the Blue Flute ceremony controlled by that clan; here the "council" was composed in Stephen's time of the Millet and Bear clan chiefs, followed by the Tribal Initiation chiefs, the Soyal, Powamu, Antelope, and Snake chiefs, and ending up with the Crier and War Chiefs.[153] The particular order at each village is sanctioned by the mythology in terms of the order of "arrival" of the clans controlling such chieftaincies or in terms of transfers of function.

The mythological sanction for the position of the Bear clan at Oraibi is found in the origin legend for that village. Matcito, a Bear clansman, quarreled with his brother, the chief of Shongopovi, and moved to Third Mesa, where he laid claim to the land. Other "clan groups" came and offered their ceremonies for rain or agreed to protect the chief in exchange for land and a position in the village. In Oraibi theory the village chief "owns" the land, and the crops and the people are considered to be his "children" and call him "father." If people withdraw from the village and fail to perform their ceremonies or other duties, they are supposed to give up their clan lands. This relation between ceremonies and land is of vital importance in understanding the events of recent years. There is considerable evidence that the difficulties at Old Oraibi were related in large measure to problems concerned with land.

In all villages the *kikmongwi*, or village chief, is supposed to watch over his people and protect them—this involves keeping a "good heart" so that the prayers for rain will be answered. In return the people are supposed to work for the village chief—and other chiefs as well—and in most villages land was set aside for the use of the chiefs of important ceremonies.

While the village chief in theory controls the land and the village, he should not participate directly in disputes or quarrels, since such activities are thought to have a deleterious effect on village welfare. Problems should be settled by other chiefs or by clan heads, if possible; only as a last resort should they be taken to the village chief unless they were directly concerned with land.

The Hopi make no sharp distinction between religious and secular duties. The welfare of the Hopi people is the basic concern of the chiefs and may be obtained in various ways—mostly religious. The nearest thing to a "council" was the chiefs' assembly which was held in connection with the Soyal ceremony.[154] But this meeting had no legislative significance and was more concerned with the ceremonial cycle of the coming year and how to maintain the Hopi way of life. The strongest deterrent force in the village is perhaps fear of the Kwan society. This group, which is particularly associated with the dead, was in former times the chief protection of the village. The Kwan chief instals the village chief, and the latter may be deposed by the Kwan society for good cause.[155] Their role in the initiation rites gives them a further measure of control over behavior.

The only chief with "police" functions was the War Chief, but he does not have the same authority that his counterparts at Zuni and other Pueblos possess. At Oraibi in recent times the War Chief was a Soyal officer, but in earlier days he was head of the War society and a member of the Coyote-Masau'u-Kokop clan group.[156] He had the duty of maintaining order and discipline, but he had no punitive powers other than those connected with his war leadership. The War Chief at Shongopovi belongs to the Sun-Reed clan group, and the Walpi War Chief to the related Reed clan; according to Curtis,[157] the latter had the duty of maintaining peace and harmony within the village, which he did by lecturing the population on the evils of adultery and other practices. With the loss of the sanctions incident to war, no additional secular sanctions have been developed to deal with witches and trouble-makers, though the former are believed to be punished in the afterworld by the Kwans who push them into underground corn-baking ovens from which they emerge as beetles.

Within the clan normally the oldest male member takes charge of the ritual duties of the clan, and the oldest female member (of the main lineage) is in charge of the clan household. Difficulties within the clan are usually adjusted by conferences, but disputes between clans over ceremonial rights or land may continue for a considerable period without solution. Violence is rare among the Hopi, so that blood feuds do not occur. According to Colton, if murder should occur, it would be the duty of the family of the murdered man to kill the murderer,[158] but actual instances of murder are very few in modern times.

Co-operation between independent villages is almost nonexistent, and the efforts of the government to develop a Hopi council to deal with matters affecting the reservation as a whole have had little success. Villages such as New Oraibi are experimenting with local elected officials, but they have great difficulty in enforcing their decisions where public opinion is divided. Titiev's summary of the situation is worth quoting:

> Within each village the lack of a strong central authority permits the growth of factions and leads to schisms; and between pueblo and pueblo there is an attitude of jealousy, suspicion, and subdued hostility. Never has any town been entirely free from strife, and never has a leader arisen to mould the autonomous villages into a co-ordinated unit worthy of being a tribe. Whatever other talents they may possess, the Hopi do not have the gift of statecraft.[159]

Conclusions and Interpretations

In the above sections we have outlined the major aspects of Hopi social organization and indicated some preliminary conclusions with reference to the subsystems. It is now possible to examine the relations between these subsystems in more detail, to outline the basic aspects of Hopi social structure, and to indicate the nature of their social integration. We can gain further insight into Hopi social organization by seeing it in historical perspective, through a reconstruction of Hopi history as seen in archeology and the documentary records and by also seeing it in comparative perspective through an examination of the social structures of the various western Pueblos.

We have seen that the Hopi kinship system might be considered as an instrument for organizing and regulating social behavior in a number of culturally defined contexts. The kinship structure is based upon a "vertical" grouping of relatives in terms of the matrilineal lineage and household; this pattern is extended on a simplified basis to clan, phratry, and ceremonial relatives, and later to the relatives of one's spouse.

The relations of the lineage to the clan—and of both to the household have been outlined above. The lineage, unnamed as it is, is of primary importance to the Hopi because it contains the *mechanism* for transmitting rights, duties, land, houses, and ceremonial knowledge, and thus it is vital with respect to status. In Hopi thinking the lineage and clan are usually considered together, but in extreme cases they may place two lineages of the same clan at almost opposite poles.[160]

The clan is the outstanding unit of social organization; in Hopi conception it is "timeless" and permanent, extending back to the period before the emergence and forward to include as yet unborn children. Deceased clansmen continue their clan affiliations and interest in the living group, and, conversely, the latter concentrate much of their ritual activities on the maintenance of proper relations with the dead. The Hopi have utilized the clan as a primitive "corporation," holding land, houses, and ceremonial knowledge and property "in trust" for future generations. Radcliffe-Brown, from whom I borrow this term, has pointed out the need for stability and continuity in the social structure and has indicated the necessity—where corporations are based on kinship—of adopting a system of unilineal reckoning of succession to achieve that purpose.[161]

The clan performs these functions relatively well but is subject to population fluctuations in both directions, independent of the total village population. Thus a clan may be reduced to a simple lineage (or further) or expand to include several lineages. The number of lineages per clan is always variable, but the custom of one "clanhouse" and a single name suggests that early Hopi social organization approximated to single-lineage clans.[162] Multiple lineages can split off as long as the socioceremonial system is expanding, but, once the pattern crystallizes, they tend to remain as subordinate groups. Here they increase stability, in that they provide some insurance against clan extinction, but they complicate clan unity through competition for land and ceremonial status.

At the next level of organization the phratry provides a similar structural situation, though its functions and origins may be somewhat different. We have noted that the phratry has no name but that kinship and exogamy are extended to the "partner" clans. The phratry group is not an economic or ceremonial unit, but it does serve as an insurance mechanism against clan extinction, since partner clans may take over the ceremonial obligations. Within the phratry group there are often sharp status differences and competition for land and prestige, as Titiev has indicated for Oraibi.[163]

The village organization among the Hopi represents a still higher level. Each major village is relatively independent and self-contained: an economic, ceremonial, and political unit. Within the village we find a complex integration; while each has a similar pattern of social structure, the particular relations between clan, society, and ceremony may vary considerably from village to village. Certain villages are colony or satellite villages which are still ceremonially dependent; others have achieved independence in pre-Spanish times—or in the twentieth century. For the Hopi tribe as a whole there is no central organization; rather each major village is a potential rival, and village "sovereignty" is jealously guarded. What tribal unity there is depends upon the extensions of the socioceremonial system and the common understandings of the culture.

STRUCTURAL PRINCIPLES

It is now possible to consider further the nature of the Hopi kinship system. We have suggested that the kinship system is the most important element in Hopi social structure and have indicated the manifold ways in which the social recognition of kinship permeates social relations of all kinds. We can gain further insight into the kinship system and its relations to other aspects of the social structure by defining the structural principles on which it is based.[164] We have noted that the Hopi system is "classificatory" in that lineal relatives are grouped with collateral relatives and that kinship covers a wide range. Radcliffe-Brown has recently pointed out that in such systems "the distinction between lineal and collateral relatives is clearly recognized and is of great importance to social life, but it is in certain respects subordinated to another structural principle, which can be spoken of as the principle of the solidarity of the sibling group."[165] The importance of the bond between siblings is fundamental in Hopi social structure; it finds expression in the equation of the father with the father's brother and the mother with the mother's sister, in the household and lineage activities, and in the clan-phratry system. It does not find expression in such institutions as the sororate and the levirate or in sororal polygyny or fraternal polyandry. Such institutions would not be efficient in terms of Hopi household organization and division of labor; their absence does call into question the frequent explanations of "classificatory" terminologies as the direct result of the sororate and levirate.

The principle of the "distinction of generation," which is characteristic of many "classificatory systems," has only limited application among the Hopi. Within the lineage (and clan) there is superordination and authority, correlative with the responsibility for transmitting the social and ritual heritage, but the mother's mother's brother is frequently relieved of this role and classed as a sibling. The grandparent-grandchild relation is one of friendliness and lack of authority; the Hopi have extended this relationship rather widely but on a lineage rather than a generation basis.

The most important structural principle among the Hopi, however, is the principle which Radcliffe-Brown has recently referred to as the solidarity and unity of the lineage group.[166] This appears to be a composite principle, built up on the basis of unilateral descent and the equivalence of siblings. The main axis for the Hopi is the mother-child relationship, particularly that of mother and daughter; correlated with this is the sibling relationship, particularly that of two sisters. The solidarity of the lineage group is indicated in the internal relations between lineage relatives and in their treatment of outsiders; the unity of the lineage group is noted particularly in the treatment of the father's and mother's father's matrilineal lineages and in the organization of relatives by marriage. The central role of a line of women in the lineage and household serves to tie together these two basic institutions. The "peripheral" roles of the brother and husband in these institutions and their variant responsibilities for training and punishment, on the one hand, and economic support, on the other, do not bind them so strongly to these institutions, and they find their major satisfactions in the society ceremonials and kiva activities, in many cases.

The organization of kindred in terms of the lineage principle involves a classification of relatives in different generations under one term. Among the Hopi the father's lineage contains "father's" and "father's sisters"; it is treated as a unit with reference to men or women marrying into it and with reference to the children of the men of the lineage. Within one's own lineage there is greater differentiation, but the lineage is a unit with regard to men or women marrying into it, or to the "children" of the lineage. The father's and mother's father's lineages are related in a similar way to one's own lineage; the father's father's lineage has no direct connections and is not recognized. This organization of kindred is extended to the clan and phratry and to ceremonial relatives as well. From the standpoint of kinship structure these "vertical" groupings of kindred represent collective or generalized relationships with definite positions and obligations. For the Hopi the kinship structure is centered primarily around the lineage; the household relationships are secondary.

The lineage principle also clarifies the differing conceptions of kinship on the part of men and women. Women occupy a central role in the kinship system, and the children of two sisters are called by the term for "child" and are normally in the same household. Men are peripherally located; their children are in separate lineages and households, and they are more closely related to their sister's children than to their own. Two sisters thus reinforce each other; two brothers have divided loyalties and obligations. A brother and a sister are united by a close bond but have differing and complementary relations to each other's children.

The relative weakness of the husband-wife bond among the Hopi is probably a structural corollary of a strong lineage principle. Where primary loyalties have developed to lineage and household it is difficult to develop strong ties between spouses, particularly with matrilocal residence and female ownership of house and land. Wives usually side with their house or lineage mates in disputes involving their husbands; in crises even grandfathers may be treated as outsiders by the lineage group.[167] Husbands often fail in the difficult adjustment to a new household, whereas wives have less adjustment to make and can rely on the support of their household in case of separation or divorce. As a husband has children and grandchildren, however, his position in his wife's household is more secure, and the husband-wife bond grows stronger. Divorce seems rarer after middle age than in the earlier periods, when less is at stake.

A significant aspect of the lineage, already mentioned, is its function of conserving and transmitting, not only the social and ritual heritage, but property rights, houses, and ceremonies, as well, from one generation to the next. Among the Hopi the women of the lineage act as trustees with reference to land and houses, holding them in trust for generations to come. They may also share in ceremonial knowledge and look after ritual paraphernalia, leadership being exercised by their brothers and transmitted to their sons.

For the clan the lineage principle is reinforced by a relationship of kinship with the clan *wuya*. Where the *wuya* is of interest primarily to the clan it is usually called "mother's brother," but where it is of major interest to all Hopi it may be called "father," "mother," or "grandmother." The extension of kinship to the phratry group is partly on the basis of clan "partnership" and partly on the basis of the relationships assumed to exist among the associated *wuya*, all of whom may be considered as kin. It is the relationship to the *wuya* which seems important in the extension of kinship to clans in other tribes.

The principle of reciprocity is of general importance in Hopi society. With regard to the kinship system the behavior patterns and terminology are usually complementary rather than symmetrical, and there are no verbal reciprocals in general use. "Relatives-in-law," men and women marrying into the lineage, use nonreciprocal terminology and have nonreciprocal relationships with the lineage group. Kinship obligations involve extensive exchanges between households and individuals at the various crises of life and in connection with ceremonies. There is, however, no organized exchange of spouses between households such as frequently occurs through such mechanisms as sister exchange and cross-cousin marriage, though families attempt some control of marriage choices.

If the kinship system is considered as organized on the basis of sociological principles, there may be instances of conflict which will necessitate a readjustment in social behavior, in terminology, or both. This readjustment may take the form of a change of generation or of kinship position or an establishment of "joking" or "respect" relationships.[168] The father's sister, for example, is in the parental generation (representing authority) which conflicts with her social behavior toward her brother's son. The Hopi have transferred her to what is essentially the status of "little grandmother" and have generalized this relationship for the lineage and clan. The father's sister's husband is likewise in a position of potential conflict as far as social behavior is concerned. In consonance with the status of the father's sister, he is classed as a "grandfather"; but the close tie between the father's sister and her brother's son is in conflict with the husband-wife relationship. Since no authority is involved, the Hopi have apparently solved the conflict by establishing a strong joking relationship which centers on their respective relationships to the father's sister. The mother's father, on the other hand, is not so strong a "joking" relative, despite being called by the same term; he partakes of his wife's central position in the household.[169]

The mother's brother is the chief "respect" relative for a man, in consonance with his position of authority. For a woman, however, the mother's brother has little direct authority, and a mild joking relationship is established concerning his relationships to his father's sister. The mother's mother's brother, while in the second ascending generation, is a close relative because of his position in the lineage, but he has generally passed on his ritual knowledge and position to his sister's son. Hence he is frequently classed as an "older brother" rather than as a "mother's brother." Women similarly may classify a mother's mother's mother, when living, as a "mother" rather than as a "grandmother."

This brief analysis suggests that the sociological principles proposed by Radcliffe-Brown are useful in interpreting the kinship system and other aspects of Hopi social organization. The lineage principle and the equivalence of siblings are utilized, along with other principles, to develop a complex structure. We can see this structure most clearly from the vantage point of the kinship system: the lineage, clan, and phratry are kinship units and depend upon kinship bonds, in part at least. When we turn to social integration, we find that associational and ceremonial bonds play an important role as well.

SOCIAL INTEGRATION

Hopi society, despite appearances, is not completely integrated. Without a political superstructure, the clan and phratry groups tend to assert their position at the expense of the village. Hopi society has been held together by kinship ties, marriage bonds, and associational structures which cut across clan lines. Rituals and ceremonies are not too highly centralized, being controlled by clans and performed by societies, for the benefit of the whole village. In the past certain external pressures have assisted in integrating the Hopi system; observation of the present process of disintegration furnishes valuable insights into the nature of that integration.

Hopi integration may be viewed from the standpoint of the major organizations: kinship, clan and phratry, society and kiva. Each of these organizations has various devices for increasing or maintaining its own social solidarity. Each system of organization also overlaps the others in terms of membership, so that an integration of the whole is achieved; the bonds holding individuals to household, clan, society, and kiva groupings interweave in complex fashion.

The primary and most important integrative factor in Hopi society is the kinship system. The strongest bonds are between members of the lineage and household groups. The clan and phratry give a primary direction to the extension of kinship; through the institution of "ceremonial father" and "doctor father," kinship is further extended to other clan and phratry groups and, in part, to society and kiva groups. From the standpoint of social integration these extensions provide a wide range, since an individual may be related in one way or another to a considerable proportion of the village, and to many people in other villages, and even in other tribes. The kinship system achieves integration primarily through establishing reciprocal duties and obligations between kindred and through developing attitudes of dependence with regard to relatives; while these obligations and attitudes become weaker with distance, they are nonetheless important.

The clan among the Hopi is stronger than elsewhere in the Pueblo area. Its social solidarity depends in part upon kinship, but the conception of the clan as a "timeless" institution, with a name, a separate tradition, ownership of land and houses, an association with one or more *wuya*, and control of ceremonies or ceremonial positions, gives it an outstanding position. Phratry solidarity is less developed, being based in part upon kinship and on a tradition of common participation and the association of the various *wuya* relating to the partnership. In a culture where lack of change is a tenet, a strong phratry grouping provides a considerable degree of permanence and stability, but the important integrative aspects of the phratry seem to be in relation to the natural environment. Through the relationships established between the clan groups and the *wuya* of the various phratry groupings, the important aspects of the Hopi universe are brought within the social system under the same rules and regulations which bind the Hopi to one another.

The various society groups cut across the clan system and help to hold it together. Integration within the society group is achieved in part through kinship but primarily through possession and performance of a ceremony or ritual on which the continued welfare of the village depends. Each society has mechanisms for insuring stability and continuity: the replacement of a man by his "ceremonial son" (or a woman by her "ceremonial daughter"), the obligation incurred by being cured, and the obligations of the controlling clan, or of related clans. While society groups are co-ordinate, there is considerable overlapping of membership, since individuals may belong to more than one society. Two or more societies may co-operate in the performance of a joint ritual or in related rituals.

The ceremony is the central activity around which the society is organized. Each ceremony, as we have noted, is thought to belong to a particular clan which holds the ceremonial paraphernalia and furnishes the chief priest as well as a portion of the society membership. The periodical performance of the ceremony reaffirms the ritual bonds between the group and their sacred objects, including the deceased members, and the kinship bonds of the living members of the society. The performance of each major ceremony is associated with the right to use a special section of land. The public performances of each society further unite them as against the rest of the village; they compete with one another in the ceremonial calendar to bring about the desired ends of Hopi life.

The major kiva groupings, as we have seen, are associated with the Tribal Initiation societies. These are active at Wuwutcim initiation, Soyal, Powamu, and Niman and during the winter Katcina season. Here there is a great deal of competition in the form of dances, games, and races, though the latter may also be organized in terms of clans. The Katcina dance cycles involve not only the kivas as units but likewise the households of the members whose female members provide food for the dancers and visitors; on certain occasions the father's sister's households are responsible for feeding the participants.

Village integration among the Hopi varies considerably in terms of circumstances but depends essentially upon the maintenance of a balance between the social and ceremonial systems and the reciprocal relations involved in each. The social organization of the Hopi provides a relatively strong and complex integration within the village, and the ceremonies provide a means of maintaining and strengthening the basic sentiments of Hopi life. That the integration has been successful is evidenced by the survival of the Hopi as a group in spite of their small population and difficult environment. But this integration has been achieved in part by relative isolation and in part by external pressures, environmental as well as human. Once these pressures were reduced and there were more alternative choices, disintegrative processes gained the upper hand in certain villages.

A strong clan system, other things being equal, is correlated with a weak political system, and vice versa. Hopi and Zuni show varying emphases in this respect; the Hopi have not achieved the same degree of centralized control that is to be found at Zuni, whereas the Hopi clan system is considerably stronger. Among the Hopi a single clan—the Bear clan—has gained a pre-eminent position, bolstered by ceremonial associations and the control of land. But Hopi ideology forbids the use of force, and quarrels are antithetical to village welfare. The achievement of unanimity by consensus is the desired end but becomes increasingly difficult to attain.

At Oraibi, the largest of the Hopi villages, a relatively weak Bear clan was unable to hold the village together in the face of white pressures and adverse economic conditions, and clan and ceremonial rivalries split the village. The six Soyal chiefs, who formed the closest approximation among the Hopi to the Zuni hierarchy, might have held the village together in the face of Bear-Spider clan rivalries, but they also divided evenly, resulting in the formation of two Soyal ceremonies and, later, of two separate ceremonial cycles.[170] At Shongopovi, on the other hand, a relatively strong Bear clan was able to hold a smaller village together in the face of similar pressures and factions and to achieve a considerable degree of unity. Here the gradual reduction in the number of clans has resulted in greater economic and ceremonial control on the part of the Bear clan. The extinction of the Bear clan on First Mesa has led to considerable reshuffling of leadership, with control lodged in several clans apparently. All villages are beset with factions which argue endlessly and disrupt the smooth operation of village life. No village has achieved a solution of the factional problem, and, where the factions become strong enough, they bring about further splitting.

The various Hopi villages are tied together by the extensions of kinship, the common clan-phratry system, and by a common ceremonial system. Neighboring villages co-operate in ceremonial activities to some extent, and there is competition in games as well as a limited amount of intermarriage. But each major village maintains its separate existence (except for colony or farming villages) and jealously guards its ceremonies. Hopi men married in from other villages are treated as outsiders until they are reinitiated into the societies. Despite their traditions of common origin and their common language and culture, the Hopi have united for common action only on rare occasions. The recent attempts of the Indian Service to create a Hopi council have been largely a failure, and the present trend is toward greater individuation and disintegration.[171]

THEORETICAL PROBLEMS

It will now be useful to re-examine certain of the problems concerned with social organization in the light of Hopi data. The Hopi kinship system belongs to the "Crow" type,[172] and Lowie has utilized Hopi data in critically examining the explanations which have been advanced to account for systems of this type and its counterpart, the "Omaha" type. Explanations of these types, for which I have elsewhere suggested the generic term "lineage" type,[173] have usually taken the form of some combination of clan and preferential marriage factors.[174] Lowie notes the far-reaching changes which have taken place in Hopi terminology in comparison with other Basin Shoshonean groups and its functional correlation with the clan system;[175] in a later paper he concludes that "linguistic conservatism has been of slight importance in the history of present Hopi nomenclature and that the clan concept has exerted a deep influence upon it."[176] Analyzing the situation in more general terms, he came to the conclusion that Crow type groupings and specific matrimonial arrangements are themselves a function of the rule of descent.[177]

With this analysis we are in agreement, but we would go a step or two further. If our interpretation of the Hopi kinship system is substantially correct, it is not merely matrilineal descent which is important but the recognition of the lineage group as a unity for social purposes. It is this "lineage" principle, along with the principle of the equivalence of siblings, which we have suggested as the basis for both the kinship groupings and the clan system.[178] From this standpoint there is no primary correlation between the kinship terminology and exogamous clans,[179] and preferential marriage patterns may or may not be present, depending on the household situation, inheritance patterns, and the division of labor.

One form of preferential marriage has caused considerable discussion with regard to the Hopi ever since Freire-Marreco erroneously reported it as regularly occurring in most of the Hopi villages. Titiev has recently summarized the problem of cross-cousin marriage among the Hopi and has reached the conclusion that in all likelihood "it was once customary for Hopi men to marry their father's clanswomen."[180] The recent information on Basin Shoshonean social organization furnished by Steward provides additional evidence for this hypothesis. Steward found several types of cross-cousin marriage among various of the Nevada and Utah Shoshoneans, including marriage with the father's sister's daughter. Cross-cousin marriage is a useful device for integrating small, relatively stable groups such as were characteristic of early Hopi history (see below). With the expansion in population, cross-cousin marriage would become a relatively inefficient method and be largely abandoned. The behavior patterns between a man and his father's sisters are intelligible, as Titiev has noted, in terms of a former pattern of marriage with the father's clanswomen, and a small percentage of such marriages still occur.[181] Alternatively, we have to account for such behavior patterns in terms of the close bond between a brother and sister and their concern for each other's children, but such an explanation does not cover the specifically sexual elements in the relationship.

Another problem of some theoretical significance is that concerned with the size of the exogamic group. Among the Hopi the phratry is the largest exogamic unit, and marriage is not permitted, in Hopi theory, within one's own, one's father's, or one's mother's father's phratry. Malinowski has suggested that the rule of exogamy is for the purpose of eliminating "sex" in workaday life, since it is incompatible with proper adjustment and cooperation.[182] Among the Hopi this might hold for the mother's and father's households but hardly for the phratry groups, since they never act as units. Empirically there is an extension of exogamy to the largest kinship unit; and exogamy is necessary if the clan-phratry structure is to be maintained. The solution to this problem requires a comparative study of a large number of tribes with similar social structures before the Hopi situation can be seen in proper perspective.

The Hopi, as well as most of the other Pueblos, use teknonymy. Kroeber has suggested that the basis for the practice among the Zuni "seems to be a very strong inclination to avoid using a person's name."[183] This explanation will not hold for the Hopi, however, since there is no such avoidance. Kroeber's own informants furnish a clue: one stated in regard to teknonymy that "the child always comes first."[184] Teknonymy may well be related to the social importance of the child in pueblo society; certainly among the Hopi he occupies a central position. Further, a husband becomes related to his wife and her relatives and vice versa) primarily through the child, so that teknonymy reflects a social situation. There is also a practical advantage in teaching the child the proper kinship terms for house mates.

The Hopi in general emphasize the use of kinship terms, but in one instance they make such usage mandatory. Once the marriage process is started, the prospective wife of a member of one's lineage and clan must be addressed as "female relative-in-law" and not by her name. Such individuals enlarge the co-operating group of kinswomen, and their assistance and good will are greatly sought.

The relative absence of self-reciprocal terminology among the Hopi is striking in comparison with the Shoshonean-speaking groups in the Basin and the other western Pueblos. Lowie has suggested that the most plausible explanation of such terms "is that they are designations not so much of the relatives as of the relationship itself,"[185] and he feels that the distribution of such terminologies in western North America is "intelligible only through diffusion."[186] The only Hopi instance of the use of verbal reciprocals occurs where men married to sisters in the same household may call one another "partner," since they have similar responsibilities with regard to its support.[187] With regard to diffusion the Hopi represent a negative instance, since they are practically surrounded by tribes with self-reciprocal terminologies.

HISTORICAL PERSPECTIVES

It is now possible to get additional insight into the nature of Hopi social organization and integration by seeing it in historical perspective—and by comparing the Hopi system with that of other Pueblos. The archeological researches of the Museum of Northern Arizona and the Peabody Museum enable us to establish a relative chronology for the Hopi region and ultimately will permit not only a detailed reconstruction of cultural development[188] but also an interpretation of the development of social structures in this region on the basis of modern social anthropological knowledge.[189]

The Hopi region at the southern end of Black Mesa was apparently not occupied during Basketmaker II times, though there are many cave sites in the Kayenta region to the north at this early period (prior to A.D. 500). The earliest occupancy of the Hopi country is represented by a few sites in the Basketmaker III period (*ca.* A.D. 500–700), and by a large number in the Basketmaker III–Pueblo I transition period (A.D. 700–800). During this latter period the pit houses became larger and more complicated, and the isolated slab-lined storage chambers were put together in contiguous aboveground association. The village structure also grows larger and more complex. At this time also there is evidence of influences from the Mogollon region, both in architecture and in pottery.

The Pueblo I period (*ca.* A.D. 700–900) is not clearly identified in the Hopi region as yet, at least in terms of developments in the San Juan. Colton notes: "Until about 900 A.D., north of the Little Colorado River, the Anasazi in Northern Arizona seemed to have had a more or less uniform culture, Kayenta Branch."[190] During this period there is evidence of considerable change: the replacement of the atlatl by the bow, improvements in metates and manos, the addition of cotton to the textile fibers, of beans to the previous corn-squash complex, and the turkey.[191] The Hopi region, being marginal to the San Juan, was possibly late in sharing in these developments, except as they may have been introduced from the south.

With the beginnings of Pueblo II (*ca.* A.D. 900–1100), culture in the Hopi region began to take on an individuality which has resulted in a separate archeological classification, the Tusayan Branch. During this period there was a definite increase in sites, on the basis of which Brew postulates an appreciable increase in population.[192] The Hopi pit houses show certain striking resemblances to the Pueblo II pit houses of the San Francisco Mountain region, and there is an influx of Tusayan wares from the Kayenta area. During Pueblo II the masonry-lined pit houses vary from circular to rectangular or D-shaped, and there is a development of a D-shaped kiva from the house types. The sites are still small, those Brew excavated varying from two to nine rooms, and are found both on the rim and on the benches.

The early Pueblo III sites are small and similar to those of the Kayenta region, except for the D-shaped kiva. The increase in the number of sites (to 124) suggests a continued increase in population. Later in Pueblo III small masonry pueblos developed, one of which (Pink Arrow) had thirty-two rooms and a kiva. During this period a number of pottery types from the Little Colorado area, particularly St. John's Polychrome, appear, and square kivas are also found. The Pueblo III period covers A.D. 1100–1300 and is divided by Colton into the Kioko, Polacca, and Hukovi foci, the determinants for which (except for pottery) have largely to be worked out. During most of this period the Tusayan Branch developed in relative isolation, according to Colton.[193]

Pueblo IV (*ca.* A.D. 1300–1600) is the first archeological culture in the Hopi region which is sufficiently comparable to the modern to be labeled "Hopi." Beginning in the fourteenth century there is a tremendous increase in the size of some of the sites (Awatovi covered over 20 acres during part of this period) and a consequent reduction in their number (to 44), though Brew believes the population continued to grow. With the abandonment of the San Juan region coincident with the great drought (A.D. 1276–99), part of the population from the Kayenta area joined their cultural (and linguistic?) relatives on the other side of Black Mesa; a little later there was an influx of population from the Winslow area. New pottery types, developed on the basis of introduced models, large masonry pueblos, rectangular kivas of the historic type, and a ceremonial life (as evidenced in kiva wall paintings) suggestive of modern practices characterize this period. After A.D. 1500 the Jeddito area was gradually abandoned, Awatovi surviving up to about A.D. 1700.

During Pueblo V (1600—present) we have considerable documentary data on the historic Hopi pueblos. The early Spanish explorations had relatively little effect on Hopi culture, though I believe the psychological effect was profound, but the introduction of missions after A.D. 1629 began to modify Hopi life in systematic fashion.[194] The Pueblo Rebellion of 1680 brought a temporary end to Spanish authority—and a considerable influx of pueblo population from the Rio Grande. A group of Tiwa-speaking people settled on Second Mesa at Payupki, where they remained until 1742, when they were removed and later resettled at Sandia, and a Tewa-speaking group came to First Mesa, where they remained as the village of Hano. Other refugees were undoubtedly incorporated into the Hopi villages—or later returned to their own.

During this period the Hopi villages moved up to the mesa tops where we now find them, except for Oraibi, which was originally settled on Third Mesa, and during this process a number of satellite villages developed: Sichomovi as a suburb of Walpi and Shipaulovi as an offshoot of Shongopovi. The Hopi were least affected by the Reconquest and managed to withstand Spanish efforts to reconvert them, except for a brief period at Awatovi. During the historic period epidemics have periodically reduced the population. Navaho and Ute pressures have restricted geographical expansion, and occasional famine periods have led to temporary migration of part of the population as far as Zuni and the Rio Grande villages.

The events of the historic period, when adequately analyzed, will assist greatly in interpreting what happened during prehistoric times. The development of Hano, outlined in the following chapter, is of particular importance in this connection, since we can see the processes by which the Tewa were gradually "Hopi-ized," while retaining partial independence. At the other end of the time scale—at the beginnings of pueblo culture in the Hopi region—we have the possibility of reconstructing the outlines of social organization through an analysis of the ecological adjustments and through a comparison with modern Shoshonean Basin groups.

Steward has analyzed the economic and social basis of primitive bands[195] and has applied this analysis to the development of society in the Southwest.[196] He notes that "a large degree of economic determinism is evident in the development of patrilineal and matrilineal bands and their later transformation into clans" and suggests the following conditions:

> First, a low culture and or unfavorable environment prevents dense population and precludes large population aggregates. It produces groups which, barring special contrary factors, are unilateral, localized, exogamous, and land owning. Descent is male or female largely according to the economic importance of man or woman in that culture.
>
> Second, increased food supply or other factors making for a denser population will produce either larger bands, occupying the same territory, more bands each occupying less territory, or multi-band villages.
>
> Third, large, multi-band villages will be produced if tribal movements, war, or some other factor dislocates the unilateral band, causing concentration, or if, in an increasing population, newly founded lineages fail to move away.
>
> Fourth, it is not inevitable that these unilateral groups become clans, but they will do so if possession of a group name, common ceremonies, or other factors create solidarity and prevent the loss of recognition of kinship in succeeding generations; or, to put it differently, if the fiction of kinship is preserved after the known connection has been forgotten.
>
> Fifth, in the course of these transformations, political autonomy passes from the localized lineage to a wider group—the Pueblo village. . . .[197]

For the first stage we have no direct evidence from the Hopi country, but the Basin Shoshoneans approximate the conditions required. While a blended Basketmaker-Pueblo culture spread northward into Utah and eastern Nevada during Pueblo I–II times, it showed many variations and local adaptations, and occupation ceased with the abandonment of the San Juan region, if not before. The modern Shoshonean-speaking peoples, according to Steward, are probably not genetically related to the earlier peoples, despite certain similarities in culture, but are largely post-Puebloan.[198] Yet at some time period a group of Shoshonean-speaking peoples on the southern margins of the Basin were influenced sufficiently to adopt a pueblo mode of life and to become the linguistic ancestors, at least, of the modern Hopi. They may have come into the Hopi country relatively early—or with the influx from the Kayenta region in the thirteenth century; not only their language survived but also, I believe, certain aspects of their social structure.

The ecology of the Basin is such that the local groups are not unilateral, localized, and exogamous for the most part. The conditions of subsistence were so severe that the individual family was the usual primary economic unit, and group activities were relatively inefficient with the techniques available. During the winter a few families congregated in a winter village where they had stored seeds and other supplies and where there was fuel and shelter.[199]

Among the western Shoshoni the local group was usually a kinship group.

> Relatives sought one another's proximity. Though exigencies of the food quest often forced related families apart, they wintered together if possible. Very small villages frequently consisted exclusively of related families and large villages had many that were related. Several marriage practices contributed to this condition. Residence was with one parent or the other, rarely independent. And if there were unrelated families in a village, their children often married one another and remained there. When brothers and sisters married sisters and brothers they all wintered at the same site if possible.[200]

Continue the process of brothers and sisters marrying sisters and brothers for another generation, and you have the beginnings of cross-cousin marriage, a convenient device for regulating marriage in a group of close kin and one very widely used. Two forms of cross-cousin marriage are reported for the region: (1) true cross-cousin marriage in a few centrally located (and isolated?) Shoshonean groups and (2) pseudo cross-cousin marriage (with a step-cross-cousin) in several others. In addition, the sororate and levirate were intensified, and both sororal polygyny and fraternal polyandry were widespread.[201]

Among some of the Basin groups, notably the Owen's Valley Paiute, the ecological conditions were more favorable in that food resources were concentrated along streams. Here the villages represented bands whose members habitually co-operated in food-gathering activities; each had a common name, a chief, and owned seed territories and sometimes hunting territories. Throughout Owen's Valley marriage between relatives was forbidden, but, since villages were large, local exogamy was ordinarily not necessary.

> In the south, however, there was a strong preference for matrilocal residence, perhaps connected with female ownership of valley seed plots. This tended to convert small villages into female lineages, which approximated but failed actually to be exogamous matrilineal bands.[202]

Here, then, is a situation in which unilateral, localized, exogamous, and land-owning groups, with matrilineal tendencies, may develop. Similar conditions, centering around the gathering of wild seeds, and later the raising and preparation of corn and other domesticated plants, may well have given a similar orientation to the small groups in the San Juan region—and later in the Hopi country.

The introduction of corn and squash—and later beans—would increase the food supply considerably and make possible a denser population.[203] In Basketmaker III times the pit-house villages were more numerous but generally small and related to the farming areas.

> Some grouping by kin is clearly indicated and it is difficult to imagine that such house clusters could have been produced by anything but a unilateral group living on its inherited land. Motives for concentration in larger villages were lacking and it is probably not rash to suggest that with increasing population, small lineages budded off and set up new house clusters at no great distance from their neighbors and former kin.[204]

The early pit-house sites in the Awatovi region are smaller than those reported by Roberts at Shabik'eschee village in the Chaco, which Steward estimates had a population of around fifty persons, but the later village (Site 264) contained seven pit houses and a large number of storage chambers, indicating a population of perhaps thirty-five.[205]

The concentration of population into larger "multiband" villages took place slowly in the Hopi country. Protected by deserts and plateau escarpments, it offered little to intruders except a fairly reliable but limited supply of water from springs and the possibility of flood-water farming once the techniques had been developed. But, as population increased, the problem of water supply became more crucial, and during drought periods groups from neighboring areas undoubtedly moved in, sometimes to stay. They undoubtedly formed separate village units at first, but the distribution of springs would require that new lineages (both foreign and domestic) stay in the vicinity—and ultimately in the village.

We have noted the small size of the Pueblo II sites, varying from two to nine rooms with associated kivas. Brew reports an early Classic Pueblo unit of three rooms and a kiva, to which an additional seven rooms were later added, and mentions storage bins, grinding bins, and fireplaces in these rooms.[206] The presence and distribution of grinding bins is of great importance, since I believe that the greater efficiency of group grinding and preparation techniques is an important factor in the development and maintenance of the extended maternal household in the western Pueblos.

Near the end of Pueblo III the sites become larger and more complex. At this time the initial building began for the great Western Mound at Awatovi. Coincident with the introduction of Black-on-Orange ware, around A.D. 1300, there was a great expansion of building in the Western Mound, with definite changes in masonry.

> The coincidence of the appearance of large numbers of potsherds showing affinity with the Little Colorado area and the beginning of massive house block construction at Awatovi adds great promise to the solution of one group of our major problems: the cause of the concentration of population evinced by the large pueblos along the Jeddito rim, and the source of this population.[207]

This influx of population, brought about by the effects of the great drought, and perhaps also of nomadic enemies, led to the development of large masonry pueblos on all the Hopi mesas. The problem of integrating large populations now faced the village leaders—problems which they had never before encountered on such a scale.

The new groups coming in from the Tsegi and Little Colorado regions came as communities or fragments of communities, such as household groups, and not as lineages or clans as such. Steward thinks the center of clan development was in the eastern San Juan because of more clearly defined groupings and more constant kiva-room ratios, with the Kayenta region showing more cultural lag and less consistency.[208] But modern Hopi social organization suggests that there must have been a strong tendency toward unilateral organization and that the matrilineal lineage principle was utilized in organizing the large pueblos on the Hopi mesas. Whether the local groups were culturally overwhelmed by the influx of population or not may be decided when Brew works out the details of development at Awatovi.

In any case the newcomers would have a common name and a socioceremonial system which would set them off from the Hopi dwellers. By utilizing matrilineal descent and matrilocal residence, they could maintain a certain amount of their group integrity and ceremonial possessions while integrating themselves with the other groups already there.[209] The clan system is a convenient device for such integration, and the later phratry system widened the sphere of integration and developed an over-all system for the Hopi as a whole.[210]

The final step in Steward's series, the transformation of political autonomy from the localized lineage to the wider group, did not take place completely in the Hopi region, if we can judge from the historic data. The village chieftaincy became associated with a single clan, the Bear clan, but political power and control were never wholly placed in the hands of the chief. Rather the village remained organized on the basis of reciprocal services performed by various groups for the benefit of all and depended on external pressures for much of its integration.

At some time in Hopi history, if our reconstruction is reasonably correct, there was a shift in the division of labor by which men took over the agricultural activities. I suspect that this shift was coincident with a change in the balance of subsistence in the direction of greater utilization of corn, beans, and squash as over against hunting and gathering, and possibly to the presence of nomadic enemies who made work in the fields a relatively hazardous occupation. I would tend to put the time of this shift relatively late, since it did not occur until after the pattern of matrilineal ownership and inheritance of land was well established—a situation I would associate with the larger aggregations of population which took place in the fourteenth century. The survival of clan lands and the female cultivation of the garden plots surrounding springs are both intelligible in terms of this hypothesis.

The failure of this shift in the division of labor seriously to modify the matrilineal-matrilocal character of Hopi society is to be accounted for, in part at least, by the nature of Hopi techniques for preparing corn, particularly the laborious grinding processes which fell to the lot of the women and which could be carried out more efficiently and pleasantly in small groups. The co-operation of the women in the household in these activities may well have been fundamental in maintaining the matrilocal character of residence.

I have included this rather extended survey of Hopi archeology because it gives us some perspective on the chronology involved in the development of the modern Hopi social structure. By looking at the social organization of the Basin Shoshoneans, we can get considerable insight into the beginnings of early Pueblo social structure in the Hopi region, and, once we can work out the history of Shoshonean groups via archeology, it will be possible to discover more precisely when the Hopi began to speak Shoshonean and the nature of the cultural continuity and variation which is found. Finally, we can make more intelligent use of the mythological materials furnished by the Hopi, an important source of data once we can properly interpret it.

Kroeber has recently emphasized the importance of residence

as over against formal social organization in the analysis of social structure.

> Instead of considering the clan, moiety, totem, or formal unilateral group as primary in social structure and function, the present view conceives them as secondary and often unstable embroideries on the primary patterns of group residence and subsistence associations.[211]

In his review of fundamental types of society, on which the above conclusion is based, Kroeber finds no instances of a matrilineal-matrilocal horde type of organization and assumes that the development of matrilineal-matrilocal groups would have to take place after larger village aggregations were established.

> Such matrilineal-matrilocal groups as exist seem to be social units or subdivisions within larger political units: clans or sibs within tribes as against the clan-tribe non-differentiation in the patrilineal-patrilocal horde. A Hopi clan is certainly matrilineal and matrilocal, but it is not autonomous; it does not possess exclusive and total ownership of a territory, and it cannot be called a tribe, nation, or state by any legitimate stretch of the meaning of these terms. It is obviously an organ in a tribe, town, or miniature state. It may be that the apparent non-horde character of the matrilineal-matrilocal group is due to its most frequent occurrence in association with agriculture, which in turn operates toward larger social integration and therefore tends to prevent the horde type of society. On this view the group which, without agriculture, becomes or remains the undifferentiated clan-tribe horde, with agriculture becomes a clan in a tribe; and the fact that normally hordes are patrilineal-patrilocal, but intra-tribe clans can be matrilineal-matrilocal, would then be due to some influence of agricultural life. At any rate, the two phenomena would be correlated.[212]

The apparent absence of matrilineal-matrilocal horde groupings is negated, in part, at least, by Steward's evidence for Owen's Valley of small villages "which approximated but failed actually to be exogamous matrilineal bands."[213] The development of agriculture on such a basis would bring about the larger social integration which Kroeber mentions, with the resultant problems we have discussed above.

But, despite the priority of the residence factor in shaping early Hopi society, it seems clear that lineage plays a more fundamental role in modern Hopi society. As in Australia, the partial coalescence of lineage and "local" groupings in the Hopi household makes their separation somewhat difficult. But residence alone has limited usefulness in integrating large blocks of population, whereas the lineage principle can be extended to cover considerable numbers. Furthermore, it is the lineage and clan, rather than the household group, which is intrusted with lands and ceremonies and which is considered to own the house itself. Important as are the ties of residence and subsistence associations, they are not the key groupings in Hopi estimation—or in terms of our interpretation.

Kroeber explicitly leaves kinship out of account in his analysis of "basic and secondary patterns of social structure," but in a sense kinship is more fundamental than either patterns of residence or formal grouping. Our analysis of Hopi kinship has suggested that both the household and the lineage organizations are encompassed in the kinship system. And it is clear that the kinship system is organized in terms of the lineage principle rather than in terms of residence.

We can agree with Kroeber that, "while one must live somewhere, one can live without artificial exogamous groupings, descent reckoning, or totems";[214] but, once a society is faced with problems of organizing an enlarged population and transmitting a substantial cultural heritage from one generation to the next, the residence factor is not enough. The Hopi have solved these problems by organizing their social structure in terms of the lineage principle; that this is a recurrent type of solution for a whole series of societies in the middle range should make us wary of considering lineage as a secondary and unstable embroidery on the primary patterns of group residence. With regard to the secondary character of clans, phratries, and totemism we would agree with Kroeber, but from a somewhat different standpoint; they are expansions of the lineage principle for integrative purposes.

MODERN CHANGES

The changes in Hopi social structure which are taking place under modern conditions of acculturation represent a complex problem which can be considered only briefly here.[215] The major villages until recently have been fairly successful in resisting modern pressures, so far as the social system is concerned, but new communities of various types have grown up near each mesa in which social and cultural change proceeds at a more rapid pace. Polacca, at the base of First Mesa, represents an unsuccessful attempt to get the Hopi to come down from Walpi, Sichomovi, and Hano; while there are many houses scattered along the foot of the mesa, their owners for the most part also maintain residence in the older villages. Near Second Mesa there is a small Christian Hopi community, made up of Baptist converts from Mishongnovi and Shipaulovi, who have been subjected to strong religious influences but are otherwise relatively isolated. On Third Mesa, New Oraibi was settled largely after the "split" of 1906 which gave rise to conservative Hotevilla and Bakavi, and since 1935 the farming village of Moencopi, some forty miles distant, has been gradually achieving independent status. In that process factional disputes have led to further splitting, so that there are now two Moencopis, Upper and Lower. A comparison of all these situations will ultimately give us detailed information on the relative influences of the school, missions, traders, and the government.

For our purposes it will be sufficient to look at some of the changes going on in a modern community such as New Oraibi. The first and most obvious change is in village structure, but there have been major modifications in other spheres of life as well. The bulk of the population of New Oraibi came directly from the parent-village on the mesa top; its early settlers came down to the valley for a variety of reasons—quarrels with the chief, new work opportunities, convenience to the school, a better water supply, and missionary and government pressures, among others. There has been some tendency to build houses in compact rows, but these are not organized on any village plan, and individual houses are scattered over a wide area. This haphazard village plan is in sharp contrast to that of the older villages, nor does it conform to the American system; it does reflect in part the relative lack of organization and integration of the village.

In this process the older patterns of matrilocal residence were modified but not obliterated. While the tendency is toward separate households for each elementary family, there is likewise a tendency for these households to be grouped in terms of the matrilineal lineage. Thus a woman and her daughters frequently live in adjacent houses and continue their co-operation in household tasks. Occasionally a son or brother will build near by as well, adding a bilateral note to the extended family grouping.

More recently ownership of houses has been shifting from women to men as the latter acquire new skills as stonemasons or accumulate sufficient wealth to hire builders. With this shift comes still further emphasis on patrilineal inheritance and patrilocal residence—and new problems for which there are as yet no cultural solutions.

The adults moving down to New Oraibi brought with them a knowledge of the whole socioceremonial system, but, having for the most part relinquished their ceremonial duties and obligations, they did not re-create the societies and the ceremonial cycle as did the migrants to Hotevilla and Bakavi. The loss of ceremonial ties was only partially compensated for by mission activities, since relatively few families turned Christian; there was a continued reduction in the extent of ceremonial relations and the associated social obligations. During the 1930's this trend was reversed to the extent of presenting Katcina and Butterfly dances, but the social rather than the ritual aspects were emphasized, and there has been no restoration of the basic Katcina cult or initiation for boys.

The clan-phratry relationships still govern marriage, though there is an increasing number of violations of clan exogamy on the part of Christians and boarding-school students. But the clan as a social and ceremonial group has lost much of its significance now that it is no longer associated with ceremonies, priesthoods, and land. Claims to clan lands are still asserted, and such lands are frequently cultivated, but the pressure of conservative Hopi opinion with regard to the correlated ceremonial duties causes considerable guilt reactions.

To the younger generation phratry relationships are little

known and clan relationships are limited. What has survived most strongly is the lineage group; this group of actual relatives in the female line still maintains a considerable unity, especially against outsiders, and frequently co-operates in various enterprises. But where these enterprises are modern rather than traditional the problem of sharing the profits becomes a crucial one and causes much conflict.

The repudiation of the chief at Old Oraibi left the new community leaderless. The first individual to settle in the valley set himself up as "Chief of the Christians" on the basis of his priority but received no support. Later a council was established but proved abortive. After the Indian Reorganization Act, however, New Oraibi elected a governor and a council; these officers have operated fairly successfully within the limitations imposed by the government.

The kinship system has undergone an interesting series of changes. While there is great variation, a comparison of different generations provides a clue to the direction in which these changes are trending. The older generations which grew up on top of the mesa can provide detailed genealogies and a description of kinship behavior and terminology which differs only in minor essentials from those secured in conservative villages. In one extended family in New Oraibi, for example, the old grandmother varied from the normal pattern only in that she showed a tendency to ignore phratry relationships and to stress "in-law" relationships at the expense of clan ties. She knows no English but was early "converted" to Christianity, so that clan and phratry ties have less meaning. She is, however, head of her lineage, and, as her daughters and grandchildren visit her daily, she has a strong influence over their lives.

Her children, except for the eldest daughter, have been well educated. A genealogy from one of her sons shows profound changes. While he knew his own and his father's close relatives, he did not know his mother's father's relatives, and his general knowledge of relatives was greatly reduced. There was a tendency to use the term "our relative" for the father's sister's children and for distant relatives on the mother's side. Relatives who were "out of the clan" on either the mother's or the father's side were frequently not called by kinship terms. These changes in terminology represent not only a reduction in extension but also a shift toward a bilateral treatment of relatives and a simplification of the terminology for distant relatives.

There were comparable changes in behavior patterns. The most significant of these was the consideration of the father's sister's daughter as a "respect" relative who could not be joked with, a pattern applied also to the father's sister. On the other hand, the mother's brother and his children could be joked with. This radical reversal of pattern is important. The rationalization given is that the father's sister and her daughter are out of one's own clan and hence cannot be joked with, whereas the mother's brother is in the clan and may be teased. But the positive influences of the school and government toward emphasizing paternal authority and the mission attitudes toward sexually tinged joking are probably the primary factors.

A series of granddaughters, daughters of her oldest daughter, have spent much of their life at boarding schools and in off-reservation employment. They have little knowledge of Hopi terminology or behavior patterns and try to adapt their terminology to American patterns. They know little of clan relationships, and there is an even greater reduction in the range of effective kinship. In general, they restrict the term "aunt" to the father's sister and "uncle" to the mother's brother, but there is a good deal of variance in the terms applied to the mother's sister.[216] The term "cousin," which is foreign to the old Hopi system, tends to be applied to all cousins, and particularly to cross-cousins; for more distant relatives the term "our relative" is used. Behavior patterns are reduced to a minimum and follow American models very considerably.

Until a larger number of genealogies have been collected and analyzed for New Oraibi it is not possible to say how typical the series of changes here sketched will turn out to be. But my observations suggest that the general trends are in these directions, though they are proceeding more slowly in most cases. Even within a lineage unit it is possible for several subsystems to exist at the same time, with resulting inconsistencies in terminology and behavior. Between different family and lineage units there are comparable differences which make kinship ties of less use in village integration.

The changes which are going on in New Oraibi are both integrative and disintegrative, but the latter are by far the stronger. To balance the loss of social and ceremonial ties as reflected in the household, clan-phratry, and ceremonial systems there is the greater economic security of the people of New Oraibi and a more effective secular government. But these are not yet sufficient to even the losses, and personal adjustment suffers in consequence.

The social disintegration of New Oraibi lends some support to our evaluation of Hopi social structure. The breakdown of the clan-phratry system to a lineage base emphasizes the importance of the lineage and the integrative functions of the clan and phratry systems, but it also suggests that the latter are a superstructure on the basic lineage pattern. The shifts in residence and ownership and the bilateral and even patrilineal tendencies in inheritance and naming have reflections in the kinship system.

We will return to these and other problems concerned with Hopi social organization after surveying the other western Pueblos and look at them from the vantage point of a comparative perspective.

Chapter III

THE SOCIAL ORGANIZATION OF HANO

Introduction

THE pueblo of Hano occupies a unique position among the western Pueblos. This Tewa-speaking group migrated to First Mesa from the Rio Grande around A.D. 1700, or soon after, as a result of disturbances brought about by the Reconquest. Reed has recently pointed out that, while the migrants came to the Hopi region from Tsawarii, on the Santa Cruz north of Santa Fe, they "were the Tanos or southern Tewa from the pueblos of San Cristóbal and San Lázaro (originally in the Galisteo Basin south of Santa Fe, moved to the Santa Cruz between 1680 and 1692)."[1] They fled the Rio Grande after the abortive revolt of 1696; a few years later they were living in a pueblo beside Walpi on First Mesa.

Their traditions state that they came at the invitation of the Walpi chiefs in order to defend Walpi against the Utes; in return they were given land, a place for their village, and various privileges and duties. This is, of course, the typical pattern for Hopi clan legends. Parsons suggests that a Hopi delegation to Santa Fe in 1700 may have been in touch with the Tano and offered them refuge; she notes the tradition as useful in preserving self-esteem.[2] Even so, they consider themselves as "protectors" of the Hopi and are so regarded by their hosts.

The village of Hano is politically independent but geographically contiguous with Sichomovi, the suburb of Walpi; it is, however, tied into the Hopi social and ceremonial system in complex ways. One of the earliest descriptions of Hano is Morfi's account, based on Escalante's visit in 1775:

On the western point of the first mesa and on the narrowest place on its eminence are situated three [villages], the first of which is that of

Los Janos (there they say Teguas). Its dwellers have a particular idiom different from the Moqui. It is a regular pueblo with its plaza in the center and with streets laid out. It has one hundred and ten families.[3]

The population indicated seems much too large; Stephen's complete census in 1893 listed only 163 individuals,[4] and there is no indication of extensive ruins but rather an extension of house-building in recent decades. Biologically there are relatively few pure Tewans; Stephen found less than 50 per cent of the adults of pure Tanoan stock and only six children (10 per cent) whose parents were both pure Tewa. Fewkes notes that this percentage of pure Tanoan is so small that in the next generation the stock will all be mixed.[5] According to Hano informants, the Hopi formerly restricted intermarriage with the Tewa, but this restriction has been breaking down at an accelerated rate, as Stephen's data for adults and children indicate. Through a rather rigid rule of matrilocal residence (Stephen's figures show no Hano women living outside the village, 23 Hopi and other men married into Hano, and 16 Hano men married in other villages), it has been possible to maintain village and linguistic autonomy despite the biological merging which has taken place.

In appearance Hano is a typical Hopi pueblo, although Mindeleff thought that there was some tendency toward a "pyramidal" structure such as is found in some of the eastern pueblos.[6] The village is divided into matrilineal, totemically named clans with some slight tendency toward linkage or phratry grouping. There are a limited number of society groups and two kivas, one located in the plaza and the other outside. The village chieftaincy is now associated with the Bear clan and follows the Hopi pattern.

The social and cultural position of Hano is thus an important one, particularly for the study of cultural change. Here, since 1700, has been a situation ideal for acculturation: close contact, intermarriage in recent decades at least, bilingualism on the part of the Tewa, and co-operation in mastering a common environment. The process of acculturation has worked both ways, as a comparison of First Mesa villages with other Hopi mesas shows, but the Tewa have made the major adjustments. Once our comparative knowledge of eastern Tewa culture is more adequate, we will have a better base for establishing the precise nature of the changes which have taken place; but the major outlines are clear. The loss of "biological" identity, while preserving linguistic and political autonomy, is related to their adjustment to Hopi social and ceremonial patterns of organization; these latter shifts in turn throw light on the nature of the lineage principle of organization.

The Kinship System

The kinship system of Hano has been outlined in exemplary fashion by Barbara Freire-Marreco,[7] though her long-promised comparative study of the eastern and western Tewa has not been published as yet. From the data available, however, it is clear that the Hano kinship system, while retaining its Tewa terminology, is structurally very similar to the Hopi and quite different in most respects from the eastern Tewa organization.[8]

TERMINOLOGY

Figures 7–10, derived from Freire-Marreco's data, present the basic structure of Hano kinship. The system is only partly "classificatory," in that the father is classed with the father's brother,[9] but a separate term is used for mother's sister, a situation which Freire-Marreco suggests may be transitional. In ego's matrilineal lineage there is a similar differentiation of relatives to that noted among the Hopi. A man differentiates his older and younger sisters, his mother, and his mother's mother in the ascending female line. In addition, there is a special term (*ko'o*) for mother's sister and her daughters, and a separate term (*papa*) for mother's mother's mother. A man's brothers are differentiated as older or younger (the same term being used for younger brother and younger sister), but all other senior males of the lineage are classed together as *maemae*, "mother's brother," though a special term is available for the mother's mother's brother where it is desirable to distinguish this relative. For junior members of the lineage below ego's generation a man uses the junior reciprocal, *maemae'e*, formed with the diminutive postfix

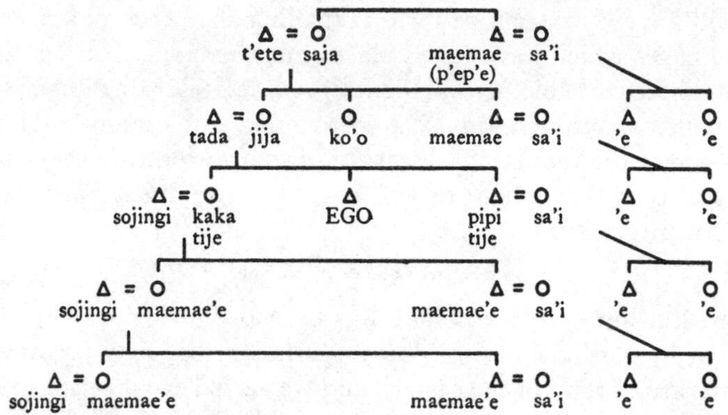

FIG. 7.—The mother's matrilineal lineage. Ego = male

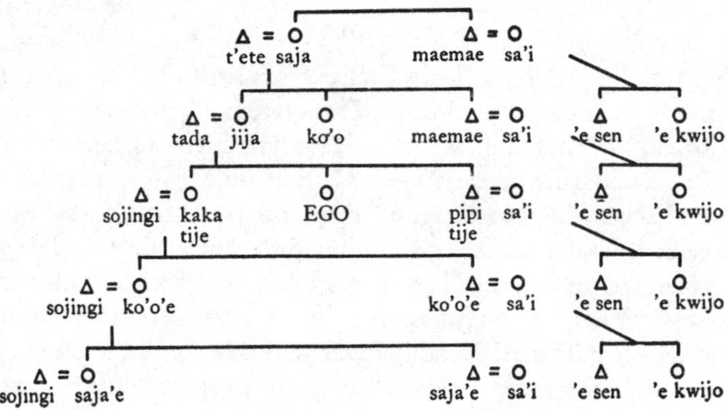

FIG. 8.— The mother's matrilineal lineage. Ego = female

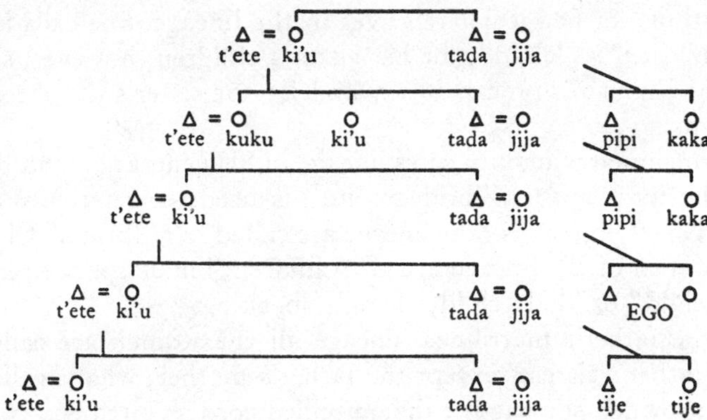

FIG. 9.—The father's matrilineal lineage. Ego= male or female

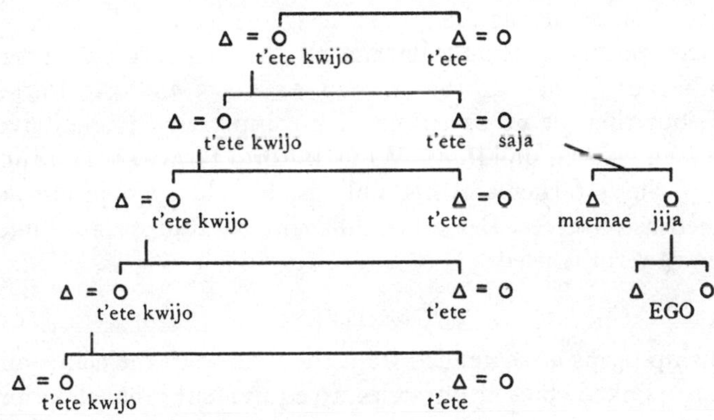

FIG. 10.—The mother's father's matrilineal lineage. Ego = male or female

'e, which by itself is used for "child."[10] A woman makes parallel distinctions for her senior relatives in the lineage. She calls her own children *'e*, "child"; for her sister's children, however, she uses the junior reciprocal, *ko'o'e;* and for the sister's daughter's children, *saja'e*.

For men marrying into ego's lineage in his generation and below, the term *sojingi*, "bridegroom," is used; correlatively all women marrying men of the lineage are called *sa'i*, "bride." Children of men of the lineage are all "children," male speaking, or "man child" or "lady child," female speaking.

In the father's matrilineal lineage all the women are called *ki'u*, "father's sister," except the father's mother, who is called *kuku* (provided she has cut the umbilical cord at birth and conducted the naming ceremony), and all the men are called *tada*, "father." All men marrying women of the father's lineage are "grandfathers"; all women marrying men of the father's lineage are "mothers"; children of men of the father's lineage are "brothers" and "sisters."

In the mother's father's lineage all the men are called *t'ete*, "grandfather," and all the women *t'ete kwijo*, "grandfather lady"; but there is no extension of kinship terms to the wives of the men or their children.[11] While kinship terms are extended to the father's father and his siblings, his clanspeople are not reckoned as relatives. For grandchildren the appropriate junior reciprocal term is used.

EXTENSIONS

Kinship terms are extended from the lineage to the clan—and further to linked clans or phratries, to equivalent Hopi clans and phratries, to equivalent Navaho clans, and to their eastern Tewa kinsmen. For one's own clan the extensions are on a simplified basis. Thus the term *ka'je* is a general term for senior clanswomen, whereas "mother" and "mother's sister" seem restricted to lineage or household or to social equivalents, and *saja* ("mother's mother") is used for the senior clanswoman and extended to any female ancestor of the speaker's clan. Similarly the term *maemae* and its junior reciprocal are used for senior and junior clansmen. In the father's clan the terms for "father" and "father's sister" are extended without regard for age or generation, as are the grandparental terms used for the mother's father's clan.

Freire-Marreco illustrates these and other extensions as follows:

Suppose that A, a Tewa Corn clan woman, married a Tewa Bear clan man and had a daughter B. B married a Tewa Cloud clan man and had a daughter C and a son D. C and D call all males of the Tewa Bear clan, Stick clan, and White-fir clan, the Hopi Bear clan, Bearskin-rope clan and Spider clan, and the Navaho Bear clan, including infants,

TEWA

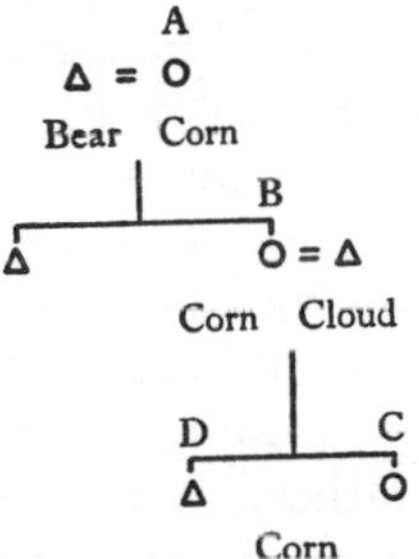

t'ete, and all females of those clans *t'ete kwijo;* and all the males and females of those clans call C and D *t'ete'e.* C and D call all the males of the Tewa Cloud clan and the Hopi Cloud clan, Water clan and Reed clan *tada* and all the females *ki'i'u;* the males of those clans claim C and D as "their children" by calling them *'e*, and the females by calling C*'e kwijo* and D*'e sen.* C and D give the title of *jija*, "mother" to the wife of any of their *tada'i*, and of "brother" and "sister" to any person whose father, like their own father, is a man of the Cloud clan; but they have no names for the wives and children of their *t'et'i*, the Bear clan men, as such.[12]

The extensions of kinship to the Navaho, with whom there is some intermarriage, are on the basis of equivalent clans; to the Hopi on the basis of clans and phratries. The Tewa from the Rio Grande villages, however, are treated as own kinsmen, being addressed as *maemae*, "mother's brother," or *ka'je kwijo*, "elder clanswoman," until more precise clan relationships are defined. Katcina families are thought to be organized on the basis of clans and are given corresponding kinship terms, and in the folk tales resourceful old women are called *saja*, "mother's mother."

Children or others living in a household will call the woman taking care of them "mother." Sick people may call in a doctor to cure them, or a child may be "given" to a strong couple "to make it live"; in such cases parent-child terms are used, and in the case of the doctor the patient may later join his society. Hosts or protectors in distant places may be called by parental terms.

There is little information regarding the selection of ceremonial parents among the Tewa. A "ceremonial father" is selected for a boy and a "ceremonial mother" for a girl at the time of Katcina initiation;[13] presumably these are from clans other than the novice's own or father's clan, and it is probable that kinship is extended to the clan of the ceremonial parent. A "ceremonial father" is likewise selected for induction into the Winter Solstice ceremony;[14] whether he is the same as the Katcina "father" is not clear. Membership in a curing society likewise involves the selection of a "doctor father," but the extension of kinship in these cases is not clear from the available accounts. The village chief is thought of as the "father" of the people and his wife as their "mother"; in the mythology the Town Chief is referred to as "our Father and Mother."[15] That kinship terms are applied to important aspects of nature, in accordance with the Hopi pattern, is probable, judging by the evidence in the mythology.

THE HOUSEHOLD

The Hano household parallels that of the Hopi in every important respect. The household is based on matrilocal residence and includes the nearest relatives. Miss Freire-Marreco gives an account of one of the two Corn clan households from the standpoint of a Tewa girl:

> The nucleus of the household, the essential and permanent part of it, consists of men, women and children of the girl's own clan. The center of the house is *na'imbi saja*, "our mother's mother," the owner and dispenser of all stores and food-stuffs, the guardian of the religious

apparatus belonging to the clan, the director of household work, the person who gives orders—so far as orders are given at all in this easy-going tolerant society.[16]

Behind the mother's mother is the tradition of her mother and all the senior clanswomen to remotest antiquity; beside her stand the mother's brothers, the men of the clan.

Maemae'i sleep, as a rule, at the homes of their wives (*na'imbi sa'i'i*, "our brides"), but they are constantly coming in and out of this, which they call their own house. They take their places at meals here as a matter of course, invite visitors to eat, behave as hosts and masters of the house; though they do not (if they are married) contribute anything to the material support of our household, since they have to supply corn, meat, and wood to their wives' homes. Their claim to obedience is a religious one—they are "our *maemae'i* who go out to see the sun before us," who give us advice "how we shall live." They consecrate our seed-corn and make prayer-feathers for us at the winter Solstice: their feather-boxes, dancing-clothes, weaving tools, jewelry are kept in our house, and they borrow our finery and ornaments as a matter of right. . . . Whatever *maemae'i* say is unquestionably right; *saja* is the only person who may ever criticise them, and she does so only on questions of practice, not of theory.[17]

Within the household seniority is generally important, with the mother or mother's sister partaking of the mother's mother's authority and carrying out her duties when she is absent. The children of these two generally address one another as "brother" and "sister," though the mother's sister's children may be called *ko'o* or *maemae* or their junior reciprocals.

The men of other clans married into the household are called "our bridegrooms."

These are the men who support, or should support, the household, bringing their yearly crops to their wives, to be stored and administered by *saja*, killing sheep (if they have any), and bringing firewood at frequent intervals. They range from *t'ete*, *saja*'s husband, who is quite a permanent, central figure in our household life, to the lately-acquired husband of my younger *ko'o*, who is still shy and sulky and inclined to shirk his duties, and must not be driven too hard for fear of a quarrel. . . .

Our *sojingi'i* sleep in our house as a rule, but they spend much of the day in their own clan houses; they have duties in the kiva where their own clans "go in," but they also dance "to help our *maemae'i* in ours."[18]

Here, in brief compass, is an exemplary account of the Tewa household sketched from actual residence within it. Besides his own household, an individual has close relations with other households in his clan, with his father's household and other households in his father's clan, with the mother's father's household and clan, and with the children of men of the clan. Outside the circle of kinship the rest of the people are "of doubtful friendliness, always capable of hostility, jealousy, and ingratitude toward us as a clan. . . . 'The people are not good' is as common a saying with the Tewa as *Hópi ka Hópi* is with their Hopi neighbors."[19]

KINSHIP BEHAVIOR

The behavior patterns between relatives can be conveniently summarized in connection with the life-cycle. Tewa social life is integrated with Hopi at many points, but until Freire-Marreco publishes her detailed observations it will not be possible to specify the similarities and differences. At birth the father's mother ordinarily comes in to assist the mother. She cuts the umbilical cord and later conducts the naming ceremony. As such she is called by a special term *kuku*, "father's mother"; this term is applied to any woman who performs these operations in the absence of the father's mother. Freire-Marreco notes that formerly at Hano the mother's mother and the child's own clanswomen used to cut the cord and give the name.[20] Since the term *kuku* is cognate with the Santa Clara term for mother's mother's mother, this is probably eastern Tewa practice, suggesting that the shift has come about through Hopi influence. The naming practices are presumably on the Hopi pattern, with the name referring to the father's clan.

The care and the training of the child are in the hands of the household—and the father's household.

My father stands in a close and tender relationship to myself and my sisters and brothers. Although, in the opinion of the elder members of the household he is not so near a relation to me as are *maemae'i*, my own clansmen, he seems to me personally nearer and dearer. *Maemae'i* give advice, instruction, and reproof, not unmixed with teasing; whereas *nabi tada* gives clothes, shoes, and toys, tells stories and sings to us

> children, caresses us and plays with us. He and my mother and my brothers and sisters and I form a little camp of our own, as it were, in the midst of the crowded household life; we sit together to eat and talk, and sleep together on my mother's own sheepskins and blankets.[21]

The men and women of the father's clan visit familiarly in ego's household. Especially close is the father's mother and the father's own sisters:

> Their house is a second home to me; they caress me, wash, comb, and cut my hair, improve my manners and morals—my youngest *ki'i'u* is modern enough to make clothes for me on the American sewing machine. From time to time my sisters and I grind corn for them; and whenever my father gives clothes to us or to my mother, we make a formal presentation of wafer-bread and other food "to pay them." My brothers kill rabbits and pile snow for their *ki'i'u'i;* when they are old enough they will go on a journey and fetch salt for them. In old times their *ki'i'u'i* would have danced with them when they took a scalp.[22]

The initiation ritual consists of a whipping by the Katcinas corresponding to the Katcina initiation of the Hopi. This initiation takes place at about the age of eight or ten during the Hopi Powamu ceremony, but in the Tewa kivas. The "ceremonial fathers" hold the boys while they are flogged, and the "ceremonial mothers" hold the girls; then they are told the secrets of the Katcina by the chief.[23]

Parsons reports an instance in which the "ceremonial father" was selected by the boy's uncle on the occasion of his first rabbit kill, his father's sisters, including ceremonial aunts, having to bake piki for the occasion.[24] She also notes a partial breakdown of the Katcina initiation ritual in recent times, with the child's father's mother or father's sister taking the child to be whipped.[25] Whether a special ritual takes place at the time of a girl's first menstruation, such as Stephen reports for First Mesa,[26] is not clear. There is no tribal initiation among the Tewa comparable to Wuwutcim; and the Tewa were said to be afraid to join the Wuwutcim societies for the most part.[27] Instead the Tewa join the Hano Winter Solstice ceremony, selecting "ceremonial fathers," observing taboos, bathing in the spring, and going after ceremonial materials.[28] Initiation into curing societies might take place at any time.

The marriage customs at Hano so far recorded closely parallel those of the Hopi. Marriage is not permitted within the clan or linked clan, or into the father's clan or phratry, a prohibition which is also extended to the comparable Hopi clans and phratries.[29] On the other hand, it is possible to marry a member of the mother's father's clan, a group into which, in Hopi *theory*, one should not marry.

There is little specific information on courtship, but the degree of intermarriage suggests familiarity with Hopi patterns. The girl's clanspeople escort her to the boy's house, the procession being led by the girl's paternal aunt and all the uncles. She grinds corn for four days; on the fifth day her hair is ritually washed by the boy's mother and clanswomen, and henceforth she is never called by name but is always referred to by the term *sa'i*, "bride"; any violation of this rule would result in the sun going down.[30]

In the meantime the boy's aunts may decide to "protest" the marriage. They gather all their clanswomen and pour mud on the boy's parents and his mother's clanswomen, accusing the bride of being lazy and unable to cook or work.[31] In one of the tales the aunts attacked the boy's father (their brother) and nearly killed him. "He said to his sisters that he had a very good *sa'i*, 'better looking than you,' he said. They dragged him to the ground, put mud on him and threw mud on the walls. . . ."[32]

After the ritual hair-washing the boy's kinsmen begin weaving the wedding garments, being fed by both households. After the garments are completed, the boy's mothers and sisters dress the girl and lead her home, where they are thanked by the girl's uncles. Early the next morning they wash the boy's head; later they make piki and take it to the boy's house. Two or three years later a further exchange takes place, including a large amount of corn meal ground by the girl for the boy's family.[33]

Both Freire-Marreco and Parsons suggest that the behavior of the father's sisters at the time of marriage may be indicative of a former custom of cross-cousin marriage, a custom which

Freire-Marreco mistakenly attributes to the Hopi as a regular practice in most villages. She points out:

> When a boy baby is brought to visit in the house of his father's clan, he is loudly welcomed as the "husband," *sen*, of one of the girls of the clan, that is, of one of his *ki'i'u'i*, whom by present-day custom he cannot marry. In the same way a girl baby is hailed as the "wife" of one of her *tada'i*. A woman speaks of her son's sons in jest as "our bridegrooms," *sojingi'i*, as if they were expected to marry some of the girls of her clan. A man must "pretend to like" his father's sister's daughters and his father's sisters. (Similarly a woman must "pretend to like" the husbands of her father's clanswomen.) When a young man's approaching marriage is announced, his *ki'i'u'i*, the women of his father's clan, are supposed to take it amiss; they "fight" one of his clanswomen and daub her with mud, or they visit his clan-house to "scold" and "talk queerly." A grown-up girl sometimes playfully warns-off other girls from her mother's brother's son, her *'e sen;* although she may not marry him, she half-seriously resents the advances of other girls toward him. In a less degree a woman is expected to resent the marriage of a man who is her *t'ete'e*, i.e., whose mother's father was her clansman: she affects a little coolness toward the young man's clan, threatens not to ask his sisters to her house, and so on.[34]

Marriage establishes a whole new series of relationships. When the husband comes to live at his wife's household, he is called "our bridegroom" by his wife's relatives. In turn he calls his wife's clanswomen *ja kwijo*, "woman relative-in-law," and her clansmen *ja seno*, "old man relative-in-law"; but he may also call his wife's household by the same terms his wife uses, though they will still call him "our bridegroom."

The position of a "bridegroom" is sketched in the section on "The Household" described above. Husband and wife terms are available but seem little used; there is some teknonymous usage, but its extent is not clear. A man expresses his relationship to his wife's clan by saying, "I am their bridegroom," and may refer to them collectively by the term *ja*. After he has children, his wife's clanspeople may refer to his mother as *saja*, "mother's mother," apparently as a complimentary reference through the child. Two men married to sisters call each other "my husband partner," possibly in reference to their joint responsibilities.

The other important relationship by marriage is that of *sa'i*, "bride," which is used for the wife of any man of the speaker's clan and by a man for his son's wife. (The reciprocal term is *ja*.) A man may also call his wife's brother's wife and wife's mother's brother's wife *sa'i*, using her terms; two women married to brothers call each other "my bride partner." The *sa'i*, who corresponds to the Hopi, *mï'wi*, is an important relative. *Sa'i* apparently means "child-bearing," and formerly she was not so called until she had conceived. Through her are produced "children" of the father's clan, and she and her husband's clanswomen aid one another on a variety of occasions.[35]

The Tewa customs with regard to death are unreported. The degree to which they may have adopted the Hopi conceptions of death and the afterworld will be a good index to the depth of acculturation; it is possible that the dead go to the Tewa lake of Emergence rather than to the Hopi underworld. So far as we know, the customs of inheritance with regard to houses, land, sheep, and ceremonial property and position follow the Hopi pattern; this is especially true in the case of Hopi-Tewa marriages. Freire-Marreco does note that a clansman's widow is called *sa'i* until she remarries, and even afterward if there have been children. A widower would normally return to his sister's household, or to the home of one of his clanswomen if he had no close relatives.

SUMMARY AND COMPARISONS

It is clear that the kinship system at Hano is organized on the lineage principle—"Tewa kinship terms belong to a clan system."[36] The lineage and household structures are closely correlated with the kinship terminology, and the behavioral patterns among relatives are consonant with the lineage and household structures. The basic patterns of kinship—both terminological and behavioral—closely resemble those of the neighboring Hopi and differ from those of the Rio Grande Tewa. Yet there is no evidence (with one possible exception) that a single kinship *term* has been borrowed by the Tewa, despite two centuries of close contact and considerable intermarriage. The terminology remains basically cognate with eastern Tewa forms, but the terminological *structure* has been radically remodeled from the bilateral generational system reported by Harrington for the eastern Tewa.[37] If we can assume that the system presented by Harrington represents the older Tewa patterns (an interpretation at variance with Freire-Marreco's),[38] then the Hano kinship system would represent a crucial case where behavior and organization have changed but terminology as such has remained much the same.

We have noted that Hano kindred are organized in terms of three basic lineages and that the extensions of kinship to the clan (and phratry) parallel those of the Hopi. A detailed comparison of the Hano terminological groupings with those of the Hopi and the eastern Tewa, based on Freire-Marreco[39] and Harrington,[40] suggests the nature and direction of certain of the changes which have taken place.

In ego's own lineage the term "mother" is not extended to the mother's sister, and the children of each are separated.[41] At Hano a special term, *ko'o* (which in the Rio Grande Tewa is used bilaterally for father's sister and mother's sister—as well as for female cousins—and, with the junior reciprocal, for brother's and sister's children), is used for mother's sister and her daughters and, as a junior reciprocal, for a woman's sister's children, all of whom are members of the matrilineal lineage. The term for "grandmother" used bilaterally in the east is restricted at Hano to the mother's mother, but it is extended to the senior head of the clan, or related clans, and all female ancestors of the clan. A special term, *ka'je*, apparently has been developed at Hano to refer to senior women in the clan.

Sibling terms at Hano have shifted from the eastern Tewa pattern of representing age but not sex toward the Hopi pattern of differentiating older brothers from older sisters, but without the further development of separate terms for male and female speakers.[42] The term *maemae* and its junior reciprocal, which in the east is used for "male cousin" primarily, is at Hano used for the mother's brother and extended to male clansmen generally. The eastern Tewa term for "uncle" (ie., father's brother or mother's brother) is occasionally used for father's brother at

Hano but is obsolescent. From *papa*, "great grandfather," a special term, *p'ep'e*, has been developed in the west to distinguish the "mother's mother's brother"; the term *papa* itself is there used primarily for relatives on the mother's side.

The eastern Tewa terms for "son-in-law" and "daughter-in law," there applied also to grandchildren-in-law on both sides, are at Hano restricted to men and women who marry into the lineage (and clan), the only exceptions being a man's son's wife and a woman's brother's son's wife.[43] The term for "child," *'e*, is at Hano extended to "brother's child" and to the children of any male of the lineage and clan, male speaking. Women distinguish the children of their brothers and clansmen as "men children" and "lady children," a differentiation which does not go so far as the Hopi one. In the Rio Grande Tewa *tu'e*, the junior reciprocal of "uncle," is used for brother's or sister's children.

In ego's father's lineage the basic patterns of organization are almost identical with those of the Hopi. The term for "father" is "applied loosely to father, elder brother, father's brother, or other relatives older than self" in the east; in the west its primary extension is to men of the father's clan and related clans, regardless of age and generation. Similarly the term for father's sister, *ki'u*, is extended to all women of the father's lineage and clan at Hano, except for the father's mother, who may be called *kuku*.[44] In the east, *ko'o* is used for both the father's and the mother's sisters, according to Harrington, though Freire-Marreco gives *ki'i* as a cognate—without, however, specifying its applications. The special term for father's brother in the east has been almost completely replaced at Hano by the term for "father."

The term *t'ete*, "grandfather," has the same basic applications at Hano and the Rio Grande villages, but it is extended to all men marrying women of the father's lineage and clan at Hano and, further, to the men and women of the mother's father's lineage and clan, regardless of generation.

The term for "mother" is likewise extended at Hano to the wives of all the men of the father's clan, regardless of age or generation; children of any of these men are "brothers" or "sisters." In the eastern Tewa the term "mother" is only extended in compounds, such as *papajija*, "great-grandmother."

The mother's father's lineage at Hano is organized in similar fashion to the Hopi. All the men are called *t'ete*, "grandfather," as noted above, and all the women "grandfather lady," a combination not used in the east. Conversely any individual whose mother's father is in the speaker's clan is called *t'ete'e*, "grandchild," a junior reciprocal which is limited to son's and daughter's children in the east.

The terms for husband and wife are similar in the two areas, but the term *ja'a* (Hano, *ja*), used in the east for "any consanguineous relative of husband or wife," is at Hano restricted to a man's wife's clanspeople and a woman's husband's clanspeople and husband's father. Further, a husband or wife may use each other's terms for their spouse's relatives, though the rules for such usage are not clear.

This comparative survey strengthens the possibility that the major changes in the *organization* of kinship terminology have taken place at Hano rather than in the eastern Tewa villages. Freire-Marreco comes to the opposite conclusion:

> At Hano, where the matrilinear clan system is in full force, the Tewa kinship terms express the facts of social life and are used consistently; in the Tewa pueblos of New Mexico, where clanship is now reckoned almost entirely by paternal descent and the clans have lost their importance, while the father-mother-and-child family has become the primary unit of social life, the same kinship terms are used inconsistently, with many local variations, and "descriptive" compound terms are being introduced to remedy the confusion.[45]

But the eastern Tewa kinship system is not the broken-down remnant of a "clan" system, if we may judge from Harrington's account, which also used her data. He presents, in a series of charts, a relatively self-consistent kinship structure which has a logic of its own.[46] It is "nonclassificatory," in that the lineal relatives are separated from collateral relatives, and essentially bilateral in its basic structure. The extensive use of the junior reciprocal, formed by adding the diminutive postfix *'e*, gives an individuality to the system; almost every term outside the elementary family is so compounded. There is, furthermore, a considerable elaboration of terms for the generation above the grandparental one, a feature which is lacking at Hano, and the use of "uncle" and "aunt" terms for father's and mother's brothers and sisters, female cousins, nephews and nieces on both sides, and more distant relatives. Such specialization does not ordinarily occur with the breakdown of a "clan" system under acculturation from either Spanish or Americans, nor is it apparent in the recent acculturation which has been taking place in the Rio Grande Valley during this century.[47]

Turning again to Hano, it is apparent that, in almost every instance, the changes have been in the direction of an adjustment to the lineage and clan pattern of organization. The Hopi pattern is approximated but not quite reached, so far as the kinship system is concerned. This is particularly true in ego's own lineage, where the elementary family is still somewhat set off and sisters and their descendants are differentiated, a situation which Freire-Marreco herself feels to be "transitional in character." Where there are variations from the Hopi pattern they are largely explicable in terms of the eastern Tewa situation.[48]

The most significant difference between Hopi and Hano is in the latter's extensive use of the junior reciprocal. These reciprocal terms, used bilaterally in the east, are almost completely fitted into the lineage pattern at Hano. In character they represent an intermediate type between nonreciprocal terminology and self-reciprocal terms, such as are used extensively among the Keresan villages and to a lesser extent at Zuni. As such we would like to know a great deal more as to their significance for social behavior, a problem which remains to be studied.

If Hano kinship terminology has been reorganized into new patterns without the terms themselves being greatly modified, we can ask what the factors are which might bring about new groupings of relatives. In the light of our Hopi analysis I would suggest that changes in kinship behavior, associated with the adoption of the Hopi household-lineage-clan pattern, represent the major factors responsible for the new terminological structure.

The Hano household, as described by Freire-Marreco, is an almost exact duplicate of the Hopi household, not only in terms of matrilocal residence, but in terms of the structural relationships of the members and their relations to other households. The line of women represents the central and permanent core; standing beside them are their brothers, who perform the rituals and give them guidance. Married in are the "bridegrooms," who cooperate in the economic support of the household, and the "brides," who furnish "children" for the clan and assist the women of the household on a variety of occasions.

With the father's household the Hopi pattern is likewise paralleled. The close and intimate relationship with the father's sisters, described above, has been considered by Freire-Marreco as an indication of a former custom of cross-cousin marriage among the Tewa.[49] I believe that the corresponding behavior among the Hopi may be so interpreted,[50] but I find no evidence among the eastern Tewa of parallel behavior. Hence, until we have further evidence, it is simpler to assume that the Hano behavior has been borrowed, through intermarriage and observation, from the Hopi. In any case, the parallel behavior performs today a different function: that of establishing a close bond between one's own and one's father's household. The classification of the husbands of the father's sisters as "grandfathers" is in accordance with Hopi patterns; it is not clear whether the special joking relationships with these "grandfathers" are in operation, but Freire-Marreco notes that the father's sisters show a more demonstrative affection for their "brother's" children than for the grandchildren in their own household. At Hano the pattern of classification of children of men of the lineage and clan does not quite approximate the logic of the Hopi where a woman calls the children of her clansmen "grandchildren," but, even so, the position of a woman is differentiated from that of a man in this position.

The behavior patterns between given pairs of relatives, as listed by Freire-Marreco, are very close, even in details, to those of the Hopi—in fact, her brief descriptions could be used for the Hopi almost without any changes. Our information on eastern Tewa kinship behavior is very meager, but, in the case of care of the newborn infant and naming practices, there is definite evidence that Hano has shifted from the eastern practice to the

Hopi system. It is probable that this has also happened with other relationships in the life-cycle.

The above analysis suggests that some of the hypotheses proposed with regard to Hano kinship organization need considerable revision—or even reversal. We will return to these problems after a consideration of other aspects of Hano social organization.

The Clan System

The social organization of Hano is built around the same institutions as the Hopi's—the matrilineal clan, phratry, society,

TABLE 4

Hano Clans

Clan Name	Population	Lineages
Bear (*ke*)	14	1
Pine (*tenyük*)	27	3
Tobacco (*sa*)	15	1
Corn (*kolon*)	25	2
Sand (*näñ*)	15	1
Katcina (*katcina*)	33	4
Cloud (*okuwañ*)	31	4
Sun (*tañ*)	1	....
Total	161	16

and kiva groupings—but the relative importance of these institutions and their relations to one another and to the ceremonial cycle varies somewhat from the Hopi pattern.

The Hano clan is similar to the Hopi clan in structure and function. Since the Tewa people came to First Mesa as a unit (neglecting the problem of the *Asa* or Mustard clan for the moment), there are no clan legends of separate clan migrations, though Parsons[51] notes a tendency of the Bear clan to set itself apart, in good Hopi fashion.

The early surveys of Stephen[52] and Fewkes[53] give us a picture of the Hano clan system at the turn of the century (Table 4). At that time the Sun clan was on the verge of extinction, and several other clans were said to have become "extinct": Crane, Stick, Pink Shell, Turquoise, Stone, Grass, and others.

Neither Stephen nor Fewkes reports any linked-clan or phratry groupings at Hano, though Mindeleff[54] gives a list of Tewa clans, bracketed in pairs, which are said to "belong together" but do not have distinctive names. A few years later (1914) Freire-Marreco mentions "groups of linked clans" and notes that kinship would be extended to "the Tewa Bear clan, Stick clan, and White-fir clan."[55] Parsons, recording Hano clans in 1920, mentions Cloud, Bear, Corn, Tobacco, Sand, Cottonwood (with Crow lineage), and Pine as a lineage of Bear. She also notes that Cottonwood (*t'eh*) is the equivalent of the Katcina clan.[56] The Bear clan is traditionally the most important clan among the Hopi, and it is interesting that the clan linkage has apparently developed first in this group, particularly as the Bear clan was practically extinct on First Mesa. It is also worth while noting that the Hano did not borrow the specific Hopi grouping, though parallel rationalizations were developed. Thus the Pine clan (which, contrary to Parsons, was not a single lineage but three lineages and considerably larger than the Bear clan) seems to be associated with the Bear clan because it owns the "Bear Clan Old Man" mask, which is said to have been brought with the Tewa from the east. The Cottonwood clan has been equated with the Katcina clan of the Hopi, apparently because of legend:

Before the migration from New Mexico, the *sumaikoli* belonged to the Cottonwood clan (because the *sumaikoli* are *okuwa* (Kachina, also clouds) and the Cottonwood clan is an *okuwa* clan. The Cottonwood clan "has Crow in their clan," i.e., one of their maternal families is Crow. That is why the *sumaikoli* wear Crow wings). Now the *sumaikoli* being blind, it was too much work to carry them in the migration. So they hid the *sumaikoli* and left them behind. But then the *okuwa* (Cloud) clan came along and found the *sumaikoli* and took them along. "That is why the *sumaikoli* were in the Cloud clan's house" on First Mesa. . . .[57]

In Hopi theory the Katcina clans came from the east and included Crow and Cottonwood, among several others;[58] the identification of Cloud as a "Katcina clan," however, is not a Hopi grouping but apparently derives from the identification of Katcina and clouds. In general, the Hano clans are considered to be the equivalent of the same or similar Hopi clans, and kinship and hospitality are extended on that basis.

The division of the Hano clans into lineages or "maternal families" is clear from the genealogies presented by Fewkes. His data suggest that the lineages are small, averaging about ten persons per lineage, though several had some fifteen persons. Normally such a group would occupy a single household, the men residing of course with their wives. Freire-Marreco gives a word picture of the two Corn clanhouses at Hano (corresponding to the two lineages listed by Fewkes). We have described one under "The Household"; the other follows:

> The other half of our clan inhabits the ancestral house from which our *saja*'s mother migrated many years ago. The old lady who presides over it is "sort of sister" to our *saja*, and addresses her sometimes as "elder sister," *kaka*, sometimes as "mother's elder sister," *ka'je*. Her daughters and daughter's children call our *saja* sometimes *ka'je*, sometimes *saja*. We address their *saja* in the same way. The members of her household are our *matu'i* (clanspeople who are not housemates of the speaker), and they ought to be our nearest friends; but there are times when a degree of coldness, or perhaps of jealousy, keeps us apart. Our *maemae'i* are not very good friends with their *sojingi'i*.[59]

Each Hano clan has a clanhouse, normally occupied by the ancestral lineage, clan masks or other paraphernalia,[60] and some beginnings of clan legends. Each clan also owns land, and certain clans are associated with springs in which their ancestral beings are said to live and which they are responsible for.[61]

The clan is also a self-conscious unit at Hano. The term *towa*, "people," is used for a great variety of groupings, including clans, in both the east and the west, but the term *matu'i*, used for a *bilateral* group of relatives descended from grandparents or great-grandparents in the east,[62] is at Hano applied to fellow-clanspeople who are outside one's own household.[63] At clan meetings ("every clan will have a meeting once in a while"), which are held in the ancestral clanhouse, the oldest man will tell the clan legends and indicate their traditional duties.[64] During the racing season races are frequently by clan, the members dressing up according to their clan emblem and at the end of the race being fed by their clanswomen. Men may also race for their sisters-in-law (*sa'i*), and women for the "children" of their clansmen.[65] Ceremonial positions and ceremonies are likewise associated with particular clans to some extent. When the Sun clan became extinct, a Bear clan family moved into the Sun clanhouse to look after the *sumaikoli* masks.[66]

The Hano clan system thus shows considerable adaptation to Hopi patterns, and there is no trace of the patrilineal dual divisions of the eastern Tewa in the clan organization of Hano. It is interesting to note that the existing Hano clans are practically all named in similar fashion to the Hopi, whereas the "extinct" clans are generally analogous to the "clan names" reported for the eastern Tewa villages. It is difficult to determine the nature of the "clan" system of the eastern Tewa today—even more difficult to decide what it may have been like in 1700. Parsons' comments in this connection are relevant:

> Of the Tewa clans that *in accordance with the Hopi tradition* were said to migrate there is no representation today among the northern Tewa. If the weakness of the northern Tewa clans today is due, as I believe, not to disintegration, but to their marginal position, then it is quite probable that at the time of the migration organization by clan did not exist.[67]

As an alternative she suggests that the concept of clanship may have spread from the Keres to the Tewa prior to the migration; they would presumably have affected the southern Tewa (from whom the Hano were largely derived) to a greater extent than the northern Tewa.

Ceremonial Organization

Hano differs more from Hopi in its ceremonial organization than in other aspects of social structure. Many aspects of the Katcina cult have been adopted and a considerable number of ritual activities, but the major Hopi ceremonies have not been borrowed, in part, because of the Hopi conception of traditional controlling clans and also because of their conservatism. Hence the Hano ceremonial calendar is for the most part a pale reflection of the Hopi, with some important differences which can be attributed to basic Tewa patterns.

The kiva organization at Hano is patterned after the Hopi of First Mesa. There are only two kivas at Hano, *mona* kiva and *tewa* kiva. *Mona* kiva is the chief kiva, and the kiva chief is a Corn clansman, the kiva being said to "belong" to the Corn clan; *tewa* kiva has a Sand clansman as chief and "belongs" to the Sand clan. Membership in the Hano kivas is said to be "according to clan affiliation," with Bear, Corn, Tobacco, and Cottonwood clansmen belonging to the chief kiva, and Sand and some Cloud and Cottonwood clansmen belonging to the *tewa* kiva.[68]

Since the Tewa do not have the tribal men's societies found among the Hopi, it is probable that kiva membership is associated either with the Katcina initiation or with the Winter Solstice ceremony, possibly the latter, since Parsons reports that "three boys, aged from eighteen to twenty, were taken into *mona* kiva" during the Winter Solstice ceremony in 1921.[69] That clan affiliation determines kiva membership is doubtful in view of Mindeleff's statement: "The membership is composed of men from all the Hano gentes, but not all of any one gens. In fact, it is not now customary for all the members of a gens to be members of the same kiva."[70]

It is probable that the Tewa kivas follow the Hopi pattern of ownership or control and are "owned" by the individual who takes the initiative in building or repairing the structure. Such an individual normally acts as kiva chief and transmits the kiva to his sister's son; Stephen gives an example of kiva transference at Hano,[71] and Mindeleff notes an instance where a dissident kiva faction set out to build its own kiva but adjusted their differences before completion.[72] A man normally attends the kiva to which he belongs, but on many occasions he may co-operate in activities initiated by the other kiva—or by Walpi and Sichomovi kivas.

The kiva is an important institution at Hano, since many of the duties which various Hopi societies carry out are assumed by the Hano kiva groups. Katcina dancing, games, racing, and other activities are frequently by kiva groups, and the Hano kivas compete both with each other and with Walpi and Sichomovi. They are also integrated into the Hopi ceremonial cycle at various points, particularly during Powamu and the Soyal ceremony.

Parsons feels that the two kivas at Hano may be a survival of the two-kiva system of the eastern Tewa, despite Stephen's mention of an abandoned kiva at Hano.[73] This may well be true, though for the available Tewa men (52 in 1894) two kivas would be quite adequate. But, despite the lack of the summer-winter "moieties" associated with kivas, there are at Hano two kiva groups competing in a variety of controlled and regulated ways, one of the major functions of dual divisions everywhere.

The ceremonial calendar at Hano has been described in detail in Parsons' *A Pueblo Indian Journal* and compared and contrasted with Hopi and eastern Tewa;[74] only certain of the organizational aspects of the ceremonies and the interrelations of clan, society, kiva, and hierarchy will be considered here. *T'ant'aii*, the Winter Solstice ceremony, corresponds to the Hopi Soyal in many respects, but the ceremonial activities and altars are kept secret one from the other. At Hano there are two Winter Solstice chiefs, the Town Chief (Bear clan) and the Sand clan chief, which Parsons considers to be survivals of the eastern Tewa dual chieftainship associated with Summer People and Winter People.[75] The Town Chief erects altars in *mona* (chief) kiva, and the Sand clan chief in *tewa* kiva; the men remain in their respective kivas for three days making prayer sticks, singing, and praying for the welfare of everything in the world. Ears of corn from every household are consecrated on the altar, and the prayer offerings are distributed by groups of clansmen to their clanspeople and to the "children" of the clan. Women from every household bring food to the kivas; that of the Bear clan household is eaten first, followed by Tobacco and Corn.[76]

Hano has a well-developed Katcina cult which is patterned after the Hopi organization. A separate initiation takes place at the time of the Hopi Powamu. The Town Chief prepares a simple altar in chief kiva. Fewkes[77] describes a Katcina initiation at Hano which parallels the Hopi whipping ritual, but Parsons[78] notes that, with the partial disruption of the Hopi ceremonial cycle, Tewa children were whipped in chief kiva by "children" of the Tobacco clan (which owns the Katcina masks used), the children being brought to the kiva by their father's mother or father's sisters. The Tewa Katcina are largely Hopi types, though there seem to be a few independent Tewa Katcina, and the organization of dances follows the Hopi pattern and is partly integrated with the Hopi dance cycle on First Mesa. Katcina dances are apparently used much more for curing purposes at Hano (and also at Walpi) than at the other Hopi villages; Parsons' journalist gives a number of instances where dances were performed for curing purposes.[79] This greater emphasis on curing at Hano may be a reflection of eastern Tewa backgrounds, perhaps reinforced by Navaho influences—it is one place where Hano has definitely influenced Hopi First Mesa culture. Since Hano has no Niman ceremony to send the Katcinas home, Katcina dancers may appear after the Hopi season is over, evidence of Hano failure to take over much of the underlying theory for the Katcina cult.

A Tewa War ceremony, the Kahbena, was formerly held in January and kept secret from the Hopi, who were not allowed to be present. The ceremony was said to be in charge of the Corn clan chief, assisted by the Town Chief and the Pine clan keeper of the Bear mask. The ceremony was held in *tewa* kiva, the men from *mona* kiva coming over, and women could be present. War songs were sung, the *kossa* (or *koyala*) and the Katcina participated, and the Corn clan furnished a drink of "corn water" medicine to every participant.[80]

The Tiyogeo', or Seasonal Transfer ceremony, is held in March. The Town Chief, assisted by the Corn clan and Tobacco clan chiefs, goes into chief kiva, where they smoke and make prayer sticks to be deposited at the springs in the four directions and at various shrines, including one representing the Tewa lake of Emergence. Parsons believes this ceremony is the equivalent of the eastern Tewa transfer from winter to summer, but the corresponding November transfer has apparently lapsed.[81]

The Summer Solstice ceremony is in the hands of the Town Chief, assisted by the chiefs of the Corn, Tobacco, and Cloud clans and the Bear clansmen (Pine maternal family) in charge of the Bear mask. They assemble in the maternal house of the Town Chief, who brings his corn-ear "mother," and all make prayer offerings for the sun so that it "will go slowly back to his house." The offerings are deposited in various shrines, and the chiefs are fed by the women of their households.

We have noted above the greater concern of the Katcina cult with curing at Hano. The surviving society groups are likewise primarily concerned with curing rather than with the production of rain and crops. None of the major Hopi societies is represented among the Tewa, though individual Tewa may belong to various of the Hopi societies.[82] Formerly a Bear curing society similar to those of the Rio Grande existed at Hano. Parsons thinks the Hano Bear mask is similar to the old Fire-curing society at Jemez and was brought by the Fire-curing society of the Tewa immigrants to First Mesa. Here it was transformed to a society of the Hopi type, so far as organization and "ownership" is concerned. And "Bear Clan Old Man," who was the first to emerge from the mythical lake and who made the "road" to Hano, has become the head of the Katcina and a "rain-maker" rather than a "doctor."[83]

The Sumaikoli is primarily a curing society which also is now organized along Hopi lines. The masks are at present in the keeping of the Cloud clan, a member of which is chief of the society, and both men and women are initiated into it. The society cures "sore eyes," and the patient either feeds the dancers or joins the society. Formerly there was a special sixteen-day ceremony held periodically in August for initiation, as well as an annual ceremony. Prayer sticks are made in the leader's house, and young men and girls dance in the kiva. Then the members come out escorting the *sumaikoli*, "blind" Katcinas, to dance in the plaza. The *sumaikoli* also appear as Walpi Katcina, but the ceremony probably was brought by the Tewa immigrants and, if the term is Keresan, originally borrowed from the latter. There is some connection between the Hano Sumaikoli society and the Hopi Yaya, the nature of which is not clear.[84]

The Yu'yuki ceremony has lapsed for some time but formerly was maintained by recruitment through sickness. A daytime dance was held near the end of February, and the members whipped one another so that the ground would freeze and the men would be brave and hardy.

The Koyala or Tewa "clown" organization also once had a regular society which belonged to the Cottonwood clan and obtained members through curing and trespass.[85] Formerly, there was a ritual in which Koyala came out and "fought" with the Katcinas in order to make them angry and send rains. The Koyala also participated in other ceremonies, particularly the Kahbena, or War ceremony. The organization is now extinct, Koyala being appointed, with a Cottonwood clansman as leader, to appear with the Katcina at either Hano or other First Mesa villages. Like the Hopi *tcïka*, they must be fed by their father's sisters when they come out.

The ceremonial activities at Hano are in the hands of a religious hierarchy headed by the village chief. The village chieftaincy at present is in the Bear clan; during Stephen's time a Tobacco clansman apparently acted as regent for Satele, who was "child" of the Tobacco clan.[86] The priority of the Bear clan is a basic Hopi pattern, and one almost certainly adopted by the Tewa after coming to First Mesa. The village chief shares with the Sand clan chief the leadership of the Winter Solstice ceremony and is considered to be in general charge of the Katcinas. His family is the "first family" of Hano, and he may be called "father" by the people, and his wife "mother."[87] In return for his ritual activity on their behalf, the people may harvest the chief's fields in October and otherwise look out for him.

The Sand clan chief shares the leadership of the Winter Solstice ceremony. In some of the myths the Sand clan plays an important role, and we have noted Parsons' suggestion that the Town Chief and the Sand clan chief represent the "Summer" and "Winter" chiefs of the eastern Tewa, an identification which has linguistic verification in the case of the Town Chief.[88] The Sand clan also "controls" *tewa* kiva.

The position of "sun-watcher," modeled after the Hopi institution, was formerly in the hands of the Sun clan, but with its extinction the Cloud clan took over the task. We have noted earlier that the Cloud clan also took over the keeping of the *sumaikoli* masks and is further concerned with the Summer Solstice ceremony.

The Corn clan chief is in charge of *mona* (chief) kiva and controls the War ceremony.

The Pine clansman in charge of the Bear mask is also an important religious official—the mask should be carried in the lead of any migration—but his precise duties, beyond assisting the Town Chief, are not clear.

The War Chief belongs in the Cottonwood clan and is responsible for guarding the village against enemies, witchcraft, and internal quarrels. That his powers are a pale reflection of those of the War Chiefs of the eastern villages is seen in the account Parsons gives of the punishment of children on First Mesa.[89]

It would be important to know much more than we do about the Hano world view. The place of the Emergence is thought to be in the east and is considered to be a lake. The Katcina, who are associated with the clouds, are thought to live in a spring to the northeast of First Mesa, and pilgrimages are made periodically to this shrine. The Tewa have adopted the concept of clan ancestor, *sena*, "old man," being used for the ancestral mask of the clan corresponding to the Hopi *wuya*. And ceremonies such as the Solstice ceremonies are devoted in part to the control of the sun, that ubiquitous pueblo deity. But there is no evidence that the Tewa have taken over the more esoteric Hopi deities or conceptions of the universe; their relative lack of interest in or participation in the Hopi ceremonies, except in terms of Katcina dances held in connection with them, suggests that they have not. Undoubtedly there will be found considerable esoteric ritual reflecting modified ancestral Tewa patterns, but that is a task for the future.

Conclusions

Not only the kinship system at Hano but the clan-phratry organization and, to a lesser extent, the ceremonial structure is remarkably like that of the Hopi, a situation to be expected in terms of the long residence of the Tewa on First Mesa. We have discussed the kinship system of Hano in its relationship to Hopi and eastern Tewa. The Hano clan system presents a similar adaptation to Hopi patterns while retaining a few Tewa names which are distinctive.

Parsons finds a good deal of confusion in the Tewa clan system:

> Possibly all this confusion in clanship is the outcome of clash between the patrilineal moiety system of the immigrant Tewa and the matrilineal clanship of their hosts, as interesting an instance of acculturation, I think, as one may find anywhere in Pueblo circles. . . . As soon as inter-marriages began between the immigrant Tewa and the Hopi, changes in the Tewa system were bound to occur. The Hopi fathers could present no moieties for their Tewa children to be born into. And so in Tewa families of mixed marriage the moiety would lapse and the clan, whether newly introduced or merely reinforced, would become the paramount unit of classification.[90]

We have discussed above her suggestion that clanship was weakly developed or absent among the immigrant Tewa. If the Tewa brought clans with them, they have been almost completely replaced by Hopi-derived clans; if they had only a patrilineal dual division, they have developed their whole clan system. In either case the process would be facilitated by the western Pueblo habit of attributing clanship to any Pueblo group. As a refugee group under the protection of the Hopi, the Tewa would be interested in accommodating their organization to that of their host's.

In the process of "borrowing" the Hopi patterns of clanship —through intermarriage and close association—the system came to approximate the Hopi clans both in organization and in names. Furthermore, the clan became, for the Tewa, not only a device for regulating marriage but a "corporation" holding ceremonies, houses, and land in trust for future generations. For the alternation of the Summer and Winter People in caring for the world and the controlled competition of the dual divisions in games and dances was substituted the co-operative activity of several clans under the direction of a hierarchy of chiefs or priests, though the two kivas continued to furnish competition for games, dances, and even ceremonies.

The Hano pattern of linked clans or phratries has not developed as far as the Hopi pattern but has developed in a comparable direction. The Hano present some evidence as to the hypothesis that the phratry organization represents in part a "safety factor" against clan extinction. The Bear clan is the most important clan at Hano and was reduced to a single lineage, with six females, in 1899; the addition of the Pine clan, with three lineages, would give added support. The Tewa had the example of the Walpi Bear clan, reduced to a single individual, and their own Sun clan, whose extinction was imminent; the Pine clan was associated with the Bear mask, which furnished the requisite tie-up. It is interesting that the *general pattern* of linkage was followed by the Tewa without taking over the specific Hopi groupings—in fact, sometimes violating them, as in the case of the equation of Cloud and Katcina as "Katcina clans." The function of phratries as integrative devices was less important in a group as small as the Tewa; the larger tie-ups with Hopi and Navaho could be accomplished by equating Hano clans in the Hopi phratral groupings, an equation which they carried out on the Hopi pattern of extending kinship and hospitality.

It is evident that the Tewa peoples came as a unit to First Mesa, but in accordance with Hopi theories as to village formation by clan migration the Tewa have developed somewhat conflicting traditions as to which "clans" were earliest. Fewkes discusses this problem and notes that the "oldest" part of Hano is inhabited by Tobacco, Corn, and Bear clans and that the Katcina and "related" Pine clans, as well as the Cloud and "related" Sand clans, are said by some to have come later. In general, if we translate "oldest" as "most important," we reach a conclusion which mirrors the contemporary situation. Fewkes himself notes that the first Tewa chief is reported by some to have been Sand clan (a view probably influenced by the control of one of the Winter Solstice chieftaincies); he rejects this view in favor of the (Hopi-derived) theory that the Tewa Bear clan "was the leading one in early times, and that its chief was also *kimoñwi* or governor of the first settlement at the foot of the mesa."[91]

The problem of the Asa or Mustard clan is a puzzling one. We have noted, in the discussion of the Hopi clan system, its marginal position on First Mesa and its probable affiliations elsewhere. All legends indicate that the Mustard clan came from the Rio Grande from the vicinity of Abiquiu and were presumably of Tewa ancestry; they are said to have come at the same time as the Hano but via Zuni. They were given a building site in Walpi, and, after a sojourn among the Navaho during a famine period, they returned to Walpi as "watchers" for the village.

The Mustard clanspeople speak Hopi rather than Tewa but consider themselves to have originally been Tewa and share a peculiar mode of hairdress with Hano. The Hano, in turn, have a legend to the effect that the Mustard clan developed from the Hano Katcina clan through a Katcina clanswoman plucking a mustard plant for her child. Both groups have a proprietary interest in Chakwaina, the woman warrior who led them against the Utes and Navaho.

It is probable that the Mustard clan represents either an early split in the Tewa migrant group or a related migration. The specific "clan" character of the group must have been acquired later, probably at Zuni; the Mustard clan does not occur among the Tewa "clan names" or, except at Santo Domingo, among the eastern Keresans. Their almost complete acculturation and absorption into the Hopi social structure make them an important group for further investigation.

The variations between the groupings of clans mentioned by Fewkes and Mindeleff and the later groupings recorded by Freire-Marreco and Parsons, along with Stephen's failure to mention linked clans at all, suggests that the development of linked clans is relatively recent. The early history of Hano was not conducive to acculturation if traditions are to be believed. According to Mindeleff, "The Walpi for a long time frowned down all attempts on the part of the Hano to fraternize; they prohibited intermarriages, and in general tabued the Hano. Something of this spirit was maintained until quite recent years."[92] And the Martinez expedition of 1716 found certain of the Hopi chiefs willing to betray the Tano to the Spaniards.[93]

It is probable, therefore, that the two groups lived side by side but relatively unmixed for some time. The success of the Tewa against the Utes and Navaho would lead to greater acceptance, however, especially as the Spanish pressures were never completely withdrawn until the American period. I would guess that it was not until the nineteenth century that intermarriage began on any considerable scale, and with it the intensive acculturation which brought about such profound changes in the kinship system, household organization, and clan system. The linkage of clans into phratry groups was apparently beginning to develop only at the end of this period and is not yet complete.

One of the important factors in this process of acculturation was undoubtedly the land situation. The lands allocated to Hano were given grudgingly and were not the best lands available, though, being in a block, they contained considerable variety. The Hopi pattern of land tenure was to maintain village boundaries and, within village lands, to allocate by clan and by households within each clan. Only if the Tewa adopted the Hopi pattern of clan lands would intermarriage be practical, since otherwise the boundaries between Walpi and Hano would soon break down. Control of land by household, and the adoption of the Hopi patterns (or expansion of Tewa patterns) of men working lands for their wives' households, must have been a fundamental factor in the organization of the household on the lineage principle.

Similarly the separation of ceremonies, jealously guarded by Tewa and Hopi alike, could be most simply achieved by tying them to particular lineages. The household, therefore, came to be associated, in its economic functions, with a portion of the clan lands and, in its ritual functions, with a ceremony and associated ceremonial apparatus. There was thus some reason for the borrowing of Hopi patterns beyond the effects of mere contact, though the direction of the reorganization was influenced by the model. It is important to emphasize that it was Tewa institutions which were reorganized, and not Hopi institutions which were borrowed as units and renamed.

The ceremonial organization has been the least affected of the major subsystems of social structure. Parsons, after a survey of Hano religion, comes to the following conclusions:

> In the ceremonial organization of Hano there is still much that is obscure but tentatively I conclude that the Hopi system of chiefly succession by inheritance within the maternal family, has been taken over, although in the conduct of ceremonies most of the chiefs participate and society members are recruited in the familiar Eastern way, through sickness or trespass.[94]

But it is rather difficult, in reading her *Pueblo Indian Journal*, to separate Tewa from Hopi activities, so thoroughly are the two interrelated from day to day. This is particularly true of the outward form of ritual activities; how far the meaning and significance are similar has not yet been determined.

The pueblo of Hano, then, offers us an instructive example of what effects close association for over two centuries can have on social organization. It seems clear that *patterns* of organization have been borrowed, rather than kinship *terms*, or clan *names*, or *particular* ceremonies—in this case. There are only a limited number of organizational forms, and the Hopi solutions have stood the test of time; in the necessity for adapting to new conditions, the Tewa would tend to borrow those solutions which were efficient. If they had settled on isolated mesas, it is possible that their patrilineal bias might have prevailed, though perhaps with matrilocal extended households; in any case they would very likely have made use of the lineage principle of organization in maintaining their socioceremonial structure.

In two major aspects the Tewa of Hano seem to differ from their Hopi neighbors: in their attitudes toward war and in their greater emphasis upon curing rather than concentration upon rain. As southern Tewa, they fought against the Spaniards and helped to drive them out; they came to the Hopi country and defeated the Utes. This is reflected in myth and ritual and in the bolder and more enterprising character of the Hano Tewa as compared with the Hopi.[95] The greater emphasis upon curing in comparison to rain is, I believe, a basic difference between the eastern Rio Grande Pueblos and the western Pueblos. Where the water supply is relatively assured, through irrigation or otherwise, rainfall becomes a relatively minor item in community welfare, and sickness, particularly in epidemic form, becomes a major factor. The Tewa of Hano have partially retained this major interest in curing rituals and have transmitted (with Navaho support) some of their concepts to First Mesa. The Hopi, in general, have considerable interest in curing but do not consider their major rituals as devoted primarily to that purpose, nor, except on First Mesa, do they utilize Katcina dances as curing devices. But, more than they perhaps realize, the Hano Tewa have absorbed the Hopi feeling for rain, and their rituals are strongly warped in that direction.

In one other feature the Hano Tewa contrast with their Hopi neighbors. They are more "acculturated" to American life, more "progressive," more interested in American schools. In 1899 there were more Tewa children in school in Keams Canyon than from all the other Hopi pueblos put together. It may be that certain habits of adaptation have carried over from their Hopi experience; on the other hand, the resulting sociocultural admixture may not be as satisfying to them as is the better-integrated Hopi sociocultural system.[96]

Tewa social integration is unusual in that it has been maintained despite almost complete loss of biological integrity. Hano is contiguous with Sichomovi, the suburb of Walpi, at present, but the dividing line in terms of households is clear, though the ceremonial line is somewhat blurred.

Hano has developed the same basic type of integration which we have found among the Hopi. The kinship system, household organization, and clan system are organized on the same pattern, and kinship extensions via linked clans and ceremonial parenthood are utilized, though not to the same extent. The society organization is tied to certain households and clans, through control of the leadership and paraphernalia, but membership cuts across clan lines despite a somewhat different and less efficient procedure for recruitment.

Tewa solidarity is based on maintenance of language, village structure, and village lands. While much of their ceremonial life is patterned after, and partially integrated with, that of Walpi, the Tewa have their own ceremonies which are guarded from Hopi eyes, their own dances, and their own ceremonial calendar. They compete against Walpi and Sichomovi in kiva races, games, and dances, as well as co-operate with them on various ceremonial occasions.

The ceremonial organization is distributed among the various clans in such a way that each clan "owns" or controls at least one ceremony or ceremonial position. The important position of the Bear clan and the Bear clan chief offers a central focus for Tewa life and results in the pre-eminence of the Bear clan. But the other chieftaincies are distributed among the clans in such a way that they are each important in turn. Thus the Bear clan chief shares the Winter Solstice duties with the Sand clan; at the Summer Solstice he is assisted by Corn, Tobacco, Cloud, and Pine; and at the Seasonal Transfer ceremony he is assisted by Corn and Tobacco. During the War ceremony, on the other hand, Bear and Pine assist the Corn clan chief. The Katcina and curing ceremonies are in the hands of still other clans, though nominally under the control of the village chief.

The Tewa hierarchy is less elaborate than the Hopi (the important "Crier chief," who notifies the deities as to the coming ceremonies, is not represented, for example, nor are the chiefs of the major Hopi ceremonies) and is not so carefully graded in importance, apparently, so that the socioceremonial system is less rigid than that of the Hopi. The War Chief, however, appears to exercise more authority than his present-day Hopi counterpart.

At the "political" level the Tewa chiefs operate independently of the Hopi and are primarily concerned with the welfare of their own village. They consider themselves the "protectors" of the Hopi, and annually at the Winter Solstice ceremony the Town Chief tells the men how they were begged to come to First Mesa by the Walpi chiefs and that they should remember this story whenever the Walpi say anything against them. The Hopi accept this tradition, and the Snake clan, at least, invites the Tewa to listen to important discussions. In ritual matters there is evidence that the Tewa defer to the Walpi chiefs, as might be expected. In recent years, at least, there has been some intermarriage of the chiefly families, the Tewa village chief marrying the sister of the Walpi chief, etc. And Kotka, the last surviving member of the Walpi Bear clan, is reported to have joined the Tewa Bear clan. These events symbolize the growing acceptance of the Tewa by the Hopi as "equals."

The Tewa as a group are at present tied firmly into the larger Hopi social structure. Intermarriage has established kinship bonds which interrelate practically every individual on First Mesa. Through the clan-phratry system, kinship is extended to the wider group of Hopi, Navaho, and other tribes. We have noted the extent to which the ceremonial systems are interlocked. The failure of Hano to develop a tribal initiation ceremony and associated societies, or to take over the major Hopi calendric ceremonies, represents a major gap in their socioceremonial structure; the activities during the solstice periods and in connection with the Katcina cult and war ritual partly take their place but do not have the same integrative significance.

Hano, then, represents one of the few documented and relatively controlled examples of acculturation in the Pueblo field. The above discussion illustrates some of the possibilities and suggestions which have emerged from the very small amount of field research so far carried out on this very interesting group. Earlier neglected in favor of the ceremonially richer and more colorful Hopi, the importance of Hano in the study of social and cultural change was first realized by Freire-Marreco and Parsons, but its potentialities have not yet been fully exploited. The reported differences in temperament and character between Hano and Hopi suggest a further important problem in the field of personality and culture which can here be studied under relatively controlled conditions.

Chapter IV

THE SOCIAL ORGANIZATION OF ZUNI

Introduction

ZUNI occupies a central location with regard to the western Pueblos and is by many considered to be the most typical —certainly it is the best known.[1] The earlier affiliations and cultural development of the Zuni Indians wait upon more precise comparative studies in linguistics and on the publication of archeological excavations. When discovered by Coronado in 1540, they occupied some six villages, but various events, particularly those concerned with the Pueblo Rebellion of 1680, led to their consolidation into a single village on the Zuni River. Today this village is still the social and ceremonial center for the tribe. We will be interested in why the Zuni have been able to maintain a greater degree of village integration in the face of stronger acculturative factors than have the Hopi.

One important factor in permitting a larger village organization in Zuni has been the water supply. The general geographical environment is much the same as that of the Hopi, with the exception of the Zuni River, which is a small but permanent stream. There are indications that rainfall is more dependable and considerably greater and the springs more numerous as well. The economic adjustment to the environment differed little from that of the Hopi, with the important exception that the Zuni early borrowed wheat from Spanish settlers, the cultivation of which involved hand irrigation in favored localities. The social and economic effects of a system of irrigation have been intensified in recent times by the erection (in 1909) of a dam by the government. Sheepherding is also on a larger scale than among the Hopi.[2]

The population of Zuni in 1941 was 2,252, making it by far the largest of the modern Pueblos. In 1910 the population was only 1,664; in 1915–16 Kroeber estimated it at around 1,700; and in 1928 it is estimated at around 1,900. For some time the men have outnumbered the women, the ratio in 1941 being 1,245 to 1,007. In recent years many of the Zuni have taken to residing in farming villages closer to their fields, but these have little independent existence. "Despite modern expansion the main village still remains a unit whose physical compactness is reflected in an intricate and closely knit social organization."[3]

Zuni is at present divided into some thirteen matrilineal, totemically named, and exogamous clans, each of which is composed of one or more unnamed lineages. Clans were formerly grouped on a ceremonial basis into phratries associated with the six directions, and there is some mythological sanction for a dual division. Certain of the larger clans are composed of named subclans, which have some resemblances to the Hopi system.

The economic unit is the household, which normally is composed of an extended family based upon matrilocal residence. The central core of the household is a maternal lineage, "a woman or group of women and their descendants through females,"[4] to which are added husbands and miscellaneous male relatives.

There is further an elaborate series of ritual organizations, the Katcina cult with its six kiva groups, the priesthoods, and the Medicine societies, which cut across clan and household groupings. This complicated structure is held together, in large part, by the bonds of kinship, so that an analysis of the kinship system may serve as a convenient basis for studying the structure, functions, and interrelations of Zuni social organization.

The Kinship System

The outstanding study of Zuni kinship is that of Kroeber.[5] Kroeber's general point of view with regard to kinship has been outlined in the Introduction to this volume; he recognized the importance of kinship in Zuni life, but in the process of re-evaluating nineteenth-century conceptions of clanship he leaned over backward in his attempts to discriminate between kin and clan. "The clans give color, variety and interest to the life of the tribe. They serve an artistic need of the community. But they are only an ornamental excrescence upon Zuni society, whose warp is the family and whose woof is the house."[6]

To the analysis of Zuni kinship, Kroeber applied the genealogical method and a set of "psychological" principles. Relying on a single genealogy and not realizing the complexities of native application, his terms are incomplete and show many ambiguities and inconsistencies. The psychological principles employed in analysis—descent and generation, affinity, sex, age, and reciprocity—did not fit the Zuni system, leading Kroeber to the conclusion: "The fact is, the Zuni cares remarkably little for system or theory. He has the broad, vague outlines of his kinship system well in mind; but he is not the least interested in following out basic principles into consistent detail."[7]

Later students of Zuni social organization—Parsons, Benedict, Bunzel, and others—have complained a bit at Kroeber's sharp distinction between blood kin and clan kin[8] and have added data here and there, but they have apparently accepted his conclusions with regard to the lack of system. From the available data, I believe it is possible to show that the kinship terminology does represent a *system* which functions in Zuni culture and that the "inconsistencies" which Kroeber finds but does not explain, either psychologically or linguistically, become intelligible, in many cases, in terms of the kinship structure and the social organization. The analysis of the kinship system which follows was developed in part before field work was carried out among the Hopi; hence the Zuni system is not being interpreted in terms of Hopi field data, although the latter throws certain points of the Zuni system into clearer relief. Since the writer has not had an opportunity to test this analysis at Zuni, it is presented as a preliminary statement and working hypothesis for further research in the field.

TERMINOLOGY

Figures 11–12 summarize the basic applications of Zuni kinship terms as given by Kroeber[9] and Parsons.[10] It may be noted that there are basic resemblances to the Hopi—and some important differences as well. The Zuni classify the father with the

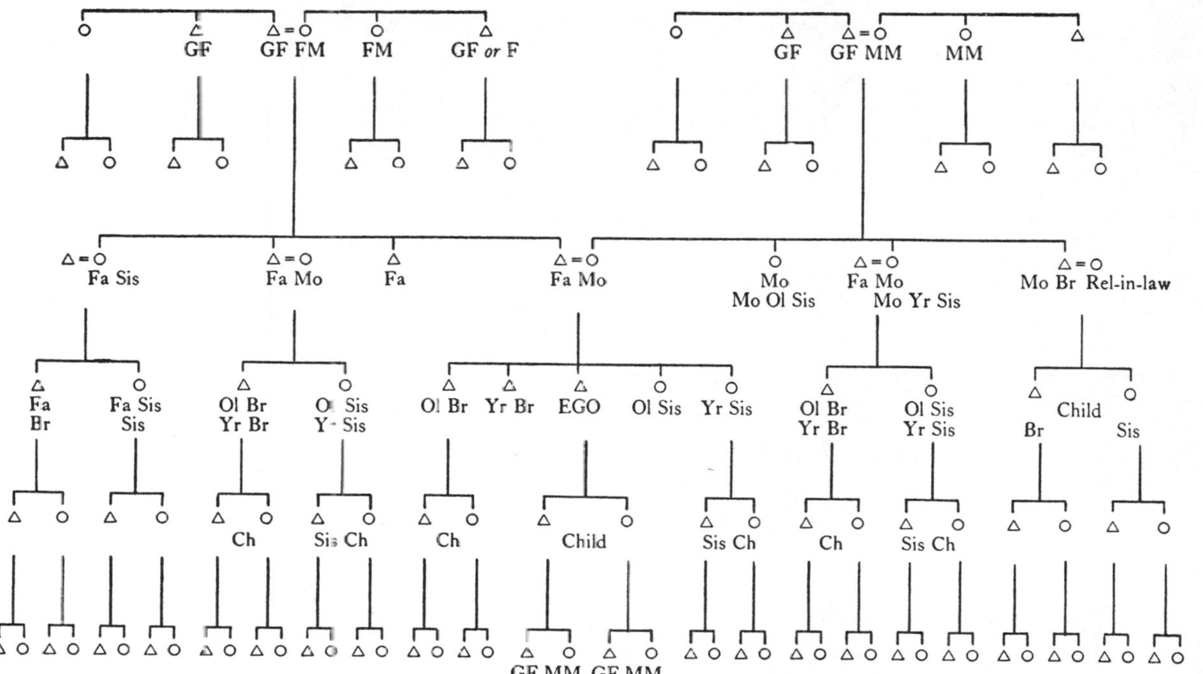

FIG. 11.—Zuni kinship terminology. Ego = male. GF = grandfather; FM = father's mother; MM = mother's mother; etc. For use of alternate terms see text.

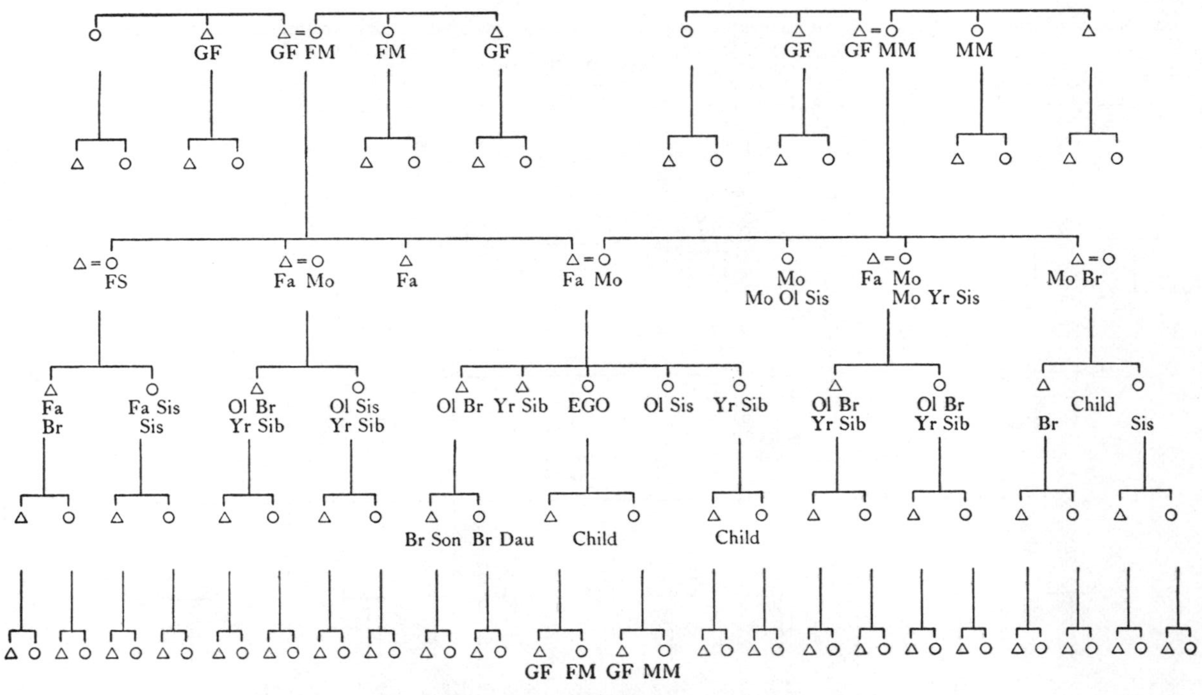

FIG. 12.—Zuni kinship terminology. Ego = female

father's brother and the mother with the mother's sister; Kroeber notes the presence of alternative terms for mother's older and younger sisters. Children are called by a collective term for "child," or distinguished as "boy" and "girl." There is one term for grandfather, but separate terms are used for father's mother and mother's mother; these terms are used reciprocally for grandchildren. Sibling terms are in accordance with the Hopi pattern and are extended to parallel cousins. There are separate terms for the father's sister and the mother's brother; their spouses are differently treated, the mother's brother's wife being considered a relative-in-law and the father's sister's husband possibly a "grandfather."[11] The pattern for father's sister's children is not clear from Kroeber; he gives "father" and "father's sister" but also indicates that sibling terms may be employed. Correlatively, the mother's brother's children are either "children" or "siblings." In systems of the general Crow type, these terms are crucial, and an additional genealogy or two would be desirable. Parsons and others indicate that "father" and "father's sister" are the normal terms for the children of the father's sister; the writer has reason to suspect that Kroeber's informant had lived for a period in his father's sister's household and thus tended to use sibling terms for his cross-cousins.[12] The important term for mother's mother's brother is not recorded by either Kroeber or Parsons; Kroeber suggests that it might be "grandfather" or "mother's brother."

Kroeber, in his analysis of Zuni terminology,[13] noted that every term denoting a lineal relative is also used for collateral relatives. Further, every term known to them is likewise applied to persons of distinct generations; this application is interpreted in terms of an age factor, where such seems relevant, though relative age as such enters only into the sibling terms. With regard to relatives by marriage, there is a complete lack, except for two generic terms, of all proper designations. Kroeber concludes that "the Zuni, a matrilinear and clan people, approximate much more nearly to the English scheme, as regards reciprocity and consistency in the use of categories, than for instance the majority of the California Indians, who resemble us in being non-exogamous and reckoning descent bilaterally or paternally."[14]

If we look at the Zuni terminology in terms of the "lineage principle," however, we find that the "vague outlines" become considerably sharper and that the basic principles of classification are "sociological" rather than "psychological." Figures 13–16 will assist in summarizing the essential features of the Zuni kinship system. It will be noted that, far from approximating the English scheme, there is a marked structural resemblance to the Crow type in general and the Hopi system in particular.

In ego's own (mother's) lineage we find a Zuni's closest relatives; here also is the greatest differentiation of kindred. Older kin are differentiated by generation and sex, though it is probable that the mother's mother's brother is classed with the mother's brother rather than with the grandfather.[15] For younger lineage relatives, however, a man uses different terms than does a woman, reflecting perhaps their different roles with regard to the lineage. A man uses the term "sister's child" for younger relatives; a woman uses "child" and "grandchild" terms, the latter differentiated according to sex and being verbally reciprocal. In one's own generation a woman classifies her younger brother and sister together, whereas a man uses two separate terms. For men marrying into the lineage (and household) at ego's generation and below there is a single term: *talakyi* (here translated as "male relative-in-law"); a correlative term, *ulani* ("female relative-in-law"), is used for the wife of any man who was "born and reared in one's home but has married out."[16] A man calls children of men of his lineage "children"; a woman uses "brother's son" or "brother's daughter" except for her own son's children, who may be called by the grandparent-grandchild reciprocals.[17]

In ego's father's matrilineal lineage the pattern is not so clear, but it is probable that all the women of the father's lineage (and household) are called either "father's mother" or "father's sister," depending on their generation and age. Since any father's clanswoman is a "father's sister," it is probable that this term is extended to all women of the father's lineage. Correlatively all the men of the father's lineage are "fathers"; this pattern is

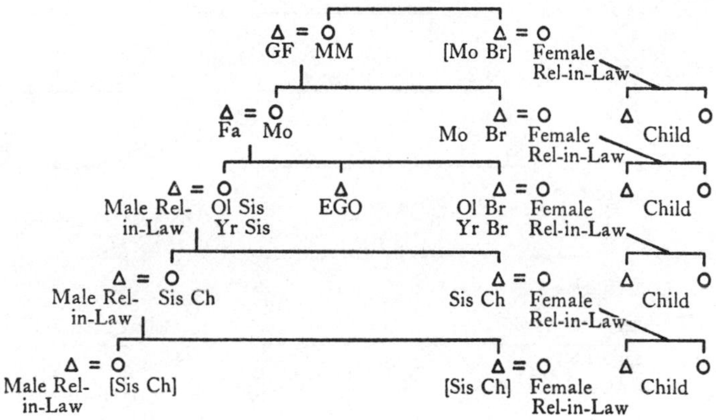

FIG. 13.—The mother's matrilineal lineage. Ego = male. Terms in brackets represent reconstructions to be tested by further field research.

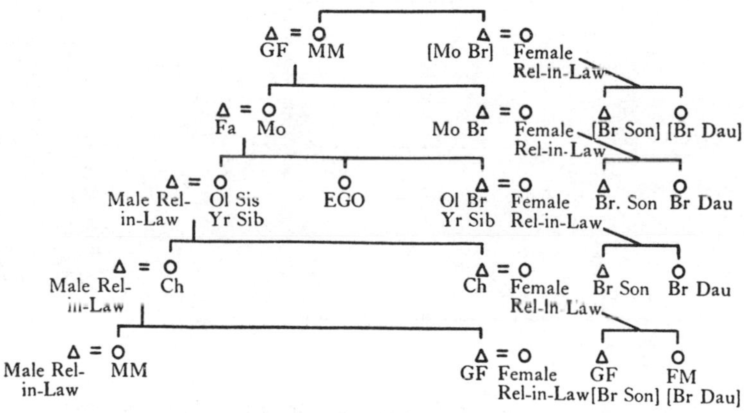

FIG. 14.—The mother's matrilineal lineage. Ego = female

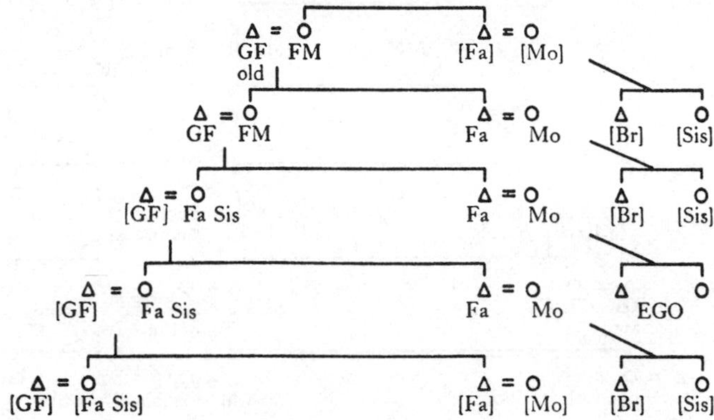

FIG. 15.—The father's matrilineal lineage. Ego = male or female

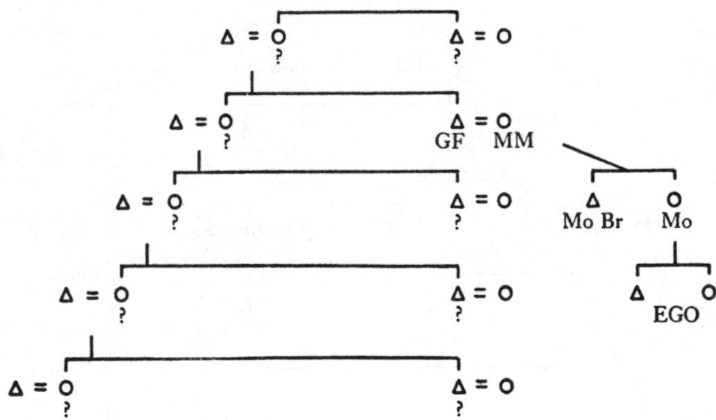

FIG. 16.—The mother's father's matrilineal lineage. Ego = male or female

probably extended to all generations, regardless of age.[18] The term (or terms) for men marrying into the father's lineage is not given by Kroeber, beyond "grandfather" for the father's mother's husband. Parsons,[19] however, gives an instance of a father's sister's husband being called "grandfather"; I suggest that this is probably the general term in such cases. The wife of any "father" is called "mother"; their children are probably "brothers" and "sisters," since they are children of the same clan.

There are no data to indicate an extension of kinship terms to the mother's father's or father's father's lineage; such lineages do not happen to be represented in Kroeber's genealogy. The extended character of grandparental terms may obscure any special relationships to these lineages, but the recognition of the mother's father's lineage among the Hopi, and also at Laguna, suggests the possibility that the Zuni may also recognize it.

EXTENSIONS

The basic kinship terms are organized in relation to the mother's and father's matrilineal lineages—and the households that develop through marriage into the lineage or lineage segment. Kinship terms are also extended, on a simplified basis, to the mother's and father's clanspeople. According to Kroeber:

> An older Zuni woman of one's clan is a mother, an older man is a kyakkya (mother's brother); to a woman of middle age, all her clan mates a generation younger are her children, to a man his kyasse (sister's children). But an exactly parallel condition holds for the father's clan: all the older men are fathers, the women kukku (father's sisters); and the men call their juniors, their clan brothers' offspring, children. What the women call their clan brothers' children, is not so clear. According to rule it should be talle (brother's son) and eyye (brother's daughter). Perhaps it is; but . . . I suspect that the women habitually accord with their brothers in calling their clan brother's progeny simply children.[20]

Kroeber points out that, while the Zuni apply kinship terms to clan relatives, "true blood relationship and clan relationship are never confused in the native mind."[21] Being concerned to demolish a now outmoded theory that "Zuni kinship terminology originated in the clans and were only secondarily applied to blood relatives," he set the clan and lineage in opposition rather than seeing the clan as an enlarged lineage. Parsons finds the boundary line between them difficult to draw—and absent entirely in the matter of marriage. She suggests that Kroeber's case against the "social functioning of the clan" would be stronger if he could show that there was no interchange of services, either econonomical or ceremonial, outside of households related by blood.[22] Kroeber says: "An individual belongs to his mother's clan but is a 'child' of the father's clan. I am Turkey-people, I am Tobacco-people their child, a Zuni will say, and will feel substantially equal relation to each."[23] The Zuni have institutionalized the concept, child of the father's clan, to a greater degree than among the Hopi. Not only is there a kinship relation with the father's clan, or between individuals whose fathers belong to the same clan, but there are almost as many occasions on which an individual is chosen for some office or duty on account of being a child of a clan as for being a clansman.[24] But, while an individual may feel closely related to both his own and his father's clan, the obligations and privileges are quite different—complementary rather than equal—as will be seen below.

The further extension of kinship to phratral and dual groupings of clans is not clear. Cushing recorded phratral groupings on a directional basis and indicated that the ritual terms for clan relatives in the associated clans are influenced by the ceremonial relations of those clans.[25] Kroeber, while conceding that the phratry—and the dual division as well—may represent symbolic groupings of clans for religious purposes, is convinced that such groupings "play no part in the social life of the people, so far as marriage, descent, and personal relations are concerned."[26] The larger clans have subdivisions which are named and which cannot intermarry, but their functions and role in daily life are not clear.

Next to blood relationship, Kroeber believes that common residence and friendship count for more than clan membership, in daily life at least. This is shown by the many nonkin relations which are expressed in terms of kinship. Normally at birth a "ceremonial father" is selected for the Katcina initiation; later other "ceremonial fathers" may be chosen for initiation into one or another of the societies. Kinship terms are applied to their households (and lineages?) but not extended to the clan as a whole. Exogamy is likewise extended to their households and to the relatives of kiva mates, as well as to all women of the same society.[27]

Marriage results in an additional set of relatives, for a man should marry outside his own and his father's clan, as well as observing other restrictions. For his wife's relatives a man uses the same terms that she employs for her household mates, and she, in turn, uses the terms that he uses; these terms are not extended to the whole clan.

Two individuals may enter into the relationship of "ceremonial friendship," *kihe*, in which their parents exchange presents and wash the children's heads. The two become "siblings" and call each other's parents, and other relatives, by kinship terms. While the relationship is primarily between the two households, neither of the *kihe* can marry into the clan of the other.[28] The various kiva groups are considered related as "elder brother" and "younger brother"; likewise certain personators from these kivas are addressed by kinship terms.

Within the village hierarchy the *ashiwanni*, or "Rain Priests," are called "fathers," and the governor and his wife are called "father" and "mother." The whole ceremonial life is pervaded by the conception of kinship; in every ceremony is found the ritual exchange of kinship terms, and deities are grouped in terms of kinship. The dead are referred to as "fathers" and "mothers," and rain clouds may be thought of as "grandmothers."[29]

There is a further extension of kinship to the world of nature. Cushing records five things that are necessary to the Zuni: the sun "father," the earth "mother," the water who is "grandfather," the fire who is "grandmother," and the corn "brothers" and "sisters."[30] In the mythology many of the animals, birds, and objects of nature have kinship terms applied to them. The Zuni equate certain of their clans with those of the Hopi and other tribes; whether kinship terms and attitudes are extended is not clear.

These various extensions result, frequently, in the Zuni standing in more than one relationship to various individuals. This may be the reason for certain of the "inconsistencies" and variations in the applications of terms in Kroeber's schedules.[31] As to the approximate order of closeness of various groups, I would hazard a guess, based on Kroeber's statements, as follows: (1) own lineage, (2) father's lineage, (3) housemates, (4) father's household, (5) own clan, (6) father's clan, (7) "ceremonial father's" households, (8) "phratry" (?). It may be noted that this order varies somewhat from Titiev's order for the Hopi, in that the father's lineage and household are put ahead of one's own clan. Marriage is theoretically forbidden with all but the last group.

THE HOUSEHOLD

In all recent discussions of Zuni social organization it is the household that is emphasized as the important unit, not the clan. What is the relationship between household, lineage, and clan? A child is born into a household and there receives his primary orientation. The core of the household is, as we have noted, a matrilineal lineage—or a segment thereof. All persons born in the household normally belong to the lineage; men at marriage move out into other households but return freely to their natal household. In turn, men from other households marry into the lineage and household, to which they have specific obligations as long as they remain married.

The household normally occupies a series of adjoining rooms. It is an economic unit owning land and the products thereof and is co-operatively organized. The line of women who own the house look to their husbands to till their fields, though they can call on their brothers for help in emergencies. But in ritual matters the husbands are outsiders; the sacred fetishes and other ritual activities associated with the house are in the care of the women and their brothers. On ritual occasions the men return to their natal household to carry out the important duties of Zuni life. The women thus normally reside throughout their life in the household in which they are born, "the slow stream of mothers and daughters forming a current that carries with it husbands, sons, and grandsons."[32] Their brothers are in a more peripheral position with divided loyalties and different residences.

Whether there is a Zuni term for one's natal household is not clear. For the household into which a man marries there is a name: *talawa*, and he calls the inmates *talakwe;* for the father's natal household there is a derivative term, *takkyikwe*. It is in these three households that a Zuni man has his major social relations; a woman is more closely centered in the household of her birth. The theoretical correlation of the household with the lineage or lineage segment can be seen in the lineage diagrams. The actual correlation is not clear; Kroeber made an analysis of the size of Zuni families and arrived at an average of over seven and a half persons per household. A census of two clans, the Coyote and Tobacco clans, gave the following results:[33]

	Coyote Clan	Tobacco Clan
No. of clanspeople	56	42
No. of houses	10	6
No. of inhabitants	58	46
No. of lineages (native view)	8	3
No. of lineages (Kroeber's est.)	4	2

Kroeber concludes, from these data, that the Zuni do not ordinarily carry relationship back very far, even within the clan, and that clan and kin are distinct things, one lightly superimposed upon the other. In this connection, Li An-che, in 1935, noted approximately the same average. He states that "characteristics of a joint household based on the kinship principle stand out very strikingly" and that unusually large households of over twenty members are not conspicuous in the minds of the Zuni.[34]

In terms of Kroeber's table it would seem that the Zuni tend to equate a lineage with a household, except in cases of recent expansion or budding off. Kinship terminology and exogamy are extended to all the households of a clan, and exogamy is certainly a social function of primary importance. But the Zuni appear not to utilize to any great extent symbolic devices such as *the* clanhouse, or "totemic" affiliations such as are involved in the Hopi clan system, to integrate the lineages and households within the clan. Kroeber did find "clanhouses" for most of the clans but without any special position or privileges.[35] Certain ceremonies are associated with particular households, however, and these are the "important families." The *ettowe* (fetishes) used in connection with these ceremonies are never removed from the house in which they are kept, and the priest is always taken from that household.[36] Kroeber notes that a number of the clan-named houses also contain the clan fetishes, though a number apparently do not. It is on the crucial point of the relations of the various households containing lineages of the same clan to the ceremonies and fetishes associated with particular households that we need more precise information. Kroeber discusses the evidence as supporting the interpretation of the clan as part of the ritualistic scheme rather than a body of kindred,[37] but the writer is not sure that this is a valid distinction.

KINSHIP BEHAVIOR

We might now turn to a brief discussion of the social relations and social usages involved in the Zuni kinship structure. For convenience, the nature of the behavior patterns between relatives will be outlined in connection with the life-cycle, since the bulk of the available source material is in terms of the round of life. Kroeber has stated that "each individual's personal status with relation to oneself is clear and fixed, and it matters very little what any and all of them are called."[38] On the contrary, I would like to suggest that there may be a fairly close correlation between the personal status of the individual, the social behavior involved, and the terminology employed, despite the greater looseness of the Zuni system.

"The individual in Zuni is fitted into an intricate and closely knit social organization."[39] The elementary family, so important elsewhere, is merged into the household group, and the specific roles of relatives are affected by their position in the social structure. A Zuni is born into a certain household, which determines his clan affiliation and kinship status and, in part, his future ceremonial roles. At birth the mother's mother supervises the delivery and looks after the mother; after the birth the father's mother comes with offerings, bathes the child, prays for its protection, and rubs its body with ashes. She then fixes a bed of hot sand for the infant beside its mother.

The father's mother continues to look after the mother and child for an eight-day confinement period, during which there are restrictions on the behavior of both father and mother. On the morning of the eighth day the father's mother takes the child into the presence of the rising sun, then bathes it and fastens it to a cradle. She then bathes both the parents' heads, and the female ("blood") relatives on both sides assemble in the child's household, the "father's sisters" bringing gifts. The mother's mother provides a feast, after which the father's sister carries the child to her household, where the father's mother prays to the sun "father" for blessing. This ceremony probably establishes the infant as a "child" of the father's lineage and clan and institutes the special relationship between an individual and his "father's sisters" which carries through life.

Girls seem to be more desired than boys. There are shrines where expectant mothers, or barren women, may go to make offerings. Twins are thought to be related to deer, because the latter always have two young; there is also an association between rabbits and children, and increase rites are held during the rabbit hunt.[40]

Naming practices vary somewhat from the Hopi pattern. Children are named later, after they give evidence of being likely to live. The father's mother normally gives the name; she may give her own name or that of some long-lived relative. Apparently there is no stock of clan names for bestowal.[41] A name is also given by the Catholic priest at baptism when this rite is observed. On initiation into the tribal Katcina society, a boy receives a kiva name from his "ceremonial father" which becomes his standing name, unless superseded by a society name given at a later initiation. The reluctance to use personal names is marked at Zuni, in contrast to Hopi; there is at Zuni a correlative elaboration of teknonymy.[42]

There is little information on the duties of parents and other relatives in relation to the training of the child. The parents should be respected and obeyed, but their precise authority is not clear. The mother's brother should also be respected but appears not to have the authority and punishing power he has among the Hopi, though Parsons gives an instance where one removed his sister's son from office. The general lack of overt authority within the household is compensated in part by the employment of bogey Katcinas and the instilling of a fear of owls and witches.[43] As children grow up, there is a general separation of the sexes. Mothers and mother's mothers are concerned with the training of a girl and keep her from running around; older girls look after their younger brothers and sisters. Boys begin to help their fathers in the fields or assist in the herding activities carried on co-operatively by groups of male relatives. The grandparents on both sides take an active interest in their grandchildren's education, telling them stories and inculcating the lore of the tribe—in fact, it is probable that grandparents play a more significant role in Zuni, in part due to the rapid shifting of spouses, than in other Pueblos.

"The ceremonial father" for the Katcina initiation is chosen by the boy's own father from the household of the father's sisters. In case a prospective mother has had bad luck with her children she may invite a successful child-rearer to blow into the newborn infant's mouth; this woman's husband then becomes the boy's "ceremonial father" at the Katcina initiation.[44] The preliminary initiation into the tribal Katcina cult formerly took place between five and six years of age. At this time the father's sister tells her clanswomen to grind corn for the "ceremonial father," to pay for the gifts he makes the child. The "ceremonial father" carries the child, who has been washed by his wife, to his kiva, where he acts as sponsor. This initiation does not teach the child any esoteric mysteries but establishes a bond with supernatural forces. The child is whipped by masked gods as a rite of exorcism. At the second and final initiation, between ten and twelve, the "ceremonial father" holds the boy while he is again whipped by the masked gods; on this occasion the secret of the masks is revealed, and the novices, in turn, whip the Katcinas. Afterward, the ceremonial father's sisters wash the initiate in yucca suds before returning him to his own home. Kinship terms are employed for the "ceremonial father," his wife, and his female relatives.[45]

A girl is not ordinarily initiated into the Katcina organization, in contrast to Hopi procedure. At puberty her mother notifies the father's mother or father's sister of the girl, and the latter takes the girl to her house, where she grinds corn all day, kneeling on heated sand and observing certain restrictions.

In case of initiation into a society the "ceremonial father" is usually the doctor who cured the individual. The patient is "given" to the society and to the doctor's household. His father's sisters and their clanswomen grind a large amount of corn for the "ceremonial father" and the society group. Both men and women belong, and it is possible to be a member of several societies.

Marriage is forbidden within one's own clan and condemned within the father's clan; we have noted above the further extensions of exogamy to ceremonial friends and their households and to kiva mates' relatives and society members. Marriage is likewise monogamous, with no institution of the sororate and levirate. Marriage "Zuni fashion" today is synonymous with any physical cohabitation without public sanction.[46] But in Cushing's and Stevenson's time, the arrangment of marriage was more complicated. Courtship was an individual matter, but the boy, once his advances were accepted, would go to the house and ask the girl's father for her hand. A series of exchanges of food and clothing then took place between the households. The husband resided in his wife's household but was without many privileges until the birth of a child; the wife made periodic visits to her husband's household with gifts of food, which were returned.[47] In Benedict's time the procedure was far more informal and the exchanges greatly reduced.[48]

Divorce is equally simple and easy. If the couple are not happy together, or if there are no children, or if the wife's mothers and sisters do not approve, the wife need merely place her husband's personal belongings on the doorstep. Usually she takes the precaution to start securing another husband, but, with the unequal sex ratio and Zuni attitudes, this is not difficult. The husband returns to his mother's house, where he and the family may weep, but there is rarely any remonstrance. "Husbands and wives abide by the rules, and these rules hardly provide for violent emotions, either of jealousy or of revenge, or of an attachment that refuses to accept dismissal."[49] Despite the ease of divorce, a large proportion of Zuni marriages endure, which Benedict notes as the more striking, because marriage cuts across the strongest social bond in Zuni—the matrilineal family.

With the departure of the husband his obligations cease, and his successor looks after his children. With the development of the herding complex, economic ties between male relatives have been strengthened. A group of male relatives herd their sheep together; they are individually owned and inherited in the male line but herded on a co-operative basis. The men of the household co-operate in agricultural labor and in housebuilding; the new house erected on the occasion of entertaining a Shalako dancer is built primarily by the kiva group of the sponsor.

Within the household, while relations are informal and "individual authority and responsibility are almost entirely lacking," the group of women hold the important position. They control the house and its furnishings, the household fields, and the produce of these fields. In any conflict with outsiders they present a united front. In this line of women the mother's mother has the greatest amount of authority. She can call on her brothers and sons for economic aid in emergencies; in turn, she is obligated to assist her brothers and her brothers' children. Sisters should co-operate with one another and obey their mother. They readily look after one another's children; in case of divorce a mother and children are supported by the household until remarriage. The ceremonial obligations of a woman to her brother's children, especially males, are important and numerous; on almost every ceremonial occasion the father's sister is involved. According to Bunzel, "there is some indication of a joking relationship between a man and a woman of his father's clan, especially his father's blood sister, who is also his most important ceremonial relative."[50]

For the Zuni the two most important groups of relatives are in one's own and one's father's households. Toward the other households of the clan the feeling of relationship and the obligations and duties are much weaker. The Zuni seem to have strengthened the ties between households united by marriage in a variety of ways: institutionalizing the concept of "child" of the clan, selecting the "ceremonial father" from the father's household, etc. They have also extended kinship ties to other households through the institution of "ceremonial friendship" and through ceremonial associations.

Illness and death are believed to be caused by witchcraft. According to Cushing, the dead were formerly cremated and their ashes thrown into the river. But now they are buried in the churchyard, with their heads to the east. The father's mother or father's sisters bathe the deceased and dress the body. The clan of the deceased and the spouse's clan are notified, as are the society mates, and relatives come to mourn. The brother or father's brothers of the deceased dig the grave and bury the body. The father's mother will carry a deceased infant to the cemetery, though one dying at birth may be buried under the floor of the house. If a wife has died, the father's sister of the husband comes to the house before the burial and takes him to his people, washing his head. He does not return to his wife's household: "Death takes two, not one," say the Zuni.[51]

Mourning continues for four days, during which time the soul of the deceased is thought to remain around the village and is a potential danger to the survivors. The Katcina mask of the deceased is buried near his grave, and offerings are made by the family. The ordinary dead go to the Katcina village in the west where they become the "rain-makers" and the bestowers of blessings.[52]

CONCLUSIONS

It is now possible to re-evaluate Kroeber's statement that "kinship is thoroughly and equally bilateral."[53]

> So far as Zuni reckoning goes . . . the sentiments of kinship and affection are the same toward father and mother, toward the brothers and sisters of each, and toward the partners and children of son and daughter. A cousin on either the father's or mother's side is identically an older or younger brother, toward whom the same degree of oneness is felt.[54]

On the contrary, I believe the evidence shows that kinship is organized on a lineage basis and that even in the "bilateral" recognition of the mother's and father's lineages there is not equality but a complementary relationship. The ritual activities are primarily in the hands of the father's household; "during the crises of individual life as well as upon public occasions it is the father's people or clan which is charged with performing the requisite rites."[55] The economic activities, on the other hand, are primarily in the hands of the mother's household and lineage, aided perhaps by her clanspeople.

Kroeber has not recognized the lineage as an important concept in relation to the household, though he states that in daily life it is "common residence and known blood" that count. The extent to which they count can best be summarized by quoting Ruth Benedict's description of the matrilineal family.

> The matrilineal family . . . is ceremonially united in its ownership and care of the sacred fetishes. To the women of the household, the grandmother and her sisters, her daughters and their daughters, belong the house and the corn that is stored in it. No matter what may happen to marriages, the women of the household remain with the house for life. They present a solid front. They care for and feed the sacred objects that belong to them. They keep their secrets together. Their husbands are outsiders, and it is their brothers, married now into the houses of other clans, who are united with the household in all affairs of moment. It is they, not the women, who learn the word-perfect ritual of their sacred bundle and perpetuate it. A man goes always, for all important occasions, to his mother's house, which, when she dies, becomes his sister's house, and if his marriage breaks up, he returns to the same stronghold.
>
> This blood-relationship group, rooted in the ownership of the house, united in the care of sacred objects, is the important group in Zuni. It has permanence and important common concerns. But it is not the economically functioning group. Each married son, each married brother, spends his labour upon the corn which will fill his wife's

storeroom. Only when his mother's or sister's house lacks male labour does he care for the cornfield of his blood-relationship group. The economic group is the household that lives together, the old grandmother and her husband, her daughters and their husbands. These husbands count in the economic group, though in the ceremonial group they are outsiders.

For women there is no conflict. They have no allegiance of any kind to their husbands' groups. But for all men there is double allegiance. They are husbands in one group and brothers in another. Certainly in the more important families, in those which care for permanent fetishes, a man's allegiance as brother has more social weight than his allegiance as husband. In all families a man's position derives, not, as with us, from his position as breadwinner, but from his role in relation to the sacred objects of the household. The husband, with no such relationship to the ceremonial possessions of his wife's house to trade upon, only gradually attains to position in the household as his children grow to maturity. It is as their father, not as provider or as their mother's husband, that he finally attains some authority in the household where he may have lived for twenty years.[56]

This clear and comprehensive statement indicates that the household had the same theoretical structure and internal organization among both the Zuni and the Hopi. The key to this structure is found, I believe, in the kinship system. Both the terminological structure and the behavior patterns are consonant, with minor variations. There seems to be in Zuni a rather clear correlation between the kinship structure, the household organization, and the social behavior of relatives, so far as the latter has been described. From this point of view, Kroeber's and Parsons' statements about the lack of system in regard to Zuni kinship indicate judgment from some arbitrary standard.

The concept of the lineage provides a bridge between the household and the clan. The clan is composed of several lineages, normally, and there is probably some division of function between them. Bunzel states:

The clan as such has no social or political functions, although each individual feels his closest ties to be with members of his clan, upon whom he calls for assistance in any large enterprise, such as harvest, housebuilding, initiations, etc.[57]

This statement seems self-contradictory, particularly when exogamy is added to the functions of the clan.

Yet there is certainly a difference in degree between Zuni and Hopi on this point. In formal terms the situation is somewhat similar: The clan is composed of matrilineal lineages organized in households, with ceremonies and ritual paraphernalia associated with particular households which are the "important families." But whereas among the Hopi the clan tie is a strong bond, among the Zuni it seems definitely weaker. Part of the answer may lie in the relative sizes of the clans—and of the village. There is also a related difference of emphasis with regard to integration. It will be useful, therefore, to turn to a more detailed examination of the clan system and the ceremonial organization.

The Clan System

Kroeber has brought together the available information on Zuni clans and analyzed it in masterly fashion.[58] There is evidence that the clan system is diminishing in importance and that it has changed in various ways. Cushing in the 1880's recorded some sixteen surviving clans grouped into phratries based on the directions, but he indicated that the phratral combinations were already modified or outgrown in his day (see Table 5).[59] According

TABLE 5

Zuni Phratral Groupings

North	Crane, Grouse, Yellowwood, or Evergreen Oak
West	Bear, Coyote, Red-Top Plant, or Spring-Herb
South	Tobacco, Corn, Badger
East	Deer, *Antelope, Turkey
Above	Sun, *Sky, Eagle
Below	Frog, *Water, Rattlesnake
Middle	Parrot-Macaw

* Extinct.

to Cushing, this organization of clans into phratries was part of a socioceremonial organization of the whole village which was not always reproduced in fact but was found in the thinking of the Zuni. The clans themselves bear the names of, and "are supposed to have intimate relationship with, various animals, plants, and objects or elements."[60] The directional groupings correspond to the Zuni conception of world organization, and each group is characterized by "peculiar fitness" for the region indicated; each is further associated with colors and with the seasons. In theory there is also a close association with town divisions, kivas, and the ceremonial organization, particularly with the medicine societies. Reference to a dual division into "Winter People" and "Summer People" is found in a myth recorded by Cushing; in a comparable myth recorded by Stevenson the division refers only to the Pikchikwe clan subdivisions, Parrot and Macaw.

Stevenson recorded the same clans as Cushing, with the exception of the Rattlesnake clan, which she classes as a society. She also noted that one man survived in the Antelope clan. Kroeber recorded the same series of clans, but his informants denied that a Rattlesnake clan or society ever existed among the Zuni. Bunzel reports only thirteen clans surviving in 1927, with the Yellowwood on the verge of extinction.[61]

At the time of his investigation Kroeber could get no information on the phratries or clan groupings:

> As with the moiety, I am convinced that phratries play no part in the social life of the people, so far as marriage, descent, and personal relations are concerned; but that in certain aspects of religion, symbolic groupings of clans are made along the lines indicated by Cushing, though these may possibly be so wholly mental as scarcely to affect even ritual.[62]

Kroeber, on the other hand, found that many of the larger Zuni clans had subdivisions recognized by the older people which were named but not functionally important in daily life (Table 6).[63] He considers that these subclans help to establish connections with the clan systems of other Pueblo groups; he also gives information which bears on the process of clan division. Except for the Raven and Macaw divisions, neither Cushing nor Stevenson discusses these groupings, and yet they are known only to the older people. Subclans of the same group may not intermarry; while generally a fourfold or twofold division is recognized, the number of actually existing subgroups is variable. It is probable that the size of the clan is an important factor. Thus the largest clan, the Pikchikwe, has apparently long been divided into two subdivisions, for which there is mythological sanction. The Corn clan was also large in Cushing's time, and there are mythological references to various of the Corn subclans; in modern times it has been reduced in population. Kroeber's information on the Badger clan indicated a migration of some of the group to Walpi

TABLE 6

ZUNI CLANS AND THEIR SUBDIVISIONS

1. PIKCHIKWE—"DOGWOOD"
   a) Pikchikwe*
   b) Macaw*
   c) Kokkokwe—Raven or Crow or God*
   d) Raven or Crow
2. EAGLE
   a) Black Eagle
   b) White Eagle
3. BADGER
   a) Badger proper*
   b) Hopi Badger*
   c) Bent over Straw
   d) Plant: Sunflower?
4. Corn
   a) Yellow Corn*
   b) Black Corn*
   c) "Sweet" Corn
   d) Corn-Ear–Water people
5. CRANE
   a) Crane
   b) Striped Pumpkin
6. DEER
   a) Deer*
   b) Antelope
7. BEAR
   a) White Bear?
   b) Black Bear?
8. TURKEY
   a) White Turkey?
   b) Black Turkey?

* Existing groups.

during a famine; on their return they were differentiated from their clanspeople. Deer and Antelope were differentiated as separate clans by some informants and coupled as subclans by others. They could not intermarry in either case.

The directional phratry grouping shows little in the way of specific resemblances to the Hopi system. There is a theoretical association of Grouse and Oak on First Mesa, if Grouse and Roadrunner are equated. Badger and Tobacco are secondarily associated at Mishongnovi but in no other village. Antelope and Deer are grouped conceptually at First Mesa, though only Deer is represented. Sun and Eagle are grouped together on all mesas, as are Frog and Water, but with different associates than at Zuni. Parrot-Macaw has parallels in all the Hopi villages.

The subclan groupings at Zuni show more precise parallels. The Macaw-Raven-God divisions of the Pikchikwe clan are clearly related to the Hopi Katcina-Crow-Parrot phratry. The distinction between Badger and Hopi Badger is paralleled at Oraibi in the distinction between (Real) Badger, Gray Badger, and Navaho Badger. The groupings of various kinds of Corn and Corn-Ear–Water is closely paralleled by the Patki-Pikyas-Corn-Water phratry of the Hopi. The grouping of Crane with the Striped Pumpkin is also common to both Zuni and the major Hopi villages.

One important factor in the decline of the phratry system as a functioning entity may well have been the extinction or near-extinction of many of the constituent clans. Cushing lists three clans as extinct and three as nearly extinct. By 1915 four of the seven phratry groups were reduced virtually to a single clan. This process went on through the accidents of male and female survival, since the population remained stationary. Population size may well be an important factor in the process of clan subdivision. The average size of the Zuni clan in Cushing's and Kroeber's time was a little over 100 persons; in Bunzel's time it had increased to about 150 persons per clan. The largest and most important clan, the Pikchikwe, had over 400 persons in 1915. The size of Hopi clans was considerably smaller. Oraibi, the largest Hopi town, before 1906 had some thirty clans for 863 people, an average of slightly less than 30 persons per clan; the nine phratry groups averaged just under 100 persons, with a range from 24 to 186 members.[64] These figures suggest that the Hopi phratry approximates the Zuni clan in size—as well as in being the kinship and exogamous units. Whether the Zuni subclan approximates the Hopi clan in size is not clear, since no clan census was made, but there probably is a rough equivalence in size. A comparative study of Pueblo clans by size, as well as by structure and function, may indicate an optimum size. Certainly the Pikchikwe, with 25 per cent of the total population, is well beyond the average for Pueblo life.

Each Zuni clan has a "fetish," which is kept in one of the households of the clan. In some cases Kroeber found that the fetish was kept in the "clan named houses"; in other cases apparently not. But he found no evidence that there was a clan head or a clan council or instances where the clan acted as a body. With regard to clan localization within the town, Kroeber's census of households shows no tendency for localization by clan but a marked tendency for each clan to be proportionately most heavily represented in the quarter to which it is assigned in Cushing's "phratral grouping."[65] This directional representation is also true of the "clan named houses"; in fact, the Coyote clan-house is in the "proper" direction, whereas Kroeber notes that "Coyote is the only clan for which the actual distribution and the phratral grouping definitely clash."[66] Furthermore, the modern movements of houses outside the town "almost invariably involve mainly a radial extension from the center of town,"[67] revealing a rather deep-rooted tendency "toward orientation of the house with reference to the town."[68]

Kroeber interprets the "phratral grouping" given by Cushing as merely the reflection of the existing distribution of clan groups in the town.[69] Being concerned with refuting the conception that the various clans had once been separate units with a life of their own, rather than the equivalent and co-ordinated dependent units that they are in fact, he gives too little attention to the possible significance of the directional grouping in Zuni life. Both Cushing and Bunzel affirm that, for the Zuni, all aspects of nature, including man, belong to one great system of related life. It is evident that the Zuni have tended to organize much of the world on the basis of the six directions; not only were the clans so organized in Zuni thinking but also kivas, societies, priesthoods, corn, prey animals, seasons, and colors. Before returning to this directional classification, it will be useful to survey the ceremonial organization of Zuni.

Ceremonial Organization

All observers have emphasized the central role of religion in Zuni life. "All of Zuni life is oriented about religious observance, and ritual has become the formal expression of Zuni civilization."[70] The foundation of Zuni ceremonialism is the cult of the ancestors. Everybody participates in their worship, and they are involved in every ceremony. They guide, protect, and nourish human life; as among the Hopi they are identified with clouds and rain. While priests and medicine men pray to special groups of ancestors, the ordinary Zuni prays to ancestors in general.

On this foundation a large number of esoteric cults have developed, "each devoted to the worship of special supernaturals or groups of supernaturals, and each having a priesthood, a body of secret ritual, permanent possessions of fetishistic power, special places of worship, and a calendric cycle of ceremonies."[71] Bunzel distinguishes six major types of cults: (1) the cult of the sun, (2) the cult of the Uwanami, (3) the cult of the Katcinas, (4) the cult of the priests of the Katcinas, (5) the cult of the War Gods, and (6) the cult of the Beast Gods. "The functions, activities, and personnel of these groups overlap and interweave in a bewildering intricacy that baffles analysis."[72]

The sun is the source of life, and daily offerings are made by the people at sunrise. The ceremonies which honor the sun take place at the solstices and are in charge of the *pekwin*, or Sun Priest, "the most revered and the most holy man in Zuni." At the solstice ceremonies all the priests participate; the *pekwin* is the keeper of the calendar and the active member of the priestly hierarchy. "He is ultimately held responsible for the welfare of the community." The *pekwin* must belong to the Pikchikwe clan, the largest Zuni clan, but the subdivision is immaterial.[73]

The cult of the Uwanami, or "rain-makers," is comprised of twelve priesthoods which are concerned with the worship of the supernaturals who inhabit the waters of the earth. Each priesthood comprises from two to six members, membership usually being hereditary in the matrilineal family residing in the house in which the fetish of the group is kept. These fetishes are the most sacred objects in Zuni and are supposed to have resided in the same household since the beginning. "In these e'to'we rest the power of the priests."[74] The priesthoods hold no public ceremonies but observe a succession of "retreats" in the households where the fetishes are kept. The most important series extends from July to September; the four chief priesthoods "go in" for eight days each, then the *pekwin* and Bow Priest, followed by the minor priesthoods for four days each. The rituals performed are secret and are primarily concerned with securing rain for the growing corn, each group being judged by the amount of rain which falls during their "retreat." The Rain Priests are considered very holy and should have no concern with worldly affairs; in particular they should not engage in quarrels.

While Bunzel indicates that membership in the main is hereditary within a matrilineal lineage, Mrs. Stevenson stated that members "must be of the clan or a child of the clan of the shiwanni (chief priest) of the division."[75] Analysis of her data makes it clear that, when a son of the chief priest inherits this position, the care of the fetishes remains in the lineage, and the clan does not permanently shift. In 1896 each priesthood was normally composed of the chief priest and four associates, the last one of which was usually a female. The distribution within clans is interesting (Table 7).[76] From this table it may be noted that the

TABLE 7

ZUNI PRIESTHOODS

Shiwanni of the North—Dogwood	Eighth Shiwanni—Dogwood
Shiwanni of the West—Dogwood	Ninth Shiwanni—Corn
Shiwanni of the South—Badger	Tenth Shiwanni (Shu'-maak-we Fraternity)
Shiwanni of the East—Eagle	Eleventh Shiwanni—Sun
Shiwanni of the Zenith (Pekwin)—Dogwood	Twelfth Shiwanni—Corn
Shiwanni of the Nadir—Eagle	Thirteenth Shiwanni—Corn
Seventh Shiwanni—Eagle	Fourteenth Shiwanni—Corn

priesthoods are concentrated in the five largest clans. Dogwood and Corn are reported as about equal in size by Cushing;[77] each has four priesthoods, though those associated with the former are the more important by far, since they include the first two groups and the *pekwin*. Three are in the Eagle clan, and one each in Badger and Sun. Two, now extinct, belonged in Coyote and Frog, respectively. The rest of the clans have no representation in the priesthoods, except temporarily through a "child" of one of the above clans.

As far as the Rain priesthoods are concerned it is clear that they are definitely associated with particular lineages which are attached to the households in which the fetishes are kept. The chief priest should be of that lineage—or a child of a member; the woman in charge of the fetishes transmits her duties to a sister or daughter. On occasions of "retreat" the members who assemble to carry out the rituals are normally all members of a lineage group. Members of the households associated with the fetishes make up the "important families" in the clan and in the town. Yet in Zuni there seems to be little that binds the particular lineages within a clan together; each seems oriented around its fetish, if it possesses one.

The cult of the Katcinas is a tribal cult, including every adult male, but normally not the women.[78] The Katcinas, in Zuni belief, represent children who were lost long ago and were transformed into beautiful and happy beings. The dead go to join them, but the identification of the dead with the Katcinas is not complete; only those intimately associated with the cult can be sure of joining them after death. The Katcina society is under the direction of a Katcina chief, his assistant, and two Bow Priests; they receive the Katcina dancers on behalf of the village and are the arbiters in matters concerning the masked dances. The society is organized into six divisions, associated with the directions; each division is associated with a special ceremonial house equivalent to the Hopi kiva. These kiva groups have their own sets of officers who decide upon the dates for dances and perform the necessary rituals. Membership in a kiva group is determined by the choice of a "ceremonial father" at birth, or later; hence there is no affiliation of kiva membership with clan membership. An individual may change his membership for violation of sexual taboos or on account of disagreement with the leaders of the kiva group.

Each kiva group is required to dance at least three times annually: in summer, in winter, and following the departure of the Shalako gods in the fall. Races are also run by kiva groups, though they may also be run by clan. The winter dance series begins after the solstice celebration and is held in the kivas. The summer series begins after the summer solstice and is primarily for the purpose of bringing rain. During this period the Katcinas are believed to be present in the village until they are sent home in November. The masks used in the dances are owned individually and represent the gods; they are highly sacred and are buried at death. "The possession of a mask is a blessing to the house; it guarantees the owner admission to the dance house of the gods, and is the means by which the spirit can return after death to delight his beloved ones on earth and assuage his own loneliness."[79] The masks are carefully guarded in a back room of the house and fed daily by a female member of the household; they are said to be "second in sacredness to the fetishes of the rain priests themselves."[80] Through them almost every household has a tangible tie with the gods.

The director of the Katcina society and his Bow Priest should belong to the Deer clan, the deputy director and his assistant should be Badger. On the occasion of the first summer solstice dances Deer and Badger women bring food, water, and yucca suds to the kiva to which the director belongs and to the house of the deputy, respectively.[81]

Bunzel treats the cult of the Katcina Priests separately from the Katcina society. While the activities of the two are intimately connected, the primary concern of the Katcina Priests is with fecundity rather than rain. The Katcina Priests are the priestly hierarchy that rules the Katchina village; the masks representing them are tribal property though kept in specific households and handed down from one generation to another. Each god has a distinct personality and name; for each god, or group of gods, there is a cult group composed of past impersonators. The impersonator is usually chosen by the priests of the cult group, generally in terms of clan and kiva affiliations. Pautiwa, the chief of the masked gods, should be impersonated by different clansmen on the different occasions he appears, according to Mrs. Stevenson;[82] by a member of the Dogwood clan, according to Kroeber's informants.[83] The mask is kept in a Dogwood household, as are the masks of several others. The *koyemci*, or sacred clowns, in Zuni the fruit of an incestuous union between brother and sister, are impersonated in turn by one of four groups of men. According to Mrs. Stevenson, the personators are chosen in terms of fraternity membership and according to their father's clan in a complicated manner.[84] The masks of the *koyemci* are kept in the house of the west priesthood, according to Bunzel; in Mrs. Stevenson's account they are in charge of a man of the Eagle clan.[85] The six *shalako* masks are associated with the six kivas but are kept in six different houses and looked after by a group of "servants"; the *sälimopia* masks are similarly treated.

At the New Year ceremony which ends the winter solstice, Pautiwa "gives his orders for the coming year." The arrangements and appointments for the Shalako ceremony are made at this time; the public ceremony is held in November in houses specially built by prominent citizens who volunteer for this service. The rituals are designed to fill the storerooms with food and the houses with children.

The masked gods appear at the solstice ceremonies and the Shalako and every four years at the Katcina initiation. The ritualistic myth recited at this time is in the keeping of four men, two Dogwood and two children of Dogwood. Further, many of the officers and activities in connection with the various ceremonies are in the hands of particular clansmen or of the children of clansmen.[86]

The cult of the War Gods is in the hands of the Bow priesthood. The War Gods, twin children of the sun, led the Zuni to victory and taught them the proper rituals. Membership in the Bow priesthood was through killing an enemy; the only escape from vengeance from the malevolent magic with which the enemy was supposedly endowed was through joining. Initiation was in connection with the Scalp Dance, at which the scalp-taker's paternal clanspeople played important roles. The Bow priesthood is in charge of the elder and younger Bow Priests, who represent the twin War Gods, assisted by the priests in charge of various fetishes, including the scalps. The Bow Priests are appointed by the *kiakwemosi*, the chief priest of the north, and may be deposed. The Bow Priests are leaders in war and the protectors of the village; they are the executive arm of the religious hierarchy and take measures against witches. The only association with clans is in connection with the annual ceremony at the winter solstice. The idols representing the elder and younger War God are carved by men of the Deer and Bear clans, respectively. Formerly there was a great public dance after the harvest.[87]

The cult of the Beast Gods is in the hands of twelve curing societies or fraternities, membership in which is open to both men and women. The cult centers around the prey animals who live in the east, control long life, and are the givers of medicine and magical power. The leaders of these prey animals are associated with the directions, and each is "elder brother" to the following one. The most powerful is Bear, who is impersonated in the curing ceremonies.

Each society practices general medicine but also specializes in certain diseases or afflictions. If an individual is seriously ill, he may be "given" to one of the Medicine societies and must later join in order to make the cure permanent. Trespass is another way of joining. While both men and women are members, the offices are mainly in the hands of men, and only the latter conduct advanced curing. According to Bunzel, all medical practice, except midwifery, is in the hands of these societies, and they have perhaps the most highly developed ritual of any of the cult groups.

The collective ceremonies of the societies are held in the fall and winter, the cult being inactive during the summer months. At the winter solstice the societies meet in their ceremonial houses, make prayer sticks for the ancients, the deceased members, and for a culture hero, and hold a ceremony for rain and fertility. Following this ceremony the societies go into "retreat" in their houses, during which the Beast Gods are invoked and impersonated, and curing powers are publicly demonstrated. Individual societies hold ceremonies irregularly on occasions of curing or initiation, other societies frequently being invited to attend. A patient who has been cured by the society is initiated into it, the doctor who did the curing becoming the society "ceremonial father." The "ceremonial father" acts as sponsor and prepares the personal fetish of the novice. The latter dances with two women of the "ceremonial father's" clan; they then wash his head and give him a new name. There are elaborate exchanges of food between the novice's family and the women of the "ceremonial father's" family. The expenses of an initiation are heavy, involving a feast for the society as well as gifts to the "ceremonial father" and his relatives.[88]

The societies have various legends to account for their origin; these follow a different pattern from the accounts of clan origins and point perhaps to the eastern Keresans as the source for the medicine societies. Certain of the societies require the head or director to belong to a specific clan; these are the four societies which were first organized. The directors of the Shiwannakwe and Saniakiakwe societies must be Turkey clansmen, those of the Newekwe and Hlewekwe are of the Crane clan, and the deputy of the latter must be Corn clan. The director of the Shumaakwe society must be Chaparral Cock, his deputy a child of that clan. Other offices or activities are filled, in part, in terms of specific clans.[89] In the above societies the society fetish is in the keeping of a household of the clan, and the ceremonies and retreats are held in the household.

The ceremonial calendar co-ordinates and interrelates the various cults and ritual activities in a complex way. Each cult has a cycle of ceremonies starting and ending with the winter solstice, where all are fitted into a twenty-day period of ceremonial celebration. In Zuni theory the ceremonial calendar of the first six months is repeated in the second half of the year, but the actual ceremonies and their relative weighting varies. The winter ceremonies are primarily concerned with medicine, war, and fertility, while the summer ceremonies are concerned with rain and crops. At the solstices there is a convergence of these various activities in honor of the sun.

The Zuni calendar is likewise a dual one, depending primarily on the position of the sun and secondarily on the moon. The year is divided into two cycles of six months each. From December to June the months are named with reference to snow and winds;

from June to December they either are named according to the order of ceremonial colors or are repeated.[90]

"Political" authority is in the hands of a council of priests[91] composed of three members of the chief priesthood and the heads of three other priesthoods. The head of this hierarchy is the "house chief," who is head of the chief priesthood (that of the north), assisted by the *pekwin* or Sun Priest, who acts as a talking chief for the priesthood. The two Bow Priests act as an executive arm; the heads of the Katcina society serve as advisers. The principal matters which come before the council relate to the appointment of secular officers, impersonations of the gods, the time of tribal initiations, changes in the ceremonial calendar, and questions of tribal policy. They have the welfare of the pueblo in their hands and are too sacred to be concerned with secular quarrels and problems. Internal crimes such as witchcraft are the concern of the Bow Priests; formerly they tortured suspects to induce confession.

The council appoints a set of secular officials: a governor, lieutenant-governor, and some eight assistants to carry out relations with outsiders and to deal with civil suits, quarrels over property, co-operative work on roads and irrigation ditches, etc. These officials hold office at the pleasure of the priests and may be removed at any time. The governor and lieutenant-governor should not be from the same clan, and their assistants are generally chosen from different clans. Whether or not this civil government is "in substance a native institution," as Kroeber believes, its activities were expanded to deal with the new problems brought about by Spanish contacts.[92]

Conclusions and Comparisons

The social organization of Zuni is perhaps the most complex to be found in the western Pueblos; the social integration here achieved is both strong and successful. The consolidation into one village, following the events of the Pueblo Rebellion of 1680–96, has been maintained down to the present. And while an adequate water supply and sufficient land were essential conditions, the key to this integration lies in the social structure. As Kroeber has noted, "it is impossible to proceed far into the complexities of the social and religious organization of Zuni without being impressed with the perception that this community is as solidly welded and cross tied as it is intricately ramified."[93] The basic binding force is the kinship system. Kroeber recognized the importance of "ties of blood and of household" but found them unorganized into any definite pattern.[94] In the section on kinship I have suggested, as a working hypothesis, that there is a definite pattern to Zuni kinship and have assembled the available evidence. Bunzel's statement summarizing the Zuni kinship system offers confirmation:

> The kinship system follows, in the main, the Crow multiple clan system, all members of one's own clan being designated by classificatory terms. There are different terms for classificatory relatives of the father's clan. Adoption is frequent, and the usual terms are applied to adopted relatives. The terms are stretched to include also all affinal relatives.[95]

The analysis of the kinship system in terms of the lineage principle clarifies the complex relationships within the household. Both the mother's and the father's lineages are important; their social and ceremonial duties are sharply differentiated. In terms of the lineage concept the clan may be seen, for *kinship* purposes, as an extension of the lineage. While Kroeber is continually opposing kin and clan, it seems clear that the basic kinship patterns are extended to the mother's and father's clans. This is true of terminology and exogamy; it is probably true of kinship behavior as well. In Stevenson's time the people of the same clan were regarded as one family and had free access to any of the households.[96] Bunzel notes that, while one's closest ties are with blood kin, especially the maternal household, each individual has close ties with the members of his clan upon whom he calls for assistance in any large enterprise.[97]

The role of the clan system in Zuni social structure is a crucial problem. While the clan is totemically named, "there is no belief in descent from or kinship or spiritual connection with the animal or object that names the clan; nor are there taboos of food or otherwise toward it, though such prohibitions are observed by the Zuni in matters distinct from clanship,"[98] according to Kroeber. One clue to the role of clans in Zuni society is contained in the mythology. In Cushing's account mankind is created from the cohabitation of the Sky Father and the Earth Mother; during the early migrations of the Zuni the gods and culture heroes named and selected the "man-groups and creature-kinds" in terms of their relations to the Earth Mother and Sky Father. The children of summer and the south, related to the Earth Mother, were divided into the Sun people, Water people (Toad, Turtle, or Frog), Seed people (First-growing Grass and Tobacco), and the Fire or Badger people. The Winter People, related to the north and the Sky Father, were chosen and named (or chose) according to their aptitudes: Bear people, Coyote people, or Deer people; Crane people, Turkey people, or Grouse people.[99] This dual division does not appear in Cushing's "Outline of Zuni Mytho-sociologic Organization," however; there the phratral groupings on a directional basis are given as a key to their sociology.[100] But even in Cushing's time this phratral organization was not in active operation; Mrs. Stevenson does not mention it, and Kroeber could find no evidence for it.

Cushing's list of the clans associated with the Summer People and the Winter People omits any reference to Pikchikwe, which he translates as Parrot-Macaw. But he does record another myth dealing with the division of the tribe into Summer and Winter People through the choice of eggs, which turned into macaws and ravens, respectively.[101] Mrs. Stevenson's account of the manner in which the clans got their names tells how the culture heroes decided that the people should be divided into clans and asked each group to choose a name. Each group chose a name from some object seen at the time. The Pikchikwe (Dogwood) clan is then divided into the Raven and Macaw subdivisions through their choice of eggs.[102]

The explanation of these discrepancies is not easy. Kroeber notes that Cushing's version is more in consonance with Zuni tradition, whereas Stevenson reflects the existing social situation more accurately.[103] It is conceivable that the Zuni once had a functioning dual division, whether exogamous or merely ceremonial. Many groups so organize that larger structure by which man and nature are brought into relationship, including the eastern Pueblos along the Rio Grande. A dual principle is apparent in the conception of sky and earth, in the opposition of life and death, in the division of the year into solstitial periods, in the priesthoods of daylight and darkness, in the culture heroes and War Gods, and perhaps in the relations of curing societies and Rain priesthoods in Zuni. But a dual organization is not an efficient device for integrating a social structure where the population is relatively large. The dual principle operates largely on the basis of opposition and rivalry and attempts to control these through organizing their expression. I would guess that Zuni may have had a dual organization of the type described in the myths in some or all of their villages prior to consolidation around 1700; further investigation in the documents of the early Spanish period may furnish evidence on this point.[104]

If there was a shift to a multiple phratry type of organization, it may well have taken place after the consolidation into modern Zuni. Such an organization would furnish a more efficient integrating mechanism for a village of this size. As Kroeber notes, clans are to be viewed as co-ordinated divisions of a communtiy with parallel and equivalent functions.[105] By grouping a number of clans into phratral units, a greater degree of stability and persmanence can be achieved. The directional basis for grouping selected by the Zuni has the advantage of being applicable to a variety of institutions: not only clans are (or were) so organized but kivas, societies, and priesthoods as well. But the directional grouping is also rather abstract and specialized, so far as the clan groupings are concerned. Relationships between the "totem" animals of a phratry is in terms of their relations to a particular direction rather than through any direct native association, as among the Hopi. Furthermore, the association between man and nature is one of parallel organization rather than of descent; animals, corn, the seasons, colors, etc., are also organized directionally. I have suggested above that the disappearance of the directional phratry system may have been in large measure the result of the process of clan extinction and the concomitant growth in size and importance of the Pikchikwe clan. By this process four of the phratry groups were reduced to virtually a single clan each. The Pikchikwe clan, not mentioned in Cushing's account of the origin and naming of the totem clans, had come to be the dominant clan in Cushing's time and represented some 25 per cent of the population in 1916. It is tempting to speculate on the possibility that Macaw and Raven, the divisional names for the Pikchikwe clan, represent the moiety "totems" described in Cushing's myth of the Summer and Winter People; this would give them ceremonial priority and perhaps account for the assignment of "Parrot-Macaw" to the middle direction, "as the all-containing or mother clan of the entire tribe."[106]

With the decline of the phratral grouping an alternative grouping seems to have developed based on the division of clans into subclans, or the equation of clans on the basis of similarities or relations between the animals or aspects of nature. In Cushing's and Stevenson's time only the Pikchikwe clan seems to have been so divided; by 1916 Kroeber found a considerable number of such groupings.[107] Since only the older informants knew much about the subclans, they must have been present before 1900; their greater importance in native consciousness is probably correlated with the increased size of certain clans and the breakdown of the directional phratry system. We have noted above the parallels with the Hopi phratry, and Hopi influence through intermarriage and other ways may be a significant factor.

The sanctions behind the complex social and ceremonial organization lie in the mythology. The mythology serves to mirror the existing (or recently existing) Zuni institutions as if they had always existed or shows them as coming into being through the activities of ancestors or culture heroes. Where institutions change, the myths are generally brought into ultimate concordance. The variant accounts of Cushing, Stevenson, and modern students make greater sense when placed in the perspective of social and cultural change; the presuppositions and problems with which they were concerned likewise have an important influence on their conclusions.

From the standpoint of social organization, the interrelations of the various ceremonial groupings can be best seen through their relations to the clan. Kroeber, who has made an exhaustive analysis of these interrelations, prefers to organize them around the fetish. He believes that

> the truest understanding of Zuni life . . . can be had by setting the ettowe [fetishes] as a center. Around them, priesthoods, fraternities, clan organization, as well as the most esoteric thinking and sacred tradition, group themselves; while in turn, kivas, dances, and acts of public worship can be construed as but the outward expression of the inner activities that radiate around the nucleus of the physical fetishes and the ideas attached to them.[108]

But all these fetishes, with few exceptions, are kept within households associated with specific clans. The lineages occupying these households are responsible for their care, and for carrying out the associated ritual, in many cases. In native theory the fetishes have been associated with the same households since the beginning of Zuni; in fact, there have been changes, as Kroeber notes.[109] In the beginning the *attowe* or fetishes were given by the gods to the leaders of the clans,[110] or became associated with the clans chosen by their possessors,[111] in the case of the Rain Priests. The clan, through the lineage principle, provides a mechanism for both stability and continuity in the group serving as trustee for the fetish; alternative mechanisms, such as "child" of the clan, are subordinate to the lineage principle of descent. Where extinction of the clan takes place, the fetish may be sealed in the house. In former times it is possible that important fetishes were transferred to surviving phratry associates—or taken over by the Pikchikwe clan as the "mother-clan" of the tribe.

The association between the clan system and the different ceremonial groupings varies in each case. The chief Rain priesthoods are associated with the directions; if there were ever an association with the directional phratries, as implied in Cushing's scheme, it has long since been lost, since three of the priesthoods are now associated with households in the Pikchikwe clan, and one each with the Badger and Eagle clans. The Katcina society is likewise organized on the basis of six kiva groups associated with the directions. While there is no relation between the kiva groups and clans, the director of the society and his deputy should belong to the Deer and Badger clans, respectively. The individual masks belonging to the Katcina gods are kept in particular households and impersonated by particular clansmen in many cases; they are frequently associated with kivas as well. The Medicine societies have both a directional and a clan association. The Beast Gods, who are the givers of medicinal and magical powers, are associated with the six directions, as follows: north—Mountain Lion; west—Bear; south—Badger; east—Wolf; above—Knife-Wing (or Eagle?); below—Gopher.[112] It will be noted that these only partly correlate with clan names; furthermore, each society is associated with all the prey animals. In Cushing's account the societies are associated conceptually with the seasons and their elements and were organized originally by the clan groups associated with particular directions;[113] Mrs. Stevenson, on the other hand, associates the first four societies with particular clans in that the original directors chose to belong to those clans.[114] One of the later societies, at least, follows the same pattern, and certain functions are carried out by clansmen. The society fetish is kept in a household of the associated clan, in these cases, and the ceremonies are likewise held there. Society membership, on the other hand, cuts across clan lines, though the controlling clan may have the largest number.

The relationships between the fetishes and the ceremonies associated with each are not too clear. Presumably the clan fetish is a symbol for the whole clan, but whether ritual activities with reference to it involve the whole clan or are carried out for its benefit by the lineage segment occupying the household in which the clan fetish is kept is not known. With regard to "clan control" of the fetishes associated with the priesthoods and the societies, it is probable that the clan is considered to be acting as a trustee for the whole community, both with reference to taking care of the fetish and in furnishing the leaders for the rituals in connection with it. Certain clans, through their possession of more than one fetish, serve as integrating agents between the social and ceremonial structures; this is particularly true where the fetishes are associated with the same household.[115]

The integrative pattern of Zuni has been analyzed by Kroeber:

> Four or five different planes of systematization cross cut each other and thus preserve for the whole society an integrity that would speedily be lost if the planes merged and thereby inclined to encourage segregation and fission. The clans, the fraternities, the priesthoods, the kivas, in a measure the gaming parties, are all dividing agencies. If they coincided, the rifts in the social structure would be deep; by countering each other they cause segmentations which produce an almost marvelous complexity, but can never break the national entity apart.[116]

This is a brilliant cross-sectional summary of Zuni social integration, but there is also an integration through time. This integration is carried out through the lineage principle, in large measure. We have noted that the lineage principle, which underlies the kinship system and furnishes the core for the clan organization, also provides a mechanism for the inheritance of ceremonial duties and obligations and the transmission and preservation of fetishes and other ceremonial paraphernalia. In Zuni this inheritance is phrased in terms of the household, but it is clear that it is the lineage segment born into the household that is important. This lineage segment, or at least the female line thereof, also owns land and holds it in trust for succeeding generations, to be worked by the men who marry into the household. In Zuni the clan is a weaker institution than among the Hopi. With regard to maintaining the socioceremonial system the clan provides an added safety factor against lineage extinction, and the phratry grouping may have operated similarly at one time, but clan control or ownership of ceremonies is not stressed. Likewise the clan does not have an economic base. In Cushing's time control of land was phrased in terms of clan, but there were already processes at work modifying this relationship.[117] Today land is controlled by households or by individuals.[118]

While the clan is weaker among the Zuni in comparison with the Hopi, tribal organization seems much stronger. One important device contributing to the relative strength of Zuni tribal integration is the grouping on the basis of the six directions. This grouping is abstract enough so that it can be used for organizing clan groups, priesthoods, kiva groups, and various aspects of nature into one conceptual system and thus contribute to total tribal unity. But the directional grouping does not provide too good a basis for organizing certain of these units; thus the phratries recorded by Cushing did not survive, although the tendencies to clan division remained. In part the directional phratry system may have been too specialized and inflexible, but a strong tribal organization frequently is incompatible with a strong clan organization. Through the directional grouping the Zuni as a whole were related to the world of nature; the individual relations between clan and "totem" groups were subordinated to this larger relationship.

With the greater emphasis on tribal as against clan organization, there is in Zuni a greater specialization in social and ceremonial control. The ultimate control of the village is in the keeping of a hierarchy of priesthoods who are responsible for community welfare. The Bow priesthood acts as an executive arm for this body in matters affecting the spiritual welfare of the group; the governor and his assistants take care of secular matters under the direction of the hierarchy. That this control is relatively efficient is evidenced by the degree of social and ceremonial integration maintained in the face of all the modern influences toward disintegration and dismemberment.

The nature of Zuni social structure and social integration can be brought out more sharply by comparing it with Hopi. In both, the kinship structures are organized on a similar pattern and utilize the same structural principles. The behavior patterns toward relatives are likewise comparable, so far as our data go, though greater variability is apparent in the Zuni system, and there is a lesser emphasis on the importance of the maternal uncles. The extension of kinship patterns among the Hopi is primarily in terms of the clan system; Zuni makes less use of the clan and more of society associations and friendship. In both groups one's most important relatives are found in the mother's and father's households; later also in one's "ceremonial father's" households and in the wife's household. Marriage is still a ritual occasion among the Hopi, with religious sanctions, but almost completely secularized and individual among the Zuni. Yet the structural relationships established seem essentially similar, and the sociopsychological problems involved in extended family life are equally unsolved.

The basic clan organization is likewise similar in Hopi and Zuni, but the Hopi have further organized their clans into phratry groupings on a totemic basis and validated the groupings through mythological sanctions. The Zuni apparently at one time also had phratry groupings on a more abstract directional basis. In both cases, however, the basic unit is the lineage, and the functions and activities of lineages in the two tribes are very similar. As Parsons remarks, "If the Zuni lineages which have distinctive ceremonial functions, the rain society lineages and a few others, were given distinctive names within the clan, one aspect of the Hopi tendency to phratry would be recognizable at Zuni."[119] I have suggested above that factors such as relative size of clan groups and greater concentration of population have been influential in the relative decline in importance and organization of the Zuni clan system, but over and above these factors have been the integrative needs of the community as a whole. As Kroeber has pointed out, "Zuni tradition is throughout concerned with the people as a whole, and, in contrast to Hopi legends, scarcely at all with the fortunes of individual clans."[120]

The similarities and differences in ceremonial organization between Hopi and Zuni have been surveyed in detail by Parsons.[121] She notes the more diversified and complex ceremonial organization at Zuni. The Katcina cult is tribal wide in both areas but is limited to males primarily at Zuni and is associated with the six kivas. Initiation is in two stages, the second corresponding in certain respects to the Tribal Initiation (Wuwutcim) of the Hopi. Both make use of a "ceremonial father," but the Zuni ordinarily select a man from the father's household and clan, whereas the Hopi normally select a nonrelative. The Katcina Priests at

Zuni represent a specialization of cult groups not found among the Hopi, as do the Shalako impersonators and the Koyemshi organization, but clan control of chieftaincy or leadership is found in both tribes.

Hopi societies are primarily concerned with rain and only secondarily with curing functions. At Zuni there are curing societies associated with the prey animals, of Keresan type, and special Rain priesthoods associated with the directions and with certain clans. The Hopi societies utilize the "ceremonial father" mechanism for the bulk of their membership, whereas the Zuni societies rely primarily on curing for recruitment. The Rain priesthoods have membership limited to four or six clanspeople associated with a particular household and go into "retreat" for the benefit of the whole community. Hopi societies are controlled by clans in that leadership and care of paraphernalia is in the hands of particular lineages and households within the clan. The Zuni curing societies have a vaguer but comparable relationship to the clan system, through tradition and through meeting in certain households. On the other hand, the relationship between the Rain priesthoods and certain clans is very close, the membership being limited to clansmen, or children of clansmen, and the fetishes being kept in certain households of the important clans. In both tribes the ceremonial calendar is controlled by the solstices, and there is a general parallelism despite numerous specific differences.

Village control is in the hands of the priests at both Zuni and Hopi. The Hopi religious hierarchy is normally associated with the priests concerned with the Soyal ceremony and with other important ceremonies; the village chief or "chief of the houses" is normally the Soyal chief and should belong to the Bear clan. The chief priest of the north at Zuni, the Kiakwemosi, or "ruler of the houses," should belong to the Dogwood clan, though a "child" of the clan may serve. This clan, the largest in Zuni, also furnishes the *pekwin* and several of the other major priesthoods. The Bow priesthood probably was paralleled by the Kaletaka organization of the Hopi, but the Zuni secular organization has no analogue among the Hopi.[122] Under the direction of the religious hierarchy the governor and his assistants settle disputes over property rights and land and look after external relations with whites and Mexicans; in recent years they are said to refuse to hear cases involving marital problems.

The general pattern of relationship between household, lineage, clan, and ceremonial organization is rather similar among the Hopi and Zuni. The Zuni emphasize the household with reference to the control of land and fetishes; the Hopi emphasize the clan ownership of land and ceremonies. But further analysis shows that the difference is one of degree. In both groups the lineage connected with the household is the important organization; the Zuni tend to emphasize the separateness of the lineage components of the clan, whereas the Hopi tend to ignore them in their thinking.[123] The relative size of Hopi and Zuni clans is an important factor in this connection.

With regard to the basic scheme of Zuni social structure which Kroeber diagrams for Zuni,[124] it would fit the Hopi without any major modifications. But there are certain emphases in social integration that differ in the two tribes. Zuni has emphasized household and village organization at the expense of a strong clan system, whereas the Hopi have reversed this emphasis. Since similar social mechanisms are involved in both cases, it is highly probable that the differences in historical development are related to these differences in integration. Modern Zuni has resulted from the consolidation of some six villages under pressure from the Spaniards and other sources.[125] The Hopi villages, on the other hand, were not subject to the same degree of outside pressure. Zuni, by developing a strong centralized organization, has been able to maintain the unity of the community under modern conditions; the Hopi have tended to split up their village at Oraibi as a result of conflict between two clans. This difference is also clearly reflected in the mythology, which usually mirrors and "explains" the existing conditions.

The type of social integration is essentially the same at Zuni and among the Hopi. In both groups kinship is the important tie. The Hopi villages give the impression of a more clear-cut organization perhaps because of their smaller size. Zuni is larger and seems more amorphous, but the strength of integration is probably greater.

Certain of the differences which exist between Zuni and Hopi are the result of a somewhat different early history; others are due to the much longer period of Spanish acculturation or to the more intensive contacts of the American period. Only when we know more about these factors can we fully evaluate the similarities and differences we have been concerned with in this chapter.

Chapter V

THE SOCIAL ORGANIZATION OF ACOMA

Introduction

ACOMA, the westernmost of the Keresan-speaking Pueblos, has occupied its mesa site since prehistoric times. Its position about midway between the Keresan villages of the Rio Grande and Zuni is reflected in its cultural position:

> Acoma occupies a position marginal both to the Rio Grande region and to Zuni, although it belongs very definitely to the Keresan pattern. Its conformity, however, is somewhat diluted because of its distance. Being close to Zuni it shows marked evidence of western influence.[1]

With regard to social structure, however, Acoma and its neighbor, Laguna, appear to have their closest affiliations with the western Pueblos.

The old village was built on the bare rock of the mesa top for purposes of defense. In recent years two summer villages, Acomita and McCartys, have been established near the main fields some twelve miles to the north; but Old Acoma is still the ceremonial center, and every family maintains a house there.

The geographical environment of Acoma is generally similar to that of Zuni and Laguna, with the exception of the water supply. Old Acoma has no constant source of water beyond small springs at the foot of the mesa, but large reservoirs on the mesa top are reported to supply the village with sufficient water. The modern economic adjustment is similar to that of Zuni. Corn and mutton are the staples; wheat, beans, alfalfa, and other crops are grown in irrigated fields. In theory all land is communally owned, but farms "belong" to particular families as long as they are cultivated. The cacique has authority to allot unused land.

The population of Acoma was estimated at 200 men in 1540. The 1910 census gives nearly 700 people, while the 1941 figures indicate a total population of 1,254, equally divided among the sexes and representing some 212 families. Acoma and Laguna represent the western dialect of Keresan and are understood with difficulty by their eastern kinsmen.

The pueblo of Acoma is an independent social, political, and ceremonial unit. The village is divided into several matrilineal and exogamous clans; there are no phratry groupings, nor are there moieties or dual divisions. The economic unit is the household—apparently of the same general type as among the Zuni and Hopi. The recent movement out to the summer farming villages, however, is bringing about changes in social organization which may be noted in many institutions. "There is a psychological disintegration taking place; the pueblo is tending to break up into family groups."[2]

The ceremonial organization centers about the Katcina cult and the Medicine societies; there are also Warrior, "Clown," and Hunting societies. But Acoma lacks the Rain priesthoods which play a central role at Zuni. White views Acoma social organization as consisting of two strata or levels: "the kinship (and clan) level and the socioceremonial level."[3] He sees kinship as the substratum upon which the ceremonial structure is reared; the two are not sharply divided but are interrelated at many points. It is this interrelationship which is responsible for the strong social integration which White notes for Acoma.[4]

The Kinship System

Despite the basic importance of kinship, there is not as yet a definitive study of the Acoma kinship system. Direct field observation of family life is not possible in Acoma, and genealogies are difficult to secure. There is enough information, however, to make it possible to reconstruct the outlines of Acoma kinship with a fair degree of assurance, particularly when the fuller data from Laguna are considered. As in the case of Zuni, the following reconstruction will serve as a working hypothesis to be tested and modified by further research.

TERMINOLOGY

Somewhat variant lists of kinship terms are given by Kroeber,[5] White,[6] and Parsons.[7] Parsons notes that Acoma kinship terms correspond rather closely in their applications to those of Laguna and Zuni.[8] The system is "classificatory" in that the father is classed with the father's brother and the mother with the mother's sister; the reciprocal terms are "son" and "daughter" (White) or "boy" and "girl" (Parsons). Siblings are differentiated by sex but not by relative age, and separate terms are used by male and female speakers; sibling terms are extended to parallel cousins and in some cases to cross-cousins. The grandparental terminology is complex; three terms are used as follows: *papa* for mother's mother and father's mother (male speaking) and mother's father and father's father (female speaking); *nana* for mother's father and father's father (male speaking); and *dyiau* for mother's mother and father's mother (female speaking). Each of these terms is used in a verbally reciprocal manner for the appropriate grandchild.

The terms for mother's brother and father's sister and their descendants show considerable variation. The term for mother's brother is used reciprocally for a man's sister's son; his sister's daughter is recorded as *naiya* (mother) by Parsons and as *nayatcani* by White. The mother's brother's children are recorded as "son" and "daughter" by White and as "brother" and "sister" by Parsons. The father's sister is recorded as *kuya* (father's sister) by Kroeber but as *naiya* (mother) by Parsons and White; the father's sister's children are "father" and "mother" (Kroeber) or "brother" and "sister" (Parsons and White).

The nature and significance of these variations can be seen in connection with Figures 17–20, which summarize the basic applications of Acoma kinship terms and indicate the general nature of the kinship structure. In ego's own matrilineal lineage a man distinguishes his female relatives as "sister," "mother," and "grandmother." The term "mother" is apparently used for alternate generations, since Parsons lists it for mother's mother's

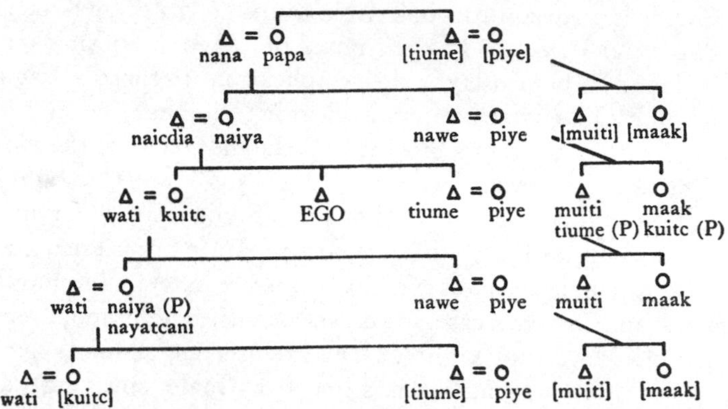

FIG. 17.—The mother's matrilineal lineage. Ego = male. The basic terms are from White; P = Parsons, K = Kroeber. Terms in brackets are reconstructions for further testing.

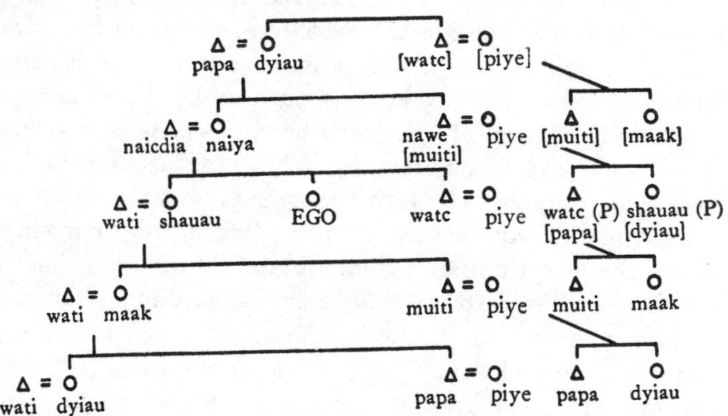

FIG. 18.—The mother's matrilineal lineage. Ego = female

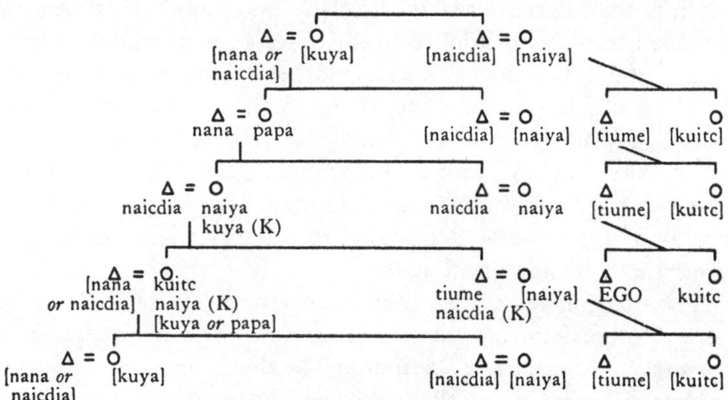

FIG. 19.—The father's matrilineal lineage. Ego = male. Presumably parallel terms are used by a female ego. Terms in brackets are reconstructions.

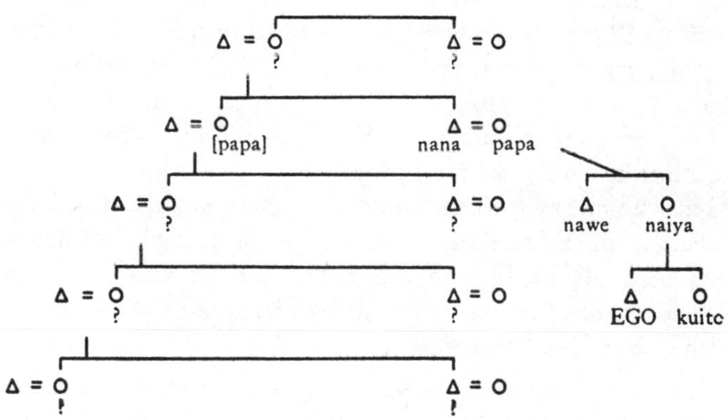

FIG. 20.—The mother's father's matrilineal lineage. Ego = male. It is not clear whether this lineage is recognized at Acoma.

mother and for sister's daughter (male speaking).[9] Ego's male relatives are differentiated as "brother" and "mother's brother," the latter term being applied to the sister's son as well. Unfortunately, the terms for mother's mother's brother and sister's daughter's children have not been recorded by any of our sources. I would guess that Acoma once followed—if it does not today—the Laguna pattern and applied sibling terms to these relatives. Such an application would maintain the patterns of alternation of generation and verbal reciprocity which seem characteristic of Acoma and Laguna.

A woman makes a greater differentiation of relatives within her matrilineal lineage than does a man. She distinguishes a "mother, "sister," and "daughter" in the female line and uses a reciprocal term for mother's mother and daughter's daughter. For males of her lineage she distinguishes a "brother," "son," and "grandson." The term for mother's brother, female speaking, is not clear; White gives *sa nawe* for mother's brother but does not differentiate male and female speakers. Parsons omits the term from her chart but gives "mother" as the term for the reciprocal: "sister's daughter (male speaking)."[10] This suggests that the correct term may be *s'amuiti*, "son," which is also the Laguna pattern. If sibling terms are applied to the mother's mother's brother, an alternation of generations parallel to that for a male ego may be noted.[11]

Men who marry into ego's lineage in his generation and below are classed together as *wati*, "male relative-in-law"; women who marry men of the lineage are *piye*, "female relative-in-law." These terms are further extended by Parsons to the kin of wife and the kin of husband, respectively.

> Affinity terms are the same as at Laguna; but their application as reciprocals appears more usual. It was definitely stated that your wife's mother or father you call *shuwati*, and all her people *shuwatitemish;* and that your husband's mother or father you call *shupiye* and his people, *shupiyetemish*.[12]

White indicates that *wati* is also applied to brother's daughter's husband and *piye* to brother's son's wife; his recording of *sak'uitc'* for mother's brother's wife is probably an error.[13]

The terms used for children of men of the lineage are incomplete, but the indicated pattern is one of classifying them as "children." It is possible that a woman follows the more complicated pattern found in Laguna; this would be probable if the terms for mother's brother and mother's mother's brother turn out as suggested.

For the father's matrilineal lineage there is, as noted above, considerable disagreement among our sources. This disagreeemnt is, I believe, intelligible in terms of changes taking place in the social structure generally and in the kinship system in particular. Kroeber recorded *naicdia* for both the father and the father's sister's son and *kuya* for the father's sister, but the latter's daughter is given as "mother." Parsons and White classify the father's sister as "mother" and her children as "brother" and "sister." However, both Parsons and White have recorded the mother's brother's children as "son" and "daughter," the reciprocals of which should normally be "father" and "mother" rather than "brother" and "sister."[14]

It is probable that the older pattern is one in which the men of the father's lineage are classed as "fathers" with the women alternating as "father's sister" and "grandmother," as in Laguna. This pattern then may have changed to that recorded by Kroeber, in which the father's sister's children became "father" and "mother." A further change in the same direction would result in the classification of the father's sister as "mother" and her children as "brothers" and "sisters," thus giving a more definite "bilateral" character to the system in place of the earlier lineage pattern.[15] The classification of men marrying into the father s matrilineal lineage is not clear; probably "grandfather" and "father" were used. Women marrying men of the lineage were probably classed as "mothers," and children of men of the lineage as "brothers" and "sisters."

There is no evidence as to whether the mother's father's or father's father's lineages were recognized as kinship units, though, since there was some recognition of the mother's father's lineage at Laguna, it is possible that this lineage was also considered as kindred at Acoma.

EXTENSIONS

The extensions of kinship at Acoma seem less widespread than among the other western Pueblo groups. Kinship terms are extended, probably on a simplified basis, to clanspeople. Parsons gives *s'awitemish*, "my mother's people," and *s'akuyatemish*, "my father's people," as referring to blood kindred but notes the usual difficulty in distinguishing between blood relations and clanspeople. The term *kuya*, "father's sister," in the latter compound strengthens the argument above for the probable classification of women of the father's lineage and clan as "father's sisters."

When a child is ready to be initiated into the Katcina cult, the parents select a "ceremonial father" for the child. Usually a clansman of the father is selected, but a friend may be chosen who is then addressed as "brother." The "ceremonial father" selects a male relative to assist him; his wife and her sisters wash the child's head and become "mothers" to the initiate. When the "ceremonial father" belongs to the father's clan, there is no new extension of kinship, though additional bonds are set up. Where the "ceremonial father" is not a member of the father's clan, White states that "the novice would not extend the use of relationship terms to clansmen of those he addressed as 'father.' "[16] Stirling's account, however, suggests that the "ceremonial father" is usually a friend of the father and that the corn meal paid to the latter is distributed among all his relatives "because this child is to become a son of all of his clan."[17] He further states that "the initiate will regard his 'father' as a real father; and all the relatives of the 'father' will be considered relatives."[18] It is probable that Stirling's account, secured in connection with the Origin Myth, represents older practice and that White's information is on current procedure.[19]

The extensions of kinship at marriage have been noted above. Kroeber states that parent terms may be used for mother-in-law and father-in-law but that "relative-in-law" terms are apparently usually applied to them and to their people. How far the latter applications extend is not clear.

When a person wishes to join a Medicine society, he selects one of the doctors to be his "father." White notes that, while they address each other as father and son, "there is doubt in this instance whether or not the new member would address all men in his 'doctor father's' clan as father and their respective wives as mother."[20]

The most important figure in Acoma mythology is Iatiku, one of two sisters, who created the people and the things they need and instructed them in their duties and responsibilities.[21] As "mother" and representative of the earth, she is held in great respect and affection. The cacique and other religious officials are her representatives in the village. The sun is called "father," and the Twin War Gods, children of the sun, are "older brother" and "younger brother."

The cacique is regarded as the "father" of the people and acts as "father" of the Katcina. The heads of the Medicine societies are also called "father," as is the War Chief during ceremonies. The corn-ear fetishes used in connection with the medicine ceremonies represent Iatiku and are called "mother"; the large flint fetishes used in these ceremonies may be called "father." There are probably many additional extensions of kinship on a ritual or ceremonial basis.

THE HOUSEHOLD

As at Zuni, the household at Acoma is undoubtedly an important social and economic unit. But in the absence of a household census for Old Acoma it is difficult to analyze the structure and composition of the ideal and average households.

The houses at Old Acoma are arranged in three long rows and are generally three stories high, the top floor being used as a living-room, the second generally for sleeping, and the ground floor for storage. White further notes that "at Old Acoma the houses are grouped somewhat according to clan."[22]

The recent census data (1941) give some 1,254 people and 212 families, an average of around 6 persons per family, a figure lower than the Zuni average. Parsons suggests that matrilocal residence is common,[23] resulting in a matrilineal extended family, but White states that "there is no fixed custom (nowadays, at least) regulating the residence of wife and husband after marriage."[24] That the older household pattern was of the compound type based on matrilocal residence is definitely indicated by a statement made in an autobiography of an elderly informant recorded recently by White:

> In the house where I first opened my eyes lived my mother and father, my mother's mother and father, three brothers and two sisters of my mother, and my mother's mother's mother. One of my sanawe (mother's brother), the oldest, was married and lived at his wife's house. My mother's eldest sister was married; her husband lived there with us. I was the oldest among my brothers and sisters.[25]

If this pattern is typical, and it corresponds closely with the household patterns of Zuni and Hopi, then there has been an important shift, in modern times, toward a more variable and simplified household grouping. It is probable that the older type of extended household is more frequently found at Old Acoma and elementary family households in the farming villages, where individual dwellings prevail.

The relations of the households to the lineage and clan is not clear. At least half the clans are probably composed of multiple lineages, whether recognized or not. There is no clan ownership of land; all land is communally owned in theory, but each farm is said to "belong" to a particular family, which means that they have the right to use it as long as they need it.[26] With regard to ceremonial prerogatives, recent information indicates that there were only four clans which were custodians of ceremonies. "Only these clans had 'clan houses' in which they met for ceremonial purposes, and in which they kept whatever ceremonial paraphernalia they might possess. The other clans 'had nothing to meet about.' "[27] These data suggest a structural relation between household, lineage, and clan comparable to that noted for the Zuni and Hopi, but the general impression given by the Acoma material is that the household and clan are subordinate to the village to a greater extent.

KINSHIP BEHAVIOR

The duties and obligations of relatives can be conveniently summarized in terms of the life-cycle.[28] During pregnancy there are various restrictions on the prospective mother. At birth the mother is assisted by a midwife, but the father's sister comes and bathes the infant and cares for him during the four-day lying-in period. During this period an ear of corn is placed beside the child, but there is no bed of hot sand as at Zuni.

Naming takes place on the morning of the fourth day. According to one of Parsons' informants, the father's mother may present the child to the sun and give it its name.[29] But the more usual custom—and the one sanctioned by the Origin Myth—is for the father to select a medicine man to carry out this ritual. He comes with his wife and sets up an altar in the house. After his wife has bathed the mother and child, the medicine man takes the infant outdoors and presents it to the rising sun, with a prayer for long life. He gives the infant its name and mentions its clan name: "Now you have become a member of such and such a clan."[30] The medicine man and his wife then return the child to the household, and, after various rituals, a feast is held. The name is usually selected by the parents and frequently refers to the father's clan.[31] Whether any special kinship relation is established between the child and the medicine man is not clear.

A Catholic ceremony of christening may be held when the infant is seven or eight months old. A godfather and godmother are chosen, and the child is given the name of the appropriate godparent, probably the Spanish name. After the christening in the church, the godparents take the child to their home and wash its head. Presents are given on this occasion and thereafter exchanged at Christmas time.[32]

The care and training of the child was distributed among various relatives. A mother might whip a child, but the father "should not," though White notes that the usual disciplinary device was the threat of a bogey.[33] The mother's brother is the head of the family and advises boys as to right conduct but does not whip his sister's children. The father and the mother's brother instruct a boy about practical matters and making a living. Older sisters take care of their younger siblings; grandfathers frequently take care of small grandchildren also. The mother's father often tells stories, as do other grandparents as well.

White notes a special joking relationship which exists between grandfathers and grandsons and between grandmothers and granddaughters. Ridicule and rivalry are emphasized: "the boy helps out his grandmother against her husband; the girl helps out her grandfather against his wife."[34] On the other hand, joking is not practiced with parents or their siblings or with the relatives of one's spouse.

In general, the father's sister is treated the same as the mother's sister; "you are supposed to be good to her." A boy should work equally for a father's sister or a mother's brother if they should ask him, and all cousins should be treated alike. This tendency to treat the father's and mother's relatives alike is in contrast to the differentiation noted for the Hopi and to some extent for the Zuni.

Initiations into the Katcina organization formerly took place when children were around the age of nine to twelve. The selection of a friend, usually of the father's clan, to act as "ceremonial father" has been described above. If the father is dead, the child's mother's brother makes the necessary arrangements. A large amount of corn meal is brought to the "ceremonial father" for distribution among his clan relatives. The initiation is considered to be initiation into the tribe, and the ceremony is held in the chief kiva where the Antelope clan altar has been erected. The ceremony is in charge of the War Chief. The "ceremonial fathers" carry their children, boys and girls, on their backs into the kiva. The children and the "ceremonial fathers" are then whipped by the chief of the Katcinas; brothers or mother's brothers of the "ceremonial fathers" then come forward, fasten some feathers in the child's hair, and give the child a name. In the account of the Katcina initiation in the Origin Myth, the "ceremonial father" is asked "if he will act as 'father' to the child, naming him with clan name."[35] The name given, therefore, probably refers to the "ceremonial father's" clan and symbolizes the new relationship established between the novice and the members of this clan.[36]

The "ceremonial father" and his wife then make new clothes for the novice, and four days later bring the child to their house, where it is told the presents are from the Katcina. The wife, or "ceremonial mother," washes the child's head and gives it a feast. The initiation is ended by a bath in front of an altar erected in the kivas by the medicine men; this ritual is designed to give the initiates new life.

Some time later on, the mother's brothers of the initiates take them to a place where the Katcina are unmasked. Here the cacique tells them about the history of the Katcina and why it became necessary for men to impersonate them. Secrecy is imposed with strong warnings of the results of revealing the secrets to noninitiates. The cacique then takes the initiates to the head Katcina and formally presents them as members of the Katcina organization.

The Katcina organization is distributed among five kivas. A boy belongs to the kiva of his own father; girls, while initiated into the organization, do not wear masks or belong to the kiva groups. While each kiva has its own officers, there is no separate organization as such. After Iatiku created the Katcina, she appointed the first-born man in the Antelope clan as cacique and father of the Katcina.[37] The Katcina organization is under the direct control of the cacique and his assistants, though certain Katcina "belong" to particular clans.

Initiation into the Medicine societies takes place through curing or through being "trapped." The "doctor father" teaches his "son" the secrets of the profession and provides him with clothing, paraphernalia, and a new name.[38] The initiation ritual as described in the Origin Myth, involves the preparation of a corn-ear fetish ("mother") for the novice and the whipping of the latter with yucca in front of the altar.[39] At the end of the initiation a public ceremony is held, attended by relatives and friends, at which the new members exhibit their accomplishments. The relatives of the novices have to prepare food for the medicine men and probably furnish gifts for the "doctor fathers."

Marriage is theoretically forbidden within one's own clan and probably not approved within the father's clan. White's analysis of marriages at Acoma shows no moiety or phratry division.[40] Men and women select their own mates, though White notes that "a young man might be advised regarding his contemplated marriage by his father and mother and by their brothers and sisters; a girl might be similarly advised."[41] The wedding is normally Catholic, and the Catholic institution of sponsorship is utilized, the sponsors taking the couple to their house after the ceremony, washing their heads, and giving them presents and advice.[42] But White indicates that many couples live together without any ceremony and that, while divorce is not recognized in theory, separation occurs in actual practice. There is a considerable amount of premarital sexual freedom, and there is no stigma attached to having children before marriage.[43]

The problem of residence after marriage and the composition of the household has been discussed above. It is probable that the older rule of residence was matrilocal but that under Catholic and modern influences the rule has broken down, particularly with regard to the farming villages.

In former times marriage outside the village was not encouraged, but White has recorded some eleven such marriages.[44] There is a ritual for welcoming a foreign bride (or groom) to Acoma. The War Chief leads the couple up the trail to the village, where the cacique embraces the newcomer, saying, "You are my daughter. You are now under my arm."[45] The groom's mother washes the heads of the couple, and, if the clan of the adopted girl is represented at Acoma, all the clanswomen come and wash her head, the oldest woman of the clan, the "mother," finishing the washing.

The accounts of death and burial vary somewhat. In the Origin Myth the medicine men prepared the first dead for burial, painting their faces in the prescribed manner and cutting their hair and attaching feathers to it. According to White, the faces of males are painted with the designs used when they were first presented to the sun at the naming ceremony; girls' faces are smeared with pollen.[46] It is not clear whether these are clan designs or not.

Burial is in the churchyard, and both the father's people and the mother's people may take part. The father makes prayer sticks for the deceased; usually a woman relative breaks a jar of water on the grave. The soul is believed to linger about the house for four days before going back to the Place of Emergence, where it joins Iatiku, the "mother" of them all. During this period a stick used to stir the fire and a flint arrowhead are placed where the deceased lay.

After four days a medicine man comes to bid the deceased to go away and to put the family through the "forgetting" ceremony. The household drinks an emetic, and the father's kindred come in and wash their heads.[47] The medicine man takes offerings and a prayer stick to a place representing the "gate to Shipapu," the Place of Emergence.[48]

Parsons notes that the heads of a widower and his children are washed by the women of his mother's household, and he may elect to return home with his mother or sister or to remain in his wife's household to look after his children. A widow or widower should wait a year to remarry; otherwise they might become ill.[49]

CONCLUSIONS

The data presented on kinship behavior reinforce, I believe, the hypotheses presented as to changes in kinship terminology. The present picture of kinship behavior is a "bilateral" one, in that there is a tendency to treat the father's and mother's relatives in a similar way. But there is also evidence of patterns of behavior differentiating the father's relatives from the mother's—patterns which parallel, in many cases, those noted for the Hopi and Zuni. That these patterns are older in every instance needs further demonstration, but they are consonant with suggested older patterns of classification, while present patterns of behavior fit current classifications.

The greatest changes in both kinship classification and behavior have taken place in connection with the father's lineage group. We have noted the probable shift in terminology from a Crow type similar to that of Laguna to a "bilateral" system, in which the father's sister is classed with the mother and the cross-cousins are siblings. There is evidence that the father's lineage and clan once performed the ritual activities on such crisis occasions as birth, initiations, and death. But at birth and naming the Medicine societies have taken over the ritually important activities; christening involves a set of godparents; the probable former role of the father's sisters in connection with the Katcina initiation has been transferred to the "ceremonial father's" wife; and at death the father's kindred share duties with the medicine man and the kindred of the deceased.

Thus there is a reduction in the number of specialized functions performed by the members of the father's household and clan, so that the father's household comes to resemble ego's household to a greater extent. The father's sister and her daughters are accorded the same treatment as the mother's sister and called by the same term, "mother." A further extension of the same process results in all cousins, whether on the mother's or father's side, being treated alike and classed as "siblings." With the breakdown of the lineage principle as a basis for organizing the father's relatives, there has probably come a corresponding change in the classification of men and women marrying into the father's lineage and of children of men of the lineage.

Within one's own lineage the changes have not been so great. The mother's brother is considered the head of the family, but he does not punish his sister's children, nor is he generally responsible for transmitting ceremonial knowledge and position to his sister's son. The cacique and the central hierarchy carry out most of such functions. The economic activities of the women are carried out under the direction of the oldest woman of the household, the "mother," but formerly, at least, the women of the village were organized into three corn-grinding groups which worked as units under the direction of a head woman called *naiy'a*, "mother."[50]

The classification of ego's maternal relatives is still in terms of the lineage principle, but it is beginning to "break" around the edges. The concept of "child" of the clan is not so institutionalized as at Zuni, and the classification of children of men of the lineage as "son" and "daughter" conflicts with the self-reciprocal terminology for grandparents and grandchildren. The "bilateral" tendency in the treatment of cross-cousins results in a conflict as to classification of the mother's brother's children.

There is a further tendency to limit the ceremonial extension of kinship. The "ceremonial father" has limited functions at Acoma, in contrast to the lifelong and complex relationship among the Hopi. The older pattern seems to have been to select a friend and to set up kinship relations with his clan; the modern tendency is to select a member of the father's clan. Where a nonrelative is selected, there is at present no extension of kinship to his clanspeople. A similar situation seems to exist with reference to a "doctor father" and his clanspeople; White notes there is some doubt as to the extension.

One important pattern at Acoma, which is characteristic of Keresan villages generally, and which contrasts with the Hopi and Zuni to a considerable extent, is the emphasis on the concept of "mother." In the Origin Myth we have seen that the central figure is Iatiku, who is the "mother" of the people whom she created and whom she receives at death. The corn-ear fetishes represent her and have her power; the cacique is her representative and is referred to as her "husband" in the mythology. In the kinship system the term "mother" is widely extended, and recent changes have extended it still further. In ritual relations the wife of the "ceremonial father" performs many of the ritual functions performed by the ceremonial father's sisters among the Hopi and Zuni. In the Scalp Dance it is the mother of the Twins who dances rather than their sister or aunts.[51]

Another important kinship pattern, which we will find more highly developed at Laguna and which is characteristic of Keresan societies, is the use of verbally reciprocal or self-reciprocal kinship terms. The use of self-reciprocal terms contributes to the pattern by which alternating generations are equated in terminology, but the latter pattern goes beyond that influence. The grandparent-grandchild terms are completely self-reciprocal as are the brother-brother, sister-sister, and mother's brother–sister's son terms. Laguna, as we shall see later, has managed to adjust the grandparent-grandchild reciprocals to the lineage pattern; I have suggested that Acoma has done the same, on the basis of the evidence so far available. The significance of the self-reciprocal terminology is not clear at present but will be further discussed in later sections.

The Clan System

The clans at Acoma are matrilineal, exogamous, and totemically named. In the Origin Myth there is an account of the origin of the clan system.[52] The two original sisters, Nautsiti and Iatiku, chose to belong to the Sun and Corn clans, respectively. After Nautsiti disappeared in the east, Iatiku married her sister's son and allotted clans to her children as they were born. The first clan mothers were: Sun, Sky, Water, Badger, and Fire; she named the rest after things she had brought to life, dividing her own clan, Corn, into Red Corn, Yellow Corn, Blue Corn, and White Corn. Clans which came into existence later (e.g., Parrot, Snake, Buffalo, and Ant) were not descended from daughters of Iatiku—presumably they came into Acoma through intermarriage or otherwise.[53]

Table 8 lists the clans as given by various investigators; of these, White's data are the best, since they are based on a complete census of Acoma. Of the "original" eighteen or nineteen clans, the majority are still in existence. Badger and Deer are not listed by any authority; the Fire clan and the Blue, White, and "Brown" Corn clans are listed as extinct by Hodge. Of the "later" clans, only the Parrot and Snake survive, with the Buffalo, Ant, and others listed as extinct.

There is no phratry grouping or moiety division of clans for exogamic purposes, as White has clearly shown by his analysis of marriages.[54] Even the surviving Corn clans do not seem to form an exogamic unit, since marriages are recorded between Red Corn and Yellow Corn. The considerable number of marriages within the Sun clan is attributed to immigration of some Sun clanspeople from Santo Domingo and Zia as well as to the breakdown of clan exogamy.[55] The problem as to whether there are functional lineages within the clans has been mentioned above; it is probable that the larger clans are composed of multiple lineages,[56] but there is little evidence that these have special functions apart from the clan.

The Acoma clans have limited economic, political, and ritual functions, in comparison with Hopi and Zuni. In the Origin Myth, however, there is a more definite allocation of duties to

TABLE 8*

ACOMA CLANS

Clan	Stirling	Bandelier	Hodge		Parsons	White
	1942	1892	1896	1907	1920	1932
Sun	×	×	×	×	×	×
Sky	×	....	×	×}	×	{×
Water	×	×	×	×}		{×
Badger	×	....	....	....	....	....
Fire	×	....	E	E	....	....
Antelope	×	×	×	×	×	×
Deer	×	....	....	....	....	....
Bear	×	×	×	×	×	×
Corn†	×	×	E†	E‡	....	....
Red	×	×	×	×	×	×
Yellow	×	×	×	×	×	×
Blue	×	×	E	E	....	....
White	×	....	E	×	....	....
Oak	×	....	×	×	×	×
Pumpkin or Squash	×	×	×	×	×	×
Roadrunner	×	×	×	×	×	×
Eagle	×	×	×	×	×	×
Turkey	×	×	×	×	×	×
Tansy Mustard	×	×§	....	....	....	....
- - - - - -	- - -	- - -	- - -	- - -	- - -	- - -
Parrot	×	×	×	×	×	×
Snake	×	×	×	×	×	E
Buffalo	×	....	E	E	....	....
Ant	×	E	E	×	E‖	....
Lizard	....	....	....	....	E#	....
Piñon-eater	....	×**	....	....	....	....

* Based on Stirling, *Origin Myth of Acoma*, Bandelier, *Final Report of Investigations among the Indians of the Southwestern United States*, Hodge, "Pueblo Indian Clans" and *Handbook of the American Indians*, Parsons, "Notes on Isleta, Santa Ana, and Acoma," and White, "The Acoma Indians." × = present; E = extinct. Order as in Stirling's *Origin Myth;* those below dotted line are of presumed later origin.

† Corn probably should be second in order but was later divided into various colors.

‡ Given as Brown Corn by Hodge.

§ Given as Ivy by Bandelier.

‖ Given as Red Ant by Parsons.

\# Listed as Lizard or Snake by Parsons.

** Probably should be Fire on the basis of meaning of native term.

various clans, which suggests a shift from clan to village control in certain instances. The clans at Acoma do not own land as such, since all land "belongs to the cacique,"[57] but, once allotted, land normally was transmitted from mother to daughter and thus might stay within a household (and lineage?) as long as it was used.[58] Since land which is allotted to a man "belongs" to him and his family, and is inherited by his widow and daughters, it is probably felt to belong primarily to the household.

White reports only four clans as custodians of ceremonies or possessing ceremonial prerogatives: the Antelope, Corn, Pumpkin, and Parrot clans.[59] Of these, the Antelope clan is the most important clan at Acoma, despite its present small size. The village cacique must always be a member of the Antelope clan; he has authority over the medicine men and the kiva chiefs and is "father" of the Katcinas. The Antelope clan, in addition to selecting the cacique and his successor, selects the other village officials and is closely associated with the Katcina cult and the head kiva and takes the lead in various important ceremonies. The Corn clan controls the Curatsa ceremony and associated Katcina, and the Pumpkin and Parrot clansmen formerly went on salt-gathering expeditions and controlled the associated rituals. Only these clans had "clanhouses."[60]

The outstanding position of the Antelope clan at Acoma, in part at least, derives from its association with the Katcina.[61] In the Origin Myth, Iatiku, after planning the first town, sent for the oldest man of the Antelope clan and said: "You are to be Tiamuni and the father of the Katcina."[62] Later, to relieve him of part of his burden of governing the village, she selected the first man in the Sky clan to be War Chief or "outside chief." Formerly this official was said to be always from the Sky clan, but at present the War Chiefs are selected without reference to clan affiliation.[63] The clan head is usually the eldest male of the clan, but, except for the clans possessing ceremonies, the head has few functions. According to Parsons' informant, disputes within the clan would be settled by the clan head.[64]

Traditionally the Hunter's society was associated with the Eagle clan. Iatiku selected the oldest male of the Eagle clan to be father of the game animals and to provide assistance in hunting. This society was associated with the directional beasts of prey: mountain lion (N), wolf (W), lynx (or jaguar?) (S), and wildcat (E), and provided the rules for the hunt and the ritual treatment of game.[65] This society is no longer in existence at Acoma, and the War Chief has taken over the necessary activities.

The Medicine societies, in the Origin Myth, are likewise associated with a clan. Iatiku this time asked the chiefs to select a man to be the first medicine man—they selected the oldest man in the Oak clan to be instructed by Iatiku as to how to set up the Fire society altar and to cure the sick. She then told Oak man that he was to select the leaders for other groups of medicine men which were to assist him: Flint, Spider, and Giant.[66] These four societies were the first to be organized; later the Ant society was formed to cure sickness caused by ants.[67] At present there are four Medicine societies at Acoma: Flint, Fire, Kabina (Spider), and Shiwanna, the latter relatively unimportant. None of these is associated with clanship.[68]

Ceremonial Organization

The ceremonial organization centers around the Katcina cult and the Medicine societies, with war and hunting once important but no longer institutionally represented. The Katcina cult is tribal wide and associated with the kiva system; both boys and girls are initiated into the cult, but only males play an important role. The Katcina themselves are anthropomorphic spirits who were created at Iatiku.[69] They live at Wenimats, under a lake southwest of Acoma, and are associated with clouds and rain. Recent information indicates that they are related to the dead, as well.[70]

Seven kivas are reported for Acoma, the head kiva used by the cacique and the Antelope clan, the ceremonial chamber of the Fire society, and five Katcina kivas.[71] Each kiva has four officers who are appointed for life by the cacique and who have charge of the Katcina organization belonging to their kiva. The chief kiva is specifically associated with the Antelope clan, but, since children join the kiva of their father, there is no clan association in the ordinary kivas. Initiation of children into the Katcina organization takes place in chief kiva under the direction of the Antelope clan and the cacique; these later tell the novices the story of the Katcinas and show them unmasked.[72]

The chief function of the Katcina cult is to bring rain to aid the crops. Associated with each kiva are a variety of Katcina; these are presented in dances at the solstices and during the summer and fall. In addition, every five years there formerly was a dramatization of the fight with the Katcinas, the kiva groups supplying the Katcina warriors, and the Antelope clansmen and the Warrior's society defending the village.[73] At the winter solstice the kiva groups go singly to dance in the chief kiva. During this period the *kopishtaiya* come—these are spirits who live in the east at the sunrise and are thought to be like Katcina. Boys who have been initiated take part in this ceremony for four years before being allowed to wear Katcina masks. The Katcina sometimes dance at the summer solstice, but the Katcina dance par excellence is the summer dance for rain given by two kivas selected by the cacique, each dancing two days. A Katcina dance may be held in the fall to celebrate the harvest.

The Katcina also participate in the fire-lighting ceremony of the Corn clan, which is held every five years around the last of July. The Corn clansmen meet in the Corn clanhouse and are assisted by their ceremonial sons and daughters in the various ritual activities which center around fire and water. Water and charcoal are distributed to each household in the village.

The society organizations comprise the Medicine societies, the Warrior's society, the Koshari, and the Hunter's society, the last three of which are extinct.[74] We have noted above the origin of the Medicine societies. Each society has a headman or "father" who is in charge of all activities and who occupies an important position in the pueblo. Members are secured both by curing and by "trapping," the novice becoming a "ceremonial son." The Fire society, traditionally the first Medicine society to be created, has its own kiva, the Flint society uses the chief kiva, and the Kabina used a room adjoining the chief kiva. The latter society became extinct in 1927, and its functions were taken over by the Flint society.

The Medicine societies "cure" illnesses due to witchcraft and purge the villages of witches at intervals. Simple cures may be performed by a single doctor, but important cases require the whole society. Altars are set up, and the medicine men cure by means of power received from certain animals: bear, mountain lion, eagle, badger, snake, and wolf.

The initiation ceremonies are concluded with a public exhibition at which the novices demonstrate their newly acquired curing powers. The Fire society concludes its initiation with an outdoor ritual in which the medicine men and the novices jump into a pit of hot coals. Communal curing ceremonies are usually held in the spring, if the cacique decides one is needed. All the Medicine societies co-operate, and the people go either to the Fire society or to the Flint society. After curing the people, the medicine men rid the pueblo of witches, "fighting" with any they find lurking about the houses. Each person in the village receives one kernel of corn and a drink of medicine.

The Medicine societies perform a number of functions in addition to curing: they assist at Katcina dances and initiations, there are certain masks restricted to medicine men, and they impersonate the heads of the *kopishtaiya.* The Kabina society formerly installed the War Chiefs, a task now taken over by the Flint society.

The Hunter's society, formerly in existence, was considered a Medicine society. At present the War Chief has charge of the communal rabbit hunts held each year for the benefit of the cacique. The Warrior's society was composed of all those who had killed an enemy in the prescribed way. On their return a scalp dance would be held. The Koshari society collaborated with the Warrior's society in the Scalp Dance. The Koshari were created by Iatiku and acted as a Clown society. During the Scalp Dance they were in complete control of the village; two groups of Koshari danced, assisted by the kiva groups. The Quiraina, the complementary Clown society in the eastern Keresan pueblos, is not represented as such in Acoma; rather the term is applied to persons who have been initiated into the Katcina organization, though individuals may be recruited to act as Quiraina on occasion.[75]

The political organization is controlled by the cacique, who is the religious head of the village, and the Antelope clan. Normally the cacique seems to be succeeded by a sister's son. He is installed in the chief kiva by the Antelope clansmen, assisted by the kiva chiefs. As father of the pueblo, as well as father of the Katcina, he is concerned for the welfare of everybody. Formerly he was assisted by a group of four "chief's helpers," who also served for life and worked for the welfare of the pueblo.[76]

The War Chief is the most important official next to the cacique; he has two assistants representing the War Twins and two cooks or helpers. There are also ten principales chosen for life by the cacique and distributed evenly among the kivas; their duty is to watch over the pueblo and see that everything goes all right and to act as liaison between the sacred and secular administrations. The secular government is composed of a governor, two lieutenant-governors, three fiskales, and a ditch boss. They are concerned with outside contacts and regulate secular activities within the pueblo.

The War Chiefs and secular officers are chosen annually by the Antelope clan from among the kiva groups. The War Chief announces the selections in advance to the medicine men and the two head men of each kiva who have a veto power; after agreement the new officials are announced to the assembled males in the public meeting-house. The War Chiefs have to be installed by one of the Medicine societies; they have the duty of preserving old customs, guarding the village, and protecting the people from witches. They and their helpers must observe continence for their period of office.

The people of the village, in turn, work a large communal farm for the benefit of the cacique and the pueblo. The War Chief has charge of the farm, and the corn raised there is stored in his house. On ceremonial occasions corn is distributed to be shelled, ground, and baked for the Katcinas. The cacique may draw on this store for his needs, and families needing help may apply to the War Chief for sufficient corn to keep them going.[77]

Conclusions and Comparisons

The position of Acoma in Southwestern culture is a crucial one. With Acoma we come to the Keresan-speaking Pueblos, a group bridging the gap between the western Pueblos and those of the Rio Grande. Thus, these Pueblos hold the key to the nature and character of the changes which may have brought about the considerable differences in social structure between the east and the west. Acoma as the most westerly of the Keresan Pueblos is of particular importance in this connection, but Laguna will furnish the most convincing evidence.

The social organization of Acoma is not as complex as that of Zuni or Hopi, but the pattern of social structure is of the same general type, and a considerable degree of social integration has been achieved by similar devices. White has emphasized the integration at Acoma and, as we have already noted, views Acoma social organization as built up on a kinship and clan substratum.

> It is on this level, too, that a great current of forces flows which influence pueblo affairs to a very great extent. These are the attractions and repulsions between person and person; the loves, hates, fears, jealousies, suspicions of the people. The alignment of individuals within the two parties, the progressives and the conservatives, is determined largely by kin and clan ties.[78]

This is an excellent statement which only needs to be extended a bit further. Not only are these "subinstitutional" forces important but also the institutionalized patterns of obligations and behavior characteristic of relatives and others occupying particular positions. While these have not been adequately studied, and cannot be under present conditions, there is enough evidence to indicate that the Acoma kinship system is definitely organized and belongs to the lineage type.

The Acoma kinship system was classified by Spier as a separate type, related more closely to the Salish than to the Crow type.[79] Whatever may be the ultimate fate of the other representatives of the Acoma type, the present analysis indicates that the

Acoma kinship system is a lineage system, primarily, and belongs in the Crow subtype. The analysis of the Acoma kinship system in terms of the lineage principle has clarified many of the apparent inconsistencies in kinship terminology and usage. We have attempted to account for other inconsistencies in terms of a hypothesis of change from a lineage to a "bilateral" system, under acculturative influences. Parallel changes are apparent, in varying degrees, in all the western Pueblos and will be discussed further in our concluding section.

The relation of the kinship system to the household, lineage, and clan seems to be of the same general order as at Hopi or Zuni. In the older pattern the matrilocal households and the matrilineal lineages were tied together through the kinship system. Through the extension of kinship patterns to the clan, the clan system was similarly tied together by kinship bonds, including the system of ceremonial kinship. The pattern of self-reciprocal terminology is probably another integrative device; only slightly developed among the Hopi and stronger at Zuni, it reaches a high degree of elaboration at Acoma and Laguna.

White has noted the changes which have taken place in Acoma culture following the recent movement from Old Acoma to Acomita Valley with its irrigation systems. There has been a shift in psychological forces and values and a gradual breakdown of tradition, and the village is beginning to break up into individual family groups.[80] These changes have been aided and intensified by modern acculturation: the Indian Service, schools, missionaries, the government farmer, the doctor, and tourists.[81] These factors have affected not only the family groupings but, concomitantly, the kinship system, the clan organization, and the ceremonial system as well. There has been a reduction in the scope and extent of the kinship system, a breakdown of the extended family organization, and a reduction in the importance of lineage and clan. In general terms, the various manifestations of the lineage principle have been replaced by a "bilateral" principle of grouping.

Unquestionably this shift in social structure has been profoundly influenced by acculturation during the last few decades.

But it is also probable that the increasing centralization of functions and control in the village at the expense of the clan (and lineage) is considerably older. Acoma has been in existence since prehistoric times, and while there has not been the necessity of integrating several communities into one, as at Zuni, there has been the task of resisting external aggression and internal dissention. In the Origin Myth there is definite evidence of the greater importance of the clan system, and the myths in general reflect older or more conservative practice.[82]

In Acoma tradition (as among the other Keres) the people came out of their underground home in the north and gradually moved southward, living at White House and other places before reaching their predestined final location. Here on their mesa top they successfully resisted nomadic enemies and challenged the Spaniards until 1598. To maintain their unity, the events of the historic period forced them to create a village organization that was flexible and centralized and able to make decisions. While this centralization has been chiefly in the realm of control, it has affected social and ceremonial life as well.

White has summarized the events of the historic period, including the conquest and destruction of Acoma by Oñate in 1598 after they had killed some of his men.[83] He notes that "the Acoma people were soon back on top of their mesa." Hammond, however, in his detailed study of the destruction of Acoma,[84] gives the punishment inflicted on the survivors.

> Oñate ordered that all males over twenty-five years of age be condemned to have one foot cut off and to give twenty years of personal service. The men between twelve and twenty-five years escaped with twenty years of service. All the women above twelve years of age were likewise doomed to twenty years of servitude.[85]

Even though this punishment may not have been carried out completely, and the numbers killed in the fighting greatly exaggerated, the social structure of Acoma must have been shaken to its foundations.

But in the next century Acoma was rebuilt, both physically and in terms of social structure, though we have few details for this period. She participated in the Pueblo Rebellion of 1680 and in the later revolt of 1696, not finally submitting until 1699. In this process of rebuilding it is probable that there was considerable reorganization and that certain functions which had been clan controlled were transferred to the central hierarchy. Thus the War Chiefs were selected on the basis of ability rather than in terms of clan membership. The position of cacique remained—or became lodged—in the Antelope clan, which gave it stability and avoided disputes over succession; the position was possibly enhanced through giving it greater control over the Katcina cult and the ceremonial system. Through centralization of the Katcina cult the kiva organizations were subordinated to the cacique and the Antelope clan.[86] Only the Medicine societies remained outside direct control, and recent information indicates that the cacique has authority over both the medicine men and the kiva heads.[87]

The process of centralization, while involving ceremonial activities, seems to have been primarily for internal control and protection. The War Chief and his assistants protected the village against enemies—external, internal, and supernatural.[88] The possibility of disputes between clans and chiefs, apparent in the accounts of Oñate's conquest, was lessened where clan solidarity was reduced. Even the Katcina cult was used to purge dissident elements in the periodic fight with the Katcinas, a procedure which seems unique among the pueblos in the extent to which it was carried out.

The ceremonial organization is streamlined in comparison with either Hopi or Zuni. There is no elaborate hierarchy of rain priesthoods associated with the directions or a calendric series of clan-controlled ceremonies. Rather there is one tribal-wide organization, the Katcina cult, which is associated with the kivas and controlled by the cacique and the Antelope clan. The kiva groupings themselves cut across clan lines, since boys normally join the kiva of their fathers, and relations of ceremonial kinship are established with sponsors and (perhaps) their clanspeople. There is no evidence that the kivas are associated with the directions, though White feels that the kiva system is like Zuni, in contrast to the eastern dual pattern. While the

Medicine societies are separate from the Katcina cult, they use the kivas for their rituals, and members of both groups are considered *chaianyi*. The Medicine societies closely resemble those of the eastern Keresan Pueblos, but their organization and interrelations are quite different. At Acoma only the War society and the Koshari were independent of central control.

This simplified socioceremonial pattern differs in certain respects from that of Hopi or Zuni. Instead of "four or five different planes of systematization" cross-cutting one another as at Zuni, or the tying-together of strong clans through kinship and ceremonial bonds, as among the Hopi, Acoma has centralized control in a single clan and subordinated societies and clans to it. By so doing, they have retained the stability and conserving power of the clan system and have, at the same time, achieved flexibility in meeting new situations. The clan system as such, however, has lost most of its functions except for exogamy, and the societies have gradually become extinct, in part through changing conditions and possibly also through loss of a clan base. The psychological and sociological results of this centralization of power and control have been perhaps as important in bringing about changes in social structure as the more recent acculturation. Together they have been responsible for the major changes which we have noted in Acoma social structure.

Despite centralization of control, Acoma has not been able to prevent the development of political factions, "conservatives" and "liberals," which are found in practically every pueblo. None of the pueblos is organized to cope with factional disputes in any constructive way. White has presented an excellent summary of these factions at Acoma; he believes that "it is simply a matter of time before the present politico-religious organization disintegrates and Acoma loses its integrity as a pueblo."[89]

The cultural position of Acoma has been stated by White as follows:

> Although differing at many points from the Keresan pueblos of the Rio Grande, Acoma resembles them very much more than she does the Hopi or Zuni of the west, or the Tewa villages of the east; Acoma is definitely Keresan in culture. Geographically Acoma is almost midway

between the eastern and the western pueblos and is decidedly peripheral to the Keresan area. One might expect to find this position reflected in Acoma culture, and one does, indeed, find a mingling of the east and the west at Acoma.[90]

But Acoma *social structure* is not merely a compromise between western and eastern types arrived at by borrowing equally from each. It is one of the theses of this study that social structures have jobs to do and that there are a limited number of stable forms, some of which are more efficient than others in doing particular tasks. The older patterns of kinship, household, and clan were organized on the lineage principle and were designed for continuity and stability, as in the other western Pueblos. The integrative pattern, while simpler and varying in emphases, is similar in type. The more recent patterns of social structure are closer to those of the eastern Pueblos, not so much because of borrowing, but because similar factors have been operating, though with different intensities and for different periods, in both regions. I would suggest, as a working hypothesis, that Keresan social organization was originally of the western type and that the greatest changes have taken place in the eastern villages, despite their reputed conservativeness.[91] Such a hypothesis can be checked both by future work at Old Acoma and the Rio Grande villages and by the proper interpretation of Laguna. For Laguna was founded in 1697 or 1698, primarily by Keresans from the Rio Grande villages, and therefore offers important evidence as to the nature and direction of the changes which have gone on in the Keresan group as a whole.

Chapter VI

THE SOCIAL ORGANIZATION OF LAGUNA

Introduction

THE pueblo of Laguna lies in the San Jose Valley some fifteen miles northeast of Acoma. Laguna was founded in historic times by Keresan-speaking peoples from the Rio Grande—primarily from Santo Domingo, Cochiti, Zia, and other villages—as a result of disturbances brought about by the reconquest of New Mexico following the Pueblo Rebellion of 1680. The date of its founding is either 1697 or 1698; a year later, in 1699, it was visited by Governor Cubero and named San José de la Laguna.[1]

Despite the eastern origins of the bulk of its original population, Laguna has close cultural affiliations with Acoma, and its social structure belongs with the western Pueblos. We have suggested, in the previous chapter, the hypothesis that the major changes in Keresan social organization have taken place in the eastern villages; the data for Laguna are thus of primary significance for this problem.

The old village of Laguna was built on a rocky knoll overlooking the river and a considerable lake, now largely drained.[2] According to tradition, a small village had been settled by Indians from Acoma shortly before; these welcomed the newcomers to the vicinity and later joined them at Laguna.[3] At present the main village is largely deserted, the population having moved out into some nine or more farming villages. This movement began sometime after 1850, when the threat of nomadic enemies began to diminish and irrigation projects were possible. In the 1870's internal dissension over new customs led to a migration of conservative families to Isleta, a migration which has had important effects on both pueblos.[4] On ceremonial occasions the people of the farming colonies return to the main village, which remains a center of ceremonial life.

The geographical conditions at Laguna are similar to those of Acoma and Zuni. The San Jose River furnishes most of the water; Gunn notes that the first irrigating ditch was constructed in 1840 and that the next ditch was taken out in 1860.[5] The farming villages have grown up around irrigable areas, some of them on streams flowing down from near-by Mount Taylor, the highest peak in the region and important in ritual and ceremony. The near-by lake, which was formed by lava dams originally, was maintained by artifical dams until around 1850, when religious disputes are said to have kept work parties away, with the result that the dams washed out and the lake was drained.[6]

The modern economic adjustment of Laguna is similar to that of Acoma and Zuni. They have a considerable amount of land and have large herds of cattle and sheep, in addition to the normal pueblo crops. Their progress in adopting modern ideas and techniques is in part a function of their location—on the main line of the railroad and later on the main highway—and in part due to a series of outstanding missionaries and teachers, some of whom married into the tribe and held office as governors of the pueblo.[7]

The population of Laguna was estimated at 600 Indians in 1760; by the end of that century it was around 800. During the present century there has been a considerable growth: 1910, 1,441 people; 1922, 1,808 people;[8] 1941, 2,600.[9] The dialect is similar to that spoken at Acoma, the two apparently forming the western dialect of Keresan, which is understood with difficulty by the Rio Grande villages.[10]

The central position of Laguna is now challenged by certain of the farming villages, notably Paguate and Mesita, but formerly it was the main political and ceremonial center, and most families maintain a house in Laguna and return for ceremonies and other occasions. The village is divided into matrilineal, exogamous clans which have totemic names and ceremonial, juridical, and economic functions. There is some slight clan linkage and a dual organization of clans in connection with ceremonial organization but no exogamous phratries or moieties. The basic economic unit is the extended maternal household. The movement out to the farming villages has brought about some instances of clan localization as well as changes in social structure which may parallel those taking place at Acoma and other pueblos.

The ceremonial organization is composed of the Medicine societies, the Katcina cult, the Kiva groups, and the "Clown" organizations. For certain dances there is an east-west division by clans according to their location with reference to the plaza. At one time there were presumably the War and Hunting societies noted for the other Keresan pueblos.

The Kinship System

Information concerning kinship—terminology, applications, and behavior—is given by Parsons in her excellent study, *Laguna Genealogies*, which is modeled after Kroeber's study of Zuni but is more complete. She used several informants, both men and women, and worked mainly in Old Laguna with relatively conservative individuals. Furthermore, she notes that kin and clan nomenclature has not been affected by white influence,[11] which makes her account of particular value in the comparative study of Keresan kinship. In the preceding chapter we have several times used inferences from the Laguna materials to suggest the probable situation at Acoma.

TERMINOLOGY

In Figures 21–26 we have taken the liberty of rearranging Parsons' data[12] in order to summarize the essential features of the Laguna kinship system as we see it. The kinship terminology is "classificatory" in that the father is classed with the father's brother and the mother with the mother's sister. Siblings are differentiated by sex but not by relative age, and separate terms are used by male and female speakers. Sibling terms are extended to parallel cousins but not to cross-cousins. The grandparental terms parallel those of Acoma: *papa* is used for mother's mother and father's mother (male speaking) and for mother's father and father's father (female speaking); *nana* for mother's father and father's father (male speaking); and *gyiau* for father's mother

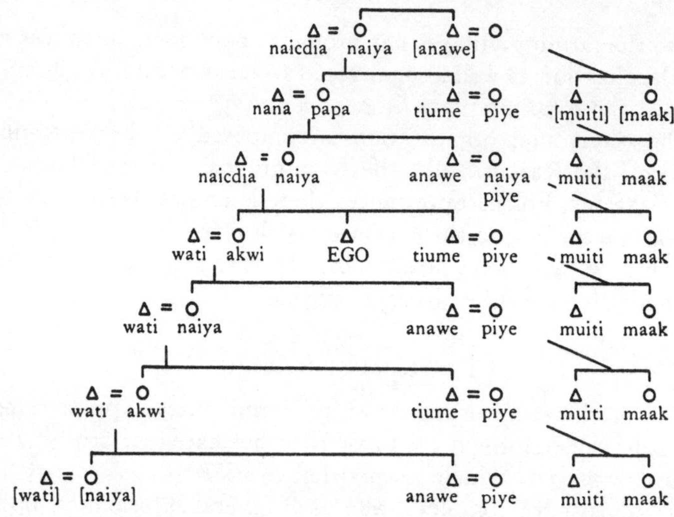

Fig. 21.—The mother's matrilineal lineage. Ego = male. Terms in brackets are reconstructions.

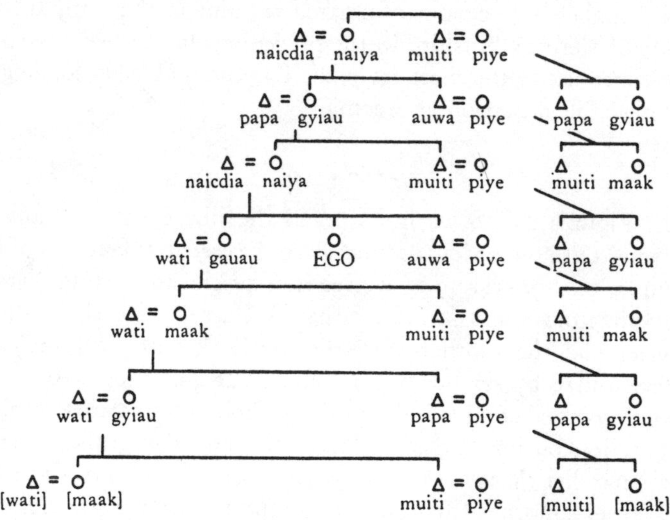

Fig. 22.—The mother's matrilineal lineage. Ego = female. Terms in brackets are reconstructions.

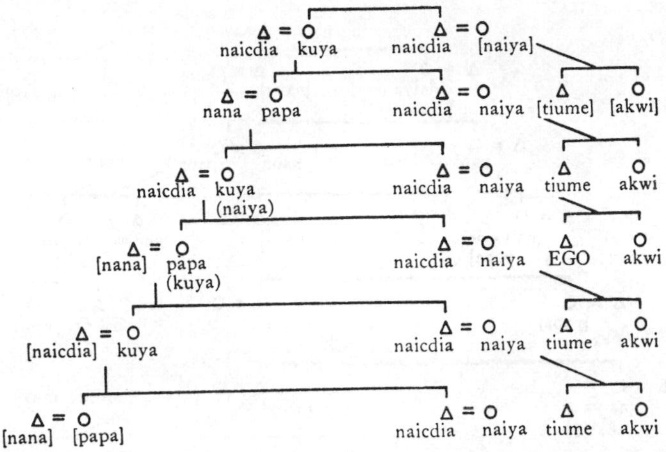

FIG. 23.—The father's matrilineal lineage. Ego = male. Terms in brackets are reconstructions; in parentheses are alternates.

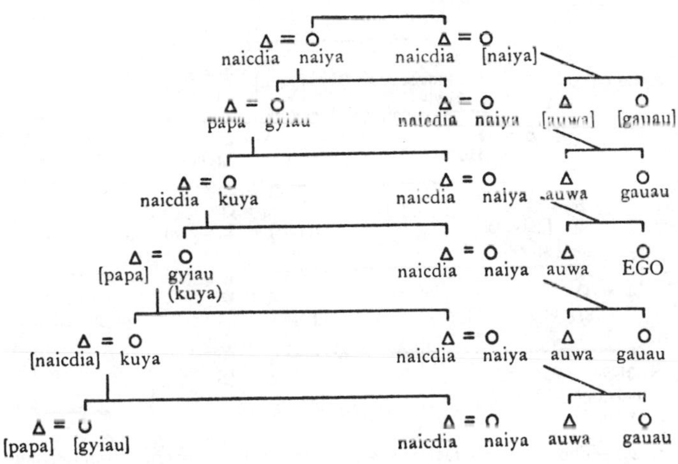

FIG. 24.—The father's matrilineal lineage. Ego = female. Terms in brackets are reconstructions; in parentheses are alternates.

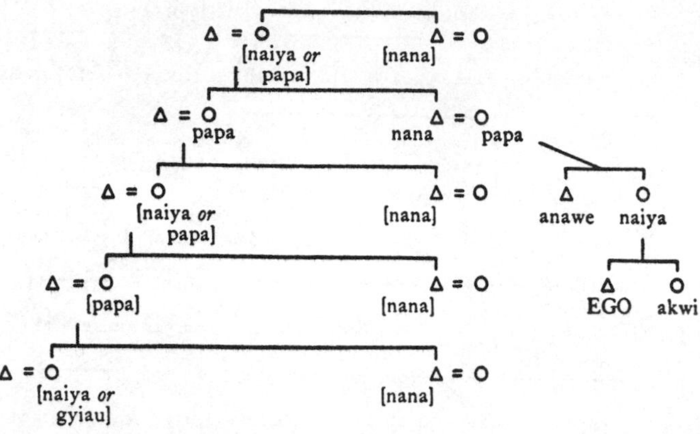

FIG. 25.—The mother's father's matrilineal lineage. Ego = male. Terms in brackets are reconstructions.

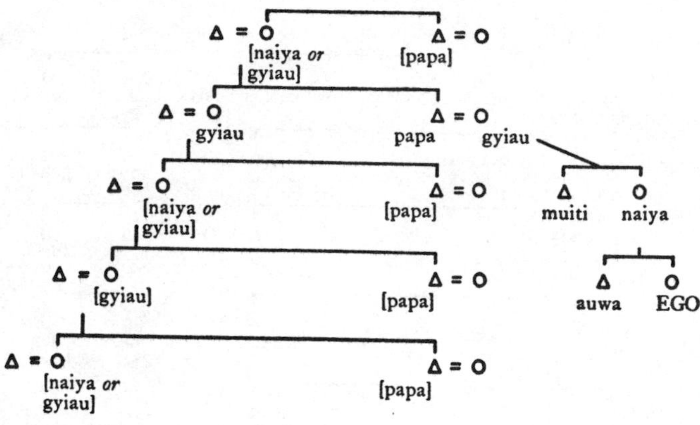

FIG. 26.—The mother's father's matrilineal lineage. Ego = female. Terms in brackets are reconstructions.

and mother's mother (female speaking). These terms are also used as verbal reciprocals for the appropriate grandchildren.

A man uses a special term for his mother's brother; this term is also used for the sister's son. His sister's daughter is called by the same term as his mother. A woman, on the other hand, calls her mother's brother by the same term that she uses for her son and her sister's son; her sister's daughter she classes with her own daughter. The father's sister is *kuya;* her children are "father" and "father's sister" or "grandmother."

These (and other) confusing applications of kinship terminology become clearer if we examine them in terms of lineage diagrams. In ego's own matrilineal lineage a man calls the women either "mother" (*naiya*), "sister" (*akwi*), or "grandmother" (*papa*); the men are either "mother's brother" (*anawe*) or "brother" (*tiume*). Alternate generations are classed together in the terminology. All women marrying men of ego's lineage are called *piye* ("female relative-in-law"), except for the mother's brother's wife, who may be called "mother"; all men marrying into the lineage in ego's generation and below are called *wati* ("male relative-in-law").[13] All children of men of ego's lineage are "son" and "daughter," regardless of generation.

Where ego is female, the situation is parallel but somewhat more complex. The women of ego's lineage are "sister," "mother," "grandmother," and "mother" in ascending generations, "daughter," "granddaughter," and (probably) "daughter" in the descending ones. The men of ego's lineage alternate between "brother" and "son," except for ego's sister's daughter's son, who is classed as a "grandson" (*papa*).[14] The terms used for men and women marrying into the lineage are the same as for a male ego, but children of men of the lineage vary—the children of "brothers" are "son" and "daughter," whereas the children of "sons" are "grandson" and "granddaughter," thus giving another pattern of alternation by generation.

The father's matrilineal lineage offers a simpler pattern of kinship terminology. For a man all the men of the father's lineage are called "father"; the women of the father's lineage are generally referred to as "father's sister" (*kuya*), but the father's mother, father's sister's daughter, and possibly the father's sister's daughter's daughter's daughter are called *papa* ("grandmother"—"granddaughter").[15] While Parsons states that *naiya* "mother," may be used for great-grandmother, irrespective of line, it is probable that this term is not used in the case of the father's mother's mother. The term *naiya* may be used for the father's sister, however. Parsons notes that "you refer to any clanswoman of your father as *s'ak'u'ya*, but in address, if the woman is your senior, you call her 'mother,' the reciprocal being, of course, 'daughter' or 'son.' "[16] The women who marry men of the father's lineage are called "mother," the terms for men marrying into the father's lineage are not clear. Parsons gives the term for father's sister's husband as "father";[17] this is consistent with the reciprocal, which is "child," on the principle that the husband adopts his wife's terminology for her relatives. On this basis the terms for father's sister's daughter's husband can be reconstructed as *nana* ("grandfather"—"grandson"), which suggests an alternating pattern for men marrying into the father's lineage. Children whose fathers belong to the same lineage are "brothers" and "sisters," regardless of generation. A woman makes parallel distinctions for the father's lineage.

Kinship terms are also applied to the mother's father's lineage apparently; Parsons' genealogies are not too clear on this point, but she notes that "you are expected to know not only the members of your parents' clans but of their fathers' clans, at least of your mother's father's clan."[18] Presumably the women of the lineage would be called "grandmother" and the men "grandfather," though a reconstruction in terms of reciprocals would suggest an alternation of "grandmother" and "mother" for women of the mother's father's lineage. To the extent that the father's father's lineage is recognized, grandparent terms would be used.

EXTENSIONS

Kinship terms are extended from the lineage to the clan on a simplified basis. One's own clanspeople are most important, but the father's clan is likewise an important group. Parsons recorded *s'a'wi*, "member of my own clan," as the only distinctive clan term she learned;[19] *s'a'wit^yemishe* refers to "my clanspeople" as a group. Senior clanswomen are called "our mother"; senior clansmen either *s'amuiti* (female speaking) or *anawe;* contemporaries use sibling terms. The father's clansmen are referred to as "father," the clanswomen as "father's sister"; a child of any man of one's own clan is considered a "child of the clan," as in the other western Pueblos. There is no further extension to phratries, and Parsons, in the one case of linked clans of which she heard, the Eagle-Sun, noted only that "the Sun clanspeople think of the Eagle clanspeople as in some way related, calling them their elders, *nawai'*."[20]

There are, in addition, a variety of collective terms for groups of kinsmen: "all my brothers," "all my sisters," etc.[21] Parsons also notes that the terms for father and mother are used "to designate individuals who are in a way in a social relation to the speaker that resembles the relations of parents to their children."[22] Thus anyone in whose house you grow up may be called "mother"; likewise parents-in-law, ceremonial parents, and others are called by parental terms. The term *naiya*, "mother," may be used in direct address for a variety of relatives, such as the father's sister, mother's brother's wife, mother's brother's daughter, and wife (teknonymy), where they are "matrons," i.e., mothers of children.

Where the Catholic rite of baptism is observed, kinship terms are used between the families concerned rather than the familiar Spanish terms. Kinship terms are also used for the wedding sponsors in the same way. The extensions of kinship at marriage will be discussed below.

Initiation into the Katcina cult involves the selection of a "ceremonial father." While Parsons was not able to secure details as to the Katcina initiation, she is fairly sure that kinship is extended to the "ceremonial father's" clan. Initiation into one of the Medicine societies does involve an extension of kinship. The head chooses a member to become the "ceremonial father" of the novice. During the initiation the latter is given a new life and a new name; his "ceremonial father" then takes him home and summons his clanswomen to wash the initiate's head and body and to give him presents. Thereafter the initiate is called "child of the clan."

Parsons lists a number of ritual extensions of kinship. Katcinas are addressed as "father," and kinship terms are used between Katcina personators. While a medicine man is addressed as "father" in ritual smoking, he is normally called "mother," as a representative of Iatiku, the great mother deity.[23] The corn-ear fetishes and altars associated with her are also called "mother"; kinship terms are likewise used for a variety of supernaturals.[24] The extension of kinship terms to the natural species after which the clans are named is not clear, though prayers are offered to these "totems" for assistance in various undertakings. Thus kinship terms are extended to express not only social relationships between people but also ritual relationships between individuals and groups and various aspects of nature.

The wide extension of kinship makes it possible for two individuals to be related to each other in a variety of ways. Parsons has discussed a number of such instances but has not attempted to work out the order of preference. She notes in several cases the preference of clan-derived terms to kin terms, particularly where the latter are on the father's side. Thus a clan term is preferred for a father's brother's child (not a close kinship relation in matrilineal lineage systems) who is also a clansman, paternal clan terms are preferred for the father's sister's son, clan terms are preferred over affinal connections, and clan terms are preferred over the "grandparent-grandchild" reciprocals for the mother's mother's brother and the father's mother's brother.[25] This priority of the lineage principle over the "grandparent-grandchild" reciprocals is of considerable theoretical interest, both in reconstructing the historical development of the Laguna kinship system and for comparative purposes.

THE HOUSEHOLD

The Laguna household corresponds in general with that of the other western Pueblos; "it tends to be of the compound family type, consisting of three rather than of two generations."[26] The normal pattern was for the married daughters to continue living at home, and in native theory the house and its furnishings belong to the women of the household. Parsons' analysis of the household census indicates the partial breakdown of these patterns under the influence of modern acculturation and the movement to farming communities.[27]

The extended maternal family ordinarily occupied a cluster of contiguous rooms, additional rooms being added as needed. This has resulted in related families within the same clan occupying adjacent houses, though there is no clan localization as such. These related family units approximate to maternal lineages, so far as the women are concerned. The Laguna household thus consists of a group of related women (a segment of a lineage), their brothers who have not yet married, their husbands who have come from other households, and their children and grandchildren. The husbands who marry into the household and lineage are at first related only through their wives; they address their new relatives by the same term their wife uses but are themselves called *wati*, "male relatives-in-law." Later, as they have children, they become a "father" and, ultimately, a "grandfather." The wives of these men, in turn, are called *piye*, "female relative-in-law," by their husband's relatives, and each ordinarily uses the kinship terms for her husband's relatives which he employs.[28] The men who marry out of their natal household still retain their lineage and household affiliations, however, and return for ritual purposes or in case of divorce or the death of their spouse.

The relation of the household to the lineage and clan is clearer than at Acoma and parallels the situation at Zuni and among the Hopi. It seems evident that there are multiple lineages for several clans, and certain of the houses are repositories for ritual paraphernalia and may be considered as "clanhouses." There is no information on the ownership or control of land by household or clan. Parsons indicates that land and other property is owned and inherited as are houses; it is probable that land has been affected by acculturative forces to an even greater extent than house ownership.[29] The larger amount of land available at Laguna may keep land from being an acute problem, so far as the community is concerned; the movement out to farming colonies has undoubtedly brought about further changes.

KINSHIP BEHAVIOR

Parsons has provided valuable observations on the duties and obligations of certain relatives, particularly in connection with the important occasions in the life of an individual. After birth the child is protected by a corn-ear "mother;" four days later the infant is presented to the sun. On the fourth morning a medicine man belonging to one of the curing societies comes and lays out an altar containing a corn-ear fetish symbolizing Iatiku, the Earth Mother deity. He gives the child a drink of medicine and sprinkles mother and child. The mother's mother[30] then takes the infant outside, accompanied by her sisters, and says a prayer. The medicine man also prays to Mother Iatiku and Father Sun, offering them the child.[31]

Naming practices are variable. In some cases the father's mother or father's sister may come on the fourth day, wash the child's head, and give it a name. Sometimes a grandfather will give his name to his grandson—in one account a deity tells a man to give his own name to his grandson "because you are getting old and you have lived for a long time."[32] American names are given at baptism by the godparents.

Names are said to have clan significance, and naming appears to be a function of the father's clan, though in some cases the names refer to one's own clan and in other cases to the father's clan. It is possible that persons receive several names at different periods, as among the Hopi, or that naming practices are in process of change. Parsons notes the use of Spanish names and the increase in the use of patronymics.[33]

The training of children was primarily in the hands of the members of the household. The grandparents are of particular importance in this connection, the grandmother or grandfather caring for the child when the mother is busy with household tasks. Girls also look after their younger siblings. The mother's brother is thought of as a "guardian" of his sister's children and has considerable authority over them. Cases are cited of maternal uncles leaving fields and ceremonial property to their nephews, though personal masks are inherited from the father. Presumably the ritual information associated with fetishes and offices is transmitted from uncle to nephew, particularly where it is clan controlled.

At initiation into the Katcina cult and the Medicine societies the ceremonial father's sisters wash the head of the initiate, and he is given a new name. The father's sister also plays an important role in the salt-gathering ritual and in hunting rituals. There is some evidence of a joking relationship with paternal relatives in general and the father's sister in particular.[34]

Marriage resulted in the acquisition of a whole new set of relatives and the beginnings of many new activities. Marriage is forbidden with one's own clan and not approved in connection with the father's clan, though clan exogamy is beginning to break down. Marriage as elsewhere in the pueblos is monogamous, but separation is fairly common, though less so than in Zuni. The sororate and the levirate do not occur. Parsons noted a tendency for brothers and sisters to marry into the same clan.

At marriage a man normally goes to his wife's household, though on occasion he may bring her to his own household or build a separate residence elsewhere. With the birth of children, the husband and wife use teknonymy, referring to their relationship to the child. Through the child the two households are brought into closer relationship; we have noted the duties of the father's sister and the mother's brother above.

A man has the task of helping to support his wife's household, but he is a "mother's brother" in turn to the children in his natal household. Husband and wife keep their own property, though they may pool their resources in land and sheep. A wife has definite responsibilities in connection with hunting; should she fail to carry them out, the hunt would be fruitless.

The old marriage ritual has not been recorded, and the present marriage ceremony is that of the Catholic church. But there is evidence of a good deal of premarital freedom, and illegitimacy is common, no disapproval being expressed beyond concern over adding an extra member to the household without a husband to aid in its support. Crane found a considerable similarity between Hopi and Laguna in connection with marriage: "Every trick and argument that the Hopi people had thrust upon me earlier, concerning the mating of their children and the control of offspring, were promptly duplicated at Laguna."[35]

Divorce or separation is common though not sanctioned by the Catholic church and frowned on by the Protestants. Laguna townspeople criticized the looseness at Zuni, but Parsons noted that "there is little if any more permanency at Laguna than at Zuni, the only difference is that the matches in early life are at Zuni frank relationships and, at Laguna, surreptitious."[36] She likewise recorded a number of changes of mates without any adverse criticism.

For serious illness a medicine man is called and cures the patient by extracting objects which witches have shot into the body. At death the medicine man comes and prepares the body for burial. A father's clanswoman, normally the father's sister, is summoned to wash the corpse; whether she gives it a new name for the afterworld is not recorded. The mother's brother or father may dig the grave,[37] and the body is buried with the head to the east. After four days the father's sisters and clanswomen come and wash the mourners' hair, and all the clanspeople of the deceased likewise wash their own hair. After the death of a wife, a husband may stay to look after his children or return to his mother's or sister's house. If the latter, he is escorted home by his wife's parents in ritual fashion.[38]

We have noted above that houses are inherited primarily by the women of the household, while fields and sheep are now divided among the children. Ritual knowledge and paraphernalia are mainly inherited in the maternal line, except for masks.

The faces of the deceased are painted "to show who it is to our mother."[39] According to some of Parsons' informants, there are special paintings for each clan; the medicine men have special facial paintings regardless of their clan. The facial paintings resemble those of Katcina impersonators, and some of the songs sung over the corpse imply an association with the storm clouds.[40] Some, at least, of the dead go to Wenimatse, the home of the Katcinas in the west near Zuni. Neither Boas[41] nor Parsons[42] believes that the dead are associated with the Katcina, though recent evidence from Acoma and other Keresan pueblos suggests such an association as possible.[43] The dead are thought to return to Shipap, the Place of Emergence, where they dwell with their mother, Iatiku.[44] On All Souls' Day the dead are elaborately fed; they are likewise fed with crumbs at ordinary meals or by bits of food put in the fire.

SUMMARY AND INTERPRETATION

Parsons, in analyzing Laguna kinship terminology from the standpoint of Kroeber's psychological principles of generation, sex, age, etc., found many inconsistencies which she could not explain.[45] She remarks on the indifference to generation, the priority of the female line with reference to seniority, the confusion of clan and kin terms, and the puzzling self-reciprocal grandparent-grandchild terms. The terminology for cross-cousins was particularly difficult to explain, since it seemed to have no close parallels in the Pueblos; hence she was forced to account for it in "circular fashion." Thus the application of the term "son" to the mother's brother by a woman "probably explains why the grandparent-grandchild terms are applied between certain cross-cousins, a Laguna anomaly; the child of anyone you call son, you naturally call grandson or granddaughter."[46] The Laguna terminology for cross-cousins is actually not anomalous—the Hopi, for example, have precisely the same pattern, except for self-reciprocal terminology. Further, the Hopi call the mother's brother by a special term, "mother's brother," so that Parsons' explanation will not fit the Hopi case.

These "anomalous" usages are clarified by organizing the terminology, not on a generation basis, but in terms of a lineage pattern. The inconsistencies in application of kinship terms largely disappear and a logical system emerges, based on the matrilineal lineage and household. The problems to be solved likewise shift from explaining isolated segments, such as cross-cousin terminology, to explaining the larger lineage patterns of grouping and alternation.

The differentiation of behavior patterns is consonant with the terminological differentiation, so far as data are available. The mother's lineage and household are responsible for training and support; the father's lineage and household for assistance at the various crises of life. The general pattern of the kinship system, in terms of both structure and behavior, is very similar to that of Hopi or Zuni; it is likewise more sharply defined than the system so far reported from Acoma.

There are two respects in which the Laguna kinship system differs from the Hopi pattern: self-reciprocal terms are used for a considerable number of relatives, and there is a tendency to link alternate generations together through the terminology to give an "alternating" type of kinship structure. These two differences seem to be related, in that the first may be a foundation for the second. The self-reciprocal pattern of kinship terminology is characteristic of the Keresan pueblos in general and is found also at Zuni and among the Tewa pueblos of the Rio Grande; it is also characteristic to a high degree among the neighboring southern Athabaskan tribes and among certain of the Basin and Plains groups. In many of these tribes the self-reciprocal terminology is associated with a bilateral generational kinship system.[47] But at Laguna it is thoroughly integrated with, and subordinated to, the lineage principle of classification. Wherever there is a conflict between the grandparent-grandchild reciprocals and the lineage principle, terms based on the latter are usually preferred.

Self-reciprocal terminology, the utilization of the same linguistic term for a pair of relatives, offers an important problem in itself. Is it a purely linguistic phenomenon, or does it have behavioral correlates? One hypothesis which has been proposed suggests that self-reciprocal terminology may be associated with some significant similarity between the two relatives in native thinking. There is not enough information given on the duties and obligations of siblings, or of mother's brothers and sister's sons, to answer the question; in regard to the grandparent-grandchild relations, however, we have noted a close association, which is reflected in a variety of activities such as care and naming, which may be significant.

The pattern of alternation of generations in the Laguna kinship system is probably carried further than in almost any other North American Indian social structure. We have noted some slight tendency to alternation of generation among the Hopi in that the terms for "older brother" and "younger brother" might be applied to the men of one's own generation, and of two generations above and below, in the lineage. At Hano verbally reciprocal equivalents are applied to the mother's brother and sister's son and extended to the men of alternate generations within the lineage. But at Laguna exact verbal reciprocals are extended by a man to his brothers, mother's mother's brothers, and sister's daughter's sons, and the mother's brother–sister's son reciprocal is likewise extended to alternate generations. Further, a man extends the term "mother" to alternate generations in his lineage and extends the term "sister" to his sister's daughter's daughter. A woman carries the process even further for the men and women of her lineage and, in addition, applies an alternating pattern to the children of men of the lineage. For the father's lineage both men and women apply an alternating generation pattern to the women of the father's lineage and perhaps to men marrying these women of the father's lineage. A reconstruction of the pattern for the mother's father's lineage suggests a similar pattern.

The explanation of these alternating patterns will ultimately come from comparative studies, since they may be associated with both lineage and generational structures. In the western Pueblos they are organized in connection with the lineage grouping; the alternating pattern is particularly appropriate to the "timeless" character of the lineage and clan, in that they are thought to extend back indefinitely into the past and forward into the future. Any particular generation is merely one of an infinite number and is of special importance only to its members.

The pattern of alternating generations probably derives from the relationship of the grandparental and grandchild generations in social life, in part at least. We have noted some evidence of an especially close relationship between these generations at Laguna. The particular relationship between the equivalence of relatives, as expressed in verbal reciprocity, and the equivalence of generations, as expressed by using the same terms for members of alternate generations, which is found at Laguna may be a special development. Zuni, with grandparent-grandchild reciprocals and other partial equivalences, has not organized them in alternating patterns or subordinated them, to the same extent, to the lineage pattern, so far as our information goes. The Acoma situation seems parallel to that of Laguna, if our reconstructions are correct; the presence of self-reciprocal terminology and alternating generations in other Keresan groups needs to be evaluated for any more general conclusions.

The question as to whether the particular combination of lineage and self-reciprocal patterns at Laguna represents an old Keresan pattern or has been borrowed in part from the western Pueblos is a crucial problem. Parsons tends to answer such questions in terms of borrowing or acculturation, and it is clear that such processes have been operating to some extent. But the Laguna kinship structure is more complex and highly organized than any of its neighbors, so that it is difficult to account for the kinship structure through contacts and occasional intermarriage. Even Acoma, on the basis of present knowledge, seems to have a less complex kinship system.

Furthermore, Laguna was founded around 1700 primarily by Keresans from the Rio Grande. Presumably early Laguna social structure reflected the Rio Grande patterns of that period. While there has been considerable contact with Acoma (witness the dialect divisions) and some intermarriage, the two pueblos have engaged in considerable conflict during the last century over land and church property.[48] There has likewise been considerable contact with Zuni and, to a lesser degree, with Hopi. One important factor in maintaining or enhancing the kinship structure has been the internal developments in Laguna. In contrast to Acoma, there has not been the process of increasing centralization at the expense of the clans; rather the reverse has happened. The clan system has thus remained important—or developed further in importance—and has thus maintained the lineage grouping of relatives and households as an important functioning group. Tentatively, then, I would suggest that the Laguna kinship system reflects earlier eastern Keresan patterns to a considerable extent. That these patterns resemble modern western Pueblo patterns is due, not so much to contact and borrowing, as to the continuation of a strong clan system. From this standpoint the greater "bilaterality" of the eastern Keresan pueblos would be the results of Spanish and American acculturation since 1700 (or before) and the greater centralization necessary to cope with internal and external affairs.[49]

Parsons has advanced the theory of onetime cross-cousin marriage to explain the situation at Laguna, where there is an identification of *papa* (father's sister's daughter, mother's brother's son, etc.) with "wife" or "husband." At present I am inclined to believe that this behavior is part of a joking relationship between a man and the women of his father's clan, parallel to that found among the Hopi. That cross-cousin marriage was once an *early* Keresan pattern is quite possible, but I doubt that it was ever practiced during the history of Laguna, except as occasional marriages in the father's clan would be between classificatory cross-cousins.[50]

The recent changes which have taken place in the Laguna kinship system can be reconstructed in part from Parsons' monograph. It is probable that the mother's father's clan is no longer of much importance, and it is not clear whether the father's father's clan was ever significant. Within the father's clan there is a tendency to *address* the father's sister as "mother," though in reference she is called "father's sister."[51] This tendency has gone much further at Acoma, and there has been a consequent classification of the father's sister's children as "brother" and "sister"; I would suggest that a parallel shift will take place at Laguna. Within one's own lineage and clan, fewer changes are in evidence as yet. But there is a tendency to classify the mother's brother's wife as "mother" rather than "female relative-in-law," and some of Parsons' informants were beginning to attempt to distinguish between "child" and "child of a clan" and between *s'amuiti*, "my son," and *amuiti*, "mother's brother" (female speaking).[52] There is some slight tendency for the terms for relatives-in-law, *piye* and *wati*, to be used reciprocally rather than nonreciprocally. These changes affect primarily the relatives who are "attached" to the maternal lineage through marriage rather than the classification of relatives within the lineage itself.

The breakdown of the household structure, which is taking place in connection with modern acculturation and dispersion, will bring about profound changes. One result will probably be to equate more closely the mother's and father's relatives, a process which has taken place at Acoma and which White has recently noted at Santa Ana.[53] There will probably be a continuing and correlative shift to a "bilateral" generational type of kinship structure, a process we have seen in various stages of development among the western Pueblos.

The Reverend Samuel Gorman, who came to Laguna in 1851 as a missionary, recorded a partial kinship system for Morgan's *Systems of Consanguinity and Affinity of the Human Family*. While the system is incomplete, the terms given are comparable with those recorded by Parsons. Gorman distinguishes grandfather, *nanăhashte*, and grandmother, *päpäkeeyon*, from grandson, *să-nănă*, and granddaughter, *să-papa*, and likewise distinguishes older and younger brother and older and younger sister.[54] These distinctions I am inclined to believe are descriptive ones; the alternative is to believe that the self-reciprocal grandparent-grandchild terms have developed since 1860, which the comparative evidence for Keresan pueblos belies.

Morgan, in his analysis of the Laguna system,[55] correctly works out some of the correlations but apparently adds a few of his own. Thus he states that "my father's sister is my mother, *Niya*," whereas no term for this relative is given in the schedules.[56] Further he states that "the relationship of cousin is unknown. My father's sister's son is my son, whence by correlation my mother's brother's son is my father."[57] Aside from the fact that neither of these terms appears in the schedules, Morgan has exactly reversed the correct usage, though he compares the Laguna system with that of the Creek, Cherokee, and other "Crow" types.[58]

The recent publication of Bourke's journal has given us new information on some of the social usages at Laguna in the 1880's, at the time when the railroad was being built across New Mexico and Arizona, and when many new changes were being introduced into the pueblo. From Pratt and Marmon, whites who were closely identified with Laguna, he received the following information:

The Pueblo of Laguna was much reduced in population by the absence of so many upon their farms outside: these farms were gentile farms. The pueblo itself was divided up into gentile quarters or wards. Children bore names referring to the clan of mother or to that of the father. The women owned the houses. Women possessed, even if they did not always exercise the right of proposing to the young men of their choice. . . . The power of the wife over property is apparent to every purchaser: upon her consent depends the closing of bargains, which she cements or breaks arbitrarily. . . .

If a man dies in Laguna or Acoma, his children are cared for by his wife's clan. Divorces are obtainable for cause, generally decided upon by the council, composed of the governor and his assistants; the man, in such cases, generally leaves home, taking with him only his blankets. . . . The people of Laguna don't have any fear of their mother-in-law: this follows as a logical consequence of their mode of marriage which requires the groom to take up his residence with his wife's people.[59]

These statements both add new information and clarify the older patterns of matrilocal residence, female house ownership, and maternal control which Parsons has noted and correctly interpreted.

When comparative data are available in greater detail from the other Keresan pueblos in the east, it will be possible to reconstruct the changes which have gone on over a longer period of time. It is encouraging to find that White, the foremost student of Keresan ethnology, has come to similar conclusions regarding the nature of changes in the kinship system from his recent work at Santa Ana and other Rio Grande pueblos. Furthermore, these changes are still in process, and some of the hypotheses may be tested by further research.

The Clan System

The clan is the most important social grouping at Laguna, being matrilineal, exogamous, and totemically named. Parsons has a detailed discussion and analysis of the Laguna clan system,[60] to which little can be added. Table 9 lists the Laguna clans as recorded by Parsons and others; it will be noted that this list corresponds rather closely to the Acoma clans and to those of other Keresan pueblos as well.

Parsons' list, based on a town census, is the most accurate, and indicates some fifteen surviving clans, with four listed as extinct. Bourke's 1881 list[61] checks rather well with her list, so far as it goes. He translates *meyo* as "Frog" rather than "Lizard" but does not mention Roadrunner, Locust, or Turquoise, and he equates Deer and Antelope. He lists "Seed-Grass" and "Sand" as extinct. Hodge's "Red Corn" and "Yellow Corn" clans represent a misinterpretation of the data, according to Parsons. The

TABLE 9*

LAGUNA CLANS

Clan	Bourke (1881)	Bandelier (1892)	Hodge (1896)	Parsons (1923)
Water	×	×	×	× (7)
Parrot	×	×	×	× (5)
Turkey	×	....	×	× (5)
Sun	×	×	×	× (4)
Bear	×	×	×	× (4)
Lizard	×	....	×	× (3)
Earth or Sand	E	....	E	....
Chaparral Cock	....	×	×	× (3)
Badger	×	×	×	× (2)
Eagle	×	×	×	× (1)
Corn	×	×	....	× (5)
Red Corn	....	....	×	....
Yellow Corn	....	....	×	....
Oak	×	....	×	× (1)
Locust	....	....	....	× (1)
Antelope	×	×	×	×
Turquoise	....	×	×	×
Coyote	×	×	×	×
Deer	E	....	....	E
Pumpkin	....	....	....	E
Wheat	E (Seed-Grass)	....	....	E
Snake	×	× (Rattle-snake)	×	E
Wolf	....	....	×	....
Mountain Lion	....	....	E	....

* Based on Table 8 of Parsons, *Laguna Genealogies*, p. 211, with additional data from Bloom (ed.), "Bourke on the Southwest," Part XII, pp. 370–71. Parsons' list is based on a household census and genealogies; the numbers in parentheses refer to the number of women household heads. × = present; E = extinct or unrepresented at Old Laguna.

extinct "Seed-Grass" clan noted by Bourke may be the prototype for the Wheat clan, an obviously post-Spanish clan name.

The Origin Myth at Laguna has not been recorded, except in fragmentary fashion, so that we have no account of the mythical origin of the clan system comparable to that of Acoma. Furthermore, the fragments recorded by Boas show much acculturation; one of the creator sisters being transformed into a brother who becomes the father of the whites.[62] Parsons, however, recorded a portion of the Origin Myth in which Mother Iatiku has three sisters who acted as creators.[63] Parsons also records a myth that the clans were led out from Shipap by the Water clan and that, after a great flood, a Water clansman from Sia and a Coyote clanswoman from Zuni settled the site of Laguna after being chased away several times by Acomans.[64] Of her own list, Parsons is inclined to doubt the former existence of the "extinct" Snake, Deer, Pumpkin, and Wheat clans; the Coyote clan, however, is said to exist at Paraje, one of the farming villages. The Turquoise clan is made up primarily of men, with no household listed, and the Antelope clan is near extinction.[65] The Snake and Pumpkin clans are represented at Acoma; the Deer clan is also mentioned in the Origin Myth there. The Coyote clan and the Turquoise clan are noted in the eastern Keresan pueblos, though the clan status of the latter is not too clear.

There is no phratry grouping or moiety organization of clans for exogamic purposes, though there is a dual organization of clans for ceremonial purposes. Parsons found a couple of instances of linked clans: the Lizard clan was also called Earth "because the lizard goes on the earth" (possibly the result of a merging of the "extinct" Earth or Sand clan?), and the Sun clanspeople think of the Eagle people as related and call them their "elders," without, however, affecting intermarriage.[66] Clan exogamy is still relatively strong, though Parsons recorded some four marriages within the clan and some nine marriages into the father's clan.

The number and the significance of lineages within the larger clans are not clear from the data available, but it is probable that the blocks of related households, in some cases at least, represent lineage units. There is a rough correlation between the number of such blocks and the women heads of households listed by Parsons.[67] Certain households are associated with ceremonial paraphernalia which were cared for by the women of the household; there are also clan rituals which are performed by the clan head, presumably in the main clan household.

The Laguna clan has definite economic, ceremonial, and juridical functions, in contrast to the more limited functions noted at Acoma. If Bourke's statements quoted above are correct, landownership was by clan, since the farms are referred to as "gentile fields." Clansmen helped one another in their fields. The clan head, on request, would ask the clansmen to come and work and prayed to the beings connected with his clan for ritual assistance.[68] The present system of landownership is one of mixed clan and individual ownership, with men owning fields and with inheritance primarily to children rather than to the maternal household.

The clan head or *nawai* was a senior male who had the proper knowledge, not necessarily the eldest clansman. Parsons recorded one account which stated that clan heads were chosen for life at clan meetings and that they went into successive retreats for rain at the summer solstice and assisted the medicine men at the winter solstice. Fetish animals and the *kotona* or perfect ears of corn, as well as other ritual paraphernalia, were also in the keeping of these clan heads.[69]

Disputes within the clan are settled by the oldest member of the clan, whether he is the clan head or not. If the dispute cannot be settled by the clan, it is taken before the governor, or other officials. Clanspeople are consulted when a man considers joining a Medicine society; presumably they have to assist him in making the payments and in other ways. There seems to be no such consultation at marriage, though the immediate households are probably involved.[70]

The clan names refer to animals, birds, or objects of nature and parallel those of other pueblos. Parsons notes that the clan head will pray to the animals or objects connected with his clan for assistance, as among the Hopi.[71]

Each clan has grinding songs sung by the women while grinding corn together. Stick races are said to have been run by clans, the sticks being painted according to clan and clan symbols being painted on the backs of the runners. We have noted above the painting of the face at death according to clan, and there is a suggestion that different colors of corn are associated with different clans.

Whether each clan had a fetish *iyatik*, "mother," kept in the clanhouse and cared for by the women is not clear; the *iyatik* in Laguna are associated primarily with the *cheani*, medicine men, but are in the custody of women who feed them daily and pass them on from generation to generation, lending them out to the *cheani* groups. Katcina masks are likewise cared for by kinswomen, usually in the natal household.[72]

The ceremonial prerogatives of clans at Laguna parallel those noted for Acoma. The Antelope and Badger clans have the right to officiate at Katcina dances, acting as "fathers" to the Katcinas.[73] Their precedence in this connection is supported by a myth as to how they brought back the Katcina when they tried to run away from the people; in the Laguna version, the Badgers succeeded when the Antelopes failed.[74] The Badger clan now controls all the Katcina masks, but originally perhaps the Antelope clan took precedence, since Parsons noted that the one remaining Antelope clansman superseded the Badger clansman as "father" of the Katcina in 1920, and in outlying colonies men are "made Antelope clan" in order to act as "fathers" of the Katcina at dances.[75] Formerly, the masks were kept in the Badger and Antelope houses when not being used. Certain of the Katcina are said to belong to particular clans—the Corn clan keeps and impersonates the *chonata* Katcina, the Parrot clan controlled the *gumeyoish* masks, etc.[76] Boas describes the procedure of a Corn clan ceremonial in which the cacique and his wife, the Katcina, and the Antelope and Badger clans play important roles.[77] The Salt Place and the gathering of salt were controlled by the Parrot clan at Laguna. The collection of salt was a ritual occasion, and Acoma and Laguna collectors went together to Zuni Salt Lake under the leadership of the Parrot clansmen. The clanswomen remaining at home prayed for their success and, on their return, sang for the Salt Woman and distributed the salt. The father's sisters carried the salt to the households of the collectors; the latter then went to their aunt's house to have their heads washed.[78]

While the various clans have migration legends accounting for their presence at Laguna, Parsons found no evidence of actual migration by clan; rather the few historical cases represent families or single women who moved to Laguna and multiplied. The Badger clan is said to be descended from a Zuni woman who came three or four generations ago, the Bear clan is attributed to a Hopi girl who escaped from the Utes, and the Sun clan is divided among four subgroups: Zuni, Hopi, Jemez, and Navaho; but Parsons believes that there were other clansmen of these groups at Laguna before the migration.[79] The general tendency to relate clans to similarly named groups elsewhere makes the equation of new groups with older ones a relatively simple matter. The migration of Laguna people to Isleta, as a result of a factional dispute in the 1870's, was on a larger scale. Some thirty to forty persons are said to have gone, representing members of some five or more clans which were accommodated to the Isletan Corn Groups.[80] The probability that some of the early settlers at Laguna were fugitives who had settled temporarily with the Hopi at Second Mesa is discussed by Crane;[81] Bancroft[82] believes that the families which Governor Anza brought out from the Hopi villages in 1780 were settled at Moquino in the Laguna region.

Ceremonial Organization

The ceremonial organization at Laguna has largely disintegrated, but it formerly centered around the Medicine societies and the Katcina cult, with the Warrior's, Hunter's, and "Clown" societies also represented. The *cheani* (medicine) orders are definitely separate from the Katcina cult, but the two are interrelated in many ways.

The Katcina cult apparently was at one time tribal wide and associated with kiva groupings; its breakdown several generations ago makes its reconstruction difficult. There are several groups of supernaturals: (1) the Katcina who came up from the Place of Emergence and live at Wenimatse in the northwest; (2) the *kopishtaya* who live in the east at the sunrise, where they went with the *kashare;* and (3) the *shiwana* who are the storm clouds and are specifically associated with the six directions.[83]

Parsons, in one account, mentions that the Katcina are divided into two groups: (1) Black—*chakwena*, and (2) Blue—*hemish*, *kohashtoch*, and *haiya* ("all kinds");[84] in another she lists three Katcina organizations: (1) *chakwena*, (2) *waiyush* ("duck"), and (3) *gwapeuts*.[85] The *chakwena* group has priority in that initiation into *chakwena* entitles a man to dance in other groups, but not vice versa. A Katcina chief is in charge of all these groups; in addition, each group has its own head and assistants. There is no evidence that headship or the kivas were associated with particular clans.

The kiva organization is no longer in operation, and information is contradictory as to the old system. Informants mention one to four kivas. In the 1870's there were two kivas, called *k'a'ach*, to the east and the west of the plaza; there were apparently also five or six rooms used by the Katcina dancers, and six or seven special rooms with decorated walls used by the *cheani* groups. Presumably these kivas had names; the last surviving kiva was called "badger house."

There is some evidence that the cacique controlled the kiva organization, as at Acoma, but the Antelope and Badger clans had special duties in connection with the Katcina cult. Children joined the kiva of their father, and women at marriage joined their husband's kiva. Novices were whipped by *tsitsinits*, the whipper Katcina (impersonated by a Flint *cheani*), and feathers made by the Badger clan were tied to their hair. The *kurena* sang, and new clothes and four ears of corn were given to the boys and girls. The ceremonial father gave the boys new names from his clan, and apparently their hair was then washed by Antelope and Badger clanswomen.[86] We have noted above the role of the Antelope and Badger clans in connection with the Katcina cult. The *chakwena* are somewhat different from the other Katcina groups. They are associated with Masewi, one of the twin War Gods, who is considered the son of Iatiku, and have some curing functions. There are also economic obligations between members. Parsons notes a tradition that the *chakwena* were introduced from Zuni, but this seems to conflict with their priority in the Katcina cult and their association with the War Gods.

The division of summer and winter is reflected in a myth in which the *shiwana* of the north and the *shiwana* of the south appear as contestants. Summer's weapons are thunder and lightning; winter's are hail, ice, and snow. In other connections the *chakwena* are associated with the "cloud spirits" of the north, while the *hemish* Katcina are associated with those of the south, all other Katcina being associated with the *shiwana* of the other directions. There are also animals and colors associated with the various directions.

The Katcina cult is concerned primarily with rain and general welfare. The Katcina dances are definitely thought to be connected with the weather, and bad thoughts or actions are rewarded with windstorms rather than rain. Dances were formerly held at the time of "retreats" during the solstice ceremonies and during the summer and fall. In recent years parallel dances have been held at various colonies, particularly Mesita.

The Medicine societies were disrupted by the split in the 1870's that sent the conservative orders to Mesita, and then to Isleta. At Laguna there were apparently the following Medicine societies:[87] (1) Osach (Sun) Cheani, (*a*) Shikane Cheani; (2) Fire Cheani; (3) Flint Cheani; (4) Shiwana Cheani; (5) Shahaiye Cheani; (6) Saiyap Cheani; and (7) Kapina Cheani. The *cheani* as a group were under the leadership of the Shikane Cheani, a leadership sanctioned by the importance of the sun.

Membership in one of the medicine orders was open to anyone, curing and trapping being the principal reasons for joining. The novice was given to an older shaman to be trained, and the initiation took place in the spring, the novice receiving a new name and being assisted by his relatives in paying the "doctor father." The whipping ritual is carried out by the Katcina, and masks are worn at initiation which belong to the *cheani* group.[88]

The Medicine societies were concerned primarily with "curing," but they also were connected with rain-making. The head *cheani* decided upon the time for the solstice ceremonies, in co-operation with the War Chiefs; formerly the societies went into "retreat," making prayer sticks, setting up altars, observing restrictions, and praying for health and welfare, rain, and good crops. In times of drought there were additional "retreats" and special pilgrimages to Mount Taylor to plant prayer sticks. During this pilgrimage the village held a communal rabbit hunt for the *cheani* and refrained from quarreling.

The Medicine societies cure through the power of their corn-ear fetishes which represent "Mother Iyatik," probably the most important deity, though the sun is thought of as the supreme power. These ritual ears of corn, we have noted, are kept in particular households and at present are loaned to surviving *cheani*. Parsons gives an account of the curing ceremony of the *Shikane*. The close relatives of both patient and shaman attend. The shaman sets up an altar[89] and uses a crystal to search for the heart of the patient which has been stolen by witches; with a bear's paw he rushes out and finds the patient's "heart." As the War Chiefs take it from him, he goes into an unconscious state and is revived by his female relatives. After the patient is given medicine, his relatives have their heads washed by the relatives of the shaman.[90]

The Medicine societies do not function as units in Laguna today; only the Shiwana Cheani are left, plus individual shamans who reside in various villages. Formerly the *cheani* groups had duties in connection with the selection and installation of the cacique and in connection with the Katcina cult, but it is difficult to tell from the data available whether these duties are old or recently acquired.

A warrior organization (*opi*) formerly existed, composed of men who had taken scalps from enemies, usually Navaho. After killing an enemy, a warrior spends four days fasting in the kiva; then his relatives bring him food and his head is washed. A Scalp Dance is then held in the plaza, during which the *opi* divide into two groups and go to the east and west kivas, with the *kashare* in charge of the east kiva and the *kurena* of the west kiva. Each group is accompanied by personations of the twin War Gods and their sister. The aunts, wives, and daughters of the *opi* stand outside the group of dancers.[91]

Nowadays the "War Dance" is danced with two groups, aligned by clan into an east and west group "according to their assignment to buildings on the east and west sides of the plaza."[92] A man may dance in both groups if his father's clan happens to be on the opposite side from his own. A similar ceremonial grouping by clans is also used for the *santu* dance.

Little is known of the hunting organization except that Caiyaik[a] and Tcaikats established the hunting rules in the Below. Mountain lion is the helper of the hunter, assisted by weasel, wildcat, wolf, and coyote.[93]

The *kashare* and *kurena* are sacred groups, designated as *cheani*, who were created in the underworld and assisted in the emergence of the people. The *kurena* at Laguna were associated with the Shikane Cheani and were said to live in the northeast; the *kashare* migrated with the *kopishtaya* to the house of the sun in the east. The two organizations have clown and war functions, as noted above; they are also in opposition to each other, alternating in their ceremonial activities. "Only *kashare* songs are sung from the winter solstice to the corn harvest. Only *kurena* songs from the harvest until the beginning of the season of *kashare* songs."[94]

The relation between these organizations and the Medicine societies is not clear. In theory members of neither organization were supposed to join the curing societies, nor could they become caciques, but exceptions have been noted in recent times, at least. *Opi* were likewise not supposed to remain members of curing societies, nor should *cheani* become *opi*. While the Medicine orders were separate from the *kurena* and *kashare*, all were known as *cheani*, as indeed were the Katcina members as well. At the winter solstice the heads of the *kurena* and *kashare* go with the Flint and Kapina shamans to the top of Mount Taylor to consult the prophetic hole there. Boas believes that "the selection of the four persons suggests that there may be a relation between *kashare* and Flint society and the *kurena* and the Kapina society, but direct information on this point is lacking."[95] The recent breakdown of ceremonial life has led to amalgamation and overlapping of function, so that it is difficult to disentangle the former situation. The Shikane and *kurena* groups apparently amalgamated after the split; the *kashare* have encroached on the *cheani* and taken over curing functions.

The Laguna sacred world is geographically organized with special homes for the major supernaturals.[96] The sun is said to be the supreme deity, but Parsons feels that "*iyatik* is the central or most authentic of all the Laguna deities."[97] She continues to live within the earth at Shipap; through her representative, the corn-ear "mother," the health and welfare of the people are maintained. The transformation of her sister into a man, Boas believes, is due to Catholic influence.[98]

The village hierarchy broke up in the middle of the nineteenth century. The last cacique, or *tiamoni hocheni*, of Laguna belonged to the Lizard clan, but his predecessors were members of other clans. The cacique is chosen by the medicine men and in theory should not be a shaman, although the last one was a Flint *cheani* as well as a War Priest. There is some evidence that the Flint *cheani* was the leading group in former times, since the Flint head, with the aid of the Shikane head, installed the new cacique and had the final choice in case of disagreement among the shamans.

The cacique was chosen for life and spent his time in prayer and sacrificed for village welfare. In return the men planted and harvested his fields, under the direction of the *kurena*, and the women cooked for him. The rabbits caught at the ceremonial solstice hunts were taken to the cacique and cooked and distributed to the Medicine society houses. For the last cacique, the people rebuilt his natal house as the chief's house.[99]

The cacique was assisted by the War Chiefs, representing the twin War Gods, who were concerned with war, hunting, and the guarding of rituals. There were possibly four "chiefs helpers" who assisted him and from among whom his successor was chosen. At the time of the religious split the cacique went to live at Mesita and his office lapsed, with some functions being taken over by the head of the Shikane-Kurena Cheani, and perhaps others by the Antelope and Badger clans and by the War Chiefs.

In recent times a group of secular officials is elected annually by a council of all the males held on January 1. The outlying colonies make nominations, and there is said to be no control of the voting. A governor and two lieutenant-governors are elected; also at this time three War Chiefs are chosen. The Shiwana Cheani now instal the new officers, transferring the cane of office from the outgoing governor to the new. The War Chiefs now take solstice observations, guard ceremonies, supervise Katcina dances, and plant prayer sticks, as well as having charge of the communal hunts.

Conclusions and Comparisons

Despite the diverse origins and relatively recent settlement of Laguna, its social structure is no hodgepodge but represents a highly integrated and specialized organization. In its essentials —kinship system, household grouping, and clan and ceremonial organization—the social structure at Laguna is composed of units similar to those of other western Pueblos and with similar functions in general. Judging by the test of *survival* as a social unit, the integration of Laguna has not been so adequate as that of Acoma, for example. But the forces bringing about social and cultural change have been much greater at Laguna than at any other western Pueblo.[100] A mission was early established and Spanish settlers were close at hand. The expansion of population and growing dependence on irrigation led to the growth of farm colonies. The main line of the railroad ran right by the pueblo for many years, to be followed by the highway. The Protestant activities were particularly strong at Laguna, and schools were early established. The inevitable conflict between "conservative" and "progressive" factions led to a crisis in which the conservatives removed from Laguna, with resultant disintegration of the ceremonial system.

But in the century and a half between 1700 and 1850, there is evidence that Laguna had welded her diverse heritage and borrowings into a well-ordered structure. Basic Keresan patterns were utilized—the kinship system was extended and elaborated, the clan system was filled in, the ceremonial organization was reconstructed, and the mythology was revised as a rationale for the resulting sociceremonial structure.

In this process kinship was utilized to a greater extent than other integrative devices; its elaboration may, in part at least, be the result of the greater difficulties in building up the clan and ceremonial systems. Unlike Acoma, which was able to centralize its organization to meet new problems, Laguna was unable to develop or to maintain a central hierarchy, and, with the breakdown of control as an aftermath of the religious split, the kinship (and clan) system remained as the chief integrative organization and is probably so today despite recent changes.

Spier correctly classified the Laguna kinship system as belonging to the Crow type.[101] It represents a specialized lineage system of the matrilineal or Crow subtype. The specializations which separate the Laguna system from the more basic Hopi and Zuni lineage systems are primarily the extensive use of self-reciprocal terminology and the pattern of alternate generations, features which, in the perspective of the total kinship systems, are relatively minor in importance.

In an earlier section we have discussed the nature of the Laguna kinship system and certain problems which are raised by the data. The relation of the kinship system to the lineage, household, and clan organizations is similar to that of the other western Pueblos. The extended household based on matrilocal residence is organized around a lineage or lineage segment, with husbands attached to it and brothers leaving it to marry into other households but maintaining privileges in their natal home. Of considerable importance also is the father's natal household which has special duties and obligations. The kinship system at Laguna seems to parallel this lineage-household organization and to reflect the ties which bind it together. Through extension of kinship patterns to the clan several lineages are united; by marriage ties the clan system is interrelated. Through the relations between house, clan, and ceremony outlined above, and through the extension of ceremonial kinship, the social and ceremonial organizations are united into a single structure.

The division of labor at Laguna is approximately the same as among the Hopi. Men farm and carry the bulk of the ceremonial activity; women are responsible for the household and its manifold duties. Women look to their husbands for economic support but to their brothers for ritual activities relating to the fetishes associated with the clanhouses.

There are certain differences, however, between the socioceremonial system of Laguna and that of the other western Pueblos. Neither Laguna nor Acoma organized their clan system into exogamous phratry groupings, and the ceremonial organization at Laguna differed with regard to the Medicine societies, the organization of the Katcina cult, and the central hierarchy. Parsons views the problem almost solely in historical terms:

> Acoma and Laguna certainly have some Zuni and Hopi traits but they cannot be understood without consideration of the eastern towns.
>
> Laguna clan heads might be similar to Hopi clan heads if only their positions were not due to the breaking down of the societies and the kiva organization. Dancing and probably kick-stick racing were obviously by clan because of the loss of the two kivas. Paraphernalia ("mothers," masks) have to be kept nowadays in a house of lineage and clan; there is no other place. If the corn-ear "mother" was originally of the clan and loaned as it is today to the shaman, that would be a very significant and exciting fact; it would clear up so much for historical reconstruction; but there is not enough evidence for this.
>
> If you reread this section in *Laguna Genealogies* from a critical historical point of view, also with comparative knowledge of *all* the other Keresan pueblos, I think you will conclude that Laguna is Keresan in its general ceremonial system, but shows Zuni-Hopi influences.[102]

We have suggested above that similarities and differences in social structure may have to be explained in somewhat different ways than similarities and differences in cultural behavior generally. It is not at all clear that the lineage *pattern* of grouping relatives, or the household *organization*, or the clan *system* are easily borrowed as such, any more than grammatical *structure* is generally borrowed. Parsons tends to treat them as phenomena of the same order as ritual behavior. She goes further and implies that structural similarities are not "similarities" because they are convergent rather than "genetically" related, an extreme historical point of view which would limit comparative work in large measure.

The clan system at Laguna is very similar to that of Acoma, and both similar to, and different from, that of Zuni and Hopi. The structural similarities, and certain functions such as exogamy, are related to the inherent nature of clan types of grouping; the relatively uniform series of clan names throughout the pueblos may involve borrowing or intermarriage, but also reflects a similar relationship to the world of nature.

Accepting Parsons' argument that Acoma and Laguna cannot be understood without consideration of the eastern Keresan towns, it is still possible that the basic Keresan pattern is found not in the east but in the west. Parsons assumes that the eastern "moiety"-society pattern was once dominant at Laguna, and, with its breakdown, the clans took over many of the functions formerly performed by kiva or society. But the evidence presented above suggests that the lineage, household, and clan were all strongly organized at Laguna. Parsons, herself, notes that when the two kivas were torn down by the progressives, "there was a meeting at which the old women in charge of what was left of sacrosant things brought them out and gave them up."[103] This does not sound like kiva control of paraphernalia but rather household and clan control. The absence of the ceremonial "moiety" organization at Acoma, and its association with war and *santu* dances at Laguna, suggests the possibility that the "moiety" pattern developed in the east as an adjustment to conditions, internal and external, in that region.

That extensive borrowing occurred in connection with the Medicine society rituals, the Katcina cult, and in other aspects of culture is clear; in fact, the amount of interpueblo borrowing is probably far greater than is generally realized, despite Parsons' extensive contributions to this problem.[104]

The lack of exogamous phratry groupings at Acoma and Laguna would presumably be interpreted by Parsons as "failure to borrow," but phratry groupings need to be analyzed functionally as well as historically. Phratry groupings are integrative devices for larger populations and represent insurance against clan extinction; it is possible that they were not needed in terms of the situation existing in Acoma and Laguna. Hano has not taken over the Hopi phratry system to any great extent despite almost two hundred and fifty years of close contact and intermarriage.

The recent history of Acoma and Laguna has been somewhat divergent. We have outlined above the process of village centralization organized in terms of the Antelope clan, which probably took place at Acoma, and suggested some of the factors involved. At Laguna there has been a process of decentralization in which the clan system has remained relatively strong, in comparison with village integration. But there is little evidence that the clan system has grown *stronger;* this would be highly improbable in view of the strong forces of acculturation involved.

The ceremonial system at Laguna, so far as it can be reconstructed, seems to have been composed of the same elements as at Acoma, but somewhat differently organized. The Katcina cult parallels in many aspects of its organization and activities that of Zuni and Hopi and has been undoubtedly influenced from these sources, if not ultimately derived from them. While there were two kivas for a period, at least, there was not the dual organization of ceremonial life characteristic in the east, and the Katcina cult remained under the control of the Antelope and Badger clans, with perhaps the cacique in over-all supervision, as at Acoma.

The Medicine societies at Laguna are basically Keresan but not too different in their organization and functions from the Zuni societies. They have both "curing" and rain-making functions at Laguna, but the latter may be incident to the breakdown of the ceremonial system, since the Acoma societies are primarily concerned with "curing" and protection against witches. The relations of the Medicine societies to the central hierarchy are different: the cacique should not be a shaman (in contrast to some of the eastern Keresans) but is chosen by the medicine men (in contrast to Acoma). The *kurena* and *kashari* organizations represent the closest approximations to the eastern ceremonial dual organization; there is some seasonal alternation in songs, and the two groups are in opposition to each other in the Scalp Dance and on other occasions. Boas suggests a possible relation between *kashare* and Flint and *kurena* and Kapina, but after the split the *kurena* and *Shikane* groups were closely associated. We have seen that the *kurena* are not represented as a separate society at Acoma, but the cognate term is applied to the Katcina group members. The *kurena* and *kashare* were on opposite sides of the "progressive"-"conservative" fight; today there is a dual division of the clans for war and *santu* dances, and the Zuni *koyamshi* have been introduced for clowning purposes.

There apparently was not at Laguna that concentration of control in the hands of the Antelope clan which developed at Acoma, a pattern which is characteristic of the western Pueblos, though other clans are involved at Zuni and Hopi. The Antelope clan does occupy an important position at Laguna in myth and ritual, however, and Parsons notes that, when the Antelope clansman took over as head of the three Katcina dance groups, he "went to Acoma to be installed by his clansman, 'the Antelope Man,' Town chief."[105] She points out that it would have been an easy matter to adopt the Acoma pattern of town chieftaincy at this time, but the secular government was too firmly established; the practical extinction of the Antelope clan at Laguna was undoubtedly a further deterring factor.

The analysis of Laguna social organization presented above helps to confirm the working hypothesis presented in the chapter on Acoma as to the character of, and changes in, Keresan social structure.[106] The kinship system, household organization, and clan system of Laguna form an interrelated unit controlling the day-by-day social relations of the individuals concerned; they are organized on a "vertical" or lineage principle and conform in all important respects to the basic social structures of the other western Pueblos.

Cutting across this basic social structure but tying into it at various points are the associational structures. Some were tribal wide, such as the Katcina cult with its kiva organization, others were restricted in membership, such as the Medicine societies. Historically they derive in part from the eastern Pueblos and in part from the western Pueblos; they utilize kinship and lineage ties to some extent but are not tied so deeply into the clan and household structure as to the west or so centralized in control as at Acoma.

The resulting type of social integration at Laguna is closest in its general form to that of the Hopi, though the specific institutions are more closely paralleled at Acoma. The intensity of integration seems somewhat lower, if we may judge from the present degree of disintegration of the pueblo. This suggests that the task of developing a strong social structure out of diverse fragments is a difficult one and takes a considerable period to accomplish. Further, no other pueblo has been subjected to such intensive acculturation during the American period.

The disintegration of Laguna, while it makes difficult the study of aboriginal patterns, offers the possibility of studying the development of new types of social structure. As Parsons notes:

> When the town was first studied, twenty years ago, its ceremonial disintegration was so marked that it presented an obscure picture of Keresan culture. But, with recently acquired knowledge of that culture in mind, today Laguna and her nine colonies offer unrivaled opportunities to study American acculturation and the important role played by miscegenation.[107]

Chapter VII

CONCLUSIONS

Western Pueblo Social Structure

WE HAVE presented the data on western Pueblo social organization in a common framework and have considered the immediate problems and relationships in the concluding sections of each chapter. It should now be possible to define the common features of western Pueblo social structure and indicate the nature of the variations which occur. The relations between the eastern and the western Pueblos can then be sketched and some hypotheses as to the nature of social and cultural change in the Southwest advanced.

The social structures of the western Pueblos so far considered, despite the variations we have noted, conform to a single general pattern: the "western Pueblo" type. This type is not limited to the Southwest but is found elsewhere in North America and, in modified form, in other parts of the world as well. This type of social structure is characterized by a kinship system of "Crow type" organized in terms of the lineage principle; a household organization on the basis of the matrilineal extended family; a formal organization based on the lineage and clan and, in some cases, the phratry group; an associational structure organized around the ceremony and its symbols, with relationships to the lineage, clan, and household; and a theocratic system of social control. There is a further relationship of the social system to the world of nature through the extension of social patterns to natural phenomena.

The basic feature of western Pueblo social structure is the kinship system. Spier, on the basis of the data then available (1925), classified the kinship systems of the groups under discussion into three separate types:[1] Crow type—Hopi, Hano, Laguna; Acoma type—Acoma; and Mackenzie Basin type—Zuni. He arrived at this classification primarily in terms of differences in the classification of cross-cousins; and in terms of the views then current as to the nature of kinship terminologies, three separate types in as unified a culture area as the western Pueblos was nothing unusual. Our analysis of the available data in terms of the total system makes it highly probable that all these tribes have (or recently had) kinship systems conforming to a single basic pattern which I have elsewhere referred to as the Crow subtype of the "Lineage" type.[2]

All these kinship systems are organized primarily in terms of the lineage principle, with other principles being subordinate to the solidarity and unity of the lineage group. These principles, while descriptive, are not merely psychological or linguistic in nature; they have sociological correlates and are reflected in social life and behavior. As such they offer a means for further analysis once their significance is clear. Thus in each tribe the matrilineal lineage represents (or recently represented) the kinship group with the strongest internal relations—this group is also treated as a unit with reference to outsiders who are related by marriage or in other ways. Within the lineage group women have a central position in contrast to their brothers, a situation which has important consequences in many spheres of life.

These lineage-type systems are "classificatory" in that lineal and collateral relatives are generally merged[3] on the principle of the equivalence of siblings. The generation principle operates primarily in one's own lineage but is modified in terms of classing older men of the lineage or clan together (Hopi, Zuni) or through the utilization of the mechanism of alternating generations (Acoma, Laguna). Verbal reciprocity, which seems to have some relationship to alternation of generations, is minimally developed among the Hopi, moderately at Zuni, and strongly at Acoma and Laguna, with Hano using the junior reciprocal. The principles of sex differentiation and seniority show considerable variation, Hopi, Hano, and Zuni recognizing age and sex distinctions among siblings and Acoma and Laguna only sex differences. But all these patterns of grouping are fitted into the lineage pattern

—an indication of the primacy of the lineage principle of organization.

The behavior patterns expectable of relatives are generally similar in the western Pueblos, so far as our data go. Everywhere the mother-daughter and sister-sister ties are important and furnish the central core for social groupings. The bonds between brother and sister are stronger than those between husband and wife, so that marriage is somewhat "brittle," particularly in early years. The relations between a man and his sister's sons are important ones; these contrast sharply with the role of the father's sister in relation to her brother's sons. Grandparents have generally similar duties and obligations in all the villages. These behavioral patterns are organized in similar systems, which reflect similar principles of organization.

The conception of the kinship system as composed of a series of behavioral patterns expectable between relatives under given conditions avoids the sterile argument as to whether there is any correlation between terminology and social behavior. The verbal behavior symbolizes the socially defined relationships; where the actual behavior diverges, a problem may be formulated in terms of social change which may give added insight into the nature of the kinship system.

The classification of kinship systems of the western Pueblo type in terms of such concepts as "overriding of generation" betrays a bias with regard to the nature of kinship systems generally and fails to get at the essential features of such systems. To define such systems in terms of the generational relations between cross-cousins is to miss the profound reorientation of the whole kinship system in terms of a "vertical" orientation and the subordination of most relationships to this fact. Such systems have characteristics different from those organized on generational lines; they are designed for continuity and for conservation, and they do not adjust very well to social change.

The discussions of western Pueblo kinship in the past have largely centered around the controversy as to "the influence of sociological factors as against the influence of linguistic factors in kinship nomenclature."[4] Parsons has provided a detailed analysis of the kinship terminologies of all the Pueblos from the standpoint of forking and merging, moiety, sex, and seniority and concludes that, "although the social organization finds expression by and large in kinship nomenclature, the tie between organization and nomenclature is elastic."[5] She goes on to point out that linguistic principles may determine certain of the "inconsistencies" she finds, particularly with reference to reciprocity and seniority, and that borrowing may have played an important role.[6]

Lowie's contribution to the controversy has already been mentioned; he concluded that "linguistic conservatism has been of slight importance in the history of present Hopi nomenclature and that the clan concept has exerted a deep influence upon it."[7] Parsons' analysis is vitiated by her failure to understand the nature of the systems with which she deals. Thus, in discussing the Laguna, she applies linguistic determination in connection with the use of the term "son" which, she believes, "leads to the anomalous application of the term for mother to a man's sister's daughter."[8] A glance at the Laguna kinship charts will show the necessity for formulating the problem in terms of the whole lineage organization rather than treating it as an isolated example of circular reasoning. In dealing with cross-cousins, on the other hand, she does see their differentiation as reflecting a "principle of clanship";[9] but she does not apply this principle to an analysis of the whole system. Thus she finds it curious, from the point of view of clanship, that the northern Tewa also classify the father's sister and the father's sister's daughter together, without taking into consideration that the two systems are based on quite different principles of grouping.[10]

The explanations offered for self-reciprocal terminologies range from Lowie's suggestion that their occurrence is a function of geographical position,[11] to Kroeber's view that "reciprocity seems essentially a thought pattern,"[12] to Parsons' statement: "Plainly enough this reciprocity system of the Tewa is the outcome of language, without reference to social organization."[13] The western Pueblo data do not support any of these explanations. Lowie's discussion of the Hopi system has emphasized the shift from Uto-Aztecan self-reciprocal systems to nonreciprocal terminology among the modern Hopi, so that language per se would not seem to be a vital factor in this case. On the other hand, the close relations between the western Pueblos, extending over a long period of time, have not led to any uniformity with reference to self-reciprocal terminologies. Nor has anyone formulated the differences in thought patterns between Hopi and Zuni or Laguna which have led to the differences noted. The covariation noted between self-reciprocal terminology and the development of alternating generation patterns suggests that these two phenomena may be correlated—as they are, for example, in a number of Australian tribes—and that they have a basis in social phenomena. It is not clear what that basis is, but it will be worth while to test Radcliffe-Brown's hypothesis that verbal reciprocity may involve some significant aspect of identity between the various pairs.

It is evident that Kroeber's rejection of sociological interpretations in favor of linguistic factors was premature. When he put the burden of proof entirely on the propounders of sociological views,[14] he had an obligation to build a better system of interpretation, which, in my opinion, he has not done. In view of the accumulated evidence since 1909, I believe that the balance has shifted and that the burden of proof should henceforth be on the shoulders of those who profess nonsociological explanations. In fairness to Kroeber, he has on occasion shown great insight into kinship problems; his discussion of the significance of "unilaterality of descent" in connection with the western Pueblo practices concerned with cross-cousin terminology is an excellent example.[15]

The problem of borrowing with regard to kinship terminology has been examined in a preliminary way by Parsons, who finds a term for grandfather at Acoma and Laguna which "is obviously borrowed from Zuni" and a term for older sister at Hano which is probably borrowed from the Hopi, as well as various Keresan and Tewa terms which are used for different purposes in different villages.[16] From the standpoint of the kinship structure the source of the term is not so important as what is done with it.

Parsons noted that the borrowed terms are fitted into the particular patterns already existing, a process she refers to as "acculturation in nomenclature."[17] If she had compared the "grandparent-grandchild" reciprocals at Zuni and Acoma and Laguna (see Table 10), she would have noted that the Acoma-Laguna

TABLE 10*

GRANDPARENT-GRANDCHILD RECIPROCALS

Term	Zuni	Acoma	Laguna
Mother's mother (female speaking)	hota	dyiau	gyiau
Mother's mother (male speaking)	hota	papa	papa
Daughter's daughter (female speaking)	hota	dyiau	gyiau
Daughter's son (female speaking)	nana	papa	papa
Father's mother (female speaking)	wowa	dyiau	gyiau
Father's mother (male speaking)	wowa	papa	papa
Son's daughter (female speaking)	wowa	dyiau	gyiau
Son's son (female speaking)	nana	papa	papa
Mother's father (female speaking)	nana	papa	papa
Mother's father (male speaking)	nana	nana	nana
Daughter's daughter (male speaking)	hota	papa	papa
Daughter's son (male speaking)	nana	nana	nana
Father's father (female speaking)	nana	papa	papa
Father's father (male speaking)	nana	nana	nana
Son's daughter (male speaking)	hota	papa	papa
Son's son (male speaking)	nana	nana	nana

* Compiled from Parsons, "The Kinship Nomenclature of the Pueblo Indians," Table I.

pattern is more complex than the Zuni one, so that it is not likely that this self-reciprocal *pattern* was borrowed from Zuni—if anything, the reverse may have happened in view of the extensive development of this pattern in all of the Keresan-speaking groups. Furthermore, if *nana* were borrowed from the Zuni, and comparative evidence makes it very likely, only certain of its applications were taken over at Acoma and Laguna, so that the "acculturation" was highly selective. How Acoma and Laguna happened to make exactly the same selection—and no others—offers a further problem of some interest.

The situation with regard to borrowing between Hopi and

Hano is quite a different one. Here almost two hundred and fifty years of residing in adjoining villages, bilingualism on the part of the Tewa, and considerable intermarriage have led to the large-scale "borrowing" of *patterns* of kinship organization. In the process of adjusting their eastern Tewa patterns to Hopi models, the actual borrowing of kinship terms is slight indeed; one term for older sister appears to have been borrowed to make the Hano sibling patterns approximate the Hopi patterns for a female speaker. The mechanism for the major readjustments which took place in Hano kinship undoubtedly involved the mixed Hopi-Tewa households; I would guess that the bilingual situation was a vital factor, since it would facilitate the establishment of equivalences. But Hano represents an exceptional situation in the western Pueblos. No other group was in such a dependent position, with possible survival depending on an adequate accommodation to the host group. Nor is there evidence that any such close association was common in the early history of the western Pueblos; in fact, the growing archeological evidence and the linguistic differentiation argues for a considerable period of separation for the existing villages.

Kinship systems have jobs to do, and we have suggested that there are a limited number of stable types, each of which is relatively efficient for certain purposes but not for others. Once the major principles of grouping are selected—by borrowing or otherwise—the elaboration of the kinship system takes place within rather narrow limits. This structural development seems to have proceeded along parallel lines in the western Pueblos, influenced at times by intermarriage, migration, trade, and other contacts and affected by the particular base with which each began. But this structural pattern as a totality is largely unconscious. Only particular aspects of it are conceptualized and thus subject to dissemination; the interrelations of the subpatterns take place within each group.

If we now turn to a consideration of the household and lineage groups and their relationship to the kinship structure, we may get further insight into western Pueblo social structure. Kroeber and Parsons have both emphasized the household as a fundamental unit in western Pueblo life; it is the basic local unit in all the western Pueblos. In theory it is—and in practice it formerly was—composed of a core of women related through the female line, plus their husbands, who normally came to reside with them, and any unmarried or unattached male relatives of the women. The women normally own the house—usually a series of adjoining rooms—and the house is the locus of both economic and ritual activities. The women look primarily to their husbands for economic support and for assistance in other ways; land is frequently associated with the household, and the crops resulting are stored there in the keeping of the women, who co-operate in their processing for food. On the other hand, the house may be a ritual center where sacred fetishes are stored and fed or where the paraphernalia for particular ceremonies is kept. The women of the household look particularly to their brothers and mother's brothers for ritual support; on special occasions the latter return to their natal household to co-operate in ceremonial activities.

The household thus takes two fundamental organizations: (1) it represents an extended family based on matrilocal residence which raises children, produces and prepares food, and co-operates in a variety of ways and (2) it represents a lineage group (or portion of such a group) who are born into the household and consider it their home, even after marriage, and who are concerned with the ritual activities associated with its sacred symbols. Among the Hopi this dual pattern is the clearest, and the central position of women is consonant with their role in both these organizations of the household. At Zuni the ritual role of many households seems considerably reduced and the economic aspects loom larger, a situation which probably has been brought about by modern conditions of acculturation and which has affected the structural relations within the household to a considerable extent. A similar situation appears to exist in the Acoma farming villages, but I would suspect that Old Acoma approximates to the Hopi pattern, though with greater centralization of ritual activities. Laguna, from the evidence available, also once had a pattern of household organization comparable to the Hopi, but the dispersal of the population to farming villages and internal dissension and migration have disrupted it considerably. But even under modern conditions of acculturation, where economic support looms larger and the household may be divided into smaller units, the lineage ties often bring about co-operation and mutual assistance.

The organization of the primary kinship patterns correlates with this dual household structure. Replace the status positions in the kinship system with actual individuals, and you have the household and lineage groupings for any particular individual. From the standpoint of the kinship system, it is the relatives born into the household (or into equivalent households) who are one's closest relatives; those attached to the household by marriage are relatives-in-law until they attain parental status. It seems clear that in the western Pueblo kinship systems the key grouping is the lineage—or lineage segment—rather than the extended family of spouses united through the female line. One important reason may be the limitations of the household group as such for purposes of wider social integration.

The lineage group is probably the basic unit for segmentary or formal organization in all the western Pueblos. There is no special name for this unit anywhere—any more than there is for the household—so that it has not had the attention it deserves. The clan is the major grouping in western Pueblo thinking. It has a name, frequently a central residence known as *the* clan-house, relations with sacred symbols, often control of ceremonies or status positions, and sometimes control of agricultural lands or other territories. Where the clan and the lineage coincide—as they do in perhaps half of the Hopi instances and undoubtedly elsewhere as well—there is no confusion, and either term may be used. But, where the clan is composed of multiple lineages, the distinction is important, since lineages within a clan may vary greatly in status and prestige. The specific mechanisms for inheritance and transmission normally reside in the lineage; the clan is normally the corporate group which holds ritual knowledge and economic goods in trust for future generations.

It is probable that an equivalence of clan and lineage is the earlier pattern, if our reconstruction of Hopi development is reasonably correct and is found to hold for other villages, as well. But with the growth of populations and the widespread migrations of the thirteenth and fourteenth—and later—centuries, the development of multi-lineage clans was almost inevitable in the western Pueblos. Multiple-lineage clans are more stable and organize a larger population, other things being equal, than do single lineages. Where there are several lineages, one of them usually controls the major functions associated with the clan, and the others are subordinate; any tendency to specific allocations of clan functions among the various lineages is made difficult by the variations which occur over even a short period of time.

Some of the western Pueblos have carried the organization of the clan system a step further. The Hopi have grouped clans into nameless phratries, or sets of linked clans, to which kinship is extended and which are the largest units for exogamic purposes; Hano has a partially developed phratry system on the Hopi model; Zuni apparently once had a ceremonial organization of clans in terms of the six directions without exogamy but perhaps with some extension of kinship. For Acoma and Laguna there is no phratry pattern, although at Laguna there is a dual grouping of clans, in terms of their relationship to the plaza, for certain dances.

We have suggested above that the organization of phratries may well have been a device to integrate larger populations among the Hopi and Zuni and that, for the Hopi, at least, the phratry organization serves as a stabilizing mechanism and as a partial protection against the effects of clan extinction. Once the phratry pattern was developed, it was maintained and expanded by a variety of processes: subdivision of clan groups, migration of women from other villages, consolidation of surviving phratry fragments, incorporation of migrant groups, and others. That the phratry groupings are relatively recent is suggested by their limited distribution and the nature of the relationships between phratry members, as well as the evidence from the Hano case.

We have suggested above that the clan organization of the

Hopi needs to be viewed from two standpoints: (1) as a classification of people for social purposes and (2) as a classification of the world of nature in its important aspects. Only when these two are seen in their proper relationship will we have an adequate understanding of the role of clanship in Pueblo life. The Hopi have organized this larger relationship primarily in terms of the phratry pattern; Zuni, in terms of a directional organization which encompassed not only clans but the central Rain priesthoods, the Katcina cult, and the curing societies as well.

Kroeber, in a brilliant analysis of the Pueblo clan system, found that in "essentials a single system of clan organization pervades all of the pueblos from Oraibi to Taos."[18] Using the Hopi data provided by Fewkes and Stephen as a basis, he discovered that it was possible to relate nearly every recorded Pueblo clan: "It is almost as if one complete pattern had been stamped upon the social life of every community in the area."[19] One key to the interpretation of this pattern was "the grouping of clans in pairs, or perhaps a tendency toward polarity within what is really one clan."[20] Kroeber believes that this principle of clan polarity may be "the basis for such moiety organization as exists among the Pueblos" and is certain that the two phenomena need to be considered together.[21]

It seems clear, from the evidence presented above as to the nature and organization of the clan systems of the various western Pueblos, that none of them supports Kroeber's organization of Pueblo clans in some dozen paired groups.[22] But Kroeber was correct with reference to the common set of clan names throughout the western Pueblos and in emphasizing the importance of duality in the Pueblos generally. In my opinion the common set of clan names must be viewed in terms of the relationship between man and nature. The aspects of the natural world which have social or ritual value for the Pueblos are similar, and the clan names reflect these aspects; the division of each village into segmentary units and their association with particular aspects of nature is a widespread technique for establishing such relationships.

The principle of duality is likewise concerned with the relationship of the pueblo group to nature but takes a different organization among the western Pueblos. Nowhere in the Pueblos are there exogamous moieties,[23] and, as Lowie has pointed out, it is essential to distinguish moieties of this type from ceremonial dual divisions.[24] The Hopi have organized their clans into a multiple phratry grouping on a semi-"logical" basis; the dual organization of Hopi life is found primarily in their conception of the organization of the seasonal and ceremonial calendar and in the relationships between the present world and the underworld—between the living and the dead.[25] At Zuni there are references in the mythology to a dual grouping of clans associated with summer and winter and some seasonal distinctions in terms of calendar and ceremonial activity. Acoma appears to have no dual groupings of consequence; but at Laguna there is some seasonal assignment of ceremonial activities and a dual organization of clans for dances, a possible substitute for a former two-kiva system. The eastern Pueblos, in contrast, have organized much of their social and ceremonial life in terms of nonexogamous but generally patrilineal dual divisions, which also are associated with a division of the year into summer and winter seasons, with transfer ceremonies for the shifting of responsibility and control. Here the important aspects of nature seem also to be grouped in dual fashion and associated with the dual divisions.

Dual organizations in a broad sense are devices to organize and regulate rivalry and opposition in order to serve the purposes of the group as a whole. Where they control marriage they offer, often in conjunction with cross-cousin marriage, a convenient way to regulate exchange of spouses, and it is possible that exogamous moieties may have been present in some early Pueblo groups. Ceremonial dual divisions have different sources than moieties. In the Pueblos they reflect differences in seasonal activities, observations of solar phenomena, and the like; they control ceremonial rivalry by regulating competition and dividing responsibility in channeled areas. We have suggested that dual organizations are not too efficient for relatively large groups, nor are they flexible enough to adjust to new conditions.

The rise of factions—*ad hoc* dual divisions—frequently results from the failure of the formal social organization to control opposition in any effective way.

The associational structures of the western Pueblos have similar organizations in most instances but vary in their major objectives and in their relationship to the clan system. The Hopi emphasize the Katcina cult and the men's Tribal societies organized in terms of the kivas; there are, in addition, a series of societies organized around ceremonies for rain which also have some concern with curing. Zuni has a series of Rain priesthoods organized on a directionally oriented basis, a Katcina cult related to the six kivas, and a dozen curing societies associated with the major prey animals. At Acoma and Laguna the Katcina cult is associated with the kivas, but the Medicine societies play a dominant role in village life. Hano approximates to the Hopi pattern but with a greater emphasis on curing, a reflection perhaps of their eastern Tewa origins. In all the western Pueblos there is a conceptual relationship between clan, society, and ceremony; this relationship is most marked among the Hopi but is present in varying degrees in each of the other groups.

In the western Pueblos the village chief is a religious official and everywhere, except at Laguna, he is a member of a particular clan. The controlling clan varies from village to village: Hopi and Hano the Bear clan, Zuni the Dogwood clan, and Acoma the Antelope clan. The last chief of Laguna was selected by the medicine men, but there is some evidence in the mythology that the Antelope clan was formerly the important clan in this village. The development of secular officials under Spanish auspices has taken place in all villages except Hopi and Hano, thus providing a mechanism for secular control and relations with outsiders. The War Chief usually handles matters of internal discipline and control.

The type of social integration among the western Pueblos follows a common pattern, although there are considerable differences in village size and dispersal at present. In all the villages the kinship system is a primary integrating factor, kinship being widely extended within the tribe and, through the clan organization, to other tribes as well. The Hopi, with their emphasis upon the clan system, have developed little in the way of centralization of control. Zuni, on the other hand, has developed a strong central hierarchy which holds this large village together; the clans have less importance and fewer functions than among the Hopi, and the phratry organization is obsolescent. Acoma has developed a strong centralized control in the hands of a single clan which has kept subsidiary organizations in line; Laguna, with a closer approximation to the Hopi pattern, has split up into a series of farming villages.

No system of social integration is perfect, but the western Pueblos have retained their group identity and a fair amount of their culture in the face of tremendous pressures for change. They have done so by tying their social structures together in intricate fashion. What Kroeber says for Zuni can stand for the western Pueblos as a whole:

> The clans, the fraternities, the priesthoods, the kivas, in a measure the gaming parties, are all dividing agencies. If they coincided, the rifts in the social structure would be deep; by countering each other they cause segmentations which produce an almost marvelous complexity, but can never break the national entity apart.[26]

The Eastern Pueblos and Their Interpretation

Turning now to the eastern Pueblos, it will be useful to review the relations between the two major divisions of Pueblo culture and to attempt to evaluate the factors responsible for the similarities and differences which are found. Our knowledge of the eastern Pueblos is incomplete and often conflicting, so that it is not possible to speak with any certainty, even as to the facts. But enough is known to suggest some working hypotheses which may be useful.[27]

The eastern Pueblos are composed of five Keresan-speaking villages: Santo Domingo, San Felipe, Cochiti, Santa Ana, and Zia; five Tewa-speaking villages: San Juan, Santa Clara, San Ildefonso, Tesuque, and Nambé; four Tiwa-speaking villages: Taos and Picuris in the north and Sandia and Isleta in the south; and one Towa-speaking village: Jemez, which includes the survivors from several Towa-speaking villages, and from Pecos, which was abandoned in 1838. These fifteen villages represent the remains of a much larger population which the Spaniards found in the sixteenth century; the Pueblo Rebellion and the Reconquest took a heavy toll, and the surviving groups have been subjected to strong acculturation since the beginning of the eighteenth century.

In contrast to the relative uniformity in social organization which we have seen for the western Pueblos it is important to note that there is considerable variation in social structure within the eastern Pueblos—as well as certain major differences between east and west. Parsons,[28] Strong,[29] and Hawley[30] have surveyed the essential features of eastern Pueblo social organization; here we shall mention only certain aspects of interest to our present study.

The Tewa villages represent a compact group with a central location along the Rio Grande and its tributaries. The outstanding feature of Tewa social organization is the dual division into Summer People and Winter People. While these divisions are generally patrilineal, they do not regulate marriage; in fact, there is some tendency to endogamy, and a woman may shift to her husband's side after marriage. There are two sets of village chiefs and their assistants each of which is in charge of the village for half the year, with Transfer ceremonies in November and March. The two groups are associated with the dual kivas and take part as teams in dances, ceremonial races, and other activities. The clan system, in contrast, is poorly developed; the so-called "clans" recorded for the Tewa are probably not clans at all.[31] They are not exogamous—an essential feature in maintaining a clan structure—nor are they kinship units. Harrington and Freire-Marreco characterize them as patrilineal, Parsons as matrilineal or patrilineal; a clue to their nature is contained in an informant's statement: "You get that Tewa name from your mother, just as you get your Mexican name from your father."[32]

The kinship system provides the best evidence that the clan system has not been important in recent years. It is "nonclassificatory," in that lineal and collateral relatives are not merged, and kinship terms are extended in bilateral fashion. Siblings are distinguished in terms of seniority but not of sex, cross- and parallel cousins are not differentiated, except in address, and the junior reciprocal is used extensively. A comparison of Harrington's ideal pattern for the northern Tewa[33] and Parsons' comparative survey[34] shows many minor variations, particularly in the extension of uncle-aunt terms to the cross-cousins, but no tendency toward organization on a lineage principle. The family organization is of the elementary type, and the major group of relatives, the *matu'i*, are the descendants on *both* sides of the great-grandparents. This latter group is usually the exogamous group, as well as the body of relatives with kinship duties and obligations. Here is a social structure which is quite different from that of the Hopi or Zuni.

The Tiwa offer some interesting variations. The northern Tiwa are the most isolated of the Pueblo groups and have had close contacts with Plains groups and with Navaho and Jicarilla Apache. The Taos data indicate a dual organization in terms of the north- and south-side divisions, with the three kivas on each side representing the ceremonial divisions. Kiva membership is by dedication rather than by inheritance, and there seems to be no regulation of marriage in terms of divisional membership. The village is controlled by the two house chiefs, who are heads of the most important kivas on their side. There are no clans at Taos—and apparently no masked Katcina cult as well. The kinship system parallels that for the Tewa in general, although there are many minor differences.[35]

Picuris, the other northern Tiwa village, is decadent but has similar social institutions. Parsons[36] noted a dual division of north-side and south-side people, but with patrilineal affiliation; a dual organization of the six kivas for racing but not for dancing; and a dual chieftaincy associated, apparently, with the solstice intervals. Kinship is bilateral and on the Taos model, though personal names have largely replaced kinship terms.

The southern Tiwa show considerable dialectic divergence from their northern relatives and a somewhat different orientation of their social structure. Isleta[37] has a dual organization with a complex method of determining membership, children belonging to the division of their parents or assigned alternately in case the parents belong to different sides. The dual division is associated with "summer" and "winter" and with the kivas, and there is a dual chieftaincy. There is, however, another all-inclusive organization of the village in terms of five "Corn" groups, which are associated with colors and directions. Individuals generally join their mother's group, but there is no exogamy involved, and a child has to be initiated or adopted into the group. The kinship system, so far as the terms have been recorded, tends to follow the northern pattern but with greater emphasis on the role of the father's sister in ceremonial and ritual relations and a profusion of alternate terms for cousins. While there are no masked Katcinas in Isleta, there is a dance which is connected with the general Pueblo Katcina cult.

Sandia, the other southern Tiwa village, is almost unknown ethnologically, though its sojourn for two generations in the Hopi country after the Rebellion suggests some interesting problems. The Laguna colony at Isleta has been studied by Parsons from the standpoint of cultural adaptation and change.

The eastern Keresan villages are characterized by matrilineal, exogamous, named clans without "totemic" affiliations or any control of land, ceremonies, or status positions. The Medicine societies are the dominant groups and control the village leadership; other societies frequently are linked with one or another of the Medicine societies in various ways. There is also a dual organization, associated with the Squash and Turquoise kivas, which has ceremonial functions; generally membership is patrilineal, but, at Santa Ana, White reports a dual grouping in terms of the matrilineal clans.[38] The kinship system tends to be "classificatory" and bilateral, with most terms cognate with those of Laguna and Acoma. Closer analysis of the kinship data for Cochiti and San Felipe suggests a lineage pattern as the earlier form;[39] White's analysis of Santa Ana kinship comes to a similar conclusion:

> It is our considered opinion that the pattern in which mother's brother is called "uncle" and his children "son" and "daughter,"

which is a characteristic of the Crow type of terminology, is the earlier of the two patterns. We believe that this pattern is breaking down and giving way to the pattern in which mother's brother is called "father" and his children "brother" and "sister."[40]

The use of the term "mother" for the father's sister, which is characteristic of the eastern Keresan systems, and which was noted at Acoma and occasionally at Laguna, would have a parallel explanation.

The Towa-speaking village of Jemez,[41] while here arbitrarily classed with the eastern Pueblos, has a social structure that approximates that of the western Pueblos in many respects. The clan organization is matrilineal and exogamous, and both the mother's and the father's clans are important as kinship units, marriage into the father's clan being disapproved. Clans have ritual functions, and the village chief and his assistants must be selected from certain clans. The chief is selected by the heads of the various societies and conducts the solstice ceremonies; land is worked for him by the villagers under the direction of the war captains. There are two kivas, children joining the kiva of their father and wives transferring to that of their husbands, but the ceremonial dual division found elsewhere is expressed largely through the two "Clown" societies. There is no formal division into Summer People and Winter People, as among the Tewa. The Katcina cult is in operation, and initiation is through a ceremonial "father" who acts as a sponsor. The societies have both weather control and curing functions and participate in periodical "retreats" for the benefit of the village.

The kinship system is not adequately recorded but appears to be a mixture of eastern and western patterns. The mother is classed with the mother's sister, but the father and his brother have separate terms. Siblings are distinguished by age and sex, and sibling terms are extended to parallel cousins. Cross-cousins may use "brother-sister" terms in address but utilize "uncle-aunt" terms for reference; on the other hand, the term for "father's sister" is applied to all the maternal kinswomen of the father, and the term for "mother's brother" applies to all the mother's maternal kinsmen of an older generation. There is evidence of a lineage pattern of grouping, particularly for the father's matrilineal lineage, but this is partially obscured by the tendency to use terms bilaterally. The household is predominantly of the single-family type, though extended families of the western pattern are found. Parsons reports houses as owned predominantly by men, but Reagan's account from around 1900 indicates female control of the house and of the crops stored therein and toleration of the husband on the Hopi pattern.[42] The descendants of the Pecos survivors maintain some differentiation but have been absorbed so thoroughly into Jemez that no details of Pecos social structure, beyond lists of clans, are available.

How are these variations to be explained? Students of southwestern cultures have offered a number of explanations in terms of the facts and theoretical knowledge then available. After reviewing these, we will add some suggestions of our own.

Parsons, who made the first modern survey of Pueblo social organization in 1924, recognized a division between east and west and noted the variations to be found in terms of clan, house ownership, and moiety. She came to the conclusion: "Between house owning according to sex, matrilineal clanship, and patrilineal moiety there appears to be among the Pueblos a definite correlation."[43] In terms of our analysis there is a relationship between the form of the household and matrilineal clan organization in the western Pueblos, but the "correlation" between the patrilineal dual divisions and house ownership is not very clear, even with Parsons' own data, since her "strong moieties" are found with ownership by men and women and the "ceremonial moieties" are associated with male ownership of houses.[44] One reason is that these patrilineal dual divisions are not directly comparable to the matrilineal clan systems.

Strong, in 1927, in connection with a survey of social organization in the greater Southwest, came to the conclusion that there was a historical relation between the Southern Californian Shoshoneans and the Pueblo and other peoples with reference to the group house, priest, and fetish complex and the moiety patterns. For the Pueblos he postulated a development of social structure in terms of patrilineal lineages and patrilineal moieties, after the Californian pattern, with a later development of matrilineal clans in the west and a continuation, with modifications, of the older pattern in the east.[45]

Steward,[46] on the other hand, has suggested that a clan system will develop from pre-existing band organizations when certain conditions are present and believes that the Californian lineages and the western Pueblo clans represent parallel developments, without any direct historical connections. We have applied Steward's hypotheses to our reconstruction of the development of Hopi social organization in chapter ii.

Hawley, who also criticizes Strong's reconstruction, but for different reasons, proposed a decade later a different historical explanation of Pueblo development, based on an evaluation of the evidence as to diversity of physical type apparent in the Pecos populations and the complex linguistic situation.[47] She believes that the history of Pueblo development has been one of migration of groups with diverse origins into the Southwest: the ancestors of the Hopi and the Zuni into Arizona and the various Tanoan linguistic groupings into the Rio Grande region. On the basis of the affiliation of Kiowa with Tanoan, she suggests the Plains as the source for the latter groups.

> The ancestors of the Eastern Pueblos may have been Plains groups who came into the Rio Grande and adjoining districts in several migrations and settled to a sedentary agricultural mode of existence with the attendant development of arts, crafts, and ceremonialism.[48]

The western Pueblos, with which Hawley includes Jemez, has four subtypes of social structure; the eastern Pueblos she divides into three subtypes, along linguistic lines:

> The linguistic groups in the east modified their old institutions and adopted new ones, but through their close inter-influence they retained a general Eastern type within their collective system of sub-types. In the west, Zuni and Hopi developed their sub-types and so influenced the isolated Western Keresan villages, the Towa village of Jemez, and the Tewa village of Hano that these modified their original social systems and acquired a distinct western veneer.[49]

I have presented Hawley's thesis at considerable length because it seemed reasonable in view of our knowledge of the archeological developments at that time. In the light of our modern knowledge of the prehistory of the Rio Grande, however, much of her hypothesis has to be radically changed. Erik Reed has recently surveyed the "Sources of Upper Rio Grande Culture and Population" and therein says:

> Up to the fourteenth century, the culture of the upper Rio Grande was closely similar in many ways to that of the San Juan drainage, in so far as can be inferred from archaeological materials. Occupation in the San Juan area apparently declined in the period 1150–1300 when that of the Rio Grande was increasing. The Anasazi abandoned the San Juan altogether at the end of the thirteenth century, just at the time of the great rise of upper Rio Grande population and culture.[50]

And on the physical side Carl Seltzer's study of *Racial Prehistory in the Southwest* shows a continuity of physical type in the Colorado Plateau "from the Basket Maker period clear up to recent times."[51] The Rio Grande region, on the other hand, shows evidence of admixture over a long period of time, but Seltzer states:

> The population in the earliest Pecos periods were more like the "Southwest Plateau" groups than the people of the later periods. The closest resemblance is to be found with the Black-on-White and Glaze I period (which exhibits important similarities with the "Southwest Plateau" groups), and as we ascend the stratigraphic sequence, the differentiation from the "Southwest Plateau" pattern becomes increasingly greater.[52]

Seltzer suggests that such groups as the Apache, Navaho, and Comanche may well have been responsible for the modifications in physical composition which Hooton observed but explained quite differently.[53]

On the basis of his archeological analyses, Reed suggests four main sources for Rio Grande population and culture: (1) the original Anasazi occupation dating from before the twelfth century; (2) a probable migration of "Chacoan" people from the eastern San Juan between A.D. 1000 and 1200; (3) the "Mesa Verde" people from the eastern San Juan around A.D. 1300; and (4) "Western Pueblo" people from the general Zuni region with glaze-paint redware and other traits who came a little before A.D. 1350.[54]

Reed tentatively correlates the Tanoan pueblos with the San Juan Anasazi and the Keresans with the redware complex. The Tiwa, most archaic dialectically of the Tanoan groups, he believes represent the original Pueblo occupants of the Rio Grande Valley; the Towa represent the "Chacoan" migration of the twelfth century, and the Tewa he correlates with the "Mesa Verde" migration. The historic Hopi, Zuni, and Acoma cultures were strongly influenced by a "Western Pueblo" complex which developed in central Arizona and which Reed believes influenced both the Hohokam and the Rio Grande; the abruptness of the change to glaze-paint redware in the latter region suggests actual immigration, and the ceramic connections between Acoma and Zuni lend some weight to the Keresan suggestions.[55]

An unpublished chart of the chronological development of Azteco-Tanoan prepared by Whorf on the basis of Whorf and Trager's "The Relationship of Uto-Aztecan and Tanoan" offers important confirmatory evidence for the major outlines of this hypothesis. The Tiwa divergence is estimated to have begun around A.D. 800, Tewa and Towa separated soon after A.D. 1000, and the Tewa dialects go back to around A.D. 1300. While these are informed guesses, they correlate excellently with the archeological evidence, as Reed points out.[56]

Accepting this correlation of evidence from archeology, physical anthropology, linguistics, and ethnography as offering a foundation for further research, what does it tell us about the dedevelopment of social organization in the Southwest? We have presented a reconstruction of Hopi social organization utilizing the concepts provided by Steward and the archeological investigations of Brew and others. The archeological evidence for Zuni and Acoma is not yet available for a similar reconstruction, but Reed believes that "the historic cultures of Hopi, Zuni, and Acoma connect up with the rectangular kiva-redware complex, which before the fourteenth century was concentrated south of the Little Colorado."[57] If this is so, it suggests that the basic similarities between Hopi, Zuni, and Acoma are not recent but have had a long period in which to develop.

Reed's interpretation of the Keresan "invasion" of the Rio

Grande in the fourteenth century fits in very well with our interpretation of the "Keresan bridge" between the eastern and western Pueblos. Hawley mentions the "remnants" of eastern Keresan social structure in the western Keresan villages.[58] I would suggest the reverse hypothesis: that the Keresan-speaking groups originally had an organization of western Pueblo type with a kinship system organized on a lineage basis, matrilineal, exogamous clans, a Katcina cult, and a series of Medicine societies with both curing and rain-making functions. After moving into the Middle Rio Grande close contact with Tewa and Towa groups resulted in the introduction of a dual ceremonial organization associated with two kivas but without the division into Summer and Winter People and the double Town chieftaincy. The variations in membership, particularly the dual grouping of matrilineal clans at Santa Ana, in contrast to the patrilineal patterns of the Tewa, suggest an incomplete adaptation of the dual division. The kinship system of the eastern Keresans was of the western lineage type, up to the time of the Rebellion, if our inferences from the Laguna situation are correct.[59] After the Rebellion the Spaniards made a deliberate attempt to acculturate the Rio Grande Pueblos to Spanish models and used a great variety of means, including force, to achieve their ends.[60] American influence in the last century has likewise been strong. As a result, the Rio Grande Keresans have shifted from a lineage system to a bilateral kinship system, and different villages show various stages in that change. If the Laguna two-kiva system and the dual grouping of clans are not recent phenomena, they may go back to the founding of Laguna and thus give us a rough measure of the order of modifications in the eastern villages.

One problem of some importance is the relationship between the society organizations of Hopi, Zuni, and the Keresan-speaking villages. The Hopi societies are primarily for rain, with secondary curing activities; the Zuni have two sets of societies; and the Keresan societies are primarily curing societies with secondary rain-making functions. White in his excellent study of Keresan Medicine societies reconstructs their historical development. He thinks that their "original" function was curing diseases and that, with the growing importance of agriculture, the curing societies undertook ceremonies for rain. Later, with the development and spread of the Katcina cult, they became involved in its activities and borrowed some of its paraphernalia.[61] Another factor that needs to be evaluated in this connection is the type of water supply. I have a strong impression that the Hopi concentration on rain rather than on curing (the curing societies are all extinct) is related to the almost complete dependence on an uncertain rainfall for the maturing of their crops, whereas the other Pueblos have access, through partial irrigation from streams, to a more dependable supply of water for their crops and can thus concentrate on curing sickness to a greater extent. That Santa Ana, Laguna, and Acoma diverge most widely from the Keresan norm may be significant in this connection, since the divergence is in terms of functions other than the curing of disease.[62]

Turning now to the Tanoan groups in the Rio Grande, we have a major task of constructing a developmental hypothesis which will fit the archeological facts and yet explain the differences which we have noted. Accepting Steward's hypothesis that the center of clan development appears to have been in the eastern San Juan region where communal houses first appeared and where population was densest,[63] and his conditions for the development of clans, we must assume that the "Chacoan" and related groups had matrilineal lineages and clans. In view of the organization of the large Chaco villages, I would further suggest that the great kivas were associated with two major men's societies, with the smaller kivas devoted to curing and rain ceremonies.

Reed's proposed correlation of the Towa group with the "Chacoan" migration would give us a continuation of Chaco social organization, in part at least. The Jemez area was one of the most conservative regions in the whole Rio Grande area; Jemez Black-on-White pottery continued to be made throughout the Glaze sequence, and there are other evidences of lack of change. That Jemez has a social structure that approximates that of the western Pueblos, plus a dual division organized around the kivas and the two "clown" groups is of significance, both in terms of a possible understanding of the past and as a means of partially controlling our analysis of the Tewa situation. Pecos, which was founded about the time of the postulated Chacoan migration, unfortunately was abandoned about a century ago, since its position on the edge of the Plains ultimately exposed it to devastating raids from the Comanche and other Plains tribes.

The Tewa are the key group in any reconstruction of eastern Pueblo social organization. Reed correlates them with the Mesa Verde phase of Pueblo III, which extended from A.D. 1150 to 1300 and was widespread over the four-corners region. The entire San Juan region was abandoned around A.D. 1300, at the time of the great drought, and Reed suggests that the eastern Mesa Verde people moved down the Rio Puerco to the Galisteo area east of the Rio Grande.[64] Black-on-White pottery of Mesa Verde type is found here, and in the northern Tewa area, dating from the fourteenth century.[65]

I would suggest that the Tewa, if they were from the Mesa Verde or adjoining regions, had a social organization of the general type we have suggested for the Towa. But the conditions under which abandonment of the San Juan took place were not ones conducive to the maintenance of a complex social structure, if the experience of the Hopi in lesser droughts is any parallel. The poorer families would leave first as they ran out of food; the later surviving groups probably moved under the leadership of their priests, but the task of staying alive in a new environment would take all their energies for a considerable period of time. During such a period the clan system would have been disrupted by extinction and the loss of leaders, and there would be a tendency to concentrate ceremonial knowledge in the hands of a few individuals. The adjustment to the new conditions in the Rio Grande would require communal effort and central direction, as well as a reorganization of the division of labor and a reorientation of the roles of the sexes in village activities.

Whether the dual organization of the population into Summer People and Winter People developed at this time—or after the extensive Spanish contacts which culminated in the Rebellion and the disruptions following the Reconquest—it would be easier to reconstitute a ceremonial system in terms of two major divisions. Their "patrilineal" tendency could well come from the conception of the "ceremonial father"; their lack of exogamy separates them from the moiety divisions elsewhere. The development of a double Town chieftaincy may have provided for the merging of fragments of former villages as well as providing regulated competition in leadership and control.

My own guess is that the dual organization began to expand soon after reaching the Rio Grande. The dual principle of organization is the simplest form of segmentary organization, beyond the band or village, and operates most effectively in relatively small groups. The organization of social, ceremonial, and political activities in terms of a dual division, and the further conceptualization of this division in terms of winter and summer, and the associated natural phenomena, suggest a fairly long period of development.

The clan system would be reduced in importance by these events but would be further affected by the extensive period of Spanish acculturation. Catholic regulation of marriage practices would take away the last remaining functions of the clan system, and intimate contacts with Spanish (and later Spanish-American) settlements would give a patrilineal tinge to the remnants. That it ended as a mere naming system under these conditions is not surprising. These same influences would tend toward the development of a kinship system on a bilateral, nonclassificatory basis and a family system on the Spanish model; more recently there has tended to be a utilization of Spanish terms as well where the contacts have included considerable intermarriage.

The Tiwa, Reed equates with the original Pueblo occupants of the northern Rio Grande; their language is the most archaic of the three Tanoan subgroups, and their surviving villages are distributed in two areas. The northern Rio Grande was a marginal area of the San Juan Anasazi and was only thinly occupied in late Pueblo times. Pit houses persisted into the twelfth century, and Black-on-White pottery continued to be made up to the historic period. There is no evidence for any dense population until the modern period.

Taos and Picuris[66] ceremonial organization, when known in detail, may well reflect the late Anasazi patterns in this region. The social organization, on the other hand, has undoubtedly undergone considerable change. The absence of clans in the Taos area may be a result of its marginal position, if diffusion from the San Juan is involved, but I would expect that a clan system was part of the cultural baggage of the Anasazi occupants of the northern Rio Grande. Taos and Picuris took a leading role in the Rebellion and suffered accordingly; several years were spent living on the Plains, and there have been intensive pressures for acculturation from Spanish sources as well as close contacts with Jicarilla Apache and other near-by tribes.

Under such circumstances a clan system is not likely to survive, since it is not flexible enough to adjust to new conditions. The same factors that we have postulated as operating in the Tewa situation would be effective in the case of Taos and Picuris—perhaps more effective, since the social organization was undoubtedly simpler to begin with.

Isleta and Sandia would be particularly useful in evaluating this hypothesis, if only we could reconstruct the development of their social organizations in some detail. The position of the "father's sisters" in kinship and ceremonial activities, and the "Corn" groups with maternal affiliation, but nonexogamous, suggest either a breakdown of former clan organization or a partial adjustment of social organization to that of their neighbors. Isleta was strongly acculturated in Spanish times, and the Spaniards took about five hundred Isletans with them to the Mexican border at the time of the Rebellion, where some of them remained at Isleta del Sur, now thoroughly "Mexicanized." Other Isletans and related groups fled westward to the Hopi country where they built Payupki, from which they were returned by the Spaniards around 1746 and settled ultimately at Sandia. With this complex historical background much more data than we have at present will be needed for an evaluation of the alternatives.

It might be argued that this is a very complicated historical hypothesis to get rid of a clan system among the Tewa and Tiwa which may never have existed in actuality. But the history of these Pueblo groups has been complex and demands a corresponding complexity of statement. It would be relatively simple to dispose of the Tanoans in terms of Plains groups who wandered into the Rio Grande and developed their dual divisions, and explain the Towa situation in terms of borrowing from the Hopi, as Hawley does.[67] But the Towa have been relatively isolated and self-contained, and this process would involve historical contacts with the Hopi of a greater intensity than we have knowledge of at present. We have tried to formulate a historical hypothesis which will fit the whole area rather than explain merely selected portions of it, and we have stated it in somewhat dogmatic fashion in order to encourage other students to examine it in terms of their special knowledge. It has the virtue of being partially testable in terms of new archeological and ethnological data and in terms of comparative linguistics. It also builds on the ideas presented by many students and will of course be subject to future restatement in terms of new data.

An independent approach to the problem of social organization in the Pueblos has recently been made by Wittfogel and Goldfrank, who have called attention to the importance of irrigation in the Southwest.[68]

> Comparative study of the social structure of agrarian societies in semi-arid or arid "oriental" countries reveals the extraordinary influence exerted by irrigation and flood control. When, in pre-industrial civilizations, water control demands large-scale cooperation, tribal, regional, or national, directing centers of authority arise and cooperative ("public") action as well as communal discipline are institutionalized. The introduction of large-scale waterworks effected a reorganization in agricultural society that is comparable only with the revolution caused by the introduction of the machine in our industrial world.[69]

Applying this hypothesis to the Pueblo data, they find that while irrigation was widely practiced it was much more intensive in the Rio Grande region and that this difference in emphasis had important effects on social structure, particularly with reference to the relative position of the sexes in various activities.

> The importance of maternal clans in Hopi, their lesser significance in Zuni, and their *gradual replacement in the east by social organizations of a different type*, certainly do not mechanically reflect the basic diversities in the structure of the miniature Pueblo waterwork societies. But variations in the irrigation pattern and the kinship systems of the different pueblos show too striking a correspondence to be dismissed easily. The assumption of some kind of interrelation between them is suggested—at least as a working hypothesis.[70]

Though I have developed the analysis above on broader grounds, the coincidence of my general conclusions with those reached by Wittfogel and Goldfrank on the basis of a more intensive analysis of the effects of irrigation practices is striking.

They go on to explore "the trend toward centralization which characterizes the growth of waterwork societies" in terms of the need for control of communal labor and indicate other factors that need to be taken into consideration: the influence of the Spaniards in setting up secular governments, the threats to survival, and the functions associated with war. All these have had important influences on the discipline and centralization which all observers of the eastern Pueblos have noted.

In our analysis of Pueblo social organization we have emphasized perhaps too little the process of borrowing or diffusion. Obviously borrowing has taken place on a large scale throughout the Pueblos—and beyond as well—in terms not only of technology and material culture but of ideas, attitudes, and concepts as well. But in the field of social structure—as with linguistic structure—the borrowing of *patterns* of organization is relatively rare, except where there is close and intimate contact accompanied by intermarriage or bilingualism. The borrowing of clan names is possible, but the essentials of a clan system are difficult to grasp; matrilocal residence can be comprehended readily, but the principle of grouping on a lineage basis is not easily formulated; kinship terms can be borrowed, but the system of organization is largely unconscious.

The "intermediate" character of the social organizations of

the Keresan villages between Hopi and Zuni, on the one hand, and the Tewa and Tiwa, on the other, has frequently been explained almost wholly in terms of borrowing. But while it is probable that the dual divisions among the eastern Keresans represent partial borrowing from their Tewa neighbors, borrowing is only part of the full explanation. The loss of certain clan functions as a result of contact is even more difficult to explain on this basis.

We have tried to see the variations in social organization in the Pueblos as a whole in terms of sociological and ecological factors and against the background of the strong and complex acculturational processes which have operated in varying degrees and for varying periods in this region. We believe, with Steward, that such an approach is far more profitable than the alternative diffusionist theory which "offers no explanation of origins, no understanding of culture change, and bases its case upon the unproved and highly dubious assumption that similarity in "arbitrary" features is proof of community of origin of unilateral institutions."[71]

The significance of our attempts to classify the social structures of the western Pueblos may now be seen in its proper perspective. By questioning the previous classifications of kinship systems and other aspects of social organization, and re-examining the data in the light of the Hopi materials, we were able to reduce the different types to variants of a single basic type of social structure. Utilizing this basic type, it was then possible to develop a hypothesis to explain the variations between the western and eastern Keresans in terms of differential acculturation and the adjustment to new conditions. This hypothesis, in turn, was then applied to an analysis of the eastern Pueblos as a whole.

At around A.D. 900–1300 the central Anasazi area probably had a social structure of essentially similar type, though with a greater emphasis on dual ceremonial organizations in the upper San Juan in contrast to the probable multiple society organization in northeastern Arizona. The later developments in the western region centered around the matrilineal lineage and correlated institutions, whereas the migrants to the Rio Grande developed the dual division as an adjustment to new conditions. The expansion of the Keresans into the Rio Grande region in the fourteenth century brought about further contacts between west and east and led to further differentiation; this latter process was intensified after the arrival of the Spaniards in 1540 and especially after the Pueblo Rebellion of 1680. Today the original Anasazi patterns survive mainly in the western Pueblos and, in modified form, in the eastern Keresan villages and at Jemez. The development of dual organizations has gone on apace among the Tewa in particular and has influenced the other eastern Pueblos in varying degrees. In broad perspective there are now two basic types of organization; if we include more details, we can subdivide each of these into several subtypes. But far more important than the classification itself is that an adequate classification allows us to formulate questions which otherwise we might not ask at all.

Wider Perspectives

Looking at the Pueblos in wider perspective, our tentative conclusions have significance both for the development of culture in the Southwest as a whole and for the comparative study of other social structures of the western Pueblo type. Steward has outlined the development of unilateral organizations in the greater Southwest in terms of ecological and sociological factors,[72] and more recently Goldschmidt has presented an analysis of the development of social organization in Native California in similar terms, including an illuminating statement on the significance of clans for social life. He concludes that "clan organization is a response to the developed institutional needs of a society under increased population, and that the clan system when fully realized offers competitive advantages as an integrating mechanism."[73]

The southern Athabaskan tribes offer an important series for the study of the factors responsible for social and cultural change. Entering the Southwest somewhere around A.D. 1300–1400, they have differentiated considerably from their original patterns, particularly with reference to social organization.

Opler[74] has not published his comparative survey, but his preliminary papers suggest that the Chiricahua Apache are closest to the aboriginal condition, the Mescalero are influenced somewhat by Plains contacts, the Jicarilla by Plains contacts and interaction with Taos, the Navaho by extensive contacts with eastern Pueblo groups and, later, with western Pueblo groups, and the Western Apache by more limited contacts with the western Pueblos. Only the Navaho and Western Apache practice agriculture on any scale, and both have matrilineal exogamous clans, with names partly derived from localities and partly totemic, and grouped into unnamed phratries that are organized in "chain-fashion" rather than in discrete groups. Both tribes also have extended families based on matrilocal residence which are grouped into larger local units based partly on lineages. The Jicarilla Apache have a dual division for opposition in games but no clans or phratries, and the kinship system is "classificatory" and bilateral, whereas the Navaho and Western Apache show some influence of the clan with regard to kinship, though there is no thoroughgoing reorientation of kindred in terms of the lineage principle.

The Havasupai, Walapai, and Yavapai form another related series which has a common linguistic and cultural background but shows variations in mode of subsistence and in contacts with other groups, the Havasupai, for example, having borrowed agriculture from their Hopi neighbors and developed a more sedentary life in Havasupai Canyon. The Lower Colorado Yuman groups and the Uto-Aztecan Pima and Papago have been subject to acculturation over a long period, and it is difficult to interpret the variations in their social structure. All have a patrilineal clan system which is exogamous among the River Yumans but not among the Pima and Papago; the latter also have a dual grouping of clans, but there is little agreement among authorities as to details.

These and other groups offer opportunities for controlled comparisons which will give us additional insights into the nature of social structure and the factors affecting their development, and such studies will ultimately contribute to a more comprehensive reconstruction of social organization in the Southwest.

Turning to a comparative view of social structures of the western Pueblo type, we find that the Hidatsa and Mandan of the Missouri River and the Southeastern tribes have social structures which are based on principles similar to those of the Hopi, while the Crow of Montana, the Pawnee, and certain of the Northwest Coast tribes have important similarities—and certain differences as well. That certain of these distant tribes are closer to the Hopi in social structure than the Hopi are to the eastern Tewa pueblos, or the near-by Navaho, illustrates the inadequacy of diffusion as a major explanation of similarities in social structure, or parallels in social structure as evidence of common origins. For the similarities are far-reaching, including even details of behavior patterns between key relatives. By comparing these social structures in terms of the conditions which underlay their development and by analyzing the principles on which they are organized, we will get increased understanding of these lineage-type systems.

We will also be able to deal with problems of change in social structures in a more fundamental way. Spoehr has made an outstanding contribution to these problems for the Southeast in his studies of the Seminole and in his comparative study of change among the Muskogean tribes.[75] I have elsewhere suggested that the Crow are transitional, so far as their social organization is concerned, between the Hidatsa parent-group and their Plains neighbors,[76] and the incomplete evidence for the Pawnee suggests a similar situation. The Pawnee may well have had matrilineal lineages and a Crow type of system without formal clans, though the evidence so far available is not conclusive. The Tlingit, Haida, and Tsimshian had certain features of a lineage-type social structure but combined it with cross-cousin marriage and residence with the mother's brother in such a way as to create a somewhat different type of structure.

By analyzing the directions of change under particular conditions, it should be possible to work out the stages by which a social system shifts from one stable configuration to another.

Spoehr has done this for the Southeastern tribes, and we have noted the data available on the Pueblo groups. To give one illustration, it surely is not accidental that the term for father's sister shifts to "mother" under conditions of change in the Southeast, among the Keresan groups in the Southwest, among the Crow and Pawnee of the Northern Plains, and among the Wichita to the south. Once such regularities in the processes of social change are formulated for various types of systems, we can use them as preliminary guides for further research.

The present volume has attempted a study of the social organization of the western Pueblos in both comparative and historical perspective, and has presented for further testing some hypotheses as to the nature of Pueblo social structures and the changes which they have undergone. The present body of materials should also be useful in examining the hypotheses and conclusions presented by Lowie,[77] Murdock,[78] and Levi-Strauss[79] on the basis of their wider surveys of social organization.

BIBLIOGRAPHY

BANCROFT, H. H. *History of Arizona and New Mexico*, in *Works*, Vol. XVII. San Francisco, 1889.

BANDELIER, A. F. *Final Report of Investigations among the Indians of the Southwestern United States*. ("Papers of the Archaeological Institute of America: American Series," Vol. III.) Cambridge, 1890.

BEAGLEHOLE, E. *Notes on Hopi Economic Life*. ("Yale University Publications in Anthropology," No. 15.) New Haven: Yale University Press, 1937.

BEAGLEHOLE, E., and BEAGLEHOLE, P. *Hopi of the Second Mesa*. ("Memoirs of the American Anthropological Association," No. 44.) Menasha, Wis., 1935.

BEAGLEHOLE, P. "Census Data from Two Hopi Villages," *American Anthropologist*, XXXVII (new ser., 1935), 41–54.

BENEDICT, RUTH. *Patterns of Culture*. Boston: Houghton Mifflin Co., 1934.

BLOOM, L. B. (ed.). "Bourke on the Southwest," Parts I–XIII, *New Mexico Historical Review*, Vols. VIII–XIII (1933–38).

BOAS, FRANZ. *Keresan Texts*. ("American Ethnological Society Publications," Vol. VIII, Part I.) New York: G. E. Stechert & Co., 1938.

BOAS, FRANZ, *et al. General Anthropology*. Boston: D. C. Heath & Co., 1938.

BOURKE, J. G. "Bourke on the Southwest," [journal ed. L. B. BLOOM], *New Mexico Historical Review*, Vols. VIII–XIII (1933–38).

BREW, J. O. "The First Two Seasons at Awatovi," *American Antiquity*, III (1937), 122–37.

———. "Preliminary Report of the Awatovi Expedition of 1939," *Plateau*, XIII, No. 3 (1940), 37–48.

BUNZEL, RUTH. "Introduction to Zuni Ceremonialism," *47th Annual Report of the Bureau of American Ethnology*, pp. 467–544. Washington, 1932.

———. "Zuni Origin Myths," *ibid.*, pp. 545–610.

———. "Zuni Ritual Poetry," *ibid.*, pp. 611–836.

———. "Zuni Kachinas," *ibid.*, pp. 837–1086.

———. "Economic Organization of Primitive Peoples," in FRANZ BOAS (ed.), *General Anthropology*. Boston: D. C. Heath & Co., 1938.

COLTON, H. S. *A Brief Survey of Hopi Common Law*. ("Museum of Northern Arizona, Museum Notes," Vol. VII, No. 6.) Flagstaff, 1934.

Colton, H. S. *Prehistoric Culture Units and Their Relationships in Northern Arizona.* (Bulletin of the Museum of Northern Arizona, No. 17.) Flagstaff, 1939.

———. *The Sinagua: A Summary of the Archaeology of the Region of Flagstaff, Arizona.* (Bulletin of the Museum of Northern Arizona, No. 22.) Flagstaff, 1946.

Cope, Leona. *Calendars of the Indians North of Mexico.* ("University of California Publications in American Archaeology and Ethnology," Vol. XVI.) Berkeley: University of California Press, 1919.

Crane, Leo. *Indians of the Enchanted Desert.* Boston: Little, Brown & Co., 1926.

———. *Desert Drums.* Boston: Little, Brown & Co., 1928.

Curtis, E. S. *The North American Indian,* Vol. XII. Seattle, Wash.: E. S. Curtis, 1922.

Cushing, F. H. "Outlines of Zuni Creation Myths," *13th Annual Report of the Bureau of American Ethnology.* Washington, 1896.

———. *Zuni Breadstuff.* ("Indian Notes and Monographs," Vol. VIII.) New York: Museum of the American Indian, Heye Foundation, 1920.

Cushing, F. H.; Fewkes, J. W.; and Parsons, E. C. "Contributions to Hopi History," *American Anthropologist,* XXIV (new ser., 1922), 253–98.

Dorsey, G. A., and Voth, H. R. *The Oraibi Soyal Ceremony.* ("Field Columbian Museum Pub. 55: Anthropological Series," Vol. III, No. 1.) Chicago, 1901.

Earle, Edwin, and Kennard, E. A. *Hopi Kachinas.* New York: Augustin, 1938.

Eggan, Fred. "The Social Organization of the Eastern Pueblos, 1932–33." (MS.)

———. "The Kinship System and Social Organization of the Western Pueblos with Especial Reference to the Hopi." Ph.D. thesis, University of Chicago. Chicago, 1933.

———. "The Kinship System of the Hopi Indians." Chicago: University of Chicago Libraries, 1936.

———. "Historical Changes in the Choctaw Kinship System," *American Anthropologist,* XXXIX (new ser., 1937), 34–52.

———. (ed.). *Social Anthropology of North American Tribes.* Chicago: University of Chicago Press, 1937.

———. "The Cheyenne and Arapaho Kinship System," in Eggan (ed.), *Social Anthropology of North American Tribes.* Chicago: University of Chicago Press, 1937.

———. "The Hopi and the Lineage Principle," in Meyer Fortes (ed.), *Social Structure.* Oxford: Oxford University Press, 1949.

———. "Archeological Cultures and Their Ethnological Backgrounds," in JAMES B. GRIFFIN (ed.), *The Archeology of the Eastern United States*. Chicago: University of Chicago Press. (In press.)

———. "Field Notes": "Second Mesa, 1934"; "Third Mesa, 1940, 1941."

FEWKES, J. W. "The Kinship of a Tanoan-speaking Community in Tusayan," *American Anthropologist*, VII (1894), 162–67.

———. "Winter Solstice Altars at Hano," *ibid.*, I (new ser., 1899), 251–76.

———. "Tusayan Migration Traditions," *19th Annual Report of the Bureau of American Ethnology*. Washington, 1900.

———. "An Initiation at Hano," *Journal of the Washington Academy of Science*, VII (1917), 149–58.

FORDE, C. D. "Hopi Agriculture and Land Ownership," *Journal of the Royal Anthropological Institute*, LXI (1931), 357–405.

———. "The Anthropological Approach to Social Science," *British Association for the Advancement of Science*, Vol. IV, No. 15 (1947).

FORTES, MEYER (ed.). *Social Structure*. Oxford: Oxford University Press, 1949.

FREIRE-MARRECO, BARBARA. "Tewa Kinship Terms from the Pueblo of Hano, Arizona," *American Anthropologist*, XVI (new ser., 1914), 268–87.

———. "A Note on Kinship Terms," *ibid.*, XVII (new ser., 1915), 198.

GOLDENWEISER, A. A. "Remarks on the Social Organization of the Crow Indians," *American Anthropologist*, XV (new ser., 1913), 281–94.

GOLDFRANK, E. S. *The Social and Ceremonial Organization of Cochiti*. ("Memoirs of the American Anthropological Association," No. 33.) Menasha, Wis., 1927.

———. "The Impact of Situation and Personality on Four Hopi Emergence Myths," *Southwestern Journal of Anthropology*, IV, No. 3 (1948), 241–62.

GOLDMAN, I. "The Zuni Indians of New Mexico," in MARGARET MEAD (ed.), *Cooperation and Competition among Primitive Peoples*. New York, 1937.

GOLDSCHMIDT, WALTER. "Social Organization in Native California and the Origin of Clans," *American Anthropologist*, L (new ser., 1948), 444–56.

GUNN, J. M. *Schat-Chen*. Albuquerque, 1938.

HACK, J. T. *The Changing Physical Environment of the Hopi Indians of Arizona*. ("Papers of the Peabody Museum of American Archaeology and Ethnology," Vol. XXXV, No. 1.) Cambridge, 1942.

HACKETT, C. W. (ed.). *Historical Documents Relating to New Mexico, Nueva Viscaya and Approaches Thereto, to 1773*. 3 vols. (Carnegie

Institution Pub. 330.) Vol. I, 1923; Vol. II, 1926; Vol. III, 1937. Washington, 1923–37.

———. *Revolt of the Pueblo Indians of New Mexico and Otermín's Attempted Reconquest, 1680–1682.* Albuquerque: University of New Mexico Press, 1942.

Hammond, G. P. "Oñate and the Founding of New Mexico," *New Mexico Historical Review*, I (1926), 42 ff., 156 ff., 292 ff. (Reprinted as a monograph.)

Harrington, J. P. "Tewa Relationship Terms," *American Anthropologist*, XIV (new ser., 1912), 472–98.

Hawley, F. M. "Pueblo Social Organization as a Lead to Pueblo History," *American Anthropologist*, XXXIX (new ser., 1937), 504–22.

Hodge, F. W. "Pueblo Indian Clans," *American Anthropologist*, IX (1896), 133–36.

———. (ed). *Handbook of the American Indians.* Bureau of American Ethnology Bull. 30. Washington, 1907–12.

———. *History of Hawikuh, New Mexico.* Los Angeles: The Southwest Museum, 1937.

Kennard, E. A. "Hopi Reactions to Death," *American Anthropologist*, XXXIX (new ser., 1937), 991–96.

Kroeber, A. L. "The Classificatory System of Relationship," *Journal of the Royal Anthropological Institute*, XXXIX (1909), 77–84.

———. "Thoughts on Zuni Religion," in *Holmes Anniversary Volume*, pp. 269–77. Washington, D.C., 1916.

———. *Zuni Kin and Clan.* ("Anthropological Papers of the American Museum of Natural History," Vol. XVIII, Part II.) New York, 1917.

———. "History and Science in Anthropology," *American Anthropologist*, XXXVII (new ser., 1935), 539–69.

———. "Athabascan Kin Term Systems," *ibid.*, XXXIX (new ser., 1937), 602–8.

———. "Basic and Secondary Patterns of Social Structure," *Journal of the Royal Anthropological Institute*, LXVIII (1938), 299–309.

Levi-Strauss, Claude. *Les Structures élémentaires de la parenté.* Paris: Presses Universitaires, 1949.

Li, An-che. "Zuni: Some Observations and Queries," *American Anthropologist*, XXXIX (new ser., 1937), 62–76.

Linton, R. "Crops, Soils, and Culture in America," in *The Maya and Their Neighbors.* New York: Appelton-Century Co., 1940.

———. "A Neglected Aspect of Social Organization," *American Journal of Sociology*, XLV (1940), 870–86.

Lowie, R. H. "Exogamy and the Classificatory System of Relationship," *American Anthropologist*, XVII (new ser., 1915), 223–39.

———. *Culture and Ethnology*. New York: D. C. McMurtrie, 1917.

———. *Notes on Hopi Clans*. ("Anthropological Papers of the American Museum of Natural History," Vol. XXX, Part VI.) New York, 1929.

———. *Hopi Kinship*. ("Anthropological Papers of the American Museum of Natural History," Vol. XXX, Part VII.) New York, 1929.

———. "Relationship Terms," *Encyclopaedia Britannica*. 14th ed. 1929.

———. "The Omaha and Crow Kinship Terminologies," *Proceedings of the 24th International Congress of Americanists*, pp. 102–8. Hamburg, 1930.

———. "American Culture History," *American Anthropologist*, XLII (new ser., 1940), 409–28.

———. *Social Organization*. New York: Rinehart & Co., 1948.

MALINOWSKI, BRONISLAW. "Parenthood, the Basis for Social Structure," in V. F. CALVERTON and S. D. SCHMAULHAUSEN, *The New Generation*. New York: Macaulay Co., 1930.

MARCSON, SIMON. "Some Methodological Consequences of Correlational Analysis in Anthropology," *American Anthropologist*, XLV (new ser., 1943), 588–601.

MINDELEFF, COSMOS. "Localization of Tusayan Clans," *19th Annual Report of the Bureau of American Ethnology*. Washington, 1900.

MINDELEFF, VICTOR. "A Study of Pueblo Architecture," *8th Annual Report of the Bureau of American Ethnology*. Washington, 1891.

MONTGOMERY, R. G.; SMITH, W.; and BREW, J. O. *Franciscan Awatovi*. ("Papers of the Peabody Museum of American Archeaology and Ethnology," Vol. XXXVI.) Cambridge, 1949.

MORGAN, L. H. *Systems of Consanguinity and Affinity of the Human Family*. ("Smithsonian Contributions to Knowledge," Vol. XVII.) Washington, 1870.

MURDOCK, G. P. *Social Structure*. New York: Macmillan Co., 1949.

OPLER, M. E. "The Kinship Systems of the Southern Athabaskan-speaking Tribes," *American Anthropologist*, XXXVIII (new ser., 1936), 620–33.

PARSONS, E. C. "Notes on Zuni," Parts I and II, *Memoirs of the American Anthropological Association*, Vol. IV, Nos. 3–4 (1917).

———. "Ceremonial Friendship at Zuni," *American Anthropologist*, XIX (new ser., 1917), 1–8.

———. "The Antelope Clan in Keresan Custom and Myth," *Man*, XVII (1917), 190–93.

———. "Zuni Conception and Pregnancy Beliefs," *Proceedings of the 19th International Congress of Americanists, 1917*, pp. 379–83.

PARSONS, E. C. "Notes on Acoma and Laguna," *American Anthropologist*, XX (new ser., 1918), 162–86.

———. "Mothers and Children at Laguna," *Man*, XIX (1919), 34–38.

———. *Notes on Ceremonialism at Laguna.* ("Anthropological Papers of the American Museum of Natural History," Vol. XIX, Part IV.) New York, 1920.

———. "Notes on Isleta, Santa Ana, and Acoma," *American Anthropologist*, XXII (new ser., 1920), 55–69.

———. "Shöhmopovi in 1920," in F. H. CUSHING, J. W. FEWKES, and E. C. PARSONS, "Contributions to Hopi History," *American Anthropologist*, XXIV (new ser., 1922), 253–98.

———. "Zuni Names and Naming Practices," *Journal of American Folk-Lore*, XXXVI (1923), 171–76.

———. *Laguna Genealogies.* ("Anthropological Papers of the American Museum of Natural History," Vol. XIX, Part V). New York, 1923.

———. "Tewa Kin, Clan, and Moiety," *American Anthropologist*, XXVI (new ser., 1924), 333–39.

———. *A Pueblo Indian Journal, 1920–1921.* ("Memoirs of the American Anthropological Association," No. 32.) Menasha, Wis., 1925.

———. *The Pueblo of Jemez.* Andover: Phillips Academy, 1925.

———. *Tewa Tales.* ("Memoirs of the American Folk-Lore Society," Vol. XIX.) New York, 1926.

———. "The Ceremonial Calendar of the Tewa of Arizona," *American Anthropologist*, XXVIII (new ser., 1926), 209–29.

———. "The Laguna Migration to Isleta," *American Anthropologist*, XXX (new ser., 1928), 602–13.

———. *The Social Organization of the Tewa of New Mexico.* ("Memoirs of the American Anthropological Association," No. 36.) Menasha, Wis., 1929.

———. "Isleta," *47th Annual Report of the Bureau of American Ethnology.* Washington, 1932.

———. "The Kinship Nomenclature of the Pueblo Indians," *American Anthropologist*, XXXIV (new ser., 1932), 377–89.

———. *Hopi and Zuni Ceremonialism.* ("Memoirs of the American Anthropological Association," No. 39.) Menasha, Wis., 1933.

———. "Picuris, New Mexico," *American Anthropologist*, XLI (new ser.,1939), pp. 206–22.

———. *Pueblo Indian Religion.* 2 vols. Chicago: University of Chicago Press, 1939.

——— (ed.). *Hopi Journal of Alexander M. Stephen.* ("Columbia University Contributions to Anthropology," Vol. XXIII.) New York: Columbia University Press, 1936.

RADCLIFFE-BROWN, A. R. *The Social Organization of Australian Tribes.* ("Oceania Monographs," Vol. I.) London: Macmillan & Co., 1931.

———. *The Andaman Islanders.* 2d ed. Cambridge: University Press, 1933.

———. "Patrilineal and Matrilineal Succession," *Iowa Law Review,* XX, No. 2 (1935), 286–303.

———. "The Study of Kinship Systems," *Journal of the Royal Anthropological Institute,* LXXI (1941), 1–18.

REAGAN, A. B. "The Jemez Indians," *El Palacio,* IV, No. 2 (1917), 24–72.

REED, E. "The Origins of Hano Pueblo," *El Palacio,* Vol. L (1943).

———. "The Distinctive Features and Distribution of the San Juan Anasazi Culture," *Southwestern Journal of Anthropology,* II, No. 3 (1946), 295–305.

———. "Sources of Upper Rio Grande Culture and Population," *El Palacio,* LVI, No. 6 (1949), 163–84.

SAPIR, EDWARD. "Central and North American Languages," *Encyclopaedia Britannica.* 14th ed. 1929.

SELTZER, CARL. *Racial Prehistory in the Southwest and the Hawikuh Zunis.* ("Papers of the Peabody Museum of American Archaeology and Ethnology," Vol. XXIII, No. 1.) Cambridge, 1944.

SIMMONS, L. W. (ed.). *Sun Chief: The Autobiography of a Hopi Indian.* New Haven: Yale University Press, 1942.

SPIER, L. "The Distribution of Kinship Systems in North America," *University of Washington Publications in Anthropology,* I, No. 2 (1925), 71–88.

SPOEHR, ALEXANDER. *Camp, Clan, and Kin among the Cow Creek Seminole of Florida.* ("Anthropological Series, Field Museum of Natural History," Vol. XXXIII, No. 1.) Chicago, 1941.

———. *Changing Kinship Systems.* ("Anthropological Series, Field Museum of Natural History," Vol. XXXIII, No. 4.) Chicago, 1947.

STEPHEN, A. M. "Hopi Tales," *Journal of American Folk-Lore,* XLIII (1930), 88–104.

———. *Hopi Journal,* ed. E. C. PARSONS. ("Columbia University Contributions to Anthropology," Vol. XXIII.) New York, 1936.

———. *The Hopi Indians of Arizona.* ("Southwestern Museum Leaflets," No. 14.) Los Angeles, 1940.

STEVENSON, M. C. "The Sia," *11th Annual Report of the Bureau of American Ethnology.* Washington, 1889–90.

———. "The Zuni Indians," *23d Annual Report of the Bureau of American Ethnology.* Washington, 1904.

STEWARD, JULIAN. "The Economic and Social Basis of Primitive Bands," in *Essays in Anthropology Presented to A. L. Kroeber.* Berkeley: University of California Press, 1936.

STEWARD, JULIAN. "Ecological Aspects of Southwestern Society," *Anthropos*, XXXII (1937), 87–104.

———. *Basin-Plateau Aboriginal Sociopolitical Groups*. (Bureau of American Ethnology Bull. 120.) Washington, 1938.

STIRLING, M. W. *Origin Myth of Acoma*. (Bureau of American Ethnology Bull. 135.) Washington, 1942.

STRONG, W. D. "An Analysis of Southwestern Society," *American Anthropologist*, XXIX (new ser., 1927), 1–61.

THOMAS, A. B. *Forgotten Frontiers*. Norman: University of Oklahoma Press, 1932.

THOMAS, W. I. *Primitive Behavior*. New York: McGraw-Hill Book Co., 1937.

THOMPSON, LAURA, and JOSEPH, ALICE. *The Hopi Way*. ("Indian Education Research Series," No. 1.) Chicago: University of Chicago Press, 1944.

TITIEV, MISCHA. *The Use of Kinship Terms in Hopi Ritual*. ("Museum of Northern Arizona, Museum Notes," Vol. X, No. 3.) Flagstaff, 1937.

———. "The Problem of Cross-Cousin Marriage among the Hopi," *American Anthropologist*, XL (new ser., 1938), 105–11.

———. *Notes on Hopi Witchcraft*. ("Papers of the Michigan Academy of Science, Arts, and Letters," Vol. XXVIII, Part IV.) New York: Macmillan Co., 1942.

———. *Old Oraibi*. ("Papers of the Peabody Museum of American Archaeology and Ethnology," Vol. XXII, No. 1.) Cambridge, 1944.

TRAGER, GEORGE. "Kinship and Status Terms of the Tiwa Language," *American Anthropologist*, XLV (new ser., 1943), 557–71.

VOTH, H. R. "Oraibi Marriage Customs," *American Anthropologist*, II (new ser., 1900), 238–46.

———. *The Oraibi Powamu Ceremony*. ("Field Columbian Museum Pub. 61, Anthropological Series," Vol. III, No. 2.) Chicago, 1901.

———. *The Oraibi Oaqöl Ceremony*. ("Field Columbian Museum Pub. 84, Anthropological Series," Vol. VI, No. 1.) Chicago, 1903.

———. *Hopi Proper Names*. ("Field Columbian Museum, Pub. 100, Anthropological Series," Vol. VI, No. 3.) Chicago, 1905.

———. *Oraibi Natal Customs and Ceremonies*. ("Field Columbian Museum Pub. 157, Anthropological Series," Vol. VI, No. 2.) Chicago, 1905.

———. *The Traditions of the Hopi*. ("Field Columbian Museum Pub. 96, Anthropological Series," Vol. VIII.) Chicago, 1905.

WHITE, L. A. "A Comparative Study of Keresan Medicine Societies," *Proceedings of the 23d International Congress of Americanists, 1928*, pp. 604–19.

———. "Summary Report of Field Work at Acoma," *American Anthropologist*, XXX (new ser., 1928), 559–68.

———. "The Acoma Indians," *47th Annual Report of the Bureau of American Ethnology, 1932*. Washington, 1932.

———. *The Pueblo of San Felipe*. ("Memoirs of the American Anthropological Association," No. 38.) Menasha, Wis., 1932.

———. *The Pueblo of Santo Domingo, New Mexico*. ("Memoirs of the American Anthropological Association," No. 43.) Menasha, Wis., 1935.

———. *The Pueblo of Santa Ana, New Mexico*. ("Memoirs of the American Anthropological Association," No. 60.) Menasha, Wis., 1942.

———. *New Material from Acoma*. (Bureau of American Ethnology Bull. 136, Anthropology Paper No. 33.) Washington, 1942.

WHORF, B. L., and TRAGER, G. L. "The Relationship of Uto-Aztecan and Tanoan," *American Anthropologist*, XXXIX (new ser., 1937), 609–24.

WIRTH, LOUIS (ed.). *Eleven Twenty-six: A Decade of Social Science Research*. Chicago: University of Chicago Press, 1940.

WITTFOGEL, K., and GOLDFRANK, E. S. "Some Aspects of Pueblo Mythology and Society," *Journal of American Folk-Lore*, LVI (1943), 17–30.

Notes

CHAPTER I

Introduction

1. Parsons, *Pueblo Indian Religion*, Vol. I, Preface.

2. Parsons has come to a similar conclusion with reference to this division: "Acoma and Laguna will be referred to as western Keres and generally accounted in the West . . ." (*ibid.*, p. 5, n. †).

3. Cf. Parsons, "Tewa Kin, Clan, and Moiety," p. 339.

4. In Sapir's proposed classification ("Central and North American Languages," pp. 138–41) Uto-Aztecan and Tanoan are grouped together, while Keresan is placed in the Hokan-Siouan stock. Zuni is possibly affiliated with Aztec-Tanoan. More recently Whorf and Trager, in their "Relationship of Uto-Aztecan and Tanoan," have refined the Aztec-Tanoan groupings and have furnished comparative data which make it possible to reconstruct the development of this stock with considerable accuracy.

5. I am particularly indebted to Radcliffe-Brown for the point of view which follows.

6. See Thomas' statement: "The social sciences are fundamentally concerned with relationships between individuals and individuals, individuals and groups, and groups and other groups. Language, gossip, customs, codes, institutions, organizations, governments, professions, etc., are concerned with the mediation of these relationships" (*Primitive Behavior*, p. 1).

7. Cf. Linton's statement: "By studying the social relations between individuals and observing the repetitive situations, it becomes possible to deduce the structural pattern of the society. This pattern tends to persist in spite of the steady turnover of the society's content . . ." ("A Neglected Aspect of Social Organization," p. 871).

8. Radcliffe-Brown has emphasized the concept of social integration in his theoretical discussions, whereas Malinowski appears to emphasize cultural integration. The concept of social integration is of more importance in considering social structure.

9. Linton expresses these ideas in the form of an analogy: "A rope can be analyzed into its component strands with respect both to its total length and to its content at any point in that length. Its structural pattern can also be ascertained by observing the spatial relations of the various strands at a series of points along its length. This pattern will persist in spite of the termination of certain strands and the introduction of others and will bear little relation to the individual qualities

of the various strands—such things as their exact length, thickness, or color. It can be described in the abstract and compared with the structural pattern revealed by other ropes. A society, in its extension through time, can be likened to a rope braided from the short strands of individual lives" (*op. cit.*, p. 871).

10. *Ibid.*, p. 871.
11. In Wirth (ed.), *Eleven Twenty-six*, p. 263.
12. *Ibid.*, p. 263.
13. See Kroeber, "History and Science in Anthropology," pp. 545 ff.
14. Eggan, "Historical Changes in the Choctaw Kinship System," p. 52, and "Cheyenne and Arapaho Kinship System," p. 95.
15. Linton, *op. cit.*, p. 872.
16. See Radcliffe-Brown, "The Study of Kinship Systems."
17. See Cushing, "Outlines of Zuni Creation Myths."
18. Fewkes, "Tusayan Migration Traditions," in particular.
19. Mindeleff, "Localization of Tusayan Clans."
20. Parsons (ed.), *Hopi Journal of Alexander M. Stephen.*
21. Cf. Kroeber, *Zuni Kin and Clan*, p. 135.
22. Kroeber, "The Classificatory System of Relationship," p. 83.
23. See, e.g., Radcliffe-Brown, *The Social Organization of Australian Tribes.*
24. Parsons, *Laguna Genealogies*, published in 1923.
25. Lowie, *Hopi Kinship* and *Notes on Hopi Clans.*
26. Lowie, *Hopi Kinship*, p. 383.
27. Parsons, "The Kinship Nomenclature of the Pueblo Indians."
28. *Ibid.*, pp. 386–87 for examples.
29. Lowie, "Relationship Terms," p. 84. Radcliffe-Brown has applied this point of view to the analysis of Australian kinship systems with important results. Cf. his *Social Organization of Australian Tribes.*
30. Radcliffe-Brown, *Andaman Islanders*, p. ix.
31. Lowie, "Exogamy and the Classificatory System of Relationship," p. 239.

CHAPTER II

The Social Organization of the Hopi Indians

1. Hack, *Changing Physical Environment of the Hopi Indians.* See also Forde, "Hopi Agriculture and Land Ownership."
2. J. O. Brew, in Preface to Hack, *op. cit.*, p. vii.
3. Village names are given as in recent literature. See the glossary in Stephen's *Hopi Journal*, II, 1199–1201.
4. See Titiev, *Old Oraibi.*
5. They co-operated in the killing of the Spanish priests in the Rebellion of 1680 and possibly in the destruction of Awatovi around 1700. Recently an all-Hopi council has been set up under the Wheeler-

Howard Act, but its effects toward unity, if any, have not yet been felt.

6. The initial field work on which the following account is based was carried out in direct collaboration with Mischa Titiev, who has also made available to me the results of his further study. Throughout we endeavored to understand the native conception of social organization and to check this conception against concrete information collected by genealogical and other methods; and, while our interpretations differ somewhat, that is largely because they are directed toward different ends. For information on First Mesa I am indebted to various accounts by Lowie, Stephen, and Parsons; for Second Mesa to Lowie, the Beagleholes, and Kennard, as well as to my own field work. See also my "Kinship System of the Hopi Indians" and "The Hopi and the Lineage Principle."

7. While we are using English terms for convenience, these terms must be understood with reference to their Hopi applications and meanings, which latter are determined by the reciprocal behavior involved. Terms used in a classificatory sense are inclosed in quotation marks. For the Hopi terms see Lowie, *Hopi Kinship;* Parsons, "Kinship Nomenclature of the Pueblo Indians"; and Titiev, *op. cit.*

8. The use of diagrams in describing kinship structures makes it possible to grasp their essentials rather easily, provided the proper diagrams are selected. Goldenweiser has pointed out that the presentation of systems of relationships should be based on the native principles of classification: "Whenever this is done the system always reduces itself to a few simple principles and can readily be presented in tabular form" ("Remarks on the Social Organization of the Crow Indians," p. 294).

9. Lowie reports this usage for First and Second Mesas (*op. cit.*, pp. 371, 373), I have found it on Second Mesa, and Titiev and I have found it on Third Mesa. Stephen and Parsons report another term (*pa'vaiya*) for Walpi, however, which is probably the third-person designation (*Hopi Journal*, II, 1044).

10. Titiev, *The Use of Kinship Terms in Hopi Ritual.*

11. Cf. Lowie, *op. cit.*, pp. 369–70.

12. Titiev, *Old Oraibi*, p. 13.

13. This conceptual unity still remains even where modern conditions have led to new housebuilding. Most censuses of Hopi villages have ignored this important grouping in favor of a count by more strictly defined "households."

14. In Hopi thinking the "clan" and the "clanhouse" are the important units. Despite the lack of specific names, the Hopi clearly differentiate the various household groups and lineages in any particular village.

15. I am indebted to Titiev for much of this material, since the original data were collected jointly, and he has placed his later notes and manuscript at my disposal. Because he has published a detailed account in his monograph, *Old Oraibi*, I am including here only a summary. Part of these data has been published in planograph form in "The Kinship System of the Hopi Indians" and, more recently, in "The Hopi and the Lineage System." I have presented the analysis of kinship in terms of the lineage rather than the clan for theoretical reasons which I think will be clear.

16. The father and the father's brothers are considered as "real fathers," since they have the same blood.

17. Based on a detailed analysis of census materials (see *Old Oraibi*, pp. 39 ff.). There is no evidence that this is a recent phenomenon connected with modern changes. There is evidence from Second Mesa villages, however, that marriage is much more "brittle" in its initial phases, with considerable stability after this period is passed.

18. In this connection it may be significant that a man has separate terms for "younger brother" and "younger sister," whereas a woman uses only one term, "younger sibling."

19. There are thought to be temperamental differences between brothers and sisters. See Kennard, "Hopi Reactions to Death," for some examples.

20. Stephen notes for First Mesa that "formerly when a girl married, her uncles and brothers went out and selected timbers for her grave and put them away preserved until her death" (*Hopi Journal*, I, 151).

21. Cf. Beaglehole and Beaglehole, *Hopi of the Second Mesa*, p. 64.

22. If Stephen is correct, the term for mother's mother's brother was also used reciprocally on First Mesa (*Hopi Journal*, II, 1044).

23. See Lowie, *op. cit.*, pp. 384–85. The Beagleholes (*op. cit.*, p. 64) report both sets of grandparents as involved in teasing.

24. Discussed in more detail in the account of the life-cycle.

25. I am indebted to Titiev for further insight into the nature of this relationship (see *Old Oraibi*, pp. 28 and 37).

26. Cf. Beaglehole and Beaglehole, *op. cit.*, p. 64.

27. Cf. the threats of castration in Simmons, *Sun Chief*, pp. 39–40.

28. The sister of the father's mother may, if young, be called "father's sister," and Lowie reports that the oldest father's sister may be called "grandmother" (*op. cit.*, p. 372).

29. This relationship of aid and co-operation is exceedingly important and works both ways. As one Hopi woman put it, "You have to *earn* your *mïwi*."

30. There is also an extension of the term "mother" to the wives of men of the father's lineage and clan, but these share in only a portion of the "real mother's" relationship.

31. Modern conditions of social change have modified the kinship structure, largely by breaking up the household organization into elementary families which are more or less independent of the household lineage. This situation will be treated in a later section.

32. See especially the reports of Voth, Stephen, Parsons, Beaglehole, Kennard, and Titiev. While there is some variation from village to village in details, the basic patterns are quite similar.

33. The confinement, presentation to the sun, and feast take place, on Second Mesa at least, even when the child dies during this period (cf. Beaglehole and Beaglehole, *Hopi of the Second Mesa*, pp. 37–38).

34. Stephen reports a similarly named deity on First Mesa, but Tuwabongtumsi (Sand Altar Woman) is reported as the mother of all living things (*Hopi Journal*, II, 978, and Glossary).

35. Cf. Parsons, *A Pueblo Indian Journal*, p. 51, n. 84, and Beaglehole and Beaglehole, *op. cit.*, p. 26.

36. Cf. Beaglehole and Beaglehole, *op. cit.*, pp. 37–38.

37. At Oraibi there are two separate initiations during Powamu—one for membership in the Powamu society which involves no whipping and which entitles the novice to act later as "father" of the Katcinas and the ordinary Katcina initiation for the bulk of the children (see Voth, *The Oraibi Powamu Ceremony*, and Stephen, *Hopi Journal*, for details).

38. Cf. Beaglehole, *Notes on Hopi Economic Life*.

39. See, especially, Stephen, *Hopi Journal*, I, 139–43; Beaglehole and Beaglehole, *op. cit.*, pp. 44–45; and Titiev, *op. cit.*, pp. 203–4.

40. I am following Titiev's suggestion in using "Tribal Initiation" for the whole ceremony, since "Wuwutcim," the generally used term, is ambiguous. There are several accounts available for First Mesa, particularly the day-by-day accounts of Stephen. Titiev has worked out the ceremony for Third Mesa, and I am indebted to him for much of the interpretation of this complex ritual (see *Old Oraibi*, pp. 130 ff.).

41. See Stephen, *Hopi Journal*, I, 96–100; Beaglehole and Beaglehole, *op. cit.*, pp. 23–24, and Titiev's account of war practices in *Old Oraibi*, pp. 155 ff. On Third Mesa, at least, every able-bodied man generally joined the War society in the old days, but few became "real warriors."

42. There are many accounts of marriage available. I am here using primarily Stephen's *Hopi Journal*, the Beagleholes' *Hopi of the Second Mesa*, and Titiev's *Old Oraibi*, in addition to my own field notes.

43. See Beaglehole, *op. cit.*, pp. 46–47, and Titiev, *op. cit.*, pp. 36 ff. There is a further restriction that two brothers should not court the same girl—even at different times.

44. Titiev, *op. cit.*, chap. iii.

45. This is particularly true in important families.

46. From an Oraibi informant.

47. Based on an analysis of over four hundred marriages (Titiev, *op. cit.*, p. 39).

48. The relation of these marriages to possible cross-cousin marriage will be discussed below.

49. The Hopi believe that the witches have a regular society and initiation. Children are stolen at night and initiated. They are thought to have two hearts, one belonging to an animal, and are able to transform themselves into that animal at will. See also Beaglehole and Beaglehole, *op. cit.*, pp. 5–10, and Titiev, *Notes on Hopi Witchcraft.*

50. Beaglehole and Beaglehole, *op. cit.*, p. 12. See also *ibid.*, pp. 11–14, for an account of "Hopi Death Customs."

51. See Earle and Kennard, *Hopi Kachinas.*

52. See Titiev, *Old Oraibi*, pp. 44–46, for a summary.

53. *Ibid.*, p. 49. Titiev adds a census of clanhouses, households, and household heads, to which should also be added clan lands.

54. Parsons, Introduction to Stephen, *Hopi Journal*, p. xxxiv.

55. Major sources: Stephen's early surveys reported in V. Mindeleff, "A Study of Pueblo Architecture," and more particularly in C. Mindeleff, "Localization of Tusayan Clans," and Parsons (ed.), *Hopi Journal of A. M. Stephen;* Fewkes, "Tusayan Migration Traditions"; Lowie, *Notes on Hopi Clans;* Parsons, *Pueblo Indian Journal;* Forde, "Hopi Agriculture and Land Ownership;" Beaglehole, "Census Data from Two Hopi Villages"; and the writer's field notes for Second and Third Mesas.

56. According to Fewkes, "Tusayan Migration Traditions," p. 604. See also Lowie, *Notes on Hopi Clans*, p. 337.

57. The last survivor, Kotka, died recently, and it will be interesting to watch the disposition of his privileges. Since then efforts have been made to get a Bear clan girl from Shongopovi to revive the group.

58. It is listed as an extinct clan at Shongopovi, however.

59. Forde, *op. cit.*, p. 375, and Eggan, "Field Notes."

60. Since partially solved by the marriage of the chief's son and successor to a Bear clan woman from Shongopovi.

61. Lowie, *op. cit.*, p. 335.

62. Beaglehole, "Census Data from Two Hopi Villages," p. 52.

63. The Katcina clan is now (1948) reduced to a single male member, but efforts are under way to revive it.

64. Later information indicates Sun and Sun's Forehead as linked but separate clans, with several lineages in each.

65. *Kokop* is variously translated as "cedarwood," "fire," "firespindle," "charcoal," etc. Whorf states that the exact translation is not known. Some Third Mesa informants said that it was the name of a small bird.

66. I was told that the Rabbit clan was formerly affiliated with Katcina-Parrot at Shongopovi.

67. Lowie's Second Mesa informants insisted there were three lineages on First Mesa: Real Corn people from Mishongnovi, Cloud people, and Sivapi people (*Notes on Hopi Clans*, p. 335).

68. This linkage with Katcina is not confirmed by my own field notes. The single male survivor is married into another Second Mesa village but returns for his ceremonial duties.

69. Some informants list all three clans as "extinct," but the absence of clan lands makes their recent presence doubtful.

70. Parsons, Introduction to Stephen, *Hopi Journal*, pp. xxii–xxiii.

71. See Titiev's parallel analysis in *Old Oraibi*, chap. iv.

72. Lowie, *Notes on Hopi Clans*, pp. 348 ff.

73. Parsons, Introduction to Stephen, *Hopi Journal*, p. xxxiv; cf. also Parsons, *Pueblo Indian Religion*, I, 60.

74. Parsons, Introduction to Stephen, *Hopi Journal*, p. xxxiv, n. 1.

75. Fewkes, "Tusayan Migration Traditions."

76. C. Mindeleff, "Localization of Tusayan Clans."

77. *Ibid.*, p. 648. His interpretations are based on both Hopi traditions and a study of Pueblo architecture.

78. See the reconstruction of Hopi history outlined below in the section on "Conclusions and Interpretations."

79. Lowie, *Notes on Hopi Clans*, p. 337.

80. Radcliffe-Brown, *Social Organization of Australian Tribes*, p. 399.

81. Titiev, *Old Oraibi*, p. 55. For convenience I will use *wuya* for both singular and plural.

82. See Parsons, *Hopi and Zuni Ceremonialism*, p. 36.

83. Cf. Lowie, *Notes on Hopi Clans*, pp. 337–38.

84. Titiev, *Old Oraibi*, pp. 56 ff.

85 See Parsons, *Hopi and Zuni Ceremonialism*, pp. 25 ff., for illustrations.

86. See Voth, *Traditions of the Hopi*, pp. 36 ff.

87. I have relied primarily on field data from Third Mesa for the following summary.

88. Voth, *Traditions of the Hopi*, pp. 36 ff.

89. Stephen, "Hopi Tales," pp. 3–6.

90. Locust is important because he comes out of the ground at a definite time. He was sent up from the underworld by Spider Woman, and, because he was very brave (did not blink his eyes), the Hopi were allowed to ascend (*ibid.*, p. 5).

91. See Titiev, *Old Oraibi*.

92. Stephen, *Hopi Journal*, p. 95, where ravens are represented as feeding upon the enemies to be slain.

93. Personal communication from Stanley Stubbs.

94. So I would interpret the Katcina (Crow) and Parrot (Katcina-Crow) lineages at Oraibi (see Titiev, *Old Oraibi*, p. 49).

95. One clan chief turned Christian and burned his ceremonial apparatus; another member was insane; etc.

96. There is an association of the two on First Mesa also (Stephen, *Hopi Journal*, p. 1072, n. 4). The Katcina initiation is concerned in part with ceremonial knowledge relating to the growth of plants.

97. Crane translates *kokop* as "ghost and bird" clan (see *Indians of the Enchanted Desert*).

98. Perhaps to "flute," since the village chieftainship and the control of the Blue Flute ceremony rested in this group.

99. Cushing, "Outlines of Zuni Creation Myths," p. 368.

100. Thompson and Joseph, *The Hopi Way*, p. 38.

101. Titiev, *Old Oraibi*, Part II.

102. Lowie, *Notes on Hopi Clans*, p. 331.

103. Kroeber, *Zuni Kin and Clan*, p. 135.

104. Fewkes, *op. cit.*, pp. 582–84. This list is derived mainly from First Mesa.

105. Forde, *op. cit.*, pp. 400–401.

106. Titiev, *Old Oraibi*, p. 49.

107. Forde, "Anthropological Approach to Social Science," p. 4.

108. I have omitted the ceremonially dependent villages of Shipaulovi and Sichomovi, as well as the recent villages derived from Oraibi, from the main discussion, though these are important in connection with a study of the process of differentiation in clan-ceremonial pattern.

109. Stephen, *Hopi Journal*, pp. 958–59.

110. See, e.g., Titiev's discussion in *Old Oraibi* (pp. 207–13) of the development of Hotevilla and Bakavi.

111. Lowie, *Notes on Hopi Clans*, pp. 343–44.

112. See Titiev, *Old Oraibi*, chap. ix, and Earle and Kennard, *op. cit.*, for an account of the Katcina cult on Third Mesa.

113. The presence of a separate Powamu kiva at Oraibi, owned by the Badger clan, is further evidence.

114. We have noted above (pp. 84–85) the association of the badger with the growth of wild plants and roots, which gives one basis for the tie-up.

115. Lowie, *Notes on Hopi Clans*, p. 346. Stephen (*Hopi Journal*, p. 1072, n. 4) quotes a Badger clansman to the effect that the Badger clan was originally of the Katcina clan.

116. This is the only exclusive Powamu kiva among the Hopi.

117. Titiev, *Old Oraibi*, chap. x.

118. Stephen, *Hopi Indians of Arizona*, pp. 18–19; see also Parsons, Introduction to Stephen, *Hopi Journal*, p. xxxix.

119. The Bear clan is thought to "own" most ceremonies at Shongopovi but allocates them to various other clans.

120. For rotation, see Parsons, "Shöhmopovi in 1920," p. 297; see also Forde, "Hopi Agriculture and Land Ownership," p. 364, Map 4.

121. Fewkes, *op. cit.*, p. 601.

122. The "Fog" clan at Shongopovi derives from a Tewa clanswoman of the Cloud clan who came from First Mesa and whose descendants have become differentiated as Fog clanspeople. See Parsons, "Shöhmopovi in 1920," p. 294, for part of the story.

123. Stephen, *Hopi Journal*, pp. 1174–76. These are probably used by Sichomovi members.

124. *Ibid.*, p. xliii.

125. Voth, *The Oraibi Oaqöl Ceremony*, p. 6.

126. Titiev, *Old Oraibi*, p. 104. Actually these two kivas are normally the same.

127. Stephen, *Hopi Journal*, p. 203.

128. See Dorsey and Voth, *The Oraibi Soyal Ceremony;* Titiev, *Old Oraibi*, pp. 142 ff.

129. Parsons, "Shöhmopovi in 1920," p. 296. My information is that the Bear clan controls the Soyal at Shongopovi.

130. See Stephen, *Hopi Journal*, pp. xxxiii and 769.

131. *Ibid.*, pp. 1 ff.

132. *Ibid.*, p. 1. Parsons was told that the distribution of prayer feathers on First Mesa was by clan (p. 46, n. 1). This is probably true on other mesas as well for this particular ritual.

133. See Titiev, *Old Oraibi*, chap. xi.

134. Stephen, *Hopi Journal*, p. 769. Parsons has here presented several exceedingly valuable historical hypotheses.

135. These associations are reversed at Shipaulovi, a colony of Shongopovi, as far as the controlling clans are concerned. Informants state that the Snake ceremony once belonged to the Snake and Sand clans; the present chief is married into the Bear clan, which may account for the present association, since the latter controls the redistribution.

136. Stephen, *Hopi Journal*, p. 580.

137. With the growing extinction of the Bear clan in the nineteenth century the Snake clan took over the Town chieftaincy temporarily and may have taken over the Antelope ceremony at that time from the Bear group.

138. Lowie, *Notes on Hopi Clans*, p. 342.

139. Titiev, *Old Oraibi*, chap. xii.

140. Parsons, "Shöhmopovi in 1920," pp. 296–98.

141. Stephen, *Hopi Journal*, pp. 83–100.

142. *Ibid.*, pp. 157–58, 182, 1073.

143. Titiev, *Old Oraibi*, p. 243, n. 6.

144. Parsons, *Pueblo Indian Religion*, I, 501 ff.

145. Titiev, *Old Oraibi*, chap. vii.

146. *Ibid.*, p. 211.

147. See Goldfrank, "Impact of Situation and Personality on Four Hopi Emergence Myths."

148. Parsons, "Shöhmopovi in 1920," p. 297.

149. Lowie, *Notes on Hopi Clans*, p. 338. That this pattern is fairly old—and variable—is suggested by a tradition recorded by Voth (*Traditions of the Hopi*, pp. 40–41) to the effect that the Town chieftaincy was held in succession by the Bluebird, Bear, Patki (Cloud) and Squash clans.

150. Parsons, "Shöhmopovi in 1930," p. 297.

151. See Titiev, *Old Oraibi*, chap. v.

152. Mishongnovi has been trying to get an acceptable village chief for some time.

153. Stephen, *Hopi Journal*, pp. 1061–64.

154. See Titiev, *Old Oraibi*, pp. 59 ff., for a discussion of the legislative and other functions of the chiefs.

155. Colton, *A Brief Survey of Hopi Common Law*, p. 22.

156. Around 1900 the Soyal War Chief was a member of the Real Badger clan.

157. Curtis, *North American Indian*, XII, 63.

158. Colton, *op. cit.*, p. 24.

159. Titiev, *Old Oraibi*, p. 68.

160. E.g., the two lineages of the Bear clan at a Second Mesa village, one of which is relatively weak, without ceremonies, and of low status, the other which is pre-eminent and controls most of the ceremonies.

161. Radcliffe-Brown, "Patrilineal and Matrilineal Succession," p. 300.

162. Cf. Titiev, *Old Oraibi*, pp. 46–48.

163. *Ibid.*, chap. vi.

164. See also Eggan, "The Hopi and the Lineage Principle."

165. Radcliffe-Brown, "The Study of Kinship Systems," p. 7.

166. *Ibid.*, pp. 9–10.

167. In the case of the Oraibi "split," however, the household proved to be a stable unit (see Titiev, *Old Oraibi*, pp. 88–89).

168. See Eggan, "Cheyenne and Arapaho Kinship Systems," pp. 75–81.

169. Beaglehole and Beaglehole (*op. cit.*, p. 64), however, report stock jokes between the maternal grandfather and the grandson, involving putative intercourse with the maternal grandmother.

170. See Titiev, *Old Oraibi*, pp. 79 ff., for a detailed account.

171. The modern situation will be discussed at greater length in a forthcoming study of Hopi social and cultural change.

172. Spier, "Distribution of Kinship Systems in North America."

173. Eggan, "Cheyenne and Arapaho Kinship Systems," p. 93.

174. Lowie, "Omaha and Crow Kinship Terminologies."

175. Lowie, *Culture and Ethnology*, pp. 176–77.

176. Lowie, *Hopi Kinship*, p. 383.

177. Lowie, "Omaha and Crow Kinship Terminologies," pp. 106, 108.

178. Lowie has recently adopted a similar type of analysis (see his *Social Organization*, pp. 69 ff.).

179. Kroeber (*Zuni Kin and Clan*, p. 86) also questioned the primacy of this correlation.

180. Titiev, "The Problem of Cross-Cousin Marriage among the Hopi," p. 111.

181. Titiev (*ibid.*, p. 110) found almost 10 per cent. But even in Shipaulovi, with only two major clans, there are relatively few such marriages, the great bulk of marriages being with Shongopovi and Mishongnovi.

182. Malinowski, "Parenthood, the Basis for Social Structure," pp. 154–56.

183. Kroeber, *Zuni Kin and Clan*, p. 72.

184. *Ibid.*

185. Lowie, *Culture and Ethnology*, p. 166.

186. *Ibid.*, p. 167.

187. The special term for mother's mother's brother noted for First Mesa may be another instance.

188. See Colton, *Prehistoric Culture Units and Their Relationships in Northern Arizona*, and Brew, "Preliminary Report of the Awatovi Expedition of 1939," and "The First Two Seasons at Awatovi." Dr. Brew has kindly outlined the development of cultures in the Jeddito region in a personal communication.

189. See Steward, "Ecological Aspects of Southwestern Society," for a pioneer treatment. For the interpretation of archeological remains see my "Archeological Cultures and Their Ethnological Backgrounds."

190. Colton, *Prehistoric Culture Units*, p. 59.

191. *Ibid.*, pp. 52–55. Cf. the determinants for the Lino and Marsh Pass Foci.

192. Brew, "Preliminary Report of the Awatovi Expedition of 1939," pp. 45–46. His analysis of sites shows 28 Basketmaker III, 25 Pueblo I, and 83 Pueblo II.

193. After the eruption of Sunset Crater (*ca.* A.D. 1066) the San Francisco Mountain region was temporarily abandoned, but the original population later returned with increments from neighboring groups. There is no evidence so far, however, that any important increments came from the Hopi region (see Colton, *The Sinagua*, pp. 258–59).

194. See Montgomery, Smith, and Brew, *Franciscan Awatovi*, for a detailed account of the historic period.

195. Steward, "The Economic and Social Basis of Primitive Bands."

196. Steward, "Ecological Aspects of Southwestern Society."

197. *Ibid.*, pp. 101–2.

198. Steward, *Basin-Plateau Aboriginal Sociopolitical Groups*, pp. 4–5.

199. *Ibid.*, pp. 230–37.

200. *Ibid.*, pp. 238–39.

201. *Ibid.*, pp. 241–46 and Fig. 13, p. 285. The systematic practice of sister exchange and cross-cousin marriage is difficult under such severe ecological conditions. Cross-cousin marriage was apparently giving way to pseudo cross-cousin marriage in some groups, resulting in a slightly wider integration.

202. *Ibid.*, p. 57.

203. Cf. Linton, "Crops, Soils, and Culture in America," pp. 34–35.

204. Steward, "Ecological Aspects of Southwestern Society," p. 95.

205. *Ibid.* For comparative purposes I have used the same figure per house (five) as Steward.

206. Brew, "The First Two Seasons at Awatovi," p. 127.

207. *Ibid.*, p. 134. Colton (*Prehistoric Culture Units*, p. 63) states that the Jeddito Focus "seems to represent the fusion of the Tsegi Focus of the Kayenta Branch with the Tusayan Branch."

208. Steward, "Ecological Aspects of Southwestern Society," p. 99.

209. See the discussion of the Tewa of Hano in the next chapter, who offer a historical instance of such an adjustment.

210. The multiple "clan names" may date from this period. It is worth recalling that the clan names were secured after the Emergence from the underworld as a result of various events occurring during periods of wandering.

211. Kroeber, "Basic and Secondary Patterns of Social Structure," p. 308.

212. *Ibid.*, p. 300.

213. Steward, *Basin-Plateau Aboriginal Sociopolitical Groups*, p. 57.

214. Kroeber, "Basic and Secondary Patterns of Social Structure," pp. 307–8.

215. The writer has in process a study of social and cultural change among the Hopi which will include an analysis of the modern situation.

216. Compare the case cited by Titiev, *Old Oraibi*, p. 20.

CHAPTER III

The Social Organization of Hano

1. Reed, "The Origins of Hano Pueblo," p. 73. The dialects of northern and southern Tewa are very similar.

2. Parsons, *Pueblo Indian Religion*, II, 913 nn.

3. A. B. Thomas, *Forgotten Frontiers*, p. 107.

4. Reported in Fewkes, "The Kinship of a Tanoan-speaking Community in Tusayan," p. 165. Excluded in these figures are some 16 Tewa men living in other villages.

5. *Ibid.*, p. 167. The present population is around 200.

6. V. Mindeleff, "A Study of Pueblo Architecture," p. 61.

7. Freire-Marreco, "Tewa Kinship Terms from the Pueblo of Hano, Arizona," pp. 269–87. I have simplified the phonetic renderings in the charts and in the discussion that follows.

8. Cf. Harrington, "Tewa Relationship Terms," and Parsons, *The Social Organization of the Tewa of New Mexico.*

9. There is an alternate term for father's brother which is sometimes used; its reciprocal is obsolescent.

10. Freire-Marreco, "A Note on Kinship Terms," pp. 198 ff.

11. Freire-Marreco, "Tewa Kinship Terms," p. 279.

12. *Ibid.*, p. 279. I have added the diagram for convenience. Freire-Marreco also notes that the junior-to-senior terms are applied to whole clans collectively but that senior-to-junior terms apply only to demonstrable relationships; i.e., a Bear clansman only calls "grandchild" those Corn clanspeople whose mothers' mothers are married to Bear clansmen, etc.. The phonetics are simplified.

13. See Stephen, *Hopi Journal*, pp. 198–201. Where a Tewa is inducted into Hopi societies, the normal Hopi procedure is followed.

14. Parsons, *A Pueblo Indian Journal*, pp. 121–22.

15. Parsons, *Tewa Tales*, p. 197.

16. Freire-Marreco, "Tewa Kinship Terms," p. 281. I have omitted diacritical marks in this and the following quotations.

17. *Ibid.*, pp. 281–82.

18. *Ibid.*, pp. 282–83.

19. *Ibid.*, p. 284.

20. *Ibid.*, p. 278.

21. *Ibid.*, p. 283.
22. *Ibid.*, pp. 283–84.
23. Fewkes, "An Initiation at Hano," pp. 152–56.
24. Parsons, *Pueblo Indian Journal*, p. 24.
25. Parsons, "The Ceremonial Calendar at Tewa," pp. 219–20.
26. Stephen, *op. cit.*, pp. 139–43.
27. However, some 18 Tewa men (out of a total membership of 147) belonged in the 1890's (*ibid.*, pp. 992–93).
28. Parsons, *Pueblo Indian Journal*, pp. 121–23.
29. Freire-Marreco, "Tewa Kinship Terms," pp. 285–86.
30. Parsons, *Pueblo Indian Journal*, pp. 32–34, 71–73, has brief accounts of Tewa marriages.
31. *Ibid.*, p. 34, n. 5.
32. Parsons, *Tewa Tales*, p. 219.
33. Parsons, *Pueblo Indian Journal*, p. 33.
34. Freire-Marreco, "Tewa Kinship Terms," pp. 286–87. We will discuss the cross-cousin marriage hypothesis in a later section.
35. Freire-Marreco (*ibid.*, pp. 280 ff.) is rather vague about the "bride" relationship, but Parsons, (*Pueblo Indian Journal*, pp. 61–62) notes races in her honor.
36. Freire-Marreco, "Tewa Kinship Terms," p. 269.
37. Harrington, *op. cit.*, pp. 472–98.
38. Freire-Marreco's interpretation depends on the analysis of the clan system and will be considered below.
39. Freire-Marreco, "Tewa Kinship Terms."
40. Harrington, *op. cit.* I have simplified the phonetics involved.
41. Freire-Marreco ("Tewa Kinship Terms," p. 276) notes that "the nomenclature for the descendants of sisters is somewhat inconsistent and perhaps transitional in character."
42. Freire-Marreco (*ibid.*, p. 276) suggests that the Hano sibling terms are not cognate with the New Mexican terms, but *tije* (Hano) seems close to *ti'u* (New Mexico). The Hano term for "older sister," *kaka*, may possibly represent linguistic borrowing from Hopi, *i-köka*, "my older sister," male speaking.
43. The other exceptions are where a man uses his wife's terms for her relatives.
44. *Kuku* is cognate with *kugu*, mother's mother's mother according to Freire-Marreco ("Tewa Kinship Terms," p. 278); the term is applied to the woman who names ego.
45. *Ibid.*, pp. 269–70.
46. Harrington, *op. cit.*, esp. Figs. 55–58.
47. The problem of the basic social structure of the Tanoan group generally, and its relationship to that of the western Pueblos and the Keresan groups, is discussed in the concluding chapter.

48. A linguistic analysis of the kinship terms of the two groups may assist greatly in settling this problem.

49. Freire-Marreco, "Tewa Kinship Terms," p. 286.

50. See chap. ii above on Hopi social organization.

51. Parsons, *Pueblo Indian Journal*, p. 122.

52. See Stephen, *op. cit.*, p. 1084, and Fewkes, "Kinship of a Tanoan-speaking Community," p. 166.

53. Fewkes, "Tusayan Migration Traditions," pp. 614–22. I have used Fewkes's population figures in Table 4.

54. Cf. V. Mindeleff (*op. cit.*, p. 39), who groups Corn and Tobacco, Bear and Spruce, House and Sun, and Cloud and Mud together on the basis of data from one informant.

55. Freire-Marreco, "Tewa Kinship Terms," p. 279.

56. Stephen, *op. cit.*, p. 1084, nn. 3 and 4.

57. Parsons, "The Ceremonial Calendar of the Tewa of Arizona," p. 210, n. 3.

58. Fewkes, "Tusayan Migration Traditions," p. 584.

59. Freire-Marreco, "Tewa Kinship Terms," p. 283.

60. Parsons, *Pueblo Indian Journal*, p. 47.

61. Parsons, "Ceremonial Calendar at Tewa," p. 212.

62. Parsons, *Social Organization of the Tewa of New Mexico*, p. 75.

63. Freire-Marreco, "Tewa Kinship Terms," p. 270.

64. Parsons, *Pueblo Indian Journal*, pp. 77–78.

65. *Ibid.*, pp. 61–62, 69.

66. *Ibid.*, p. 47.

67. Parsons, Introduction to Stephen, *Hopi Journal*, p. xlv. She uses northern Tewa for the surviving eastern Tewa.

68. Parsons, "Ceremonial Calendar at Tewa," p. 211, n. 9.

69. *Ibid.*, p. 213. There may be a special kiva grouping at the Winter Solstice ceremony (*ibid.*, p. 216).

70. V. Mindeleff, *op. cit.*, p. 134.

71. Stephen, *op. cit.*, p. 1176.

72. V. Mindeleff, *op. cit.*, p. 134.

73. Stephen, *op. cit.*, pp. 483–84. Stephen says that smallpox reduced their numbers to such an extent that they did not need more kivas.

74. Parsons, "Ceremonial Calendar at Tewa."

75. *Ibid.*, pp. 224–25. The Solstice ceremonials are less important in the east than the Transfer ceremonies.

76. *Ibid.*, p. 212. These may be the oldest clans if Fewkes is correct ("Winter Solstice Altars at Hano," p. 257).

77. Fewkes, "An Initiation at Hano," pp. 152–56.

78. Parsons, "Ceremonial Calendar at Tewa," pp. 219–20.

79. Parsons, *Pueblo Indian Journal*, pp. 65, 71.

80. Parsons, "Ceremonial Calendar at Tewa," pp. 216–18. This ceremony is held after the Winter Solstice ceremony but is related to it in certain ways.

81. *Ibid.*, pp. 225–26.

82. See Fewkes, "Tusayan Migration Traditions," pp. 622–30, for a census of First Mesa societies. Cf. Stephen, *op. cit.*, pp. 992–93. The latter indicates that about one-third of the Tewa men belong to the Wuwutcim societies.

83. Parsons, "Ceremonial Calendar at Tewa," pp. 227–28.

84. *Ibid.*, pp. 222–23.

85. Parsons (*Pueblo Indian Journal*, p. 68) notes that formerly the Koyala were called *kossa*, the northern Tewa term for one of the clown groups.

86. Stephen, *op. cit.*, p. 1130.

87. In Parsons, *Tewa Tales*, p. 197, the Town Chief is referred to as "our Father and Mother"; in the eastern Tewa the Winter Chief is referred to as "father" and the Summer Chief as "mother."

88. Parsons, "Ceremonial Calendar at Tewa," p. 225.

89. *Ibid.*, p. 227, n. 45.

90. Parsons, Introduction to Stephen, *Hopi Journal*, pp. xliv–xlv. It should be noted that the patrilineal "moieties" are ceremonial dual divisions and not exogamous.

91. Fewkes, "Winter Solstice Altars at Hano," p. 257.

92. V. Mindeleff, *op. cit.*, p. 37. Hano informants report a similar situation.

93. See Parsons, *Pueblo Indian Religion*, II, 915.

94. *Ibid.*, p. 923.

95. *Ibid.*, p. 917, n. *. They should be less susceptible to witchcraft also.

96. This problem is under investigation as part of a long-range study of Hopi acculturation.

CHAPTER IV

The Social Organization of Zuni

1. Of the early students of Zuni life, Cushing and Stevenson are outstanding; more recent students include Benedict, Bunzel, Kroeber, and Parsons. Irving Goldman's summary, "The Zuni Indians of New Mexico," will be found useful as an introduction. Leslie Spier has been kind enough to read this chapter, and I have incorporated several of his suggestions.

2. Bunzel, "Introduction to Zuni Ceremonialism," pp. 473–76. The Hopi raise irrigated wheat only at the farming village of Moencopi, and it will be important to study its effects there. Spier believes that canal irrigation from springs in the Zuni area is probably pre-Spanish.

3. *Ibid.*, p. 476.

4. Bunzel, "Economic Organization of Primitive Peoples," p. 352. See also her "Introduction to Zuni Ceremonialism," pp. 476–80, for a general summary of Zuni organizations.

5. Kroeber, *Zuni Kin and Clan*, pp. 51–88.

6. *Ibid.*, p. 49.

7. *Ibid.*, pp. 76–77.

8. Cf. Parsons, "Notes on Zuni," Part II, p. 258.

9. Kroeber, *op. cit.*, pp. 51–75. See the "Summary List of Terms" on p. 52. Since the actual terms are readily available, I have not included them here.

10. Parsons, "The Kinship Nomenclature of the Pueblo Indians," Table 1, p. 380.

11. Kroeber, *op. cit.*, p. 57, indicates that the husband of a father's mother's older maternal half-sister's daughter might be called grandfather.

12. Kroeber states (*ibid.*, p. 51) that, "while two or three genealogies would have been preferable to one, this one seems sufficient to establish practically every trait of the system accurately." His genealogy omits his informant's mother's relatives completely and gives no information on the mother's father's relatives.

13. *Ibid.*, pp. 75–81.

14. *Ibid.*, p. 81.

15. Kroeber's suggestion (*ibid.*, p. 63) of mother's brother is more probable, since it refers to "a male relative of the mother older than the speaker" and is also used for older unrelated males of one's own clan. It is possible to clarify many of the applications which Kroeber finds puzzling in terms of the clan, though he does not "see any need of going beyond kinship in the search for an explanation," in most cases.

16. Kroeber (*ibid.*, p. 67) with reference to the term *talakyi* states that "it transcends both the matrilinear principle and the kinship factors most important in the Zuni mind, and illustrates pregnantly the influence of the house."

17. From Bunzel (through Kennard) I get confirmation of the classing of the mother's mother's brother's children as "child," since they are "children of the same clan."

18. Kroeber, *op. cit.*, p. 53, notes that the father's mother's younger brother is called "father" but says that "by usual rule" it should be "grandfather."

19. Parsons, "Notes on Zuni," Part II, p. 256, n. 2. Kroeber, *op. cit.*, p. 71, gives "grandfather" or "father."

20. Kroeber, *op. cit.*, p. 74–75. My own guess is that women differentiate their brother's children.

21. *Ibid.*, p. 73.

22. Parsons, "Notes on Zuni," p. 258, n. 1.

23. Kroeber, *op. cit.*, p. 48.

24. *Ibid.*

25. Cushing, "Outlines of Zuni Creation Myths," p. 372.

26. Kroeber, *op. cit.*, p. 96.

27. Information from Bunzel via Kennard.

28. Parsons, "Ceremonial Friendship at Zuni," p. 4. While Parsons presents evidence that this custom is a recent innovation, it has been rapidly assimilated into both the kinship and the ceremonial patterns.

29. Parsons, "Notes on Zuni," Part II, pp. 249–54, has a discussion of "Kinship in Communal Ceremonialism." It will be important to find out whether these usages are merely verbal or associated with attitudes and behavior patterns.

30. Cushing, *Zuni Breadstuff*, p. 19.

31. See, e.g., Parsons, "Ceremonial Friendship at Zuni," p. 1. Kroeber apparently never asked the Zuni *why* they used inconsistent terms. Among the Hopi, Titiev and the writer were able to resolve practically all cases of variation in the application of terms by reference to ceremonial, clan, and phratry relationships.

32. Kroeber, *op. cit.*, pp. 47–48. Bunzel's "Economic Organization of Primitive Peoples," has the best description and analysis of households.

33. Kroeber, *op. cit.*, pp. 123–32.

34. Li An-che, "Zuni: Some Observations and Queries," p. 75.

35. Kroeber, *op. cit.*, pp. 133–34.

36. Information from Bunzel via Kennard; see also Bunzel, "Introduction to Zuni Ceremonialism," pp. 490–92.

37. Kroeber, *op. cit.*, p. 167, n. 2. Recent information indicates that we have greatly underestimated the number and importance of the clan fetishes.

38. *Ibid.*, p. 73.

39. Goldman, *op. cit.*, p. 320. The main sources for kinship behavior are Parsons and Stevenson (see Bibliography). Bunzel has not yet published her detailed account of Zuni household life.

40. Parsons, "Zuni Conception and Pregnancy Beliefs," pp. 381–82.

41. Cushing, "Outlines of Zuni Creation Myths," p. 371, mentions such a stock of clan names, however.

42. There are widely contradictory accounts of naming in Zuni. The above summary is based mainly on Parsons, "Zuni Names and Naming Practices," pp. 171–76.

43. Spier reports that every elder in the household exercised almost equal supervision over the children and that this held by extension for all adults in the community.

44. Parsons, "Zuni Names and Naming Practices," p. 173. Stevenson, "The Zuni Indians," p. 65, considered the latter practices as the rule, an erroneous generalization according to Parsons.

45. Based mainly on Bunzel, "Zuni Katcinas," pp. 975–1001, and Benedict's summary in *Patterns of Culture*, pp. 62–65.

46. Li An-che, *op. cit.*, p. 73. Note the contrast with Hopi custom.

47. Stevenson, *op. cit.*, pp. 304–5.

48. Benedict, *op. cit.*, p. 67.

49. *Ibid.*, p. 68.

50. Bunzel, "Introduction to Zuni Ceremonialism," p. 478.

51. Parsons, "Notes on Zuni," Part II, p. 258.

52. Cf. *ibid.*, pp. 257–58, and Bunzel, "Introduction to Zuni Ceremonialism," pp. 482–83.

53. Kroeber, *op. cit.*, p. 48. If Kroeber means, by "equal," equivalent but not identical, then we are not so far apart.

54. *Ibid.*

55. Parsons, "Notes on Zuni," p. 258.

56. Benedict, *op. cit.*, pp. 75–76. It is not clear whether this ideal pattern is limited to the fetish-holding "important" families or is more general; nor whether it is still maintained in the face of long acculturation.

57. Bunzel, "Introduction to Zuni Ceremonialism," p. 478.

58. Kroeber, *op. cit.*, pp. 91–188.

59. Cushing, "Outlines of Zuni Creation Myths," pp. 367–73; *Zuni Breadstuff*, pp. 126–28.

60. Cushing, "Outlines of Zuni Creation Myths," p. 368.

61. See Kroeber's discussion and comparative lists, *op. cit.*, pp. 93–97; Bunzel, "Introduction to Zuni Ceremonialism," p. 477.

62. Kroeber, *op. cit.*, p. 96.

63. *Ibid.*, pp. 100–103.

64. Calculated from Titiev's figures given in *Old Oraibi*, p. 52, Chart VI. For the Hopi tribe as a whole the average population per clan was around fifty persons (1900–1910); for the phratry perhaps two hundred individuals. Titiev's figures may not include children.

65. Kroeber, *op. cit.*, pp. 118–19.

66. *Ibid.*, p. 119.

67. *Ibid.*, p. 122.

68. *Ibid.*

69. *Ibid.*, p. 118. This point of view neglects the whole mythological background and does not explain why the directional grouping is applied to other aspects of Zuni society and the world.

70. Bunzel, "Introduction to Zuni Ceremonialism," p. 509. This study offers the best introduction to the complex subject of Zuni ceremonialism.

71. *Ibid.*, p. 511.

72. *Ibid.*

73. Kroeber, *op. cit.*, p. 165.

74. Bunzel, "Introduction to Zuni Ceremonialism," p. 513.

75. Stevenson, *op. cit.*, p. 165.

76. *Ibid.*, pp. 167–68.

77. Cushing, *Zuni Breadstuff*, p. 127. Cushing gives the order of rank (size) as follows: Parrot, Corn, Badger, Sun, Eagle, Turkey, Crane, Deer, Bear, Coyote, Frog, Grouse, Tobacco, Spring Vine, Yellowwood.

78. Females are initiated "to save their lives," in cases of mental sickness believed to be caused by supernatural beings. The ritual is the same as for boys in such cases.

79. Bunzel, "Introduction to Zuni Ceremonialism," p. 517.

80. *Ibid.*

81. Stevenson, *op. cit.*, p. 162.

82. *Ibid.*, p. 127. Parsons, "Notes on Zuni," Part I, p. 163, confirms Mrs. Stevenson's statement.

83. Kroeber, *op. cit.*, p. 164, n. 2. Kroeber neglected Mrs. Stevenson's fuller statement on the following page.

84. Stevenson, *op. cit.*, p. 235. Cf. Parsons, "Notes on Zuni," Part I, pp. 183–84. The *koyemci*, in representing their father's clans, are repaid by the father's clanswomen bringing meal and prayer feathers to the father's sister's household and by the clansmen presenting mutton and prayer sticks (*ibid.*, pp. 205–6).

85. Bunzel, "Introduction to Zuni Ceremonialism," p. 523; Stevenson, *op. cit.*, p. 142. Only the ordinary *koyemci* masks are referred to in Stevenson's account. The masks of the leaders of the *koyemci* may be kept separately.

86. See the summary of Mrs. Stevenson's references to functions of clan members in Kroeber, *op. cit.*, pp. 162–65.

87. Bunzel, "Introduction to Zuni Ceremonialism," pp. 525–28. Bunzel notes that the Bow priesthood is organized in similar fashion to the Medicine societies. This is quite possibly because one of its prime functions, according to Spier, is protection of the village from the malevolent magic embodied in enemies and strangers.

88. Bunzel, "Zuni Ritual Poetry," pp. 791 ff., has a detailed account of the initiation.

89. Kroeber, *op. cit.*, pp. 158–60, has a summary of Stevenson's references to clan-fraternity affiliations.

90. Cope, *Calendars of the Indians North of Mexico*, p. 152. Cushing gives the summer months in terms of colors; Stevenson as repeated.

91. Bunzel, "Zuni Katcinas," pp. 978–79, gives the clearest summary; Stevenson, *op. cit.*, p. 289, lists the heads of the six directional

priesthoods plus some others; Kroeber's informants restricted the appointing body to the first four.

92. Consult Kroeber, *op. cit.*, pp. 178–80; also Cushing, "Outlines of Zuni Creation Myths," p. 332, for a statement of Spanish origin of the civil government.

93. Kroeber, *op. cit.*, p. 183.

94. *Ibid.*, p. 184.

95. Bunzel, "Introduction to Zuni Ceremonialism," pp. 477–78.

96. Stevenson, *op. cit.*, p. 164.

97. Bunzel, "Introduction to Zuni Ceremonialism," p. 478. When Bunzel's detailed information on social organization is available, we will have a much clearer conception of the kinship system and its interrelations with household and clan.

98. Kroeber, *op. cit.*, p. 48.

99. Cushing, "Outlines of Zuni Creation Myths," pp. 386–87.

100. *Ibid.*, pp. 367 ff. The summer grouping coincides with the clans of the south, above, and below (with one exception, Grass or Tansy Mustard, which is here grouped west but elsewhere south); the winter grouping with the north, west, and east.

101. Cushing, "Outlines of Zuni Creation Myths," pp. 384–86.

102. Stevenson, *op. cit.*, pp. 40–41.

103. Kroeber, *op. cit.*, p. 96.

104. Since writing the above, I have reread Hodge (*History of Hawikuh, New Mexico*, p. 55) and discovered Mota Padilla's account: "They reached Tzibola, which was a village divided into two wards. . . " While this may merely refer to the house blocks, it may also have referred to a social division.

105. Kroeber, *op. cit.*, p. 182.

106. Cushing, "Outlines of Zuni Creation Myths," p. 368.

107. Bourke, in 1881, stated that he was "pretty certain that their clans are combined into phratries" (see Bloom, "Bourke on the Southwest," Part IX, p. 199).

108. Kroeber, *op. cit.*, p. 167–68.

109. *Ibid.*, pp. 173–74.

110. Cushing, "Outlines of Zuni Creation Myths," p. 387.

111. Stevenson, *op. cit.*, p. 164. The actual history of the association may, of course, be quite different, in that the clan-fetish relationship may be secondary.

112. Bunzel, "Zuni Origin Myths," p. 528.

113. Cushing, "Outlines of Zuni Creation Myths," pp. 370–71, 387–88.

114. Stevenson, *op. cit.*, p. 40.

115. See Kroeber, *op. cit.*, Table 12, where fetishes of different groups are kept in the same household in certain instances.

116. *Ibid.*, p. 183.

117. Cushing, *Zuni Breadstuff*, pp. 132 ff.

118. Forde, "Hopi Agriculture and Land Ownership," pp. 383–84, notes "little evidence of the importance of the clan in the distribution and acquisition of fields." However, when a man owned fields, they should properly be inherited by his daughter's and his sister's children; "where a man had no son or daughter, his land was usually claimed by his relatives of *his* own clan."

119. Parsons, *Hopi and Zuni Ceremonialism*, p. 75, n. 276. She underestimates Hopi phratry organization. See Titiev, *op. cit.*, chap. iv, and chap. ii above.

120. Kroeber, *op. cit.*, p. 96.

121. Parsons, *Hopi and Zuni Ceremonialism.*

122. Kroeber, *op. cit.*, p. 178, thinks Zuni civil government to be "in substance a native institution," but Parsons leans toward a Spanish derivation (see her *Pueblo Indian Religion*, I, 147 ff.).

123. See, e.g., Parsons, *Hopi and Zuni Ceremonialism*, p. 83, n. 310, where she shows that the same feelings toward trusteeship of ceremonial properties may exist in the two tribes.

124. Kroeber, *op. cit.*, p. 185.

125. Kroeber, "Thoughts on Zuni Religion," p. 270, notes that the exceptional and complete concentration of the Zuni into one town was "almost predestined to emphasize the solidary communal aspects of life."

CHAPTER V

The Social Organization of Acoma

1. White, "Summary Report of Field Work at Acoma," p. 568. White is the outstanding student of Acoma and the Keres generally, and much of the following account is based on his "The Acoma Indians," and *New Material from Acoma*. Parsons' "Notes on Acoma and Laguna" and Stirling's *Origin Myth of Acoma* also contain valuable information on this highly conservative pueblo.

2. White, "The Acoma Indians," p. 58.

3. *Ibid.*, p. 140.

4. *Ibid.*, pp. 140–41.

5. Kroeber, *Zuni Kin and Clan*, p. 84, gives a combined Acoma-Laguna list.

6. White, "The Acoma Indians," p. 40.

7. Parsons, *Laguna Genealogies*, pp. 199–201, has an incomplete list of terms; a more detailed list is given in her "Kinship Nomenclature of the Pueblo Indians," Table I.

8. Parsons, *Laguna Genealogies*, p. 199.

9. *Ibid.*, p. 200. This is also the Laguna pattern.

10. *Ibid.*

11. Parsons also gives mother's mother's mother as *naiya* ("mother") and the reciprocals as "boy" and "girl" which conforms with the alternating pattern ("Kinship Nomenclature of the Pueblo Indians," Table I).

12. Parsons, *Laguna Genealogies*, p. 201.

13. White, "The Acoma Indians," p. 40. All other applications given for *sa k'uitc'* are for siblings or for parallel or cross-cousins.

14. Parsons, *Laguna Genealogies*, p. 199, n. 2; White, "The Acoma Indians," p. 40.

15. Parallel changes under acculturation have taken place in the Crow-type systems of the Southeast. See Spoehr, *Changing Kinship Systems*, for examples.

16. White, *New Material from Acoma*, p. 319.

17. Stirling, *op. cit.*, p. 109.

18. *Ibid.*, p. 112.

19. This shift is in keeping with other changes in social structure. If the father's clan has absorbed the functions of the "ceremonial father," and the wife of the father's clansman—rather than the father's sisters—washes the initiate's head, this is further evidence of a shift in social organization toward a more bilateral system.

20. White, *New Material from Acoma*, p. 319. It is probable that a contraction of kinship extension parallel to that noted for the "ceremonial father" is in process.

21. See Stirling, *op. cit.*, for an account of the role of Iatiku in Acoma thinking.

22. White, "Summary Report of Field Work at Acoma," p. 561.

23. Parsons, "Notes on Acoma and Laguna," p. 177.

24. White, "The Acoma Indians," p. 136.

25. White, *New Material from Acoma*, pp. 327–28.

26. White, "The Acoma Indians," p. 34. In *New Material from Acoma*, p. 315, he states that "land was transmitted, as a rule from mother to daughter, but if there were no daughters, a son could inherit the land."

27. White, *New Material from Acoma*, p. 314.

28. Material on the life-cycle and kinship obligations is given in White, "The Acoma Indians," pp. 132–38, and *New Material from Acoma*, pp. 318–25; and Parsons, "Notes on Acoma and Laguna," pp. 174–82.

29. Parsons, "Notes on Acoma and Laguna," p. 174.

30. Stirling, *op. cit.*, pp. 41–42.

31. White, *New Material from Acoma*, p. 175.

32. Parsons, "Notes on Acoma and Laguna," p. 175.

33. White, *New Material from Acoma*, p. 320.

34. *Ibid.*, pp. 320–21.

35. Stirling, *op. cit.*, p. 109.

36. During certain Katcina dramatizations the Antelope clansmen are assisted by their "ceremonial sons."

37. Stirling, *op. cit.*, p. 17.

38. White, *New Material from Acoma*, p. 319.

39. Stirling, *op. cit.*, pp. 38–40.

40. White, "The Acoma Indians," pp. 34–38.

41. White, *New Material from Acoma*, p. 320.

42. Parsons, "Notes on Acoma and Laguna," p. 175.

43. White, "The Acoma Indians," pp. 135–36.

44. *Ibid.*, p. 35, Table 2,

45. White, *New Material from Acoma*, pp. 321–22.

46. *Ibid.*, p. 322.

47. Parsons, "Notes on Acoma and Laguna," p. 177. One informant stated that both one's own and one's father's clanspeople wash the heads.

48. There is no evidence that the dead become Katcina; in fact, the Origin Myth provides for the separate creation of the Katcina by Iatiku.

49. Parsons, "Notes on Acoma and Laguna," p. 177. These statements offer further evidence for a pattern of matrilocal residence.

50. White, *New Material from Acoma*, p. 316.

51. See Stirling, *op. cit.*, p. 89.

52. *Ibid.*, pp. 4, 13–14.

53. There is a formal ritual for the reception of a foreign spouse (see White, *New Material from Acoma*, pp. 321–22).

54. White, "The Acoma Indians," pp. 35–38.

55. *Ibid.*, p. 38.

56. The average size of the surviving clans is around a hundred individuals per clan.

57. White, *New Material from Acoma*, p. 315.

58. Stirling, *op. cit.*, p. 91.

59. White, *New Material from Acoma*, pp. 313–14.

60. *Ibid.*, p. 314.

61. The Antelope clan was not in the first group of clans created. White ("The Acoma Indians," p. 39, n. 26) and Parsons ("The Antelope Clan in Keresan Custom and Myth") have discussed the problems of the position of the Antelope clan.

62. Stirling, *op. cit.*, p. 17; see White, "The Acoma Indians," pp. 154–56, for a variant account.

63. Stirling, *op. cit.*, p. 25. At present the War Chief and his assistants are selected every year, along with the secular officials (see *ibid.*, pp. 99–108).

64. Parsons, *Laguna Genealogies*, p. 214, n. 5.

65. *Ibid.*, pp. 20–25.

66. Stirling, *op. cit.*, pp. 28–42.

67. *Ibid.*, pp. 75–76. Inferentially the Ant society was connected with the Ant clan.

68. White, "The Acoma Indians," p. 107.

69. Stirling, *op. cit.*, p. 15.

70. White, *New Material from Acoma*, p. 311.

71. White, "The Acoma Indians," pp. 30–31; Stirling, *op. cit.*, p. 45, n. 16. Earlier writers report six kivas.

72. White, "The Acoma Indians," pp. 71–75; Stirling, *op. cit.*, pp. 108–12.

73. This is one of the most dramatic of all pueblo ceremonies. White ("The Acoma Indians," pp. 88–94) and Stirling (*op. cit.*, pp. 70–75) give a description and rationale.

74. White, "The Acoma Indians," pp. 96–102, 107–25.

75. *Ibid.*, pp. 97–101.

76. White, *New Material from Acoma*, pp. 305–6.

77. *Ibid.*, pp. 315–16.

78. White, "The Acoma Indians," p. 140.

79. Spier, "The Distribution of Kinship Systems in North America," pp. 74–75. Spier was forced to rely on incomplete data for Acoma.

80. White, "The Acoma Indians," p. 58.

81. Ibid., pp. 55–60.

82. "With this myth, according to Acoma ideology, everything in the universe must harmonize" (Stirling, *op. cit.*, Preface).

83. White, "The Acoma Indians," pp. 23–28.

84. Hammond, "Oñate and the Founding of New Mexico," chap. vii (monograph).

85. *Ibid.*, pp. 461–62. The number of casualties is reported as between six and eight hundred (probably far too high), with seventy or eighty warriors captured. Of the latter, twenty-four were said to have been mutilated by having a foot cut off.

86. This hypothesis is not necessarily in conflict with the origin legend, since the latter is usually brought into conformity with important changes in the socioceremonial structure. A comparative study of Keresan pueblos will ultimately help us test this hypothesis.

87. White, *New Material from Acoma*, p. 305.

88. White (*ibid.*, pp. 332–34) presents a vivid account of how skeptics were kept in line a few decades ago.

89. White, "The Acoma Indians," p. 63.

90. *Ibid.*, p. 141.

91. White, "Summary Report of Field Work at Acoma," p. 568, believes Acoma never had certain of the Rio Grande characteristics, such as those related to the moiety principle.

CHAPTER VI

The Social Organization of Laguna

1. Bancroft (*History of Arizona and New Mexico*, p. 221) states that, around 1697, "rebel Queres of Cieneguilla, Santo Domingo, and Cochiti formed a new pueblo four leagues north of Acoma. . . ." Hodge (quoted in Hackett, *Historical Documents Relating to New Mexico . . .*, p. 29, n. 108) adds Sia and Acoma to the list of contributors. According to Fray Lezaún, writing in 1760, "Father Miranda, a very apostolic man, went through all the land . . . collecting the wandering sheep of numerous nations. With them he founded a mission called Señor José de la Laguna. They spoke many languages but all have learned that of the Queres, forgetting their native tongues" (*ibid.*, p. 469).

2. For a description of Laguna in the eighteenth century see Thomas, *Forgotten Frontiers*, pp. 102–3.

3. Gunn, *Schat-Chen*, pp. 42–43.

4. Parsons, "The Laguna Migration to Isleta," pp. 602–13.

5. Gunn, *op. cit.*, p. 100.

6. *Ibid.*, p. 15.

7. Crane, *Desert Drums*, chap. iii.

8. Crane (*ibid.*, p. 65) indicates the distribution as follows: Old Laguna, 391; Paguate, 540; Seama, 279; Paraje, 181; Mesita, 173; Encinal, 152; and Casa Blanca, 92.

9. Made up of 1,345 males, 1,255 females, and 537 families, an average of almost 5 per family.

10. Boas (*Keresan Texts*) has collected a large amount of material on the western dialect, but much remains to be done by way of linguistic analysis.

11. Parsons, *Laguna Genealogies*, p. 141.

12. *Ibid.*, pp. 147 ff. English terms are used for convenience wherever possible; the full phonetic forms of native terms can be found in Parsons.

13. These terms do not alternate with generation.

14. Here is an instance of conflict between the general principle of alternating generations and the self-reciprocal terminology for grandparents and grandchildren. Unfortunately the terms for the children of this "grandson" are not given.

15. The reciprocals of these terms are likewise *papa*, which suggests that this alternation is correct.

16. Parsons, *Laguna Genealogies*, p. 209.

17. *Ibid.*, p. 197.

18. *Ibid.*, p. 209.

19. *Ibid.*, p. 208.

20. *Ibid.*, p. 232. There is also an extension of kinship to clanspeople in other tribes.

21. *Ibid.*, p. 167.
22. *Ibid.*, p. 159.
23. *Ibid.*, p. 165. I have standardized the spelling of "Iatiku."
24. *Ibid.*, pp. 159–60.
25. *Ibid.*, pp. 210–12.
26. *Ibid.*, p. 175.
27. *Ibid.*, pp. 235–53.
28. *Piye* and *wati* may be used as reciprocals, but Parsons (*ibid.*) says that this application is rarely made.
29. *Ibid.*, pp. 177, 195.
30. In contrast to the father's mother among the Hopi.
31. Parsons, "Mothers and Children at Laguna," pp. 34–38, gives a detailed account of the ritual.
32. Parsons, *Laguna Genealogies*, pp. 180–81. Boas' informant indicates that the medicine man gives the name (*op. cit.*, pp. 201–3).
33. Parsons, *Laguna Genealogies*, p. 174.
34. *Ibid.*, p. 196.
35. Crane, *op. cit.*, p. 61.
36. Parsons, *Laguna Genealogies*, p. 176.
37. Boas, *op. cit.*, p. 296, notes that "men of the maternal family of the deceased dig his grave."
38. Recorded from Hopi informants.
39. Parsons, *Laguna Genealogies*, p. 216.
40. *Ibid.*, pp. 216–19.
41. Boas, *op. cit.*, p. 277.
42. Parsons, *Laguna Genealogies*, p. 218, n. 6.
43. White, *The Pueblo of Santo Domingo, New Mexico*, pp. 198–99; *New Material from Acoma*, p. 311.
44. See Boas, *op. cit.*, pp. 203–4, for an account of funeral ritual.
45. Parsons, *Laguna Genealogies*, pp. 169–73.
46. *Ibid.*, p. 151.
47. See Parsons, "The Kinship Nomenclature of the Pueblo Indians"; White, *The Pueblo of Santa Ana, New Mexico;* Harrington, "Tewa Relationship Terms"; Opler, "The Kinship Systems of the Southern Athabaskan-speaking Tribes"; Steward, *Basin-Plateau Aboriginal Sociopolitical Groups;* and Eggan (ed.), *Social Anthropology of North American Tribes.*
48. See Gunn, *op. cit.*, pp. 93–100; Crane, *op. cit.*, pp. 317–51.
49. White, *The Pueblo of Santa Ana, New Mexico*, p. 159, has some evidence which bears on this point. He finds two patterns for the mother's brother and his children: (1) mother's brother is called "uncle" and his children "son" and "daughter," and (2) mother's brother is called "father" and his children are "brother" and "sister." "We believe that the presence and use of these two patterns at Santa Ana today

indicate a transition from one type of kinship system, or pattern, to another. It is our considered opinion that the pattern in which mother's brother is called 'uncle' and his children 'son' and 'daughter,' which is characteristic of the Crow type of terminology, is the earlier of the two patterns. We believe that this pattern is breaking down and giving way to the pattern in which mother's brother is called 'father' and his children 'brother' and 'sister.' We believe that we have sufficient reason and evidence in support of this view, but we must reserve discussion of it to another time and place."

50. This is a complex problem which depends on much comparative evidence. I have dealt with the Hopi situation above, and we will return to the problem in the next chapter.

51. Vocative terms or terms of address usually are more sensitive to change than are terms of reference.

52. Parsons, *Laguna Genealogies*, pp. 157, 209.

53. White, *The Pueblo of Santa Ana, New Mexico*, p. 161.

54. Morgan, *Systems of Consanguinity and Affinity of the Human Family*, p. 262 and schedules.

55. *Ibid.*, pp. 261–62.

56. *Ibid.*, pp. 262, 322.

57. *Ibid.*, p. 262.

58. It may be that Morgan had additional information. However, he was worried about the position of the Pueblos and the difficulties of getting information, and I am inclined to believe that he was "forcing" the evidence a bit.

59. Bloom (ed.), "Bourke on the Southwest," Part XII, pp. 373–75. Both Pratt and Marmon had married into Laguna and had unusual opportunities for obtaining information. Bourke's journal likewise gives us much insight into the changes going on at Laguna during the early 1880's.

60. Parsons, *Laguna Genealogies*, pp. 206–35.

61. Bloom (ed.), *op. cit.*, pp. 370–71.

62. Boas, *op. cit.*, p. 221.

63. Parsons, *Notes on Ceremonialism at Laguna*, pp. 114–16.

64. Parsons, *Laguna Genealogies*, pp. 234–35.

65. *Ibid.*, pp. 232–34.

66. *Ibid.*, pp. 231–32.

67. *Ibid.*, pp. 211, 251–52. Thus Parsons notes four (or more) blocks of Corn clan families and five women heads of households; four blocks of Sun clan families and four women heads; etc.

68. *Ibid.*, pp. 212–13. There is no reference to the former theoretical ownership of land by the cacique.

69. *Ibid.*, pp. 213–14. Parsons was unable to verify this statement. The informant got the information from his father who had migrated to Isleta, and his account may be colored by Isletan practices.

70. Boas, *op. cit.*, pp. 196–97, gives an autobiographical account of marriage which indicates that clan relatives were once consulted.

71. Parsons, *Laguna Genealogies*, pp. 212–13.

72. *Ibid.*, pp. 254–56. Parsons was able to locate some ten *iyatik* fetishes distributed among eight houses.

73. *Ibid.*, pp. 219–21.

74. Boas, *op. cit.*, p. 222.

75. Parsons, *Laguna Genealogies*, pp. 222, 278.

76. Parsons (*ibid.*, p. 256) notes that masks and fetishes which are associated with a clan are kept in an old house of the clan.

77. Boas, *op. cit.*, p. 282.

78. Parsons, *Laguna Genealogies*, pp. 225–26. The Parrot clan at Zuni is also associated with salt.

79. *Ibid.*, pp. 232–34.

80. Parsons, "The Laguna Migration to Isleta," pp. 602–13.

81. Crane, *op. cit.*, p. 60.

82. Bancroft, *op. cit.*, p. 266.

83. Boas, *op. cit.*, pp. 277–83.

84. Parsons, "Notes on Acoma and Laguna," p. 182.

85. Parsons, *Laguna Genealogies*, pp. 223–24; cf. Parsons, *Pueblo Indian Religion*, for additional details.

86. Parsons, *Laguna Genealogies*, pp. 253, 264–65.

87. See Boas, *op. cit.*, pp. 290–91; and Parsons, *Notes on Ceremonialism at Laguna*, pp. 109 ff.

88. Parsons, *Laguna Genealogies*, pp. 164–65.

89. The *cheani* altars have directional color associations.

90. Parsons, *Notes on Ceremonialism at Laguna*, pp. 118–22.

91. Boas, *op. cit.*, pp. 289–90, has an account of the warrior's initiation and the Scalp Dance. The warrior also chose a "brother" from among the members of the organization.

92. Parsons, *Laguna Genealogies*, p. 229. In the east group: Sun, Corn, Turkey, Water, and Turquoise clans; in the west group: Bear, Parrot, Coyote, Chaparral Cock, and Oak clans.

93. Boas, *op. cit.*, pp. 28–33, 285, 296–98. Ceremonial rabbit hunts were held at the solstices.

94. *Ibid.*, p. 294. The *kurena* (winter) group was later associated with the "progressive" faction, while the *kashare* was anti-American.

95. *Ibid.*

96. *Ibid.*, pp. 276–77.

97. Parsons, *Notes on Ceremonialism at Laguna*, p. 95.

98. Boas, *op. cit.*, p. 221.

99. *Ibid.*, pp. 288–89; Parsons, *Notes on Ceremonialism at Laguna*, pp. 109–12.

100. See Parsons' summary in *Pueblo Indian Religion*, II, 888–90.

101. Spier, "The Distribution of Kinship Systems in North America," p. 74.

102. Parsons, personal communication, on reading an earlier draft of the present study.

103. Parsons, *Pueblo Indian Religion*, II, 889.

104. See, especially, *ibid.*, chaps. viii–ix.

105. *Ibid.*, p. 890.

106. Recent archeological evidence indicating an eastward spread of Keresan-speaking peoples is important in connection with this problem and will be further discussed in our general conclusions.

107. Parsons, *Pueblo Indian Religion*, II, 890.

CHAPTER VII

Conclusions

1. Spier, "The Distribution of Kinship Systems in North America," pp. 73–77 and Pl. I.

2. Eggan, "The Cheyenne and Arapaho Kinship System," p. 93, Table 2.

3. Zuni has alternate terms for mother's sisters which may be associated with greater social differentiation within the household; Hano differentiates the mother's sister and her descendants, a carry-over of eastern Tewa practice. The extension of the term for mother to the father's sister at Acoma, and occasionally at Laguna, is probably a recent development.

4. Parsons, "The Kinship Nomenclature of the Pueblo Indians," p. 377.

5. *Ibid.*, p. 385.

6. *Ibid.*, pp. 386–89.

7. Lowie, *Hopi Kinship*, p. 383.

8. Parsons, *op. cit.*, p. 386.

9. *Ibid.*, p. 385.

10. *Ibid.*, n. 14.

11. Lowie, *Culture and Ethnology*, p. 167.

12. Kroeber, "Athabascan Kin Term Systems," p. 606.

13. Parsons, *op. cit.*, p. 386.

14. Kroeber, "The Classificatory System of Relationship," p. 83.

15. Kroeber, *Zuni Kin and Clan*, pp. 86–87.

16. Parsons, *op. cit.*, pp. 387–89.

17. *Ibid.*, p. 389.

18. Kroeber, *Zuni Kin and Clan*, p. 135.
19. *Ibid.*, p. 140 and Table 10.
20. *Ibid.*, p. 142.
21. *Ibid.*, p. 143.
22. Parsons, *Laguna Genealogies*, p. 232, likewise found no confirmation at Laguna, except for one instance.
23. *Ibid.*, p. 231.
24. Lowie, "American Culture History," p. 427.
25. Cf. Titiev, *Old Oraibi*, pp. 173 ff.
26. Kroeber, *Zuni Kin and Clan*, p. 183.
27. I have drawn primarily on an unpublished manuscript on "Eastern Pueblo Social Organization" for the following accounts, as well as on the indicated literature.
28. Parsons, "Tewa Kin, Clan, and Moiety."
29. Strong, "An Analysis of Southwestern Society."
30. Hawley, "Pueblo Social Organization as a Lead to Pueblo History."
31. Freire-Marreco ("Tewa Kinship Terms from the Pueblo of Hano, Arizona") thinks the Tewa clans have lost their former importance.
32. Parsons, "Tewa Kin, Clan, and Moiety," p. 334.
33. Harrington, "Tewa Relationship Terms."
34. Parsons, *The Social Organization of the Tewa of New Mexico.*
35. Trager has recently made available his recording of Tiwa kinship terms and indicated their value for historical reconstruction in his "Kinship and Status Terms of the Tiwa Language."
36. Parsons, "Picuris, New Mexico," pp. 206 ff.
37. Parsons, "Isleta."
38. White, *The Pueblo of Santa Ana, New Mexico*, pp. 142–43.
39. Goldfrank, *The Social and Ceremonial Organization of Cochiti;* White, *The Pueblo of San Felipe.*
40. White, *The Pueblo of Santa Ana*, p. 159.
41. Parsons, *The Pueblo of Jemez;* see also Reagan, "The Jemez Indians," for insights into an earlier period.
42. Reagan, *op. cit.*, pp. 33–37.
43. Parsons, "Tewa Kin, Clan, and Moiety," p. 339.
44. See also Marcson, "Some Methodological Consequences of Correlational Analysis in Anthropology," pp. 588 ff.
45. Strong, *op. cit.*
46. Steward, "Ecological Aspects of Southwestern Society."
47. Hawley, *op. cit.*, pp. 504 ff.
48. *Ibid.*, p. 521.
49. *Ibid.*, p. 519.

50. Reed, "Sources of Upper Rio Grande Culture and Population," p. 163; see also his "The Distinctive Features and Distribution of the San Juan Anasazi Culture," pp. 303–4.

51. Seltzer, *Racial Prehistory in the Southwest and the Hawikuh Zunis*, p. 25.

52. *Ibid.*, p. 30.

53. *Ibid.*, pp. 30–31.

54. Reed, "Sources of Upper Rio Grande Culture and Population," p. 176.

55. *Ibid.*, pp. 178–79.

56. *Ibid.*, p. 182.

57. *Ibid.*, p. 179.

58. Hawley, *op. cit.*, p. 519.

59. See "Conclusions" to chap. vi above.

60. Hackett has collected a number of documents from the Reconquest period which illustrate the extent to which the Spaniards went (see his *Revolt of the Pueblo Indians of New Mexico* and *Historical Documents Relating to New Mexico*).

61. White, "A Comparative Study of Keresan Medicine Societies," pp. 618–19.

62. *Ibid.*, p. 619.

63. Steward, *op. cit.*, p. 99.

64. Reed, "The Distinctive Features and Distribution of the San Juan Anasazi Culture," p. 303.

65. Reed, "Sources of Upper Rio Grande Culture and Population," p. 178.

66. Taos and Picuris dialects are mutually intelligible and they are more archaic, Taos apparently most so. Sandia and Isleta are almost identical and can understand the northern dialects, but the reverse is not true (Trager, *op. cit.*, p. 557).

67. Hawley, *op. cit.*, p. 513.

68. Wittfogel and Goldfrank, "Some Aspects of Pueblo Mythology and Society."

69. *Ibid.*, p. 20.

70. *Ibid.*, p. 27. (Our italics.)

71. Steward, *op. cit.*, p. 101.

72. Steward, *op. cit.*

73. Goldschmidt, "Social Organization in Native California and the Origin of Clans," pp. 454–55.

74. See especially Opler, "The Kinship Systems of the Southern Athabaskan-speaking Tribes."

75. Spoehr, *Camp, Clan, and Kin among the Cow Creek Seminole of Florida* and *Changing Kinship Systems*.

76. Eggan, "The Cheyenne and Arapaho Kinship System," p. 94.
77. Lowie, *Social Organization.*
78. Murdock, *Social Structure.*
79. Levi-Strauss, *Les Structures élémentaires de la parenté.* The last two volumes were published after the text was substantially completed.

Index

PRINTED IN U.S.A.